ORGANIZATIONAL CHANGE

Visit the *Organizational Change*, *fourth edition* Companion Website at **www.pearsoned.co.uk/senior** to find valuable **student** learning material including:

- Chapter overviews
- Case study feedback
- Annotated links to relevant sites on the web

WITHDRAWN
FROM THE LIBRARY OF
UNIVERSITY OF ULSTER

100562344

PEARSON

We work with leading authors to develop the strongest
educational materials in business and management,
bringing cutting-edge thinking and best learning practice
to a global market.

Under a range of well-known imprints, including
Financial Times Prentice Hall, we craft high quality print
and electronic publications which help readers to
understand and apply their content, whether studying
or at work.

To find out more about the complete range of our
publishing, please visit us on the World Wide Web at:
www.pearsoned.co.uk

Fourth Edition

ORGANIZATIONAL CHANGE

Barbara Senior

Stephen Swailes

Financial Times
Prentice Hall
is an imprint of

PEARSON

Harlow, England • London • New York • Boston • San Francisco • Toronto
Sydney • Tokyo • Singapore • Hong Kong • Seoul • Taipei • New Delhi
Cape Town • Madrid • Mexico City • Amsterdam • Munich • Paris • Milan

100862344
658·
406
SEN

Pearson Education Limited

Edinburgh Gate
Harlow
Essex CM20 2JE
England

and Associated Companies around the world

Visit us on the World Wide Web at:
www.pearsoned.co.uk

First published 1997
Second edition published 2002
Third edition published 2006
Fourth edition published 2010

© Barbara Senior 1997, 2002
© Barbara Senior and Jocelyne Fleming 2006
© Barbara Senior and Stephen Swailes 2010

The rights of Barbara Senior and Stephen Swailes to be identified as authors
of this work has been asserted by them in accordance with the Copyright,
Designs and Patents Act 1988.

All rights reserved. No part of this publication may be reproduced, stored in
a retrieval system, or transmitted in any form or by any means, electronic,
mechanical, photocopying, recording or otherwise, without either the prior
written permission of the publisher or a licence permitting restricted copying
in the United Kingdom issued by the Copyright Licensing Agency Ltd,
Saffron House, 6–10 Kirby Street, London EC1N 8TS.

ISBN 978-0-273-71620-4

British Library Cataloguing-in-Publication Data
A catalogue record for this book is available from the British Library

Library of Congress Cataloging-in-Publication Data
Senior, Barbara.
  Organizational change / Barbara Senior. Stephen Swailes. -- 4th ed.
    p. cm
  Includes bibliographical references and index.
  ISBN 978-0-273-71620-4 (pbk.)
  1. Organizational change. I. Swailes, Stephen. II. Title.
  HD58.8.S456 2010
  658.4'06--dc22
                                                        2009043566

10 9 8 7 6 5 4 3 2 1
13 12 11 10

Typeset in 9.5/13 pt Stone Serif by 30
Printed and bound by Graficas Estella, Navarro, Spain

The publisher's policy is to use paper manufactured from sustainable forests.

Contents

Part One
THE CONTEXT AND MEANING OF CHANGE

Part Two
CHANGING ORGANIZATIONS

Part Three
STRATEGIES FOR MANAGING CHANGE

Supporting resources

Visit **www.pearsoned.co.uk/senior** to find valuable online resources

Companion Website for students
- Chapter overviews
- Case study feedback
- Annotated links to relevant sites on the web

For instructors
- Power Point slides of key learning points, objectives and activities
- Chapter overviews and synopsis
- Feedback on activities and key areas of discussion
- Case example notes
- Possible session structures

For more information please contact your local Pearson Education sales representative or visit **www.pearsoned.co.uk/senior**

List of illustrations, figures and tables

Illustrations

Figures

Tables

About this book

Introduction

Those of us who work in organizations, some time or another, get caught up in the need for change, along with all the rationalizing, the arguments, the politics and the emotions that accompany it. Understanding the triggers that lead people to think changes are needed, and what happens when managers try to make changes, is essential given the volatile world that we live in. The impetus for writing this book comes from our belief that organizations must co-exist with change or they will drift out to the margins of survivability and perish. Its content derives from our experience in helping to meet the learning needs of management students with respect to the way people in organizations approach and deal with change, and with managing and working with change in a variety of organizations.

The aim of this book

The overall aim of this book is to provide a discussion of change in relation to the complexities of organizational life. The text takes both a theoretical and practical approach to the issue of organizational change in seeking to meet both the academic and applied aims of most business and management courses.

More specifically this text aims to be:

- *Comprehensive* in its coverage of the significant ideas and issues associated with change from operational to strategic levels. Change is also examined in terms of its effects at the individual, group, organizational and societal levels.
- *Conceptual* in the way it explores and critiques theory and research on organizations and change.
- *Critical* through its recognition of the limitations of much of the change literature and its inclusion of critical management perspectives.
- *Practical* through descriptions and worked examples of different approaches to 'doing' change.
- *Challenging* through asking readers to undertake activities relating to their work contexts. Each chapter is punctuated with activities intended to personalize ideas from the text and to reinforce learning. End of chapter discussion questions, assignments and case examples ask for longer and more detailed responses.

- *Balanced* in its use of case studies and examples, drawn from various types of organizations – public, private and voluntary sectors, small and large.

Who should use this book?

The book is intended for all those who are interested in exploring, organizational change and how to deal with it.

- *Undergraduate students* in the final year of business and management programmes should find it sufficiently structured to provide an understandable route through the subject.
- *MBA students* who need to relate theory to the workplace will find the blend of theory and practice closely linked to the demands of their practical/ programmes.
- *Students* on specialist Master's programmes should find sufficient practical examples in the text, and cases to illustrate theory even if they have little practical experience of management and business themselves.
- *Students on professional courses* that include organizational change.
- *Practising middle and senior managers* who wish to know more about change theory, models of change and its complexity in relation to organizational functioning.

Readers will benefit if they have some prior knowledge of organizational theory and behaviour and of experiencing the murky waters of change in organizations. However, we have tried to make the book accessible to readers without prior knowledge.

Distinctive features

- **Clear structure.** The book is structured into three parts. The first considers the nature of organizations operating in complex environments and responding to the 'winds of change'. The causes of change and different types of change are discussed. Part Two, opens up the organization to explore issues that are crucial to an understanding of organizational change and how it happens. Part Three addresses the more practical considerations of designing, planning and implementing change.
- **Chapter summaries and learning objectives.** Each chapter begins with a short summary of the chapter content and the learning objectives.
- **Boxed illustrations and activities.** Illustrations that expand or give examples of points made in the text are used throughout. They include summaries of research papers and short case examples. Each chapter has several activities that invite readers to think about theory and practice in relation to their own experiences of change in organizations.

- **End of chapter discussion questions and assignments.** Each chapter ends with questions that are intended to promote a more lengthy consideration of issues raised in the text. Many of the questions are set in 'examination'-type terms and can be used as preparation for such tests that might be associated with a particular course.
- **End of chapter case examples.** The chapters in Parts One and Two include, at the end, a short case example and case exercise, which helps readers apply concepts, theories and ideas introduced in the chapter to a real example of change. Questions on these cases are intended as a guide to thinking about the different aspects of the situation described in relation to ideas and themes, not only in the chapter in which they appear, but elsewhere in the book.
- **Indicative resources for the reader.** Further readings are suggested at the end of each chapter.
- **Website links.** At the end of each chapter several websites giving further information and support are provided.
- **Academic sources and references.** Full details of references used are given at the end of each chapter and in the author index at the end of the book.
- **Lecturer's Guide and PowerPoint slides.** A Lecturer's Guide is available, downloadable from **www.pearsoned.co.uk/senior**, to those lecturers adopting this textbook. It includes commentaries on each chapter, in particular how to use the activities and the kinds of responses to be expected from students carrying out the activities and answering the discussion questions. Additional study work is suggested and PowerPoint slides are provided.

How to use this book

The book has a simple structure. Readers new to the subject of organizational change will find the chapters in Part One essential. Readers with little knowledge of organizational behaviour will find Part Two especially important and for those who have already studied organizational theory and behaviour Part Two explores power, culture and leadership with special reference to change. Part Three provides methodologies for planning and implementing changes and closes with review of current trends and issues in change theory and research.

Activities are distributed throughout all chapters embed ideas and concepts in the text. Sometimes they invite readers to reflect on their workplace, other times they invite application of concepts and ideas to work situations. A useful strategy is to read through a chapter quickly first then, on a second reading, carry out the activities.

Discussion questions, assignments and case examples enable readers to write at length on issues associated with organizational change. They are particularly useful as preparation for completing assignments and examinations.

About the authors

Barbara Senior, BA (Hons), MA, D.Occ.Psych, C.Psychol

Barbara is Director of Highfield Consultants. She supervises doctoral students for the Open University. She is a Chartered Occupational Psychologist and a Member of the Chartered Institute of Personnel and Development (CIPD). Her past experience is varied. After working in administration and running her own dressmaking and tailoring business, she entered the academic world, researching, teaching and directing courses in organizational behaviour and change at Liverpool John Moores University, the Open University and the University of Northampton, where she was Director of the Postgraduate Modular Scheme. She is the author (with John Naylor) of two previous books on work and unemployment and has contributed to *Introduction to Work and Organisational Psychology*, by Nik Chmiel (Blackwell, 2000). She has published many papers on her research into teamworking and cross-cultural management.

Stephen Swailes B.Sc. (Hons), DMS, MPhil., MBA, PhD

Stephen is a Senior Lecturer at Hull University Business School where he teaches undergraduate and postgraduate management modules in the UK and overseas. Starting his career in scientific research Stephen worked in the water industry and later for a research and consulting organization. During this time he became interested in the study of management - trying to understand what was happening around him - and completed a Diploma in Management Studies and an MBA. After working in business and market research he moved into teaching and was awarded a PhD for research on employee commitment in organizations and how changes in the workplace influence the nature and expression of commitment. He has published over 30 papers in the fields of organizational commitment and, with Barbara Senior, on team performance. He has contributed several book chapters on organization structure, teams and teamwork, and how organizations use technology. His main research interest now is on talent management and, in particular, how the idea of talent is constructed. Stephen's scientific background and time in manufacturing laid down a lasting interest in graduate employability and he is co-author with Simon Roodhouse of *Employers, Skills and Higher Education* by Kingsham Press.

Acknowledgements

Barbara

This fourth edition of the book is dedicated to my late husband Gerry, without whom this project would not have happened. As always, my children David and Jayne as well as various friends have listened with patience to my accounts of researching, writing and checking. Their moral support has been important to me.

I am delighted to welcome Stephen, who I have known and worked with for many years, as my co-author for this 4th edition. His important contribution to this edition has made it happen.

Finally, Stephen and I have tried to be true to the large amount of research and work already accomplished in the subject area of organizational change. Every effort has been made to trace and acknowledge ownership of copyright.

Stephen

Although Barbara and I have worked together for nearly 20 years I would like to take this opportunity of thanking her for inviting me to co-author the fourth edition of this popular book. Barbara has been a good colleague and friend without whom some of the things I have achieved would never have been possible. I am also indebted to Elizabeth my wife for her patience and support while writing for this book and to Thomas and Nicholas whose working lives will see change on a grand scale.

Publisher's acknowledgements

We are grateful to the following for permission to reproduce copyright material:

Figures

Figure 1.2 from *Creative Management*, Prentice Hall (Goodman, M. 1995) 38; Figure 2.1 from *Implementing Strategic Change*, Kogan Page (Grundy, T. 1993); Figure 2.2 from *Exploring Strategic Change*, FT Prentice Hall (Balogun, J. and Hailey,V.H. 2004); Figure 2.2 from *Exploring Strategic Change*, Pearson Education (Balogun, J. and Hope Hailey, V.H. 2004); Figure 2.3 from Radical change accidentally: The emergence and amplification of small change., *Academy of Management Journal*, 50(3), 515–543 (Plowman, D. A, Baker, L.T., Beck, T.E., Kulkarni, M., Solansky, S.T. and Travis, D.V.); Figure 2.4 from Evolution and revolution as organizations grow, *Harvard Business Review*, 41 (Greiner, L.E. 1972); Figure 3.1 from *Management and Organisational Behaviour*, 7, FT/Prentice Hall (Mullins, L.J. 2005) 612; Figure 3.5 from Morgan, G. (1989) *Creative Organization Theory. A Resource Book*, London, Sage, p.66; Figure 3.9 from The effective organization forces and forms, *Sloan Management Review*, 32, part2, 55 (Mintzberg, H. 1991); Figures on pages 82 and 83 from www.unilever.com/ourcompany/newsandmedia, Unilever Plc; Figure 4.2 from Measuring organizational cultures: a qualitative and quantitative study across twenty cases, *Administrative Science Quarterly*, 35, 291 (Hofstede, G., Neuijen, B., Ohayv, D.D. and Sanders. G. 1990); Figure on page 135 adapted from *Exploring Corporate Strategy, Texts and Cases*, 7, Pearson Education (Johnson, G., Scholes, K. and Whittington, R. 2005) 201–5; Figure 4.3 from Managing Cultures: Making Strategic Relationships Work (Hall, W., 1995, p.58), Chichester, Wiley, © 1995, copyright John Wiley & Sons Ltd, reproduced with permission; Figure 4.4 adapted from A competing values framework for analysing presentational communication in management contexts, *Journal of Business Communication*, 28(3), 213–232 (Quinn, R.E. 1991); Figure 4.5 from Managing Change Across Corporate Cultures (Trompenaars, F. and Prud'homme, P., 2004, p.67, figure 2.6), Chichester, Capstone Publishing, © 2004, copyright John Wiley & Sons Ltd, reproduced with permission of John Wiley & Sons Ltd on behalf of Capstone Publishing Ltd; Figure 4.7 adapted with permission from *Cultures and Organizations*, McGraw Hill (Hofstede, G. 1991), copyright © Geert Hofstede; Figure 4.8 from *A European Management Model Beyond Diversity*, Prentice Hall (Calori, R. and De Woot, P. 1994) 20; Figure 4.10, 4.11 and 4.12 Reprinted from *Organizational Dynamics*, Summer, Schwartz, H. and Davis, S.M., "Matching corporate strategy and business strategy", p. 36, 41 and 44, copyright 1981, with permission from Elsevier; Figure 6.5 from *Beyond Rational Management: Mastering the Paradoxes and Competing High Demands of High Performance*, Jossey-Bass (Quinn, R.E., 1988); Figure 6.7 from The strategic management of corporate change, *Human Relations*, 46(8), 908 (Dunphy, D. and Stace, D. 1993); Figure 6.9 adapted from Creating readiness for organizational change, *Human Relations*, 46(6), 681–704 (Armenakis, A.A., Harris, S.G. & Mossholder, K.W. 1993); Figure 8.2 from *Doing Action Research in Your Own Organization*, Sage Publications (Coghlan, D. and Brannick, T. 2007) 35; Figure 8.7 from "The Pugh Matrix", from Course P679 Planning and Managing Change, Block 4, Section 6, Copyright © The Open University; Figure 9.1 adapted from Organizational Change Capacity in Public Services: The Case of the World Health Organization *Journal of Change Management*, 8(1), 57–72 (Klarner, P., Probst, G. and Soparnot, R. 2008)

Tables

Table 1.1 from *Working Futures 2004–14 National Report*, Institute of Employment Research, University of Warwick (Wilson, R., Hominedou, K. and Dickerson, A. 2006); Table 2.1 from *The Essence of Change*, Prentice Hall (Clarke, L. 1994); Table 4.1 adapted with permission from Cultural constraints in management theories in *Academy of Management Executive*, February (Hofstede, G. 1993), copyright © Geert Hofstede; Table 5.1 from Understanding Power: Bringing about Strategic Change, *British Journal of Management*, 7 (special issue), S3-S16 (Hardy, C. 1996); Table 9.1 from Organizational Discourse and New Organization Development Processes, *British Journal of Management*, 19 Special Issue, S7-S19 (Marshak, R.J. and Grant, D. 2008)

Text

Illustration 3.14 from *Organizations: A Guide to Problems and Practice*, Sage Publications (Child, J., 1998); Illustration 4.12 from On a wavelength with the Danes, *Financial Times*, 23 October 2000, 15 (Frank, S.), reprinted with permission of Sergey Frank, International Management Consultant; Illustration 5.11 from Sociological Paradigms and Organisational Analysis, Heinemann Educational Books (Burrell, G. and Morgan, G., 1979);

The Financial Times

Case Study on pages 65–66 from NHS revolution breathes new life into private sector *Financial Times*, 3 May 2004, 6 (Timmins, N.); Figures 2.5, 2.6 from Breakpoint: how to stay in the game, *Financial Times Mastering Management*, Part 17 (Strebel, P. 1996), 1st March 1996; Figure 6.11 from Choosing the right path, *Financial Times Mastering Management*, Part 14, p.17 (Strebel, P. 1996), 9th February 1996

In some instances we have been unable to trace the owners of copyright material, and we would appreciate any information that would enable us to do so.

Part One

THE CONTEXT AND MEANING OF CHANGE

Even before the recent financial crisis and economic recession the rhetoric of business was telling us that the pace of change was accelerating and all organizations, if they are to survive, have to anticipate and respond to change. Now that recession and credit problems are affecting public spending and consumer demand in many developed countries the pressures for change to ensure organizational survival are probably even greater.

Part One of this book examines what is meant by organizational change and the reasons why it happens. Chapter 1 begins by proposing a model of organization in which organizational life is influenced by many factors, mainly those originating outside the organization. A metaphor of the 'winds of change' is used to show how organizational activities are the outcomes of historical developments as well as the results of the day-to-day vagaries of political, economic, technological and sociocultural influences. Chapter 2 investigates the nature of organizational change in more detail.

Chapter 1

Organizations and their changing environments

In this chapter, organizations are defined as systems comprising elements of formal organizational management and operations as well as elements of the more informal aspects of organizational life. Organizational systems are conceptualized as operating in three types of environment – temporal, external and internal – whose elements interact with each other to create the 'triggers' of change.

Learning objectives

By the end of this chapter you will be able to:

- describe the general characteristics of organizations;

- identify triggers for change in a range of organizations;

- discuss the concept of organizations as systems operating in multi-dimensional environments and the implications for understanding the causes of organizational change;

- analyze the level of turbulence in organizational environments.

A view of organizations

At the simplest level we can think of organizations as the physical spaces that we work in and interact with. 'Who do you work for?' is a common question in small-talk and our replies give a name and place to the organization that we identify with and which pays our salaries. Tony Watson (2002, p. 45) summarized definitions of organizations and noted that a common factor is the idea that organizations have goals which act as a glue holding together the various systems used to produce things. As well as systems arranged to meet goals Watson also points out that management actions come after the goals have been set.

So organizations can be seen as people interacting in some kind of structured or organized way to achieve some defined purpose or goal. However, the interactions of people, as members of an organization, need some kind of managing to give shape and direction to their activities. This implies some kind of structuring of their activities that picks up the idea of organizational roles. In addition, the activities of individual organizational members and their interactions with one another imply processes through which work gets done in order to achieve the organization's purposes or goals. Thus we have organizations as entities and organization as a way of organizing. Above all, there is the requirement for decision-taking about the processes (the means) by which the goals (the ends) are achieved.

Organizations also have geographic and product/market boundaries yet Butler (1991) saw boundaries as 'abstractions' (see Illustration 1.1). However, boundaries are real, even if sometimes diffuse, and draw attention to the concept of an organization's environment. By this is meant all those influences that may act to disturb organizational life but are not considered directly part of it.

Illustration 1.1

The meaning of organization

A typical working definition of an organization might say it is: (1) a social entity that (2) has a purpose, (3) has a boundary, so that some participants are considered inside while others are considered outside, and (4) patterns the activities of participants into a recognizable structure (Daft, 1989). Although organizations are real in their consequences, both for their participants and for their environments, they are essentially abstractions. The hospital, the firm or the school have physical aspects to them, the buildings, the plant and equipment and so on, but to understand how organizations work we need to go further than this. The factory has something real and physical about it but this is not the organization; people are doing tasks to which there is a pattern, raw materials are taken in, converted and distributed to markets; capital is provided by banks and other financial institutions; systems provide information for decision making and coordination; people are talking about matters that do not necessarily appear to have anything to do with the job; some people remote from the physical plant, perhaps a continent away, are making decisions critical to our factory.

Source: Butler, R. (1991) *Designing Organizations. A Decision-Making Perspective*, London: Routledge, pp. 1–2.

This view of organizations draws on the concept of an organization as a system of interacting subsystems and components set within wider systems and environments that provide inputs to the system and receive its outputs. This is shown in Figure 1.1, which identifies the main elements of most organizations and their functioning. These are grouped into two main subsystems – the formal and informal. Thus elements of the formal subsystem include the organization's strategy, whether this is devised by a single person, as might happen in a small owner–manager company, or by a board of directors and top management group. Other components include the organization's goals and the means of achieving them through the production of goods or services. Management, as the formal decision-making and control element, is of course present in all organizations.

It is clear from any examination of complex systems like organizations that some kind of structuring of activities is required and the concept of organizational structure is central to that of organizational systems. However, nearly 40 years ago Child (1973) drew attention to other, more intangible elements of organizational life such as the political behaviour of organizational members.

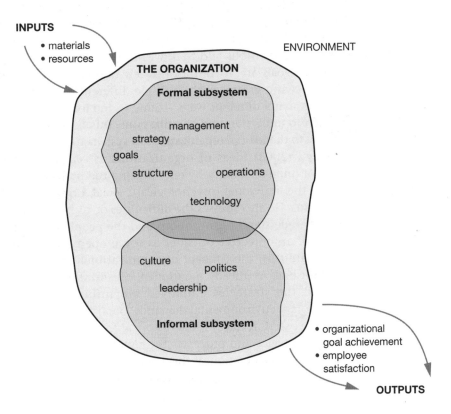

Figure 1.1 The organization as a system

Nadler (1988) included the informal organization (patterns of communication, power and influence, values and norms) in his systems model of organizational behaviour and Stacey (2003) coined the phrase 'shadow system' to describe these less predictable and more intangible aspects of organizational life. Thus the idea of the 'informal subsystem' encapsulates the more hidden elements of organizational culture and politics and the rather less hidden element of leadership – including those who are led.

These relatively stable subsystems and elements of organizational functioning interact with each other in some kind of transformation process. This means taking inputs such as materials, capital and knowledge and transforming them into product or service outputs. However, while the outputs can be thought of as the legitimate reason for the organization's existence, an output that is particularly relevant to the informal subsystem is employee behaviour and job satisfaction. This is reinforced by Storey, Edwards and Sisson (1997, p. 1) who note that: 'Given that technology and finance are increasingly internationally mobile and that innovations can be copied rapidly, it is the unique use of human resources, which is especially critical to long-term organizational success.'

However, the concept of organizational systems as open systems has not gone without criticism. Silverman (1970) challenged the idea of organizations as systems since the notion rests on an assumption that defining an organization's goals is uncontentious and that, within the organization, there is consensus as to what its goals are. A contrasting view of organizations as being composed of individuals and groups with multiple different interests – who construe their actions in many different ways – came to the fore. Known as the 'social action' approach to understanding organizations, this became recognized as an alternative view to the idea of organizations as systems.

Stacey's (2003) ideas of organizations as *complex* systems emphasize the notion of unpredictability by emphasizing the multitude of interactions in and between the individual (psychological), social, organizational and environmental domains. He also stresses the difficulties or, as he sees them impossibilities, of trying to understand organizations and the people within them from the point of view of an objective outsider as some open systems theorists have done. Having said this, the concept of organizational systems as *open* systems is an important one. As already mentioned, organizations transform inputs into outputs and the strategies employed are influenced by both historical and contemporary environmental demands, opportunities and constraints.

The next section traces some historical trends, which have influenced organizational strategies and processes through time. This tracing of history acts as a prelude to a consideration of the more immediate environment of organizations today and as they might present themselves in the future.

The historical context for change

The forces that operate to bring about change in organizations can be thought of as winds which vary from warm summer breezes that merely disturb a few papers to hurricanes that cause devastation to structures and operations that require reorientation of purpose and rebuilding. Sometimes, the winds subside to give periods of relative calm and organizational stability. During the agricultural age which prevailed in Europe until the early 1700s (Goodman, 1995) wealth was created in the context of a society based on agriculture that was influenced mainly by local markets for both produce and labour punctuated by uncontrollable factors such as bad weather and epidemics. During this time the cycle of activities required to maintain life was predictable even if for most people life was little more than at subsistence level.

Maintaining the meteorological metaphor, stronger winds of change blew in the Industrial Revolution and the industrial age beginning in the late 1700s which drove industrial output in the UK and later in America well into the twentieth century. It was characterized by a series of inventions and innovations that reduced the number of people needed to work the land and, through the factory system, provided the means of mass production. To a large extent demand and supply were predictable, enabling companies to structure their organizations along what Burns and Stalker (1966) described as mechanistic lines – as systems of strict hierarchical structures and lines of control.

This situation prevailed into the late twentieth century and of course still exists in some organizations. Demand came largely from domestic markets and organizations strived to meet consumer demand and the most disturbing environmental influence on organizations of this time was the demand for products which outstripped supply. Henry Ford's remark that 'Any customer can have a car painted any colour so long as it is black', summed-up the supply-led state of the markets. Apart from any technical difficulties of producing different colours of car, Ford did not have to worry about customers' colour preferences: he could sell all that he made.

Figure 1.2 characterizes organizations of this period as 'task oriented', with effort being put into increasing production through more effective and efficient production processes. The push during this period for ever-increasing efficiency of production supported the continuing application of the earlier ideas of Taylor (1911) and Scientific Management allied to Fordism that was derived from Henry Ford's ideas of assembly-line production (see Wood, 1989). This was a period mainly of command and control, of bureaucratic structures and the belief that there was 'one best way' of organizing work for efficient production. However, as time passed, this favourable period for organizations began to wane as people became more discriminating in the goods and services they wanted and as technological progress brought about increased productivity to the point where supply overtook demand. A consequence of this was that organizations began increasingly to look abroad to open up new markets for their outputs.

At the same time, organizations faced increasing competition from abroad for their own products and services. In the West, this forced the shrinking or near elimination of some high labour cost manufacturing sectors (like textiles and clothing) and a shift from manufacturing to services such as banking and

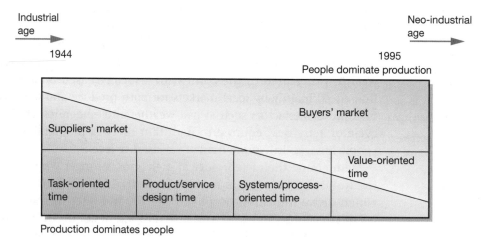

Figure 1.2 Market factors impacting on operations of Western organizations
Source: Goodman, M. (1995) *Creative Management*, Hemel Hempstead: Prentice Hall, p. 38.

insurance, real estate, healthcare and education. In the neo-industrial age of the advanced economies the emphasis has moved towards adding value to goods and services – what Goodman calls the value-oriented time (see Illustration 1.2) in contrast with the task-oriented, products/services-oriented and systems-oriented times of the past.

Illustration 1.2

Value-oriented time

Customers

As competition becomes more severe and markets oversupplied, organizations must find products and services that are differentiated not only by purpose and form but also by the 'added value' which attaches to them. This means identifying potential customer expectations and then exceeding them. In other words, organizations must constantly increase customers' perceived value for money.

As product life cycles shorten, organizations are under increasing pressure to introduce new products and hence there is a need for constant innovation. Innovation is, however, not only associated with the product itself but also with ways of supplying and marketing. What may differentiate one product offering from another is not the product itself but the innovative production techniques, quality and relationship marketing – skills that are difficult for competition to copy.

Production

Of the production processes of the future, Goodman (1995, p. 49) says:

> On the supply side, production will continue to get leaner and more responsive to customer demand. Lean production appears to do the impossible. It delivers the great product variety once associated with craft production at costs that are often less than those associated with mass production. Furthermore these benefits are provided together with products of high quality by sophisticated networking processes.

Knowledge

The economies of the West can no longer rely on mass production. Knowledge has become increasingly important and through intelligence and creative thinking organizations will improve competitiveness. Information and communication technology are of more importance than mass production systems which gave competitive advantage in the past. People as human capital have become the most important asset to most organizations as only people have the inherent capacity to solve complex problems. To quote Goodman again (1995, pp. 49–50):

The successful product packages of the future will result from the exposure of creativity to complex, curvilinear, messy, fuzzy logic-type problems. As demand grows for such value packages, so individuals will respond by having ingenious ideas. This will challenge organisations, with their liking for structure and order, as intensive creativity usually arises out of chaos and disorder conditions . . . Thus, old mind-sets and rule books will have to give way to new organisational patterns that continuously encourage individuals to have ideas.

The impact of the information age which began around 1970 is captured in the comments of Jones, Palmer, Osterweil and Whitehead (1996):

. . . the pace and scale of the change demanded of organizations and those who work within them are enormous. Global competition and the advent of the information age, where knowledge is the key resource, have thrown the world of work into disarray. Just as we had to shed the processes, skills and systems of the agricultural era to meet the demands of the industrial era, so we are now having to shed ways of working honed for the industrial era to take advantage of the opportunities offered by the information age . . . Organizations are attempting to recreate themselves and move from the traditional structure to a dynamic new model where people can contribute their creativity, energy and foresight in return for being nurtured, developed and enthused.

Activity 1.1

Consider how you would describe an organization that you know well in terms of its wealth-creating capacity. For instance:

- Which business sectors does it operate in?

- Does the organization operate at a local, regional, national or international level?

- Does it supply domestic or international markets – or both?

- In what ways does the organization need creativity and innovation to survive?

- What is the mix of employees – unskilled, skilled, professional?

- Can it attract and keep high-performing employees?

- How much autonomy do employees have over the work they choose to do and how they do it?

- How much is decision-taking devolved to the lowest level possible or kept in the hands of top management?

 **An uncertain future**

Your responses to Activity 1.1 may show an organization operating in a fairly predictable environment with a sense of security about the future – where the winds of change are light to moderate. Other responses may suggest more uncertainty about markets, demand, the ability to attract and retain good employees and whether employment will increase or decrease – an environment where the winds of change are stronger. If creativity, innovation, and working in teams to solve complex problems are indicative of the organization it has already moved into value-oriented time (see Figure 1.2).

Most commentators on organizations agree that business is becoming ever more uncertain as the pace of change quickens and the future becomes more unpredictable (Furnham, 2000). One of the best-known management thinkers, the late Peter Drucker, writing in 1988, maintained that future organizations would be almost wholly information-based and that they would resemble more a symphony orchestra than the command and control, managed structures prevalent in the past (see Illustration 1.3).

Illustration 1.3

Organizations as symphony orchestras

Writing about the way that information technology is transforming business enterprises and how they would look today, Drucker observed:

A large symphony orchestra is even more instructive, since for some works there may be a few hundred musicians on stage playing together. According to organization theory then, there should be several group vice president conductors and perhaps a half-dozen division VP conductors. But that's not how it works. There is only the conductor-CEO – and every one of the musicians plays directly to that person

without an intermediary. And each is a high-grade specialist, indeed an artist.

(Drucker, 1988, p. 48)

A contemporary study of a conductorless orchestra (think about that for a moment) emphasized creativity by all musicians and the relationship between trust and control – specifically trust in the competence of others and trust in their goodwill (Khodyakov, 2007). The orchestra metaphor is useful to help us imagine how work organizations could work, if only . . .

With this vision of how organizations would change Drucker predicted the demise of middle management and the rise of organizations staffed almost exclusively with high-grade, specialist staff. Middle management has been a victim of the downsizing so popular in the past 20 years (McCann, Morris and Hassard, 2008; Thomas and Dunkerley, 1999) yet the culling did not reach Druckerian proportions. However, for the United Kingdom, the projected growth in the numbers of professionals and knowledge-based workers and the decrease in numbers of lower-skilled workers is supported by data published by the Institute for Employment Research (see Table 1.1).

Table 1.1 Percentage share of UK employment, 1994–2014

	1994	2004	2009	2014
Managers and senior officials	13.6	15.3	16.0	16.6
Professional occupations	10.0	11.8	12.6	13.5
Associate professional and technical	12.0	14.3	14.7	15.2
Administrative and clerical	14.8	12.6	11.8	11.0
Skilled trades	13.6	11.4	10.9	10.5
Personal services	5.6	7.5	8.0	8.5
Sales and customer service	7.0	8.0	8.4	8.9
Machine and transport operators	9.7	7.9	7.5	7.2
Elementary occupations	13.7	11.3	10.0	8.7

Source: Wilson, R., Hominedou, K. and Dickerson, A. (2006) *Working Futures 2004–14 National Report*, Institute for Employment Research, University of Warwick.

While the percentages shown in Table 1.1 may not appear particularly gripping at first sight, think about the numbers of people behind the percentage changes shown. We will see significantly more people in managerial and professional posts and in sales and personal services. In contrast, we will see big falls in administrative and skilled jobs along with machine operators and people doing elementary work. These adjustments to the UK labour force represent a response by employers to the skills they need if they are to respond to global competition.

Activity 1.2

Linking to Illustration 1.3, if you work in an organization, think about the people you work with. What are your impressions of your trust in their goodwill and their competence? What might your colleagues think of you in this regard? What do your impressions mean for the likelihood of successful change in the organization?

Clarke (1994, p. 1) maintained that the 1980s were a time when change was an 'accelerating constant'. This view was echoed later by Dawson (2003, pp. 1–2) in his discussion of a 'new bias for organizational action', meaning that managers needed to be leaders of change or else, in an increasingly competitive environment, their organizations will cease to exist.

This somewhat dramatic tone was supported by Nadler and Tushman (1999, p. 45), who observed: 'Poised on the eve of the next century, we are witnessing a profound transformation in the very nature of our business organizations. Historic forces have converged to fundamentally reshape the scope, strategies, and structures of large, multi-business enterprises.' Continuing to use the 'winds of change' metaphor, the expectation is of damaging gale-force winds bringing the need for rebuilding that incorporates new ideas and ways of doing things.

What seems uncontestable is that the public and private sectors are facing fast-moving change even if the exact nature of the changes needed is not always clear. In the next section we look in more detail at the environmental winds that disturb organizational life and analyze the factors which trigger organizational change.

Environmental triggers of change

When we were writing this new edition in 2008 two extraordinary things happened. The first was a near meltdown of the banking and financial structures in western developed economies which, although a few had predicted it, came upon us with speed and surprise. Lehman Brothers, the fourth largest investment bank in the US, went into what was then the world's biggest bankruptcy. *The Times* (2008) considered the collapse to have been avoidable and blamed it on an aggressive chief executive who was quick to talk yet slow to listen, backed up by weak board members. Other organizational pillars of the financial community fell or were baled out. Confidence fell and fear spread among the business community.

The investments that we thought were in safe hands in prudently managed institutions quickly turned out to be anything but. Investments and pension fund values plummeted and the UK and US governments were forced into fast and decisive action – pumping billions into their financial systems to recapitalize the banks, keep them afloat and save themselves. Queues of people waiting to take their money out of high street banks would surely have led to the government's quick demise. What long-term changes will the credit crunch force on governments, institutions and investors? Capitalism came close to imploding; new rules and regulatory frameworks for financial institutions seem needed at least.

The other momentous change was the election of Barack Obama as President of the United States of America. Throughout the presidential race both Senators Obama and McCain called for change. 'Vote for me and things will change' was the rallying cry to voters. Quite what would change and in what way did not seem so emphatically spelt out. When Senator Obama's victory was assured there seemed a great sense of relief in the media and in large sections of America. Something new had happened; America had woken up to a black president and surely this would lead to new ways of seeing things; to change. By the time you are reading this book we will know to what extent the nation's hopes were met.

While these great events were unfolding in the UK we read and heard of the truly awful case of 'Baby P' whose short life ended when he died from neglect and abuse from those who should have been looking after him. Despite being seen 60 times by social workers from Haringey Council a mixture of bureaucracy, blame culture and incompetence conspired to seal the poor child's fate. Not many years before another child in Haringey had met a similar end and this must raise concerns about how much, if anything, the Council had learned from the first occurrence. We also read of a whistleblower who wrote to inspectors six months before 'Baby P' died who was claiming that her life had been ruined. The former social worker claimed that after she accused the organization of negligence her bosses conspired to undermine her. Are people in organizations more concerned with protecting their own reputations and taking vengeance than intervening and making changes to ensure the safety of children obviously at risk? It seems so in this case. Touched by public outrage the case was debated in parliament, with promises made to ensure it cannot happen again. But it will happen again unless fundamental changes take place in and amongst the organizations responsible and in the attitudes of the people involved.

We see from these episodes that change is triggered by large and momentous events and by events touching a single individual that are so unacceptable that something has to be done – or at least appear to be done. In the latter case, it is as if people tolerate what they know are unacceptable situations, idly waiting for the critical incident that will act as a change trigger. Yet while we are all used to hearing calls for change, Burnes (2005) observes that while change is all around us examples of successful change are 'elusive' (p. 73). Because it is so often a mantra of politicians and managers, change has attracted much theory development in an effort to explain how successful change works.

Figure 1.1 depicts an organization as a system receiving inputs from its environment and releasing outputs back into it. The view of organizations existing as systems of interrelated elements operating in multi-dimensional environments has a number of supporters. The work of Peter Checkland (1972), for instance, is well known for the pioneering development of the soft systems model – an approach designed specifically for analyzing and designing change in what Checkland terms 'human activity systems', most frequently, organizational systems. Nadler (1988) has proposed a systems model applied to organizational behaviour and Stacey (2003) uses systems concepts in his discussion of organizations and change. However, before reading any further in this chapter, please have a go at Activity 1.3.

Activity 1.3

For an organization that you know well, what are the main reasons why it has attempted to make changes to products, services, systems and/or structure?

Brooks (2004, p. 4) sees the environment as 'a general concept which embraces the totality of external environmental forces which may influence any aspect of organizational activity'. It is worth noting that while some environmental changes are objective, even measurable, it is the ways that people interpret events that determine how an organization responds (Mason, 2007). Thus to some extent the environment is a construction of reality. Similar organizations in the same sector while battling with the same forces may construct the significance of events quite differently. The different constructions arise from the following:

- The characteristics and experiences of the people filtering information from the environment.
- Organization culture – what recipes does the culture have for interpreting the events?
- Organizational politics and structures.
- How the organization has developed in the past.
- How the business sector as a whole interprets the information.

When you completed Activity 1.3, did you list anything that falls under any of the following headings?

- changing customer requirements;
- changing demand for products/services;
- government or regulatory bodies;
- trade union activity;
- actions by competitors;
- business performance (falling incomes or revenues);
- economic climate;
- technological advances;
- marketing techniques;
- prices of inputs (materials, labour);
- computing and information systems developments;
- the growth of e-commerce and use of the Internet.

An organization's environment also includes broader influences such as the internationalization of trade, the prevailing political ideology, attitudes to trade unions, changes from public to private ownership or vice versa, demographic changes and changes in family structure. We now consider the environment in more detail and draw attention to the way changes in the organizational environment can trigger consequent changes in some or all of the ways an organization and its constituent components operate.

An analytical framework

A common way of grouping different environmental factors uses the PEST mnemonic; political, economic, social and technological factors. Legal and ecological factors can be considered as well (PESTLE). Figure 1.3 illustrates the PEST

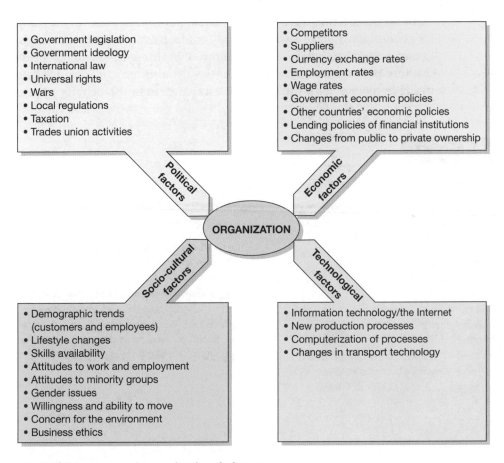

Figure 1.3 PEST factors and organizational change

factors that, at some time or another, impact upon an organization's formal and informal subsystems and their components as well as the product/service it offers and the markets it serves.

Political triggers

A plethora of national and international bodies, elected and unelected, influence organizational life to a greater or lesser degree. Consequently, not only do changes in the political environment influence organizations directly, they also interact with changes in the economic environment. Examples include the government-inspired privatization of previously publicly owned institutions such as the UK programme of privatizing utilities and railways, and/or the cooperation of different governments to stimulate trade.

Perhaps the most important role for governments is the bringing of economic prosperity to their countries. They also act as lawmakers, passing legislation that requires employers to make changes. Consider how employers have responded to legislation addressing discrimination, equal pay and flexible hours, for instance. All governments have influence and control over their healthcare systems. Consequently they influence their countries' health policies and practices and the health of their populations. Illustration 1.4 demonstrates the complexity of issues arising from what some might regard as a change in health delivery policy.

Illustration 1.4

Health reforms approved in France

The French parliament approved controversial healthcare changes aimed at cutting the debt burden. Changes include the following:

- a new charge of one euro for seeing a doctor;
- an increase in the levy payable by pensioners and companies;
- a new reimbursement system to reward patients who use a doctor rather than going straight to a specialist;
- incentives for patients to choose generic drugs over more expensive branded varieties;
- cracking down on fraudulent sick leave;
- new health 'ID' cards to stop abuse of prescriptions.

The moves were part of an attempt to trim the budget deficit, which exceeded EU limits for three years in a row. An official report said the standard of care provided by French doctors was among the best in the world, but the system was badly regulated and badly governed. Some of the reforms have been criticised by health workers, who accuse the government of creeping privatisation.

Source: BBC News (2004).

The general election in the UK in 1979 proved to be a turning point and is a good example of how political decisions influence organizations. The 1970s were characterized by poor industrial relations, ongoing strikes, stoppages and disputes. Union influence on the government and on employers and employees was high. With a clear mandate from the electorate, successive governments under Prime Minister Thatcher introduced legislation to curb union powers and to increase the level of democracy in union-related workplace decisions. The manager's right to manage was asserted as was the primacy of market forces. Business had to stand in the face of market forces or it would be allowed to fall. Government intervention through subsidies to prop up fundamentally unprofitable enterprises was no longer an option. The demise of coal mining in the UK bears testimony to this principle. The Labour government that was swept to power in 1997 did nothing to change the prevailing government philosophy on this issue.

The collapse and break-up of the former Soviet Union led to the opening of fledgling market economies and thus to opportunity. Some former Soviet bloc countries are now in the European Union – unthinkable 20 years ago. Spurred on by the political belief that certain public assets would be far more efficiently managed in the private sector the privatization programmes begun under Mrs Thatcher forced huge changes in the sectors affected. Competition was introduced into telecommunications, gas, electricity and water supply among other sectors. Managers faced new challenges and had to learn quickly if their organizations were to survive. Job security changed as did the working patterns and routines of staff.

Thatcherism and policies from subsequent Labour governments have forced big change upon public sector organizations. Frameworks for inspection and audit have flourished and ways were found to evaluate and rank the performance of public organizations. League tables of hospitals, local authorities and police forces, for instance, put organizations into the spotlight. If nothing else this must raise the pressure on managers to act. We often see public sector managers on TV apologizing, explaining or justifying some action by their organization – this rarely happened before save for the worst of disasters. The media is very quick to jump on even a minor failure of policy and put some poor manager under scrutiny.

The UK government acted decisively in winter 2008 to save the country's financial systems and similar actions were taken by other world leaders. Whereas 30 years ago the new attitudes ushered in deregulation of financial systems it does look as if deregulation went too far and allowed too many 'toxic' products that brought the sector to the brink. With governments taking a stake in their leading banks it looks like some things are going to have to change – restrictions on this type of product and the links between performance and employee reward perhaps. Indeed, at least one of the authors hopes the whole concept of performance in the financial sector is revisited!

Political decisions also influence the ability of organizations to operate and trade on an increasingly international scale. Multinational companies in particular have to grapple with issues such as dealing with a far more diverse workforce and the need to assimilate multiple cultures.

Activity 1.4

Look back at Figure 1.3 and your answer to Activity 1.3.

What do your conclusions tell you about the interconnections between the various aspects of the PEST environment?

Can you make any interconnections between decisions made outside your country that will affect the country you live and work in?

Economic triggers

Activity 1.4 may show that some factors can be categorized in more than one way. This is normal and simply illustrates the fact that aspects of the organizational environment are interrelated and operate in a complex way to trigger change within organizations. However, because organizations operate in the main to make profits or, in the case of public sector organizations to operate within budgets, some of their more serious concerns are with triggers for change in the economic environment. This includes a concern for competitors and other issues, such as exchange rates, corporation tax, wage rates and skills availability which determine their ability to compete.

Political and economic environments are closely related since political decisions shape economic fortunes and economic changes influence political decisions. In general, governments in developed countries at least work to keep four key economic indicators in balance (Cook, 2004):

- increasing output of goods and services (economic growth);
- healthy balance of payments (more exports than imports);
- low inflation;
- low unemployment.

After a long period of stability in the UK, inflation and unemployment rose sharply in 2008 and national output began to fall; recession had arrived. A casualty of recession is confidence. Organizations become less confident about the future; people start to worry about job security and their ability to provide for their dependents. Attitudes change too – what seemed a good idea yesterday is not so appropriate today. Priorities change, projects are shelved and structures change as organizations regroup and reposition in their competitive environment.

Changing economic structure in the past 30 years has led to more flexible career patterns. Whereas having several jobs within a single lifetime career was normal, a response to contemporary market conditions is to have several jobs in several careers in a working lifetime. There has also been a shift in attitudes away from the paternal employer having the responsibility to look after employee development and offer job security towards employees being much more responsible for their own development and for ensuring their own employability. At the root of this are changes to the psychological contract between employer and employee – the sets of mutual expectations that each party has of the other (Rousseau, 2001, 2004).

Socio-cultural triggers

All the socio-cultural factors listed in Figure 1.3 influence the way organizations are set up, run and managed as well as their capacity to attract people to work within them. Examples of how changes in the socio-cultural environment influence attitudes to work and trigger changes are:

- expectations for continuous increases in the standard of living;
- demographic changes such as the age composition of the workforce;
- changes in family structures and the roles of men and women which influence preferences for working hours and provision of child care;
- heightened awareness of equality and intolerance of unfair and unethical practices;
- heightened awareness of and sensitivity to cultural and religious differences.

Business practices in long-established organizations have an historical pedigree and in light of socio-cultural changes need to be reviewed to ensure they do not contain any practices that could be seen as discriminatory. Recruitment, selection and promotion policies are particularly vulnerable here. Organization cultures can tolerate, even promote, sexist or racist banter and where this happens managers have to act to eliminate it. For example, the Metropolitan Police have received steady criticism for being 'institutionally racist'; criticisms which seem slow to go away despite apparent efforts by managers to change the culture among officers.

Geert Hofstede pioneered a better understanding of how national cultures differ which we discuss in Chapter 4 and his framework and others like it suggest that different cultural groups have different approaches to organizing. This influences the nature of relationships between employees and thus the ways that organizations are structured as well as preferences for teamwork or individualism. A key implication is that what an organization does successfully in one country will probably not work so well if it simply attempted elsewhere without at least being sensitive to cultural differences.

Changing population demographics influence the availability of skills and they influence markets. Healthcare providers are of course at the sharp end of demographics. Life expectancy continues to rise and increases demand for services while new treatments stemming from technological progress can be beyond their budgets. This puts pressure on government health spending which is overshadowed by the health of the economy (or lack of it). Media interest in patients denied treatment forces healthcare providers to justify their rationing decisions. With new treatments becoming ever more costly, unless governments simply inject more money into healthcare, major changes will be needed to the decision processes and policies that govern who receives potentially lifesaving or life-prolonging treatment.

Activity 1.5

Take the list you made when doing Activity 1.3 and categorize each factor according to whether you consider it to stem from the political, economic, technological or socio-cultural forces.

Are there any factors that do not easily fit into these categories?

Technological triggers

Examples of technology triggering change are many and varied and often of a long-run effect on the shape of society and organizations. Investment in technology is seen as a driver of productivity at the level of the organization and, by aggregating organizational output, a driver at national level. It drives productivity and change by replacing labour and at the same time it creates new types of jobs. It enables new products to be marketed – good examples are communication technologies and biotechnology. Consider for a moment the business opportunities created by the Internet in the past ten years.

In terms of technology use organizations can be seen in two ways. Most just use technology to help in the production and delivery of what they produce. But some exist through the creation of technology itself – consider Microsoft, pharmaceutical manufacturers and telecoms companies for instance. Their business is technology-driven and they invest heavily in research and development in order to remain competitive.

Illustration 1.5

Spooks in the office?

The ease with which organizations can monitor how their employees use email and the Internet raises questions. Monitoring is easily done and, in the UK at least, organizations perhaps take a lead from a parliament that is routinely arguing why it should inflict ID cards and storage of mobile telephone records and Internet searches on the people. Yet organizations need to be upfront about the surveillance they are doing. They should give reasons for monitoring how employees use email and the Internet and clarify the extent to which they do it. If employees are disciplined over Internet use they would have a strong defence if their employer had not followed above-board procedures and made them clear. Human rights and data protection legislation lurk in the background.

Source: C. Smith (2006) 'At Work with Big Brother', *Financial Times*, 11 December, p.13.

The technologies that organizations use affect how they decide their structure for optimum efficiency. They affect the knowledge and skills that employers want and which employees need and lead to retraining and career change. Information and communication technology (ICT) enables teleworking which contributes to efficiency and influences work-life balance. It also shrinks time and space, enabling employees to communicate in new ways, for example as members of virtual teams. It allows employers to carry out surveillance on employees' use of emails and the Internet, raising questions about privacy and human rights. ICT has also influenced the relationships between citizen and state, at least in the UK. Our shopping trips, car journeys and Internet usage (amongst other things) are monitored. Advances in human biology are raising questions about the ethics of medical research, for example on human embryos, and seem likely to have a huge impact on health spending.

What is clear is that there is no one rationale for the way in which organizations react or interact with triggers for change coming from the PEST environment and perhaps constraints coming from their own histories and the influences of their temporal environments. External and internal politics play a part in decisions to change. While rational decision making may seem attractive, and many persuade themselves that this is what they are involved in, personal circumstances, attitudes and emotions influence the way change is attempted. In addition, not only do triggers for change come from outside, forces for change originate inside organizations – and these also need to be managed.

Illustration 1.6

Future trends

Some of the trends that managers predict will affect UK organizations in the near future are identified below.
The UK becoming a much more knowledge-based economy.
Skilled employees becoming more demanding of their employers.
Increasing difficulty recruiting and keeping talented employees.
The working population is aging and becoming more diverse.
Greater sensitivity to ethical practices and corporate social responsibility.

Greater concern for workers' quality of life and personal fulfilment.
More individualised (less standardised) relationships between employers and employees.
Greater importance put upon the ability to communicate ideas and persuade others.

Source: Environmental Scanning: Trends Affecting the World of Work in 2018 (2008). Executive Summary, Chartered Management Institute.

Activity 1.6

Think about the future trends in Illustration 1.6. What sorts of things will organizations have to do to respond to them? Can you think of any sectors that will not be influenced in some way by these trends?

Internal triggers and big ideas

So far we have presented change triggers as things that happen but at this point we need to introduce another trigger – the power of big ideas. To make this point we draw on what is arguably one of the most powerful ideas ever to occur to a human mind – Darwin's thoughts on natural selection (Dawkins, 2008). For the best part of 2,000 years Christian society had an easy answer to questions about why the earth exists and why it contains such a diversity of species – God created it all. The Koran also tells us how the earth was created, and all religions have a creation story.

Following his travels around the world and his studies of finches and iguanas, English naturalist Charles Darwin wondered why God had created so many different types of the same thing. It occurred to Darwin that life forms were not fixed; they evolved to adapt to their environments. Some finches had narrow, fine beaks to tease out tiny seeds, others had large, strong beaks to crack open bigger seeds. Darwin's theories of evolution were a first step in replacing one set of powerful ideas with another and this really is what change is about. But big ideas need big evidence. Even so, Darwin could not explain how species evolved – the fossil record, DNA and genetic modification were not understood for another 100 years or so. Nevertheless, despite much resistance at the time and since, Darwin's ideas have endured.

In giving this example we do not mean to deny Creationists their beliefs. Perhaps God did create the universe and then allowed things to evolve. The point of the example is to show how a new idea can mean that it is no longer necessary to adhere to established explanations of things. Big ideas don't have to have all the answers if they can stimulate changes to the way we think and the research that we do.

Activity 1.7

Hopefully provoked by this example – what do you think are the five most powerful ideas to occur to the human mind? How did they change society?

As far as work goes, can you identify a particularly big idea that has led to change?

Returning to more mundane matters, the following are indicative of internal triggers for change (Stewart, 1991; Paton and McCalman, 2000; Huczynski and Buchanan, 2007; Johnson, Scholes and Whittington, 2008):

- decisions to recognize or not recognize a union;
- a new chief executive or other senior manager;
- realization that operating structures are performing poorly;
- the redesign of jobs and working relationships among a work group;
- the redesign of a factory or office layout;
- the adoption of new technology;
- a new marketing strategy;
- a decision to sell or acquire a business unit;

- a cut in overtime working;
- labour shortages or surpluses.

It is difficult to separate completely internal from external triggers for change since decisions that appear on the surface as internal may be responses to some external event or in some way fit with the organization's strategy which is aimed at responding to external forces. This argument is taken up in more detail in Chapter 3. Meanwhile, as the next section shows, there are other ways of categorizing organizational environments that are more focused on organizations and change.

Organizational responses to change

Thus far the discussion suggests that organizations operate in at least three types of environment, which together make up the total 'operating environment' (Sadler, 1989, p. 174). The first consists of the historical developments bringing changes over time. These range from those activities that are mainly sector focused to those which rely more on knowledge and human capital – what Handy (1994) calls 'focused intelligence', that is the ability to acquire and apply knowledge and know-how. These can be categorized as the *temporal environment*. This is an environment that influences organizations in at least two ways. The first is in a general way, through the cycles of industry-based innovation, which move organizations through a major series of developments such as shown in Figure 1.2. The second is in a more specific way through the life cycle of the organization itself. This includes its particular history built up from its founder days through periods of expansion and decline, all of which are instrumental in helping to explain an organization's 'idiosyncrasies' of strategy and structure, culture, politics and leadership style.

The second type of environment is the *PEST framework* and the third is the organization's *internal environment* which, to some extent, consists of those organizational changes that are the first-line responses to changes in the external and temporal environments. Figure 1.4 is a stylized depiction of the concept of organizations as systems operating in multi-dimensional environments, with all that this means for organizations and change. However, this way of conceptualizing the organizational environment to some extent misses its dynamic nature and the degree of *strength* of the winds of change.

Environmental turbulence

The dynamics of any organization's environment have also been described in terms of the degree of environmental turbulence. Ansoff and McDonnell (1990) state that a firm's performance is optimized when its aggressiveness and responsiveness match its environment. They propose five levels of environmental turbulence:

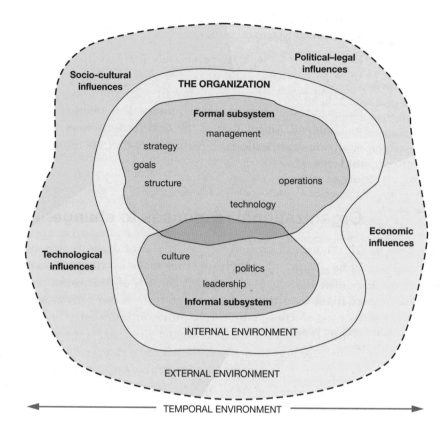

Figure 1.4 The organizational system in multi-dimensional environments

- *Level 1: Predictable.* A repetitive environment characterized by stability of markets; where the challenges repeat themselves; change is slower than the organization's ability to respond; the future is expected to be the same as the past.
- *Level 2: Forecastable by extrapolation.* Complexity increases but managers can still extrapolate from the past and forecast the future with confidence.
- *Level 3: Predictable threats and opportunities.* Complexity increases further when the organization's ability to respond becomes more problematic; however, the future can still be predicted with some degree of confidence.
- *Level 4: Partially predictable opportunities.* Turbulence increases with the addition of global and socio-political changes. The future is only partly predictable.
- *Level 5: Unpredictable surprises.* Turbulence increases further with unexpected events and situations occurring more quickly than the organization can respond.

These levels can be compared to three different kinds of change situation proposed by Stacey (1996), namely: closed change, contained change and open-ended change which are described in Illustration 1.7.

Illustration 1.7

Closed, contained and open-ended change

Closed change

When we look back at the history of an organisation there are some sequences of events that we can clearly recount in a manner commanding the widespread agreement of the members involved. We are able to say what happened, why it happened, and what the consequences are. We are also able to explain in a widely accepted way that such a sequence of events and actions will continue to affect the future course of the business. We will call this a closed change situation.

Such closed change would normally apply to the continuing operation of an existing business. For example, consider a business that supplies music to the teenage market. Managers in that business are able to say with some precision how the number of customers in that market has changed over the past and furthermore how it will change for the next 15 years or so. Those customers already exist. The managers can establish fairly clear-cut relationships between the number of customers and the number of CDs they have bought and will buy.

Contained change

Other sequences of events and actions flowing from the past are less clear-cut. Here we find that we are able to say only what probably happened, why it probably happened, and what its probable consequences were. The impact of such a sequence of events upon the future course of the business has similarly to be qualified by probability statements. For example, the music supplier will find it harder to explain why particular bands sold better than others. That supplier will find it somewhat difficult to forecast what kinds of music will sell better in the future; but market research, lifestyle studies and statistical projections will enable reasonably helpful forecasts for at least the short term.

Open-ended change

There are yet other sequences of events and actions arising from the past and continuing to impact on the future where explanations do not command anything like widespread acceptance by those involved.

The music company may have decided in the past to diversify into film by acquiring another company already in that business. That acquisition may then become unprofitable and the managers involved could well subscribe to conflicting explanations of why this is so. Some may claim that the market for film is too competitive. Others may say that diversification was a wrong move because it meant operating in a different market with which they were not familiar. Others may say that it is due to a temporary decline in demand and that the market will pick up in the future. Yet others may ascribe it to poor management of the acquisition, or to a failure to integrate it properly into the business, or to a clash of cultures between the two businesses. What that team of managers does next to deal with low profitability obviously depends upon the explanation of past failure they subscribe to.

Source: Based on Stacey, R.D. (1996) *Strategic Management and Organisational Dynamics* (2nd edn), London: Pitman, pp. 23–24.

Both Ansoff and McDonnell's levels of environmental turbulence and Stacey's closed, contained and open-ended kinds of change situation can also be related to Stacey's concepts of 'close to certainty' and 'far from certainty' (1996, p. 26). Thus, close to certainty describes a situation where organizational members face closed and contained change or, in Ansoff and McDonnell's terms, when the environment resembles Levels 1 to 3. As the degree of environmental turbulence moves from Level 4 to Level 5 or, in Stacey's terms, to a situation of open-ended change, organizations can be said to be far from certainty. These changing situations have significant implications for the actions of managers as they attempt to choose appropriate strategies to deal with them.

Activity 1.8 offers the opportunity to carry out an environmental assessment of one or more organizations. It is a challenging activity and you will almost certainly say you need further information. However, organizations always exist in situations of imperfect knowledge and managers have to do their best in the circumstances. A start may be made by (simply?) identifying whether the forces for change are strong, moderate or weak. Strebel (1996) describes a strong change force as one causing a substantial decline or a substantial improvement in performance. He identifies a moderate force for change as one causing only a minor impact on performance, while a weak force is one whose nature and direction are difficult to discern.

Activity 1.8

Think about two or three organizations with which you are familiar. Carry out an environmental assessment for each organization. To help you with this, consider:

- *the PEST factors and the organizations' internal environments;*

- *how past historical developments (either in societal or organizational terms) have influenced the organizations' strategies and operations.*

Using Ansoff and McDonnell's (1990) framework, make a judgment about the level of environmental turbulence prevailing for each organization.

Match these levels to Stacey's (1996) types of change situations.

Identify the similarities and differences in the three organizational environments.

What lessons can you draw about the probability of each organization responding to future environmental triggers for change?

The strength of the forces for change can be related to the degree of turbulence in the environment: the stronger the force the more probable it is that the environment is moving to Ansoff and McDonnell's (1990) Level 5. What this implies is that the ability to plan and manage change becomes ever more difficult as the forces and levels of turbulence increase. This is related to, but complicated further by, the different types of change that can be experienced by organizations.

Conclusions

Organizations operate in multiple environments (temporal, external and internal). The key task for organizations is to work with and try to manage them – in Schein's (1988, p. 94) words, organizations have continually to achieve 'external adaption and internal integration'. In addition, they need to be 'quick on their feet' to anticipate, where possible, opportunities and threats and react with knowledge to the 'unpredictable surprises' that Ansoff and McDonnell (1990) speak of. The purpose and focus of efforts to do so are, essentially, what managing organizational change is all about. This means understanding more fully how the formal aspects of organizational life respond to pressures from the internal, external and temporal environments – that is how change is leveraged through strategy, structure and operational processes. In addition, it means understanding the more informal processes such as power, politics and conflict, culture and leadership.

Having said this, it can be argued that all scanning tools are limited in some way. It is difficult to identify all the determinants of change, which will make it difficult to prescribe appropriate strategies. Furthermore, the information gathered is subjective and personal to the researcher at any one time.

Albright (2004) argues, however, that if managed effectively and applied progressively a continuous process of identifying, collecting and translating progressive information about external influences will benefit strategic decision making towards establishing a preparatory stance to environmental factors.

This chapter has commented on the winds of change as they blow variably and, to a degree, unpredictably. Having set the organizational environmental scene in this chapter, Chapter 2 looks in more detail at the impact of the winds of change upon organizations with a more detailed examination of the nature of change itself.

Discussion questions and assignments

1 To what extent do you think the open systems concept is helpful in understanding how organizational change might happen?

2 Give examples of environmental forces for change that are likely to affect, significantly, the way organizations operate over the next ten years. Justify your choices.

3 How realistic do you think it is to categorize types of change within an organization? What might be the advantages and disadvantages of doing this?

Discussion questions and assignments *continued*

4 Carry out an 'environmental scan' of an organization you know well. The following steps should help:

(a) Using the PEST framework, the results for one of the organizations chosen for Activity 1.8 and the suggestions in Figure 1.3, list those factors you consider could affect the future performance of the organization and/or the way it operates. Concentrate on those factors external to the organization.

(b) Indicate on your list where there are linkages between the various factors. Doing this with a mind map may help.

(c) Star those factors that are critically important to the organization. Consider where they fit in the PEST framework they are from. Are they also linked to the general movement of organizations into value-oriented time?

(d) Finally, list the starred factors and rank them according to the volatility of the external environment. Consider whether this volatility provides an opportunity or a threat to the organization and its future performance.

Through carrying out this process you may have realized how much you know about the organization's environment but also how much you do not know! The outcome of this activity may be, therefore, not only an increased understanding of the environmental forces facing the organization, but also a realization that environmental scanning requires continuous vigilance and collection of information that must then be used creatively to help predict necessary changes within the organization itself.

Case example ●●●

Nokia not so Mobile?

This Finnish company has dominated mobile telecoms but has been slow to recognize recent challenges to its market share. A customer who has used Nokia products for over ten years broke his Nokia allegiance and bought an updated camera phone from a competitor. The Nokia product portfolio does not seem to have changed its look over the past ten years. Its European share in the market is beginning to decline, and even in the company's native Finland (where loyalty is very high), the share is down from 93 per cent to 80 per cent.

A Finnish retail mobile phone chain commented that other brands, such as Samsung and Sony Ericsson, have colour screens that are so sharp, and the clam shell (folding design) is extremely handy. Nokia appears to be facing its greatest challenge since it transformed itself from a sprawling conglomerate to a highly focused telecommunications group in the early 1990s. The US share is also thought to have gone down due to competition from Motorola and LG of South Korea.

Nokia is also suffering because of a desire by mobile phone operators to launch a superior 'look and feel' over that of the handset maker. Vodafone and T-Mobile are large operators looking for differentiation in the market. Exclusivity has never been a Nokia strategy. Co-branding is becoming more common, again a strategy not yet taken by Nokia.

If Nokia were to continue to lose its share in the market, the 'tremor would be felt throughout Finland'. This company has helped put Finland on the map as a technological leader, and due to its size the employee numbers are considerable.

Source: Based on Christopher Brown-Humes and Robert Budden (2004) 'Not so Mobile: will Nokia now get the message of changing consumer tastes, new technology and stronger rivals?' *Financial Times*, 7 May 2004.

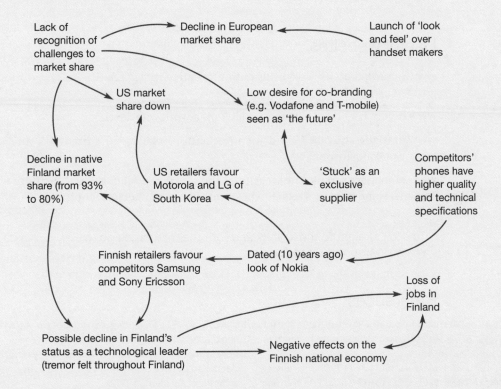

Case exercise   Analyzing the causes of change

Situations of change such as this draw attention to the complexity of the change environment. However, it is not sufficient merely to *identify* these triggers for change. Analyzing the relationships between them – in other words, their systemic nature – is even more important. The multiple-cause diagram in the case example is an attempt to do this.

Such diagrams have the power to capture the complex dynamics of change situations. They help bring about a deeper understanding of how interventions in one variable can have far-reaching effects in other parts of the situation. They act, therefore, not only in a descriptive mode, but also as an analytical tool for understanding and managing change.

1 Write a brief account of how different elements of the temporal and PEST environments interact to influence the situation described in the case.

2 Consider how you could use multiple-cause diagrams to 'picture' the multiple and interacting causes that bring pressure for change in your own organization or one you know well.

Indicative resources

Brooks, I., Weatherston, J. and Wilkinson, G. (2004) *The International Business Environment*, Harlow: Pearson Education. This text gives a detailed exploration of PEST factors and provides additional perspectives on the business environment.

Useful websites

www.guardian.co.uk Useful for current affairs articles relating to IT, politics and business.

www.ft.com Useful for business updates on a worldwide level.

www.statistics.gov.uk Useful for information relating to current UK and some European comparisons.

www.managers.org.uk The website of the Chartered Management Institute which contains summaries of research reports on a range of management issues.

To click straight to these links and for other resources go to
www.pearsoned.co.uk/senior

References

Albright, K. (2004) 'Environmental Scanning: radar for success', *The Information Management Journal*, May/June, pp. 38–45

Ansoff, I. H. and McDonnell, E.J. (1990) *Implanting Strategic Management*, Englewood Cliffs, NJ: Prentice Hall.

BBC News (2004) 'Health Reforms Approved in France'.

Brooks, I. (2004) 'The International Business Environment', in Brooks, I. Weatherston, J. and Wilkinson, G. *The International Business Environment*, Harlow: Pearson Education, pp. 3–36.

Brooks, I. Weatherston, J. and Wilkinson, G. (2010) *The International Business Environment* (2nd edn), Harlow: Pearson Education.

Brown-Humes, C. and Budden, R. (2004) 'Not so Mobile: will Nokia now get the message of changing consumer tastes, new technology and stronger rivals?', *Financial Times*, 7 May.

Burnes, B. (2005) 'Complexity Theories of Organizational Change', *International Journal of Management Reviews*, 7(2), pp. 73–90.

Burns, T. and Stalker, G.M. (1966) *The Management of Innovation*, London: Tavistock.

Butler, R. (1991) *Designing Organizations: A Decision-making Perspective*, London: Routledge.

Checkland, P.B. (1972) 'Towards a System-based Methodology for Real-world Problem Solving', *Journal of Systems Engineering*, 3 (2).

Child, J. (1973) 'Organization: a choice for man', in Child, J. (ed.) *Man and Organization*, London: Allen & Unwin.

Clarke, L. (1994) *The Essence of Change*, Hemel Hempstead: Prentice Hall.

Cook, M. (2004) 'The International Economic Environment', in Brooks, I. Weatherston, J. and Wilkinson, G. *The International Business Environment*, Harlow: Pearson Education, pp. 87–146.

Daft, R.L. (1989) *Organization Theory and Design* (2nd edn), St. Paul, MN: West Publishing.

Dawkins, R. (2008) 'The Genius of Charles Darwin', broadcast on Channel 4, 4 August.

Dawson, P. (2003) *Reshaping Change: A Processual Perspective*, London: Routledge.

Drucker, P.F. (1988) 'The Coming of the New Organization', *Harvard Business Review*, January/February, pp. 45–53.

Furnham, A. (2000) 'Work in 2020: prognostications about the world of work 20 years into the millennium', *Journal of Managerial Psychology*, 15 (3), pp. 242–254.

Goodman, M. (1995) *Creative Management*, Hemel Hempstead: Prentice Hall.

Handy, C. (1994) *The Empty Raincoat*, London: Hutchinson.

Huczynski, A.A. and Buchanan, D. (2007) *Organizational Behaviour* (6th edn), Harlow: FT Prentice Hall.

Johnson, G., Scholes, K. and Whittington, R. (2008) *Exploring Corporate Strategy: Text and Cases* (8th edn), Harlow: FT Prentice Hall.

Jones, P., Palmer, J., Osterweil, C. and Whitehead, D. (1996) *Delivering Exceptional Performance: Aligning the Potential of Organisations, Teams and Individuals*, London: Pitman.

Khodyakov, D.M. (2007) 'The Complexity of Trust-Control Relationships in Creative Organizations. Insights from a Qualitative Analysis of a Conductorless Orchestra', *Social Forces*, 86(1), pp. 1–22.

Mason, R. (2007) 'The External Environment's Effect on Management and Strategy: a complexity theory approach', *Management Decision*, 45(1), pp. 10–28.

McCann, L., Morris, J. and Hassard, J. (2008) 'Normalised Intensity: the new labour process of middle management', *Journal of Management Studies*, 45(2), pp. 343–371.

Nadler, D.A. (1988) 'Concepts for the Management of Organizational Change', in Tushman, M.L. and Moore, W.L. (eds) *Readings in the Management of Innovation*, New York: Ballinger, pp. 718–732.

Nadler, D.A. and Tushman, M. L. (1988) 'A Model for Diagnosing Organizational Behavior', in Tushman, M. L. and Moore, W. L. (eds) *Readings in the Management of Innovation*, New York: Ballinger, pp. 148–163.

Nadler, D.A. and Tushman, M.L. (1999) 'The Organization of the Future: strategic imperatives and core competencies for the 21st century', *Organizational Dynamics*, 28(1), pp. 71–80.

Paton, R.A. and McCalman, J. (2000) *Change Management: Guide to Effective Implementation* (2nd edn), London: PCP.

Rousseau, D. (2001) 'Schema, Promise and Mutuality: the building blocks of the psychological contract', *Journal of Organizational and Occupational Psychology*, 74, pp. 511–541.

Rousseau, D. (2004) 'Psychological Contracts in the Workplace: understanding the ties that motivate', *Academy of Management Executive*, 18(1), pp. 120–127.

Sadler, P. (1989) 'Management Development', in Sisson, K. (ed.) *Personnel Management in Britain* (2nd edn), Oxford: Blackwell.

Schein, E.H. (1988) 'Coming to a New Awareness of Organisational Culture', *Sloan Management Review*, 25(2), pp. 3–16.

Silverman, D. (1970) *The Theory of Organisations*, London: Heinemann Educational.

Stacey, R.D. (1996) *Strategic Management and Organisational Dynamics* (2nd edn), London: Pitman.

Stacey, R.D. (2003) *Strategic Management and Organisational Dynamics* (4th edn), Harlow: FT Prentice Hall.

Stewart, J. (1991) *Managing Change Through Training and Development*, London: Kogan Page.

Storey, J., Edwards, P. and Sisson, K. (1997) *Managers in the Making: Careers, Development and Control in Corporate Britain and Japan*, London: Sage.

Strebel, P. (1996) 'Choosing the Right Path', *Mastering Management*, Part 14, *Financial Times*.

Taylor, F.W. (1911) *Principles of Scientific Management*, New York: Harper & Row.

The Times (2008) 'After the Lehman Disaster', 6 September, p. 2.

Thomas, R. and Dunkerley, D. (1999) 'Careering Downwards? Middle managers' experiences in the downsized organization', *British Journal of Management,* 10(2), pp. 157–169.

Watson, T.J. (2002) *Organizing and Managing Work*, Harlow: FT Prentice Hall.

Wood, S. (1989) 'The Transformation of Work?' in Wood, S. (ed.) *The Transformation of Work*, London: Unwin Hyman, chapter 1.

Chapter 2

The nature of organizational change

This chapter introduces the different ways of conceptualizing the types of change that organizations encounter. A basic distinction is made between *convergent* change and *radical* change that is organization-wide and which is characterized by transformations of strategy, mission and values as well as structures and systems. We also discuss *planned* change and *emergent* change and summarize complexity theory which challenges the viability of planned change. The chapter concludes with an examination of the different change situations that organizations experience and provides an appreciation of their relationship to the way change might be designed and implemented – as a link to Part Three where different methodologies for designing and implementing change are discussed in more detail.

Learning objectives

By the end of this chapter, you will be able to:

● describe and discuss the multi-dimensional nature of organizational change;

● analyze change situations in terms of the different types of change experienced;

● explain limitations to the 'common-sense' approach to managing change arising from cultural, political and leadership influences;

● critically evaluate the theoretical perspectives relating to the types of change that organizations experience.

Types of change

The former British Prime Minister Benjamin Disraeli (1804–1881) observed that 'change is inevitable in a progressive country. Change is constant'. His remark is often reported as 'the only constant is change'. Many of us accept this as a truism yet it is important for organizations to strike a balance between both the forces for stability and inertia and the forces for change. Where the right balance lies, however, will vary from situation to situation. Change is also far from a homogenous concept – it comes in many forms.

A starting point for considering the nature of organizational change is Grundy's (1993) three 'varieties of change' as shown in Figure 2.1.The first, 'smooth incremental change', is change that evolves slowly in a systematic and predictable way. Grundy maintains that this type of change is mainly reminiscent of developed economies from the 1950s to early 1970s, but it became less common by the 1990s. The vertical axis in Figure 2.1 represents the *rate* of change not the *amount* of change. Thus, smooth incremental change, at whatever level, happens at a constant rate.

The second variety, 'bumpy incremental change', is characterized by periods of relative tranquility punctuated by acceleration in the pace of change. Grundy likens the 'bumps' to 'the movement of continental land masses where the "fault" enables periodic readjustment to occur without cataclysmic effect' (Grundy, 1993, p. 24). Triggers for this type of change are from both the environment and internal changes such as the periodic reorganizations that organizations go through to improve efficiency. One way of categorizing both types of incremental change is to see them as change that is associated more with the *means* by which organizations achieve their goals rather than as a change in the goals themselves.

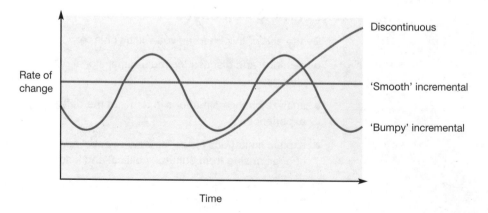

Figure 2.1 Grundy's major types of change
Source: Grundy, T. (1993) *Implementing Strategic Change*, London: Kogan Page, p. 25.

Grundy's third type is 'discontinuous change' which he defines as 'change which is marked by rapid shifts in strategy, structure or culture, or in all three' (p. 26). An example given is the privatization of previously publicly-owned utilities such as electricity generation and distribution. Another example is what Strebel (1996a) calls a 'divergent breakpoint' which is change that results from the discovery of a new business opportunity, such as new ways of communicating and new classes of medicines.

However, not all instances of discontinuous change are linked to technological innovations. Health scares rendering some food products temporarily unsaleable can have cataclysmic effects throughout an industry, as can a sudden lack of confidence in a financial institution. Thus discontinuous change can be likened to change in response to higher levels of environmental turbulence.

The pace and scope of change

Grundy's three types of change make intuitive sense but they are somewhat simplistic and appear to be based largely on observation alone. While this also appears to be the case with Balogun and Hope-Hailey's (2004) identification of change 'paths', they go further by suggesting four types of change. The two dimensions are scope (incremental or big-bang) and the scale (realignment or transformation) – see Figure 2.2.

Tushman, Newman and Romanelli (1988), on the basis of numerous studies and case histories, proposed a model of organizational life that consists of 'periods of incremental change, or convergence, punctuated by discontinuous changes' (p. 707). They suggest there are two types of converging change: fine-tuning and incremental adaptations. Both these types of change have the common aim of maintaining the fit between organizational strategy, structure and processes. However, whereas fine-tuning is aimed at doing better what is

Nature of change	End result: *Transformation*	End result: *Realignment*
Incremental	Evolution	Adaptation
Big bang	Revolution	Reconstruction

Figure 2.2 Types of change

Source: Balogun, J. and Hope Hailey, V.H. (2004) *Exploring Strategic Change*, Harlow: FT Prentice Hall.

already done well, incremental adaptation involves small changes in response to minor shifts in the environment.

Both fine-tuning and incremental adjustments to environmental shifts allow organizations to perform more effectively and optimize the consistencies between strategy, structure, people and processes. Yet Tushman *et al.* show how, as organizations grow and become more successful and develop internal forces for stability, these same forces eventually produce resistance to hold back further change. Thus at times of major change in an organization's environment, incremental adjustment will not bring about the major changes in strategy, structure, people and processes that might be required. At times like these Tushman *et al.* maintain that most organizations will be required to undergo discontinuous or frame-breaking change. Thus, in any organization's life cycle, periods of relative tranquillity will be punctuated with (probably shorter) periods of frame-breaking change. Illustration 2.1 summarizes the definition of frame-breaking change advanced by Tushman *et al.*

Illustration 2.1

Frame-breaking change

The need for discontinuous change springs from one or more of the following:

- *Industry discontinuities* – sharp changes that shift the basis of competition. These include: deregulation, technologies that lead to replacement (substitution) of the products or processes used, the emergence of industry standards or dominant designs, major economic changes (e.g. oil crises), legal shifts (e.g. patent protection, trade/regulator barriers).
- *Product/life cycle shifts* – changes in strategy from the emergence of a product to its establishment in the market, the effects of international competition.
- *Internal company dynamics* – as organizations grow beyond the person-centred organization built around the founding inventor–entrepreneur they give way to more bureaucratic management and a revised corporate portfolio strategy that can alter the role and resources assigned to business units.

The scope of frame-breaking change includes discontinuous change throughout the organization. Frame-breaking change is usually implemented rapidly. Frame-breaking changes are revolutionary as opposed to incremental changes of the system. Frame-breaking change usually involves the following features:

- *reformed mission and core values* – new definition of company mission;
- *altered power and status* – reflecting shifts in the bases of competition and resource allocation;
- *reorganization* – new strategy requires a modification in structure, systems and procedures, change of organization form;
- *revised interaction patterns* – new procedures, work flows, communication networks, decision-making patterns;
- *new executives* – usually from outside the organization.

Frame-breaking change is revolutionary in that the shifts reshape the entire nature of the organization. It requires discontinuous shifts in strategy, structure, people and processes concurrently. Reasons for the rapid, simultaneous implementation of frame-breaking change include:

- *synergy* – the need for all units of the organization to pull together;

- *pockets of resistance* – these have a chance to grow and develop when frame-breaking change is implemented slowly;
- *pent-up need for change* – when constraints are relaxed, changes in fashion;
- *riskiness and uncertainty* – the longer the implementation period, the greater the period of uncertainty and instability.

Source: Based on Tushman, M.L., Newman, W.H. and Romanelli, E. (1988) 'Convergence and Upheaval: managing the unsteady pace of organizational evolution', in Tushman, M.L. and Moore, W.L. (eds), *Readings in the Management of Innovation*, New York: Ballinger.

Figure 2.3 taken from Plowman *et al.* (2007), shows how organizational change can be mapped in terms of its pace (continuous or episodic) and its scope (convergent or radical). Each of the four categories of change differs on the following dimensions.

PACE \ SCOPE	Convergent	Radical
Continuous	**1** *Driver*: minor system instability *Form*: small adaptations within an existing framework *Nature*: emergent and local as people improvise and learn *Feedback*: positive, encouraging deviations and adaptations *Connections*: loose coupling which helps local conditions from amplifying	**4** *Driver*: major system instability *Form*: frame-bending adaptations *Nature*: emergent and system-wide as adaptations accumulate into patterns *Feedback*: positive and negative feedback which pulls in two directions *Connections*: light coupling which enables local adaptations to amplify into radical change
Episodic	**2** *Driver*: minor inertia *Form*: minor replacement within an existing frame *Nature*: intended and local *Feedback*: negative, highlighting the need for minor replacement *Connections*: loose coupling which requires local minor replacements	**3** *Driver*: major inertia *Form*: dramatic frame-bending replacement *Nature*: intended and system-wide *Feedback*: negative, highlighting need for major replacement *Connections*: light coupling which requires system-wide radical replacement

Figure 2.3 Four types of change

Source: Plowman *et al*. (2007) 'Radical Change Accidentally: the emergence and amplification of small change', *Academy of Management Journal*, 50(3), pp. 515–543.

- The driver of change, namely instability or inertia.
- The form of the change, namely adaptation or replacement.
- The nature of the change, namely emergent or intended.

- Types of feedback; negative feedback discourages deviations from the organization's current position whereas positive feedback encourages deviation.
- Types of connections in the system which are loose or tight.

The four quadrants portray four types of change.

1 *Continuous and convergent* change which is slow and which is channelled into improving systems and practices. Change happens within an organizational template; the template itself is not altered.
2 *Episodic and convergent* change occurs more quickly and perhaps as a result of a specific shock or crisis. Negative feedback pushes minor changes and keeps the template in shape.
3 *Episodic and radical* change happens quickly in response to a major shock or crisis. The template is altered through, for instance, a new top management team or new strategy.
4 *Continuous and radical* change arises out of an accumulation of small changes that gather momentum and lead to a new template being formed. If successful the new template becomes established and is reinforced by new rules, values and norms.

An example of frame-breaking change springing from the changes in the political conditions in Europe is NATO (North Atlantic Treaty Organization). This organization was founded shortly after World War II in an atmosphere of anxiety largely because of Soviet expansion into Europe. The first frame-breaking change for NATO, testing its longevity, was the collapse and break-up of the Soviet Union in 1991. This brought about the subsequent demise of the Warsaw Pact which left NATO with no obvious enemy. It had to reconfigure to incorporate new countries, in particular countries that were once seen as potential aggressors. NATO also changed its strategy, attempting to foster a more proactive approach to 'out of area' activities – arguing that instability in any part of Europe would constitute a threat to its members.

The NATO Permanent Joint Council was established in May 1997 to give Russia a consultative role for discussion in matters of mutual interest. There have been other political incidents that have forced NATO to re-evaluate its role, for today and in the future. The September 2001 attack on the World Trade Center and the Pentagon was another pivotal moment as the US did not involve the NATO alliance in the international 'war on terror' that followed.

Russia's supportive reaction following the attacks of 2001 proved to be a catalyst for a thaw in relations and saw yet again a change in direction for the organization. Russia is now a member of the decision-making team on policies to counter terrorism and other security threats.

Once again a change was to take place as there were disputes between Germany, France and the US over the invasion of Iraq in March, 2003. NATO's leadership was tested. Since the invasion, analysts perceive NATO to be shaping a new role for itself. There have been joint plans relating to the rapid reaction team that was jointly designed for swift deployment to anywhere in the world.

The first test of this partnership is the role the alliance is playing in stationing armed forces in Afghanistan. NATO is clearly an organization that needs to be seen as proactive. However, political and environmental factors often happen so fast that there is a constant need for it to evaluate its role as an effective and responsive organization.

Fine-tuning to corporate transformation

Grundy (1993) does not claim any particular status for his typology of change conceding that it is not empirically tested. The typology proposed by Tushman *et al.* (1988) is supposedly based on more rigorous research which is also the case with the typology put forward by Australian academics Dunphy and Stace (1993), discussed in Chapter 6, although the four descriptions that represent their scale of change are shown in Illustration 2.2.

Dunphy and Stace's scale types 1 and 2 are typical of Grundy's concept of smooth incremental change, while their scale types 3 and 4 are reminiscent of Grundy's bumpy incremental and discontinuous types of change respectively. The benefit of the Dunphy and Stace model, though, is in the detailed descriptions of each scale type and its testing with the executives, managers and supervisors of 13 Australian service sector organizations. Organizations operating scale 1 and 2 type changes were in the minority in their small sample.

Illustration 2.2

Defining the scale of change

Scale type 1: Fine tuning

Here, organizational change is an ongoing process characterized by fine-tuning of the 'fit' or match between the organization's strategy, structure, people and processes. Such effort typically occurs at departmental/divisional levels and deals with one or more of the following:

- refining policies, methods and procedures;
- creating specialist units and linking mechanisms to raise output and better focus on quality and cost;
- developing personnel better suited to the present strategy (improved training and development; tailoring award systems to match strategic priorities);
- fostering individual and group commitment to the company mission and the excellence of one's

own department;
- promoting confidence in the accepted norms, beliefs and myths;
- clarifying established roles (with their associated authorities and posers), and the mechanisms for allocating resources.

Scale type 2: Incremental adjustment

Here, organizational change is characterized by incremental adjustments to a changing environment. Such change involves distinct modifications (but not radical change) to corporate business strategies, structures and management processes, for example:

- expanding sales territory;
- shifting the emphasis among products;
- improved production process technology;
- articulating a modified statement of mission to employees;

▶

- adjustments to organizational structures within or across divisional boundaries to achieve better links in product/service delivery.

Scale type 3: Modular transformation

Here, organizational change is characterized by major realignment of one or more departments/divisions where radical change is focused rather than on the organization as a whole, for example:

- major restructuring of particular departments/divisions;
- changes in key executives and managerial appointments;
- work and productivity studies resulting in significantly reduced or increased workforce numbers;
- reformed departmental/divisional goals;
- introduction of significantly new process technologies affecting key departments or divisions.

Scale type 4: Corporate transformation

Here, organizational change is corporation wide, characterized by radical shifts in business strategy and revolutionary changes throughout the whole organization involving the following features:

- reformed organizational mission and core values;
- altered power and status affecting the distribution of power in the organization;
- reorganization – major changes in structures, systems and procedures across the organization;
- revised interaction patterns – new procedures, work flows, communication networks and decision-making patterns across the organization;
- new executives in key managerial positions from outside the organization.

Source: Dunphy, D. and Stace, D. (1993) 'The Strategic Management of Corporate Change', *Human Relations*, 46(8), pp. 905–920.

However plausible Illustration 2.2 appears, care must be taken with schema like this based on a small sample of 13 organizations from one sector only. Having said this, Dunphy and Stace are not alone in suggesting the types of change they do. For instance, their typology is similar to those of Tushman *et al.* and Plowman *et al.* (2007). It is fairly clear that Dunphy and Stace found the same two types of change as are grouped by Tushman *et al.* under the concept of converging change. Both used identical names – 'fine-tuning' and 'incremental adjustment'. Where Dunphy and Stace go beyond Tushman *et al.* is in, apparently, splitting what Tushman *et al.* termed 'frame-*breaking*' change into two types – 'modular transformation' and 'corporate transformation'. This is a useful development in detailing more clearly the different levels at which frame-breaking change can take place. It still recognizes the implications of these types of change for goals and purposes, but identifies the fact that these may have different meanings at the departmental/divisional level than at the corporate/organizational level.

So far we have analyzed change basically in terms of its size and scope and have not looked at how it arose. An assumption perhaps underlying the above types and typologies is that change can be *planned* – but as the next section shows this is not always the case.

Activity 2.1

Look again at Dunphy and Stace's types of change in Illustration 2.2. Position an organization with which you are familiar on the following scale:

Fine-tuning   Incremental adjustment   Modular transformation   Corporate transformation

←——→

Tushman et al. (1988, pp. 713–714) observe:

The most effective firms take advantage of relatively long convergent periods. These periods of incremental change build on and take advantage of organization inertia. Frame-breaking change is quite dysfunctional if the organization is successful and the environment is stable. If, however, the organization is performing poorly and/or if the environment changes substantially, frame-breaking change is the only way to realign the organization with its competitive environment.

Does the type of change now being experienced by your organization fit the environment in which it is currently operating and that is likely to prevail in the foreseeable future?

Illustration 2.3

Explaining types of change

We have introduced some new terms in this chapter and for convenience they are summarized below.

Convergent – this is fine-tuning of an existing configuration. The organizational configuration or template is not itself changed.

Radical – breaking away from a position such that a very different position is reached. Organizations or parts of them can be seen as being transformed from one template or blueprint to another. Also known as frame-bending.

Planned – deliberate actions designed to move an organization or part of one from one state to another; discrete beginning and end points. Change is seen as something that managers can control.

Evolutionary – as its name suggests, slow adaptation of existing systems or structures. Also termed continuous change. Although small in nature, changes are not trivial and are cumulative. They can trigger radical change.

Revolutionary – fast paced, which affects all or most of an organization at the same time. Typically a planned move from one strategy and/or structure to another. It incorporates the idea of episodic change which is intentional but is infrequent, not continuous.

Emergent – if the organization is seen as an evolving system then change arises out of experimentation and adaptation. Change is seen as something that managers create the right climate for.

Planned and emergent change

Fine-tuning and incremental change are features of all organizational life and, while they can be planned, are frequently associated with change as it *emerges* out of ongoing operations. The idea of emergent change has been linked with the concept of organizations as open systems (Wilson, 1992). Kast and Rosenzweig (1970), von Bertanlanfy (1971), Checkland (1972) and McAleer (1982) among others have produced detailed discussions of the concept of organizational systems. Briefly, these discussions include the idea of organizations striving to maintain a state of equilibrium where the forces for change are balanced by the forces for stability. Therefore, organizations viewed as systems will always strive to restore equilibrium whenever they are disturbed. According to this view, the organizational system is constantly sensing its environment in order to continuously adjust to maintain its purpose and optimum state.

Illustration 2.4

Holy breakfasts! Accidental radical change

Churchgoers at a US city church were discussing new things to do. The group decided to offer hot breakfasts on Sunday mornings to homeless people. This idea was quickly implemented and soon volunteers were providing over 200 breakfasts. Within a few months a volunteer who was a doctor began to see people who wanted to discuss health questions. Shortly after, full-scale medical, dental and eye clinics were in place. Within a few years and with the support of grants the Church was running a day centre to help thousands of homeless people. Legal and job search support services were added.

Homeless people began to attend church services and this led to changes in dress codes and in the style of music – quite a shock to a church that had always attracted worshippers from the wealthiest corners of society. The Church's mission was changing and this brought conflict with the local business community for whom the influx of homeless people into the district was unwelcome. These radical changes were not planned – a 'cycle of continuous radical change' had emerged.

Plowman and colleagues argue that existing theories of episodic or continuous change (Weick and Quinn, 1999) and convergent or radical change (Greenwood and Hinings, 1996) do not explain how small changes escalate and become radical. Whereas radical change is usually seen as occurring in episodes, i.e. with beginning and end, the case of the Church appears to show continuous radical change. No leadership crisis or financial crisis arose to trigger these changes – just an idea to serve hot breakfasts.

Source: Based on Plowman *et al*. (2007) 'Radical Change Accidentally: the emergence and amplification of small change', *Academy of Management Journal*, 50(3), pp. 515–543.

In an ideal world, organizational sensing of the environment would be so effective as to render frame-breaking change unnecessary. If organizations responded continuously to the need for change, they would have no need for the periodic upheavals that sometimes seem inevitable. In other words, through their continuous assessment of the environments, change should emerge almost 'naturally'.

However, Tushman *et al*. (1988), Johnson (1988) and Johnson, Scholes and Whittington (2008) describe a phenomenon whereby managers and other personnel become so comfortable with 'how we work here' and 'what we hold important here' that they also become impervious to warning signs of impending difficulties from the environment. According to Tushman *et al*., this is the effect of what they call the 'double-edged sword' of converging periods of change. Thus the habits, patterns of behaviour, finding out the best way to do things and commitment to values that have been built up during periods of converging change can contribute significantly to the success of the organization. However, the organizational history built up during this period can also be counterproductive in restricting the vigilance needed towards the environment and may become a source of resistance to the need for more radical forms of change.

Johnson (1988, p. 44) refers to the organizational 'paradigm' to describe the core set of beliefs and assumptions held commonly by the managers of an organization. He says:

> This set of beliefs, which evolves over time, might embrace assumptions about the nature of the organizational environment, the managerial style in the organization, the nature of its leaders, and the operational routines seen as important to ensure the success of the organization.

The fact that the paradigm is widely held is taken for granted and is not, therefore, seen as problematical means that signals from the environment are filtered through it. These signals are only made sense of in terms of what Johnson (1988, p. 44) calls 'the way we do things around here'. Therefore, when signals for change come from the environment, he says:

> [Their] relevance is determined, not by the competitive activity, but by the constructs of the paradigm [and] in these circumstances it is likely that, over time, the phenomenon of 'strategic drift' will occur: that is gradually, probably imperceptibly, the strategy of the organization will become less and less in tune with the environment in which the organization exists. (Johnson, 1988, p. 44)

As the process of strategic drift continues, an organization's strategy, structure and processes gradually move further away from a path that would take account of the triggers for change coming from the environment. It is at these points that more frame-breaking or revolutionary change becomes necessary to realign the organization's purposes and operations with environmental imperatives.

From the discussion so far, it is clear that the process of strategic drift forces organizations into a more conscious deliberate *planning* of change, for instance the four-stage processes of exploration, planning, action and integration discussed by Burnes (2004). Planned change describes situations where a change agent takes deliberate actions with the aim of moving an organization or part of one from one state to another, e.g., to a new structure, to more commercial behaviour or to altered working patterns. It contrasts with emergent change which is change that arises out of ongoing activities. Of course, things do not always go to plan in planned change and some 'unintended consequences' occur.

Illustration 2.5

Change: accelerant or retardant?

Beck and colleagues (2008) conceptualize change as 'discrete modification of structural organizational elements' (p. 413). Whether planned or emergent, a popular theme in change research is to examine the effects of past change on the likelihood of future change. A core assumption is that change leads to increased chances of further change; change today is more likely to lead to change tomorrow. Beck *et al*. identify three commonly analyzed change events,

- Change of markets, e.g., finding new groups of customers and/or new products/services.

- Change of organizational leadership.
- Changes to rules and routines that comprise the basic structure of organizations.

The theory behind the 'change leads to change' assumption is that the more an organization changes things the more it learns about how to do it successfully. People increase their competences at making changes of a particular type and raise their confidence as well. As competence and confidence rise then the recipes will be applied to an increasing range of situations.

▶

The alternative view put forward by Beck and colleagues is that since change is aimed at improving things; if it works there should be less need to change after change has been made. Not all change leads to improvements of course but even unsuccessful change should enable people to modify the way they attempt it again. They tested these two views and found that when conventional research methods were used the first view was supported. When an improved method was used change led to deceleration rather than an acceleration of future change. So it seems that we still don't have a clear answer to this question.

Source: Based on Beck *et al.* (2008) 'Momentum or Deceleration? Theoretical and methodological reflections on the analysis of organizational change', *Academy of Management Journal*, 51(3), pp. 413–435.

However, the distinction between emergent and planned change is not clear-cut. Wilson (1992) criticizes the idea that change can be planned logically and systematically. He argues that planned change is a management concept which relies heavily on a single view of the way change ought to be done. This view assumes that the environment is known and, therefore, that a logical process of environmental analysis can be harnessed in the service of planning any change. Wilson says this view emphasizes the role of human agency, that is, that chief executives and managers are able to invoke the changes they feel are necessary and that this process is not problematic. His argument is that this view does not take account of the context in which change must take place; for instance, the cultural and political components that influence most, if not all, implementations of any planned change.

Jian (2007) provides an interesting account of what happened during one planned change episode and in particular to the unexpected outcomes that were seen as shown in Illustration 2.6.

Illustration 2.6

Unintended consequences of planned change

Unintended consequences are those things that would not have happened if an actor (e.g. a manager) had acted differently and are not what the actor had intended (Jian, 2007, p. 6). The scene for this Illustration is a US insurance company. As a result of some acquisitions the (new) top management team engaged consultants to tell it that it needed to cut costs and restructure. And so a plan was hatched.

Top management explained why change was needed and how important it was to keep the company's stock (share) price high. 'If we don't cut costs then we won't be able to generate the new business that we need' – was the general thrust of the message from the top. The basic message precluded consideration of other change paths and in doing so positioned top management as a dominant force. Employees were assured that they would be told of important things as soon as top management knew them. Much was made of not communicating before the communication was clear. Employees were assured that they would hear first and that this was important to ensure consistency. But top management was only going to communicate something that had been decided – not what things were being decided.

This positioned top management as being privileged to know things and to debate them and to decide on the best way forward. Employees were simply expected to execute their wishes. This background, Jian writes, sowed the seeds for the unintended consequences. Jian points out that in this case top managers were deciding on new structures and systems but it was up to employees to make sense of them; to figure out what the changes mean to them. To help them do this, employees used a grapevine to communicate the contradictions and stories around them. The picture constructed along the grapevine was one of management secrecy, betrayal as people were losing their jobs and unfairness because of cutbacks or increased prices to a range of employee benefits provided by the company.

Mass meetings of staff and management did little to help things and were occasions where top management reiterated its position without appearing to appreciate employee concerns. Despite the well-intentioned information releases by management, rumours quickly followed them. This widened the trust gap between management and employees. Other unintended outcomes were higher stress and a loss of productivity as employees diverted energy into analyzing their situations rather than winning new business or cutting costs.

The key lesson from this real case is that managers need to appreciate the meaning of change as seen by employees. They need to help employees make sense of change and help translate new ways of doing things into everyday practice.

Source: Based on Jian, G. (2007) 'Unpacking Unintended Consequences of Planned Organizational Change', *Management Communication Quarterly*, 21(1), pp. 5–28.

Quinn (1980) has also criticized the idea of planned change as something that is deliberately and carefully thought through and then implemented. His research into the decision-making processes of a number of organizations demonstrated that most strategic decisions are made in spite of formal planning systems rather than because of them. Reinforcing this idea Stacey (2003, p. 71) summarizes the key points made by Quinn as follows:

1 Effective managers do not manage strategically in a piecemeal manner. They have a clear view of what they want to achieve and where they are trying to take the business. The destination is thus intended.

2 But the route to that destination, the strategy itself, is not intended from the start in any comprehensive way. Effective managers know that the environment they have to operate in is uncertain and ambiguous. They therefore sustain flexibility by holding open the method of reaching the goal.

3 The strategy itself then emerges from the interaction between different groupings of people in the organization, different groupings with different amounts of power, different requirements for and access to information, different time spans and parochial interest. These different pressures are orchestrated by senior managers. The top is always reassessing, integrating and organizing.

4 The strategy emerges or evolves in small incremental, opportunistic steps. But such evolution is not piecemeal or haphazard because of the agreed purpose and the role of top management in reassessing what is happening. It is this that provides the logic in the incremental action.

5 The result is an organization that is feeling its way towards a known goal, opportunistically learning as it goes.

Quinn terms this process 'logical incrementalism' in that it is based in a certain logic of thinking but is incremental in its ability to change in the light of new information and the results of ongoing action. Opportunism plays an important part in this process (see Illustration 2.7).

Illustration 2.7

Proactively managing incrementalism in the development of corporate strategies

Quinn (1979) makes the following statement to illustrate how executives proactively manage incrementalism in the development of corporate strategies.

Typically you start with general concerns, vaguely felt. Next you roll an issue around in your mind until you think you have a conclusion that makes sense for the company. You then go out and sort of post the idea without being too wedded to its details. You then start hearing the arguments pro and con, and some very good refinements of the idea usually emerge. Then you pull the idea in and put some resources together to study it so it can be put forward as more of a formal presentation. You wait for 'stimuli occurrences' or 'crises', and launch pieces of the idea to help in these situations. But they lead toward your ultimate aim. You know where you want to get to. You would like to get there in six months. But it may take three years, or you may not get there. And when you do get there, you do not know whether it was originally your own idea – or somebody else had reached the same conclusion before you and just got you on board for it. You never know. The president would follow the same basic process, but he could drive it much faster than an executive lower in the organization.

Source: Quinn, J.B. (1979) 'Xerox Corporation (B)', copyright case, Hanover, NH: Amos Tuck School of Business Administration, Dartmouth College.

Predictable change

In some respects change could be viewed as neither wholly emergent nor planned. As cycles of growth and activity are an essential part of living, so the concept of an organizational life cycle (Greiner, 1972; Kimberley and Miles, 1980) has been used to describe the stages organizations go through as they grow and develop. Figure 2.4 illustrates these in terms of the size and maturity of organizations.

Greiner maintains that, as organizations mature and grow in size their activities go through five phases, each of which is associated with a different growth period in an organization's life. In addition, as each growth period moves into the next, the organization goes through a shorter-lived crisis period. These are, respectively, the evolution and revolution stages shown in Figure 2.4. Illustration 2.8 is a brief description of a typical life cycle pattern that is complemented by Clarke's (1994) useful categorization of the characteristics and crisis points associated with each phase of growth (see Table 2.1).

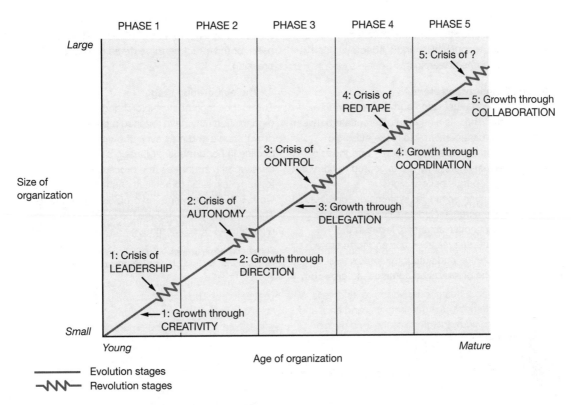

Figure 2.4 The organizational life cycle

Source: Reprinted by permission of *Harvard Business Review*. Greiner, L.E. (1972) 'Evolution and Revolution as Organizations Grow', July–August, p. 41. Copyright © 1972 by the Harvard Business School Publishing Corporation. All rights reserved.

Copyright © 1972 by the Harvard Business School Publishing Corporation. All rights reserved.

Illustration 2.8

A typical life cycle pattern

1. The entrepreneurial stage

In this first (often entrepreneurial) stage, the primary task is to provide a service or make a product. Survival is the key strategy. Organizational culture is fashioned by the founding entrepreneur. It may be a new organization, a new subsidiary or part of an established, larger organization. Success brings growth and the need to recruit more staff. Staff need managing and the question of future organizational strategy becomes more complex. The alternatives are to limit growth and remain small (but risk being unable to sustain competition) or to grow and recruit professional managers.

2. The collective stage

The organization begins to take 'shape'. Departments and functions begin to be defined and the division of labour is the dominant theme. The professional managers recruited tend to be strong leaders who share the same vision as the founders. Further growth brings the need for management control and delegation. The organization has begun

▶

to establish its position; internal tasks are allocated and who has responsibility and autonomy to carry them out become pre-eminent.

3. The formalization stage

Systems of communication and control become more formal. There is a need to differentiate between the tasks of management – to make strategic decisions and to implement policy – and those of lower-level managers, who are expected to carry out and oversee operational decisions.

Bureaucratization occurs as systems of coordination and control emerge, including salary structures, reward and incentive schemes, levels in the hierarchy, reporting relationships and formalized areas of discretion and autonomy for lower-level managers. The organization continues to grow, but

burdened by the process of bureaucratization the need for the structure to be 'freed up' becomes pressing.

4. The elaboration stage

This is the stage of strategic change. The organization may have reached a plateau in its growth curve and may even show the first stages of decline in performance. Managers used to handling bureaucratic structures and processes usually have to learn new skills to achieve change, such as team work, self-assessment and problem confrontation. This stage may also include the rapid turnover and replacement of senior managers.

Source: Based on Greiner, L.E. (1972) 'Evolution and Revolution as Organizations Grow', *Harvard Business Review*, July–August, 50, pp. 37–46.

Activity 2.2

Consider an organization you know well. Using the descriptions in Illustration 2.8 and Table 2.1, position the organization on the graph in Figure 2.4.

Table 2.1 Characteristics of Greiner's phases of growth

	Phase 1 Creativity	Phase 2 Direction	Phase 3 Delegation	Phase 4 Coordination	Phase 5 Collaboration
Structure	• Informal	• Functional • Centralized • Hierarchical • Top down	• Decentralized • Bottom up	• Staff functions • Strategic business units (SBUs) • Decentralized • Units merged into product groups	• Matrix-type structure
Systems	• Immediate response to customer feedback	• Standards • Cost centres • Budget • Salary systems	• Profit centres • Bonuses • Management by exception	• Formal planning procedures • Investment centres • Tight expenditure controls	• Simplified and integrated information systems
Styles/ people	• Individualistic • Creative • Entrepreneurial • Ownership	• Strong directive	• Full delegation of autonomy	• Watchdog	• Team oriented • Interpersonal skills at a premium • Innovative • Educational bias

Table 2.1 Characteristics of Greiner's phases of growth continued

Strengths	• Fun • Market response	• Efficient	• High management motivation	• More efficient allocation of corporate and local resources	• Greater spontaneity • Flexible and behavioural approach
Crisis point	• Crisis of leadership	• Crisis of autonomy	• Crisis of control	• Crisis of red tape	?
Weaknesses	• Founder often temperamentally unsuited to managing • Boss overload	• Unsuited to diversity • Cumbersome • Hierarchical • Doesn't grow people	• Top managers lose control as freedom breeds parochial attitudes	• Bureaucratic divisions between line/staff, headquarters/field, etc.	• Psychological saturation

Source: Clarke, L. (1994) *The Essence of Change*, Hemel Hempstead: Prentice Hall.

Greiner's model is useful for identifying an organization's situation and providing warnings of the next crisis point it may have to face. It therefore helps in the planning of necessary change. It also helps managers and others realize that change is, to some extent, inevitable; organizations must of necessity change as they grow and mature. It therefore helps legitimize the need for change and may be useful in discussions aimed at combating resistance to change.

So far in this chapter we have seen several ways of analyzing and describing change and the idea that change can be planned or can emerge out of what people do. Another very important spotlight on change, and in particular an antidote to theories of planned change, is provided by complexity theory.

Complexity theory

Burnes (2005) provides a readable review of complexity theory which we draw on below. Complexity theory is a set of ideas stemming from the study of natural systems such as weather patterns and animal behaviour and which draws on mathematical principles to help explain how organizations behave. Like natural systems, it sees organizations as highly complex entities where a natural order comes to exist. One of the best known proponents is Stacey, who together with colleagues identified three cornerstones of complexity theory (Stacey *et al.*, 2002).

1 Chaos theory – chaotic systems are characterized by constant transformation analogous to the ways that species evolve. Events in chaotic systems are not proportional to the sum of causes and effects. Small events or perceptions of small events in an environment can lead to large changes in patterns of behaviour. These new structures and patterns are known as dissipative structures.

2 Dissipative structures – these need energy and impetus from outside otherwise they reduce to next to nothing (dissipate). Analogous to natural systems they can withstand large forces acting on them or undergo radical self-reorganization in response to small events. The new structures adopted are unpredictable but are stable arrangements arising from the constituents of the system.

3 Complex adaptive systems – these are made up of agents each of which conforms to its own principles that shape its behaviour in relation to other agents. If we can understand how the agents (e.g. employees) behave individually then this will help to understand how the entire system will behave. An illustration of this occurs in the popular TV documentaries of meerkat colonies. The colony (system) functions as a result of different agents including dominant males, females caring for youngsters, juveniles, foraging parties and sentries.

What does this mean for organizational change? If we see organizations as complex entities where things do not happen in a linear fashion and where the people in them have the wherewithal to self-organize, then top-down, directive and hierarchical efforts at change (planned change) will not work. If so, then managers need to 'promote self-organizing processes and learn how to use small changes to create large effects' (Burnes, 2005, p. 82).

In place of bureaucracy delimiting what can and cannot be done, experimentation needs to be encouraged and mistakes/mishaps have to be accepted as part of the adaptive change processes. This of course is not especially new and is reminiscent of the advice given by Peters and Waterman (1982) and Kanter (1989). Burnes however proposes three implications of applying complexity theory to organizations.

1 There is a need to move beyond 'narrow employee participation in change' towards much more democracy and equalization of power. This gives employees the scope to act.

2 The extremes of incremental change and large-scale transformation are not realistic and do not work. Between the two extremes lies a continuous approach based on self-organization to improving products and processes.

3 To fuel the continuous change ideal, self-organization needs the presence of 'order-generating rules'. These rules evolve and are part of the processes of self-organization.

Despite its origins in natural sciences and its reliance on mathematical principles, as far as understanding organizations goes complexity theory does not give or attempt to give mathematical explanations for behaviour. Rather it is a set of ideas that act as a metaphor for understanding how change happens and how it is sustained. The metaphor gives managers new insights into how their organizations work and how they, the managers, can conceive change and the actors in it in a new way.

Classic thinking about strategic change assumes that planning processes rely on the ability to join-up causes and effects, for example, the assumption that certain actions will lead to certain outcomes. This model underpins the top-down approach to strategy analyses and implementation. Complexity theory, however, holds that change will occur in systems that are some distance away from the simple equilibrium model. A more realistic description is that organizations exist in non-equilibrium conditions where cause and effect break down (Stacey, 1995). Any organization at a moment in time:

> . . . is a result of every detail of its history and what it will become can only be known if one knows every detail of future development, and the only way one can do that is to let the development occur. The future of such a system is open and hence unknowable until it occurs. (p. 491)

Stacey argues that while managers and leaders can decide what their next action will be and have a go at implementing it, they cannot determine the eventual outcomes of those actions in future time. An implication of this, and quite a big one, is that if complexity theory is an accurate portrayal of organizational life and behaviour, then it is not possible to use theory-testing, hypotheses-testing research to identify things that lead to success and then generalize from them. Hence, recipes for strategic change are all doomed to illusion and failure.

Illustration 2.9

How a decision to marry changed England

King Henry VIII is one of England's most well-known monarchs, partly because he had six wives but also because of changes that occurred during his reign that transformed England and set in train further radical changes. His older brother Arthur, who was expected to be King, married Catherine of Aragon but died soon afterwards. Henry married his brother's widow in 1509 even though she was older than him and shortly afterwards he was crowned King. However, by the time her child-bearing days were over Henry did not have the son he wanted who would inherit the throne. The Pope refused to grant Henry a divorce from Catherine which pushed him to consider drastic action. The outcome was a break from the Catholic Church such that the monarch became supreme head of the Church of England. Religious freedom increased and one hundred years later these same freedoms fuelled confrontation between parliament and the monarchy, the English Civil War and establishment of the right of parliament to govern. The point of this historical interlude is to show how events or decisions which appear normal and harmless at the time can lead to radical change later. If Henry had not married Catherine, if Catherine had born a son . . . Of course there are many 'What ifs?' in this case but it is only because of particular decisions which at the time seemed normal that a chain of events occurred that transformed the role of the monarchy and the Church which shaped England for the following 500 years at least.

ITS MINE :) University of Ulster LIBRARY

While various n-point recipes for successful change are popular we urge managers to exercise great care if ever tempted to use them. While they may contain some good ideas and things to think about, the 'one best way' approach is an illusion. There are simply too many variables impacting upon change coupled with the fact that every change effort is unique. Even in the same sector in similarly-sized organizations of similar age attempting the same change, there will be big differences in the experiences and attitudes of the people involved and in their social relationships and the resources available to support change. There is such a bewildering array of differences between change efforts that recipes, we suggest, are siren calls. That said, we are not arguing against the idea of good practice. Involvement of people and explanation of intentions are important at least for their courtesy value – they are the sorts of things that change agents should be doing simply out of respect for others. If an organization has to downsize then some ways of doing this are better than others, at least if a socially responsible perspective is adopted.

Houchin and Maclean (2005) suggest that complexity theory can be used to understand organizational change since it gives us insights into how patterns of order develop and how organizations learn and adapt. It views organizations as existing in a state of non-equilibrium; a state in which forces of adaptation are acting on the parts of the system, pushing it towards an equilibrium that is rarely, if ever, reached. It rejects the notion that change from one stable state to another can proceed through a series of linear steps.

Since complexity theory has its origins in the study of natural and biological systems there has to be some doubt over its relevance to explain human behaviour. Houchin and Maclean (2005) point out though that rather than see complexity as a distinct theoretical approach it can usefully be seen as a 'metaphor giving us new insights' into how change happens (p. 152). They give an account of change in a newly formed agency made up from several predecessor organizations with a remit to handle environmental regulation and protection. Their ethnographic study found differences between the intended outcomes of the change and the actual equilibrium states that formed over three years. The key differences were:

- hierarchical organization not wide spans of organization;
- emphasis on professional specialization not employee flexibility;
- bureaucratic procedures not delegation and empowerment;
- focus on cost control not value for money;
- independent regional branches not a strong centre.

Why had this alternative equilibrium state come to exist? Among the 500-plus employees some were excited by new organization and others were anxious about the future and prospects. Strategies to reduce anxiety were taken by individuals to help them feel in control and as ways of reducing conflict. These strategies gradually led to individuals reducing the amount of interactions with others (e.g., project groups, consultation, training events) which meant that actions designed to lead to new ways were infrequent and ineffective. Houchin and Maclean also proposed that the order that developed did not emerge within the organization's legitimate systems. A 'shadow system' consisting of the old network that employees had before the new organization was formed still existed and this meant that employees could, to a point, continue with their established working ways. In sum, the order that emerged in the new organization was pretty much the same as that which had existed in the organizations it was made up from.

It seems therefore that an understanding of the shadow system is crucial to understanding change. Logical-rational approaches of course emphasize the logic of the formal/legitimate systems. Anxieties prevent a social system such as a work organization from reaching equilibrium and they are overlooked in logical-rational approaches. Anxieties arising from restructured power relationships, new targets and expectations are feelings that people naturally dislike and want to replace. When the logical-rational system neglects the resolution of anxiety then people compensate in the informal, shadow system. Borrowing a biological analogy, it is rather as if a particular equilibrium, if disturbed or threatened by outside agents, defends itself again attack in the form of a desired and articulated new equilibrium. Menzies' (1960) work on social systems defending themselves against anxiety was an early recognition of this phenomenon.

Another complexity theory concept that helps us to understand change is the idea of a tipping point (Boyatzis, 2006). Here, events occur and are contained within a system which lead up to and which culminate in a tipping point. A good example of this is the recent UK story relating to finance and property markets. Several years of 'easy' money, available finance and rising property prices seemed to suit lenders and borrowers alike. But these halcyon days led to unsafe lending in America (sub-prime lending) which eventually caused great turbulence as the frailty of heavily interconnected financial systems was exposed. In September 2007 the UK bank Northern Rock went almost overnight from being a competitive institution to a complete lame-duck when it asked the Bank of England for assistance. This erosion of confidence led to the first run on a bank (people queuing *en masse* to withdraw their money) in over 100 years. A government loan of £25 billion (yes, billion) was needed to sustain the bank and to protect the investments of its customers. Other financial institutions were compromised by collapsing share prices. The UK government was rocked (no pun intended) by the changes that happened. Short of war, financial meltdown must be the one thing politicians fear the most.

Share values in banking and finance crashed, the supply of money for lending fell and the terms and conditions of borrowing were tightened, making home ownership even harder for first-time buyers. The seeds of the UK credit crunch were sown when the generally prudent and careful building societies in the UK converted to banks around 20 years previously. Senior managers were in the enviable position of receiving bonuses beyond the comprehension of lesser mortals if their organizations met targets and yet massive compensation if they failed to meet them or were sacked for pretty much any reason. Prudence had gone out of the window and in the language of change the 'butterfly effect' was set in train. The butterfly metaphor captures the idea that tiny variations in air pressure caused by the beat of a butterfly's wings in one place can, in theory, set in motion a chain of weather events that lead to a hurricane on the other side of the world.

Illustration 2.10

Equitable Life: creating chaos out of order

A good case of chaos emerging out of order is shown by the Equitable Life Assurance Society. For 200 years Equitable was a 'safe pair of hands' looking after life insurance and pensions typically for society's professionals – doctors, engineers, teachers and managers. However, in the years before 1988 it sold policies to some investors that guaranteed the pay out of certain benefits. Time passed and interest rates rose and fell. A situation built up in which Equitable did not have enough money to keep paying out to those to whom it had guaranteed returns. Realizing this, Equitable tried to stop paying out the rates it had guaranteed. But people with the guaranteed return policies would have none of this. Legal action was taken, ending up in the House of Lords where the Law Lords ruled that the policies had to be honoured. But where could Equitable find the money to honour its promises? Its answer was to take money from its policy holders who did not have guaranteed return policies and give it to those with guarantees.

The Lords' decision caused Equitable to close to new business, not that anyone in their right mind would have taken out a new policy with them. Most of its policy holders were worried about their investments and many looked to transfer their policies to a secure institution. Equitable's 200-year-old world collapsed and along with it the well-being of thousands of policy holders. Investors who decided to transfer their money out to another

investment company saw the value of their policies reduced by transfer penalities. Even so, many investors cut their losses and transferred to what they hoped would be a safer investment company. The Lords' decision forced Equitable to seek a buyer but with a £1.5 billion gap in its funds it was not an attractive proposition.

The point of this case is to illustrate how ongoing operations which seemed quite acceptable, even very desirable, built up an organizational time bomb that one day exploded. The events central to this case appear to be traceable to decisions taken by 'top' managers under the influence of environmental forces. That said, if the Law Lords had come to a different decision then perhaps Equitable would have avoided so big a crisis. So some environmental 'throw of the dice' was at play. We can also see how warning signs and signals were ignored. Before the turmoil, the Treasury had realized that Equitable would be insolvent if it had to find cash to meet its guarantees (Senior, 2001). Furthermore, the true poor performance of Equitable was an open secret in financial circles yet it continued to pay out relatively high bonuses (and so top the league tables) in preference to putting aside funds that could be used when markets were less prosperous (Miles, 2000). The Board, in what now seems to be a rather pathetic action, thought about suing former executives, financial advisors and auditors.

Having looked at how change is conceptualized and at how it might be possible to predict the next turning or crisis point (through application of the organizational life cycle concept), more needs to be done to develop ways of bringing about the necessary changes from one stage to another. It is useful therefore to have models and techniques for diagnosing the type of change situation prevailing at any one time in order to determine what kind of change approach to take.

Diagnosing change situations

> Those who pretend that the same kind of change medicine can be applied no matter what the context are either naive or charlatans.
>
> (Strebel, 1996b, p. 5)

Strebel goes on to say, 'Thus, change leaders cannot afford the risk of blindly applying a standard change recipe and hoping it will work. Successful change takes place on a path that is appropriate to the right situation' (p. 5). Pettigrew and Whipp (1993, p. 108), reporting on their study of a range of UK companies across four industry sectors, said: 'One of the central characteristics of the firms under study, therefore, is that the management of strategic and operational change for competitive success is an uncertain and emergent process.'

Being able to diagnose change situations is, therefore, important if organizations are going to have any chance of responding to and managing change successfully. However, diagnosing any organizational situation is far from being an exact science. There are, though, some tools and techniques that can help. For instance, Greiner's model of the organizational life cycle is useful for drawing attention to periods when organizational change is likely to be needed. In addition, techniques such as stakeholder, SWOT and PEST analysis can lead to planned change and can increase awareness of the need for continuous incremental change. Multiple-cause diagrams which help understand the relationships among events leading to outcomes can lead to a better understanding of the interactions between the many different and often simultaneous causes of change.

There are, however, a number of other methods that can be used for anticipating when change is imminent and for deciding an appropriate approach to use for its management and implementation.

Looking for breakpoints

To help organizations focus on environmental scanning for signals that could trigger change within organizations, Strebel (1996a) suggested a model of industry behaviour which is similar to Greiner's in the concept of a cycle of behaviour. However, while Greiner links his model mainly to changes in the structure and management of organizations, Strebel links his model more to an organization's competitive environment (see Figure 2.5). He uses the concept of the 'evolutionary cycle of competitive behaviour' to introduce the idea of 'breakpoints', that is those times when organizations must change their strategies in response to changes in competitor behaviour.

The cycle of competitive behaviour involves two main phases. One is the innovation phase when a new business opportunity is discovered. This triggers a breakpoint to introduce a phase in the evolutionary cycle that causes a *divergence* in competitors' behaviour as they attempt to exploit the new opportunity with innovative new offerings. Strebel (1996a) says this phase corresponds to variety creation in the evolutionary cycle and he gives examples of the first Apple computer, microchips and software, all of which triggered breakpoints. He goes on to say (p. 13):

> Divergent competitive behaviour aimed at enhancing the value of offerings continues until it becomes impossible to differentiate offerings because value innovation has run its course and imitation of the competitors' best features has taken over. As the offerings converge and the returns to value innovation decline, someone sees the advantage of trying to reduce delivered cost. Competitors converge on total quality management, continual improvement, and re-engineering or restructuring of the business system in an attempt to cut costs and maintain market share.

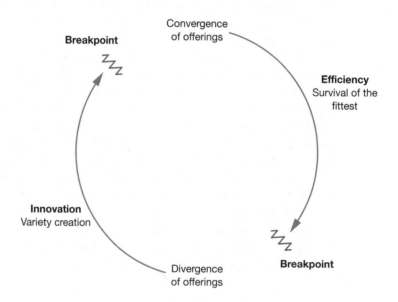

Figure 2.5 Evolutionary cycle of competitive behaviour

Source: from 'Breakpoint: how to stay in the game', *Financial Times Mastering Management*, Part 17 (Strebel, P. 1996) 1st March 1996

This brings about the second of the two phases – *convergence*. During this phase, the least efficient leave the scene and only the fittest survive. This is a phase of cost cutting and consolidation until the returns from cost reduction decline and people see the advantage of looking for a new business opportunity – bringing a new breakpoint with the cycle starting all over again. In summary (Strebel, 1996b, p. 5) the competitive cycle suggests that there are two basic types of breakpoint:

- Divergent breakpoints associated with sharply increasing variety in the competitive offerings, resulting in more value for the customer.
- Convergent breakpoints associated with sharp improvements in the systems and processes used to deliver the offerings, resulting in lower delivered cost.

It should be noted that although the competitive cycle repeats itself, the industry continues to evolve and Strebel illustrates this with respect to the computer industry (see Figure 2.6).

The vertical axis in Figure 2.6 represents the innovation–variety creation phase of the cycle of competitive behaviour; the horizontal axis represents the efficiency–survival phase. The vertical arrows denote periods of innovation (following divergence breakpoint) while the horizontal arrows denote periods of efficiency seeking and cost cutting (following convergence breakpoint). Over time, industries move up the diagonal with increasing customer value and lower delivered cost. Clearly some industries (e.g. those based on commodities) offer less opportunity for innovation and customer-value creation. Others (e.g. clothing and fashion) offer fewer opportunities for cost reduction. They evolve mainly through innovation.

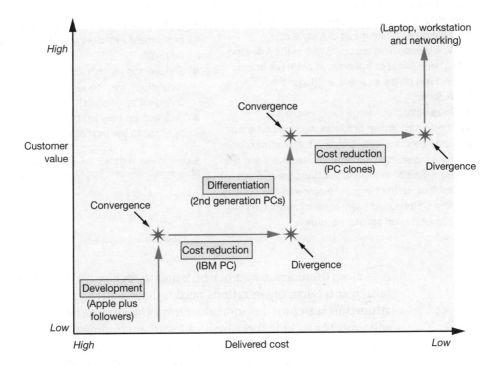

Figure 2.6 Breakpoint evolution of personal computer industry

Source: from 'Breakpoint: how to stay in the game', *Financial Times Mastering Management*, Part 17 (Strebel, P. 1996) 1st March 1996

Strebel's model is very useful in explaining the external environment in which organizations operate as is his advice on how to detect patterns in the environment that indicate a breakpoint might be imminent – see Illustration 2.11.

Illustration 2.11

Looking for breakpoints with leading indicators

The timing of breakpoints is impossible to predict because they might be triggered by many different factors and because they require both a latent market and a supplier with the right business system. However, with an understanding of an industry's evolution it is possible to look for patterns indicating that a breakpoint may be imminent. Specifically, the competitive cycle can be used to look for leading indicators of a potential breakpoint.

The tendency of the competitive cycle to oscillate between divergence (variety creation) on the one hand and convergence (survival of the fittest) on the other provides the framework.

Convergence is usually easier to anticipate because it is built on an offering that already exists.

Typical indicators are contained in the following list. When several of these are in place, all that is needed is a player, or event, to trigger the breakpoint:

- *Competitors*: convergence is visible in increasingly similar products, service and image.
- *Customers*: the differentiation between offerings looks increasingly artificial to customers and the segmentation in the market starts breaking down.
- *Distributors*: the bargaining power in the industry often shifts downstream to distributors who play competitors off against each other.

- *Suppliers*: they cannot provide a source of competitive advantage because everyone knows how to use their inputs.

Divergence is more difficult to anticipate because it is based on a new offering that does not yet exist. However, if the following are in place, the industry is ready for a new offering that breaks with the past.

- *Customers*: an increasingly saturated market is accompanied by declining growth rates and restless customers.
- *New entrants*: restless customers are attracting new entrants.
- *Competitors*: declining returns may force them to experiment with new offerings or look elsewhere for profits.
- *Suppliers*: new resources and, especially, new technology are frequently the source of a divergent breakpoint.
- *Distributors*: they lag behind because they have to adapt to the new offering.

Source: Strebel, P. (1996a) 'Breakpoint: how to stay in the game', *Mastering Management*, Part 17, *Financial Times*.

It is clear there are a number of issues associated with the identification of breakpoints. First, organizations need to have both formal and informal systems attuned to searching for indicators from the environment. The formal systems will probably include those involved with environmental scanning, benchmarking and data collection and interpretation. In addition, the way in which organizations are structured must help, rather than hinder, these activities.

As important are the more informal aspects of organizations, such as open attitudes on the part of managers and personnel, a degree of cooperation rather than destructive competition between divisions and departments, and a culture supportive of innovation and change. Part Two of the book discusses these factors in more detail but before then we describe another way of assessing both the impact and the magnitude of impending change as an essential tool in determining the most appropriate methodology for carrying out the change management process. However, rather than diagnosing change by scanning the organization's competitive environment this approach characterizes organizational problems (and therefore the need for change) in terms of their complexity, variability, people involvement and how much consensus there is on what constitutes the problem and what might bring a solution.

Hard (difficult) and soft (messy) problems

The discussion so far shows how situations forcing change vary in complexity and seriousness. A minor event in some part of an organization's environment can bring about small-scale or large-scale change. Disturbances from the external environment will have a much more wide-ranging impact on an organization's strategy, structure and processes.

In the preceding section, reference was made to identifying industry breakpoints. Sometimes, however, the signals arriving on managers' desks are not as clearly categorized as implied, neither can they always be separated easily into those concerned with competitors, customers, suppliers and distributors. These signals are frequently confused and diffuse and it is not easy to see clearly just what type of situation prevails – the only thing managers perceive are 'problems'. These problems may vary in complexity and seriousness, ranging from minor upsets to major catastrophes, from temporary hitches to gnawing 'tangles'. Paton and McCalman (2000) use the terms 'hard' and 'soft' to describe, respectively, these two types of problems. Alternatively, the Open University (1985) uses the terms 'difficulties' and 'messes', the latter term based on Ackoff's (1993) article entitled 'The Art and Science of Mess Management'.

Illustration 2.12 demonstrates some differences between difficulties and messes and shows how difficulties are simply more limited sorts of problems while messes are larger and much more taxing for those who want some kind of change to 'solve' the problem. However, messes are not just bigger problems, they are qualitatively different from difficulties.

In distinguishing between these two types of problem the Open University uses the concepts of 'hard complexity' as characteristic of difficulties and 'soft complexity' as characteristic of messes.

> Complexity is not just a matter of there being many different factors and interactions to bear in mind, of uncertainty concerning some of them, of a multitude of combinations and permutations of possible decisions and events to allow for, evaluate and select. It is not only a computational matter – such as operational researchers deal with. Complexity is also generated by the very different constructions that can be placed on those factors, decisions and events.
>
> (Open University, 1985, p. 18)

The consequence of these different interpretations of complexity is to describe hard complexity as characteristic of those problems that lend themselves to quantification and an optimal solution – an example is working out the best timetables for workers on production lines to achieve the most output. Soft complexity, by way of contrast, is indicative of situations where the description of events is ambiguous and there is a 'tantalizing multiplicity of different interpretations and reconstructions' (Open University, 1985, p. 18) that can be put upon a problem, let alone its possible solution.

Illustration 2.12

Difficulties and messes

Difficulties are bounded in that they:
- tend to be smaller scale;
- are less serious in their implications;
- can be considered in relative isolation from their organizational context;
- have clear priorities as to what might need to be done;
- generally have quantifiable objectives and performance indicators;
- have a systems/technical orientation;
- generally involve relatively few people;
- have facts that are known and which can contribute to the solution;
- have agreement by the people involved on what constitutes the problem;
- tend to have solutions of which the type at least is known;
- have known timescales;
- are 'bounded' in that they can be considered separately from the wider organizational context and have minimal interactions with the environment.

Messes are unbounded in that they:
- tend to be larger scale;
- have serious and worrying implications for all concerned;
- are an interrelated complex of problems that cannot be separated from their context;
- have many people of different persuasions and attitudes involved in the problem;
- have subjective and at best semi-quantifiable objectives;
- have an absence of knowledge of factors and uncertainty as to what needs be known;
- have little agreement on what constitutes the problem let alone what might be possible solutions;
- have usually been around for some time and will not be solved quickly, if at all; bringing about an improvement may be all that can be hoped for;
- have fuzzy timescales;
- are 'unbounded' in that they spread throughout the organization and, sometimes, beyond.

The introduction of new working practices is an example of a messy problem involving soft complexity. For instance, not everyone will agree there is a problem and a need for new working practices. Some will interpret this action as a hidden agenda such as a desire to reduce the workforce or an attempt to split up certain work groups. Others may view this optimistically in terms of getting extra experience and perhaps new responsibilities. Management is likely to think it a 'good thing' while any trade union will want to know the implications for its members.

What is more, if the changes have implications for pay and status, the possible 'losers' will see the world very differently from the possible 'winners'.

Activity 2.3

1 *Note three 'difficulties' you have faced at work or in similar situations elsewhere.*

2 *Note two or three 'messes' you have faced or been involved in.*

3 *Using Illustration 2.12, list the ways in which the difficulties differ from the messes. What might this tell you about ways of dealing with them?*

The change spectrum

Asking a number of questions about a change situation may help to identify whether it is likely to involve hard or soft complexity and whether it can, therefore, be seen to be more of a difficulty or more of a mess. Using the terms 'hard' and 'soft' to distinguish these two types of problem, Paton and McCalman (2000) have devised what they call the 'TROPICS' test to help locate a change situation on a continuum from hard to soft. Illustration 2.13 presents the TROPICS factors as dimensions on which a change situation can be positioned, according to whether it is further towards the hard or soft end of each factor.

The TROPICS test, as with any analysis of problems according to the lists in Illustration 2.12 and Illustration 2.13, can only be a guide to the nature of the problem. What is important is to have undertaken exercises like these to understand more clearly the type of change situation faced, in order to guide the design, planning and implementation of any change. This is because problem solving and managing subsequent change is not simply an intellectual problem. As situations move away from being difficulties and towards a mess, they encompass not only issues that can be addressed through the application of intellect, but also issues which have emotional and social dimensions requiring different kinds of approaches to resolve them. Simplistically, these approaches can be categorized as hard and soft and there are a number of models of change that, in broad terms, attach to these different approaches. These are considered further and in much more detail in Part Three, when the issues of 'doing' change are addressed.

Illustration 2.13

The TROPICS factors

Hard		*Soft*
Timescales clearly defined/ short to medium term		Timescales ill-defined/ medium to long term
Resources needed for the change clearly identified		Resources needed for the change uncertain
Objectives clearly stated and could be quantified		Change objectives subjective and ambiguous
Perceptions of the problem and its possible solution shared by all		No consensus on what constitutes the problem/ conflicts of interest
Interest in the problem is limited and defined		Interest in the problem is widespread and ill-defined
Control is maintained by the managing group		Control is shared with people outside the managing group
Source of the problem originates from within the organization		The source of the problem originates from outside the organization

Activity 2.4

Take each example you thought of in answer to Activity 2.3 and apply the TROPICS test to it. To do this, put a cross on each line according to whether your example is nearer to one end or the other of the factor. When you have done this for all factors for each example, make a judgement as to whether your example is, overall, a hard or soft problem/change situation.

Did the TROPICS test confirm or refute your judgement of what is a difficulty and what is a mess in terms of your answer to Activity 2.3?

● ● ● ● ● How change has changed

As we near the end of this chapter it is useful to summarize how change has itself changed over the past 50 or 60 years of management research and we attempt this in Table 2.2. Key differences found in traditional and contemporary discourses are a move away from managerialist approaches to leading episodes of change caused by environmental and competitive triggers towards a state in which change is more of a 'taken for granted' aspect of organizational life in climates of continuous improvement in contrast to problem solving. We are not suggesting that this is the way organizations have changed necessarily – anecdotally we hear of many traditional approaches being used. The differences in the table reflect changes in the way change is discussed in the management research literature (Oswick *et al.*, 2005).

Table 2.2 The changing nature of change

Comparator	Traditional discourse	Contemporary discourse
Temporality	Episodes of change with discrete beginning and end points (e.g. see Lewin's model of freezing and unfreezing in Chapter 6)	A philosophy that continuous organizational change is necessary to cope with the environment
Ethos	Fixing problems, focusing on negative events	Recognizing that things working well can be improved, improving already positive situations
Inputs	Analysis of data, 'running the numbers'	Constructive ongoing dialogues about what's working
Targets	Tangible features of the workplace, systems, structures	In addition to traditional targets the less tangible areas of organizations such as reputation and image
Drivers	Top and middle management	Involvement of people at all levels
Narratives	Managerialist, top-down, recipes for change	Debating what works, more focus on rhetoric of change in the particular organizational setting

Source: Based on Oswick *et al.* (2005) 'Looking Forwards: discursive directions in organizational change', *Journal of Change Management*, 18(4), pp. 383–390.

Conclusions

Organizational change can be categorized in three dimensions; pace, scope and planned-emergent. As the typologies reviewed here show, not only are there different types of change, change also appears differently at different levels of an organization. Planned change can lead to unintended outcomes that can lead to escalating positive or negative events. Complexity theory questions whether planned change is possible. Of course managers can plan, but to what extent are the changes that are seen connected to their plans?

There is still doubt around the question of whether change today makes change tomorrow more or less likely – more research is needed in this area. Strebel's model of change at the industry level is useful in looking to the wider environment for triggers for change. This model, together with the TROPICS test, can be used to analyze situations where change is considered desirable in order to understand which approach might be adopted in order to make it happen.

Chapter 1 examined the different environments in which organizational life and death take place. Table 2.3 summarizes the similarities between the theories and research discussed in Part One which sets the scene for the more detailed discussion of issues of change in Part Two.

Table 2.3 Environmental conditions and types of change

Environmental forces for change			Types of change				
Ansoff and McDonnell (1990)	Strebel (1996a)	Stacey (1996)	Tushman et al. (1988)	Dunphy and Stace (1993)	Balogun and Hope Hailey (2004)	Grundy (1993)	Stacey (1996)
Predictable	Weak	Close to certainty	Converging (fine-tuning)	Fine-tuning	Adaptation	Smooth incremental	Closed
Forecastable by extrapolation	Moderate	Close to certainty	Converging (incremental)	Incremental adjustment	Evolution		Contained
Predictable threats and opportunities				Modular transformation	Reconstruction	Bumpy incremental	
Partially predictable opportunities	Strong			Corporate transformation	Revolution		
Unpredictable surprises		Far from certainty	Discontinuous or frame breaking			Discontinuous	Open ended

Discussion questions and assignments

1 Discuss the proposition that: 'All change can be categorized as either incremental or radical.' Use examples from your own experience to support your argument.

2 To what extent are Dunphy and Stace's four types of change helpful in working with 'real-life' examples of change? Illustrate your answer with examples from organizations you know well.

3 Discuss Quinn's (1979) contention that change occurs through a process of 'logical incrementalism'. Give examples to support your argument.

4 To what extent do organizational messes get treated as if they were difficulties? What are the organizational consequences of this? Does it matter how change situations are classified?

5 To what extent do you think the environmental scanning tools are effective in diagnosing the environment for organizations? Are there situations when they might not be effective?

Case example ●●●

NHS revolution breathes new life into private sector

The government is turning to outside health providers in its determination to cut hospital waiting times.

A revolution is taking place in the private health sector that could see its hospital activity double in less than 10 years. Ironically, it is the determination of the government and the National Health Service to secure big cuts in waiting times for patients that has breathed new life into the sector. But the remarkable shake-up taking place in the private sector is not all good news for those companies established in the market. Expansion will come at a price as consultants see their fees squeezed and could even threaten some of the main medical insurers' business. William Laing, who for 25 years has been the leading analyst of the private sector and its relationship with the NHS, says: 'It is the biggest change in the sector that there has ever been. And it is a real change if they [the government] go through with it.'

The government's decision to turn the NHS less into a direct provider of services, and more into a purchaser of care has big implications for the private hospital groups as overseas providers are brought in to supply waiting list operations and diagnostic procedures. It is also changing the NHS itself as elective, waiting list care is increasingly separated from more urgent work. NHS consultants, whose rates for private work are the highest in the world, are beginning to see their fees squeezed. And for private patients there is the potential for the cost of treatment to fall, at least in real terms, as the government begins to create a genuine market in healthcare supply. In the longer term, however, the market could threaten the business of BUPA and other private medical insurers. According to two of Britain's big four private hospital suppliers – the market is being transformed by the arrival of the NHS as a bulk purchaser of care from the private sector.

The change has come in two stages. The first was the government's decision to bring in overseas suppliers to compete for chains of fast-track treatment centres to provide 250,000 operations a year for NHS patients. When the deals were announced, almost all the preferred bidders came from overseas – from South Africa, Canada and the US – on the grounds of price and innovation. Home-grown operators, which include Bupa and General Healthcare's BMI hospitals, lost out. The second breakthrough came when the private sector reacted to the threat to their business. Capio, which is Swedish owned, and Nuffield won the deal to provide 25,000 operations this year by offering prices that neither they nor the NHS would disclose in detail. However, John Reid, Health Secretary at the time, said they were 'on a par with equivalent NHS prices'. That compares with the premium of 20 per cent to 46 per cent over NHS costs that the service has been paying for the 60,000 to 80,000 procedures a year that it has bought from UK private hospitals. The competition is starting to make private treatment affordable for the NHS.

Direct comparison of private sector and NHS prices is fraught with difficulty; and NHS prices are expected to rise as they become more accurate as a result of being used internally to pay hospitals. But with contracts for a second wave of treatment centres expected to be announced in the summer, by 2008 the private sector looks set to be treating a minimum of 600,000 NHS patients a year – approaching a ten-fold increase on the numbers last year. Mr Reid has said perhaps 15 per cent of NHS operations could be privately provided – that would amount to 1m a year out of the 7m-plus that the NHS is projected to provide towards the end of the decade. And that figure would match the current total size of the private sector.

There is an undoubted irony that it is a Labour government presiding over the biggest expansion in privately provided care since the NHS was founded in 1948. Some doubt it will last. Not all the overseas contracts have been signed. Some providers have been dumped and swapped for others. These are either teething troubles as the NHS seeks the best price going, or a sign of more fundamental problems. Among the sceptics the chief executive of

Case example *continued*

General Healthcare said: 'The big question is sustainability' – an issue that worries other private hospital executives. This company has undertaken significant cardiac work for the NHS but has yet to win one of the big contracts. The treatment centre deals run for five years. But he queried whether the money would be there to pay for them when the current period of 7 per cent real terms growth for the NHS ended in 2008. In addition, to achieve its current cuts in waiting times 'the NHS is sprinting. But this is a marathon. And you can't keep sprinting over a marathon.' However, growth of the NHS seems set to continue – there seems no end to the demand for healthcare.

Source: from 'NHS Revolution Breathes New Life into Private Sector', *Financial Times*, 3 May 2004 (Timmins, N).

Case exercise   Is this 'frame-breaking' change?

1 To what extent do you consider this change to be 'frame-breaking' change? Justify your view.

2 In your opinion, which sectors and elements of the environment do you consider to have had the most influence on the decisions detailed in the case? Justify your conclusions.

3 From your knowledge and experience of the NHS and private healthcare providers, analyze the effects that will be felt by doctors, other medical staff and administrators in the NHS and other healthcare providers.

4 What effects, if any, over the longer term might these changes have for patients?

●●●● Indicative resources

Balogun, J. and Hope Hailey, V. (2004) *Exploring Strategic Change* (2nd edn), Harlow: Financial Times Prentice Hall. This book focuses on the change process itself and is a good text for considering change at the strategic level.

●●●● Useful websites

www.pwc.com This site for PriceWaterhouseCoopers contains papers and advice on a range of business issues including managing change.

www.ft.com *The Financial Times* website has a useful search facility to find examples of organizations that are responding to change.

To click straight to these links and for other resources go to
www.pearsoned.co.uk/senior

References

Ackoff, R.L. (1993) 'The Art and Science of Mess Management', in Mabey, C. and Mayon-White, B. (eds) *Managing Change* (2nd edn), London: PCP.

Ansoff, I.H. and McDonnell, E.J. (1990) *Implanting Strategic Management*, Englewood Cliffs, NJ: Prentice-Hall.

Balogun, J. and Hope-Hailey, V. (2004) *Exploring Strategic Change* (2nd edn), Harlow: Financial Times Prentice Hall.

Beck, N., Bruders, J. and Woywode, M. (2008) 'Momentum or Deceleration? Theoretical and methodological reflections on the analysis of organizational change', *Academy of Management Journal*, 51 (3), pp. 413–435.

Boyatzis, R. (2006) 'An Overview of Intentional Change from a Complexity Perspective', *Journal of Management Development*, 25(7), pp. 607–623.

Burnes, B. (2004) *Managing Change: A Strategic Approach to Organisational Dynamics* (4th edn), Harlow: Financial Times Prentice Hall.

Burnes, B. (2005) 'Complexity theories and Organizational Change', *International Journal of Management Reviews*, 7, pp. 273–290.

Checkland, P.B. (1972) 'Towards a Systems Based Methodology for Real World Problem Solving', *Journal of Systems Engineering*, 3(2), pp. 87–116.

Clarke, L. (1994) *The Essence of Change*, Hemel Hempstead: Prentice Hall.

Corzine, R. and Adams, P. (1996) 'Shell May Face Fresh Pressure Over Nigerian Oil Discovery', *Financial Times*, 8 March, p. 1.

Dawson, P. (1994) *Organizational Change: A Processual Approach*, London: PCP.

Dunphy, D. and Stace, D. (1993) 'The Strategic Management of Corporate Change', *Human Relations*, 46, (8), pp. 905–920.

Greenwood, R. and Hinings, C.R. (1996) 'Understanding Radical and Organizational Change: bringing together the old and new institutionalism', *Academy of Management Review*, 21(4), pp. 1022–1054.

Greiner, L.E. (1972) 'Evolution and Revolution as Organizations Grow', *Harvard Business Review*, July–August, 50, pp. 37–46.

Grundy, T. (1993) *Managing Strategic Change*, London: Kogan Page.

Houchin, K. and Maclean, D. (2005) 'Complexity Theory and Strategic Change: an empirically informed critique, *British Journal of Management*, 16 (2), pp. 149–166.

Jian, G. (2007) 'Unpacking Unintended Consquences of Planned Organizational Change', *Management Communication Quarterly*, 21(1), pp. 5–28.

Johnson, G. (1988) 'Processes of Managing Strategic Change', *Management Research News*, 11 (4/5), pp. 43–46. This article can also be found in Mabey, C. and Mayon-White, B. (eds) *Managing Change* (2nd edn), London: PCP.

Johnson, G., Scholes, K. and Whittington, R. (2008) *Exploring Corporate Strategy: Texts and Cases* (8th edn), Harlow: Financial Times Prentice Hall.

Kanter, R.M. (1989) *When Giants Learn to Dance: Mastering the Challenges of Strategy, Management and Careers in the 1990s*, Unwin: London.

Kast, F.E. and Rosenzweig, J.E. (1970) *Organization and Management: A Systems Approach*, New York: McGraw-Hill.

Kimberley, J.R. and Miles, R.H. (1980) *The Organizational Life-cycle*, San Francisco, CA: Jossey-Bass.

McAleer, W.E. (1982) 'Systems: a concept for business and management', *Journal of Applied Systems Analysis*, 9, pp. 99–129.

Menzies, I. (1960) 'A Case Study in the Functioning of Social Systems as a Defence Against Anxiety', *Human Relations*, 13, pp. 95–121.

Miles, R. (2000) High Bonuses Masked High Performance, *The Times*, Money Section, 16 December, p. 5.

Open University (1985) Block 1, 'Managing and Messy Problems', Course T244, *Managing in Organizations*, Milton Keynes: Open University.

Oswick, C., Grant, D., Michelson, G. and Wailes, N. (2005) 'Looking Forwards: discussive directions in organizational change', *Journal of Change Management*, 18(4), pp. 383–390.

Paton, R.A. and McCalman, J. (2000) *Change Management: Guide to Effective Implementation* (2nd edn), London: Sage.

Peters, T.J. and Waterman, R.H. (1982) *In Search of Excellence: Lessons from America's Best Run Companies*, Harper and Row: London.

Pettigrew, A. and Whipp, R. (1993) *Managing Change for Competitive Success*, Oxford: Blackwell.

Plowman, D.A., Baker, L.T., Beck, T.E., Kulkani, M., Solansky, S.T. and Travis, D.V. (2007) 'Radical Change Accidentally: the emergence and amplification of small change', *Academy of Management Journal*, 50(3), pp. 515–543.

Quinn, J.B. (1979) 'Xerox Corporation (B)', copyright case, Hanover, NH: Amos Tuck School of Business Administration, Dartmouth College.

Quinn, J.B. (1980) 'Managing Strategic Change', *Sloan Management Review*, Summer, pp. 3–20.

Senior, A. (2001) 'Equitable May Sue Advisors and FSA', *The Times*, Money Section, 20 October, p. 12.

Stacey, R. (1995) 'The Science of Complexity: an alternative perspective for strategic change processes', *Strategic Management Journal*, 16(6), pp. 477–495.

Stacey, R. (1996) *Strategic Management and Organisational Dynamics: The Challenge of Complexity* (3rd edn), Harlow: Financial Times Prentice Hall.

Stacey, R. (2003) *Strategic Management and Organisational Dynamics: The Challenge of Complexity* (4th edn), Harlow: Financial Times Prentice Hall.

Stacey, R., Griffin, D. and Shaw, P. (2002) *Complexity and Management: Fad or Radical Challenges to Systems Thinking*, London: Routledge.

Strebel, P. (1996a) 'Breakpoint: how to stay in the game', *Mastering Management*, Part 17, *Financial Times*.

Strebel, P. (1996b) 'Choosing the Right Path', *Mastering Management*, Part 14, *Financial Times*, 16 October.

Timmins, N. (2004) 'NHS Revolution Breathes New Life into Private Sector', *Financial Times*, 3 May, p. 6.

Tushman, M.L., Newman, W.H. and Romanelli, E. (1988) 'Convergence and Upheaval: managing the unsteady pace of organizational evolution', in Tushman, M.L. and Moore, W.L. (eds), *Readings in the Management of Innovation*, New York: Ballinger.

von Bertanlanfy, L. (1971) *General Systems Theory*, Harmondsworth: Penguin.

Weick, K. and Quinn, R. (1999) 'Organizational Change and Development', *Annual Review of Psychology*, 50, pp. 361–386.

Wilson, D.C. (1992) *A Strategy of Change*, New York: Routledge.

Part Two

CHANGING ORGANIZATIONS

The idea of organizations as systems operating in a wider environment was developed in Part One. However, organizations are not simply the hapless victims of the winds of change because of the internal environment created to cope with disturbances. The strategy an organization pursues and the way in which it is structured have a big influence upon the capacity to respond to and initiate change.

Strategy and structure can be thought of as the more formal, overt aspects of how organizations function. As important, however, are the more informal, covert aspects of organizational life such as organizational culture (set in the context of its national culture), organizational politics and issues of power, cooperation and conflict, as well as the way the organization is led.

Part Two investigates these aspects of organizational life in terms of their relations with the external environment and the opportunities and constraints for change. The four chapters in Part Two reflect this focus and prepare the ground for the more practically oriented material on the designing and implementing of change coming up in Part Three.

This chapter looks at how organizations structure their activities while Chapters 4 and 5 concentrate on the less tangible contexts of culture and politics and their significance for the success of change processes. Chapter 6 discusses leadership and its impact on change.

Chapter 3

Organizational structure, design and change

This chapter introduces the characteristics of different organizational designs and structures. Advantages and disadvantages of each are given in relation to organizational performance and the ability of organizations to introduce and implement change. Network and virtual organizational forms are examined in the context of best-fitting contemporary business environments. Strategy, size and technology are examined in relation to their influences on structure.

Learning objectives

At the end of this chapter you will be able to:

- define what is meant by organizational design and structure;

- explain the organizational forms that are commonly found;

- discuss the relationship between strategy and structure;

- evaluate the contingency relationships between organizational structure, size, technology and the external environment;

- assess the extent to which different structures can cope with and adapt to a variety of change processes.

The meaning of organization structure

Social systems usually group people in different ways to get work done. In order to achieve goals and objectives, organizations need ways of dividing work up and allocating it to members of the organization. The allocation of responsibilities, the grouping of workers' activities and their coordination and control are basic elements of structure.

At a simple level, structure is something managers design to enable efficient production and delivery of the organization's outputs. It 'describes the way an organization is configured into work groups and the reporting and authority relationships that connect individuals and groups together' (Swailes, 2008, p. 191).

Is there a difference between organization structure and design? There is and it is worth noting. Design refers to the way a structure might be drawn on an organization chart. Design shows the formal reporting relationships and areas of responsibility drawn to impress the organization's various stakeholders. Yet readers who have worked in organizations will know that very often employees ignore the design to get things done – they use the operating structure not the formal design. So we can see structure as the incarnation of a design with 'patterned regularity' being a dominant feature of structure (Willamott, 1981, p. 470).

Organizational designs are 'managerialist responses' to the contingencies thrown up by the environment and the main framework for understanding organizational design is called contingency theory (Clegg, Kornberger and Pitsis, 2008, p. 528). Large organizations, for instance, typically organize around centralized decision making; here the contingency (size) is shaping the response (centralization).

Keeping the design/structure distinction in mind is also important since the real working structure of an organization can be seen as something that is socially constructed (Bate *et al.*, 2000). Changes to design can have no impact on the social structures that are overlaying them. 'Empty restructuring' is the phrase used by Paul Bate (1995) to describe what happens when managers change designs but disregard the social interactions that are overlaying them.

Social structures can be seen as informal structures that are not designed by management but are the outcome of friendship and interest groupings as well as those which serve political purposes, not always related to the organization's goals. These issues are taken further in the discussions of culture, power and politics and the leadership of change.

The dimensions of structure

Organization structure can vary in many ways but a classic study identified the following six primary dimensions of structure (Pugh, Hickson, Hinings and Turner, 1969):

1 *Specialization*: the extent to which there are different specialist roles and how they are distributed.
2 *Standardization*: the extent to which an organization uses regularly occurring procedures that are supported by bureaucratic procedures of invariable rules and processes.
3 *Formalization*: the extent to which written rules, procedures, instructions and communications are set out for employees.
4 *Centralization*: the extent to which authority to make decisions lies with the apex (top) of the organization. Decentralization refers to attempts to push decision making down to lower levels in the hierarchy.
5 *Configuration*: the shape and pattern of authority relationships; how many layers there are and the number of people who typically report to a supervisor.
6 *Traditionalism*: how many procedures are 'understood' in contrast to being written; how commonly accepted is the notion of 'the way things are done around this organization'.

Derek Pugh and his colleagues established four underlying dimensions:

1 *Structuring of activities*: the extent to which there is formal regulation of employee behaviour through the processes of specialization, standardization and formalization.
2 *Concentration of authority*: the extent to which decision making is centralized at the top of the organization.
3 *Line control of workflow*: the extent to which control of the work is exercised directly by line management rather than through more impersonal procedures.
4 *Support component*: the relative size of the administrative and other non-work-flow personnel performing activities auxiliary to the main workflow.

Support for these dimensions was provided by John Child (1988) who made some additions of his own:

- the way sections, departments and divisions are grouped together;
- systems for communication, the integration of effort and participation; and,
- systems for motivating employees such as performance appraisal and reward.

It is clear from this that structure is a multi-dimensional concept such that organizations can be structured in many different ways according to where they fit on the dimensions above. Every organization has a unique structural 'finger-print'. Despite this it is possible to discern similar ways of designing organizations and to identify some general patterns. There is also evidence to show that some types of structures are a better fit with environments than others and we discuss this later. First it is necessary to understand the broad range of structures used.

Models of structure

Bureaucratic structure

One of the best-known forms of organization structure is the bureaucratic form and we are indebted to the German sociologist Max Weber – one of the founding fathers of organization theory. Three ideas that are central to the concept of bureaucracy: the idea of rational legal authority; the idea of 'office' and the idea of 'impersonal order' (from Henderson and Parsons' translation of Weber (1947) found in Pugh, 1990).

These ideas are based on:

- a continuous organization of official functions bound by rules;
- a specified sphere of competence, i.e. differentiation of function;
- the organization of offices (i.e. positions) follows the principle of hierarchy;
- the separation of members of the administrative staff from ownership of production or administration;
- no appropriation by the incumbent of their official position;
- administrative acts, decisions and rules are formulated and recorded in writing, even in cases where discussion is the rule or is essential.

Illustration 3.1 summarizes the characteristics of the pure form of bureaucratic structure.

Illustration 3.1

Bureaucracy

Weber specified several characteristics of his ideal organization structure of which the main four are:

1 Specialization and division of labour. Work is finely divided between well-defined and highly specialized jobs or roles.
2 Hierarchical arrangement of positions. Roles are hierarchically arranged with a single chain of command from the top of the organization to the bottom.
3 A system of impersonal rules. The incumbents of roles (or positions) carry out their duties impersonally in accordance with clearly defined rules.
4 Impersonal relationships. Coordination of activities relies heavily on the use of rules, procedures and written records and on the decision of the lowest common superior to the people concerned.

Other characteristics of a bureaucracy identified by Weber are: the selection of officials solely on the basis of technical qualifications; appointment not election; remuneration by fixed salaries with a right to pensions; only under certain conditions can the employing authority terminate an employment; the employee can leave at any time; and a system of promotion according to seniority or achievement or both.

Source: Based on Weber, M. (1947) *The Theory of Social and Economic Organisation*, Free Press, translated and edited by Henderson, A.M. and Parsons, T. in Pugh, D. (1990) *Organization Theory. Selected Readings*, Penguin. (German original published in 1924.)

The bureaucratic form of organization structure is an enduring one still found in most if not all large public sector organizations. For instance, McHugh and Bennett's (1999, p. 81) account of an attempt to bring about change in a large public sector agency describes organizations like it in the following way:

> A rigid bureaucratic maze typified structural formation within many such organizations with the majority of members having narrowly defined and highly specialized jobs, and being protected from making decisions through their constant deference to authority and reference to their rule books.

The difficulties expressed by McHugh and Bennett regarding the problems of changing such a structure are consistent with Weber who was convinced of the case for the bureaucratic form. For instance, he says (Pugh, 1990, p. 12):

> It would be sheer illusion to think for a moment that continuous administrative work can be carried out in any field except by the means of officials working in offices . . . For bureaucratic administration is, other things being equal, always, from a formal, technical point of view, the most rational type. For the needs of mass administration today, it is completely indispensable.

Illustration 3.2 is a brief description of a construction company called the Beautiful Buildings Company (known as the BB Company). The organization chart illustrates its current bureaucratic structure. The BB Company is used later in this chapter to illustrate other types of organizational structures that try to overcome problems of bureaucracy.

Illustration 3.2

The Beautiful Buildings Company

The Beautiful Buildings Company designs and builds a variety of different buildings. It is known for its imaginative designs and the construction of a range of factory and other industrial buildings and prides itself on having won contracts to build a new civic hall in one of the world's leading cities. Just over 12 months ago it took over a smaller building company specializing in home building for middle- to higher-income families. It would like to develop further into the area of commercial office buildings.

During the past 20 years the company has grown from operating solely in the UK to securing contracts in Australia and North America, and it has footholds in a number of mainland European countries.

The BB Company is headed by Gillian Lambeth, the daughter of the previous owner. There are a number of directors reporting to Gillian who are each in charge of one of the company's main functions. Marcos Davidson, the Marketing Director, has been the person most involved in promoting the company's activities outside the UK.

Currently the company is structured on typical bureaucratic lines as illustrated in the simplified chart shown below.

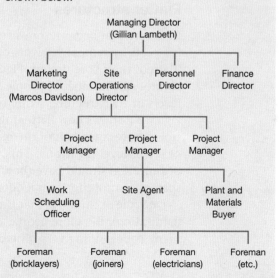

Activity 3.1

● *Obtain an official organization chart for an organization that you know well. To what extent would you regard the organization's structure as indicative of a bureaucratic structure and indicative of what really happens? How much of a match is there between the chart and the BB Company's bureaucratic structure? To what extent does the organization of work conform to Weber's bureaucratic principles?*

● *For organizations structured as bureaucracies, what barriers might exist to adaptation in response to environmental forces?*

Of particular interest are the differences between individual perceptions of organization structures and the formal design chart and the stories told by senior management. Jackson and Carter (2000), for instance, offer a strong argument for the view that structure is not, in the case of organizations, something *concrete* and *objective*, but essentially *abstract*. Adopting what they term 'a post-structuralism' approach to explaining structure, they maintain (in contradiction to Weber) that there is no obvious and *natural* way of ordering the management of organizational activities. What is more, they maintain that what one person perceives or experiences as (say) an authoritarian, oppressive structure, another person perceives as a structure that is democratic and which treats everyone fairly according to the rules.

It is certainly the latter of these two views of bureaucracies that was part of Weber's thinking. Weber's bureaucracies were intended to portray neutrality and fairness in the way people were treated. However, the term *bureaucracy* has, more recently, taken on negative connotations of undesirable and burdensome rules and regulations, and an overwhelming feeling of control.

Flatter structures

In a search for better responsiveness to markets and sometimes to reduce operating costs by removing layers of management some organizations have tried to 'flatten' their core design. Figure 3.1 demonstrates how widening the span of control (the number of people reporting to a supervisor) reduces the number of levels in the structure, while retaining the same number of staff. By contrast, Figure 3.2 shows how flattening the structure through doubling the span of control removes over half of the management positions while retaining the number of lower-level positions. This, however, does not reveal how many levels an organization should have (how vertically differentiated it should be) or what the span of control (horizontal differentiation) should be at each level.

One rule of thumb is that the more similar jobs are at any one level (job standardization), the more people a manager can coordinate and control. Managing many people doing very different kinds of jobs requires more managerial attention. As task ambiguity increases there is an increase in the number of problems a manager has to solve and these add to managerial overload (Butler, 1991). Another rule of thumb is that the more decision making is decentralized and therefore reducing the burden on each manager, the broader the span of control. Other factors that affect the span of control are the physical location or geographical spread of subordinates, the abilities of subordinate staff and the ability and personal qualities of the manager concerned (Mullins, 2005).

With regard to the number of levels in the structure of the organization (the 'scalar chain' or 'chain of command'), Drucker (1999) suggests that these should be as few as possible. Too many levels bring difficulties in understanding and communicating objectives both up and down the hierarchy. In a study of over 300 US companies Rajan and Wulf (2006) found that the number of managers between the CEO and the lowest managers with profit centre responsibility fell by over 25 per cent between 1986 and 1998. Possible explanations include:

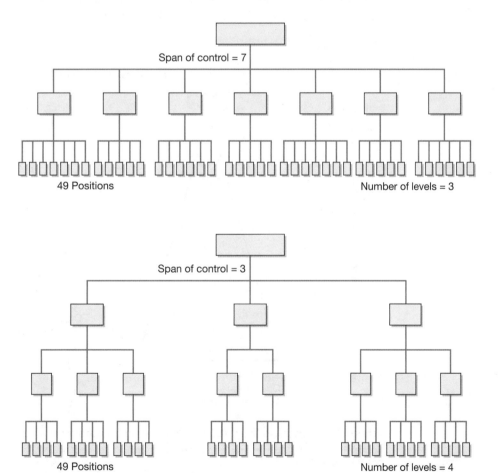

Figure 3.1 Flattening the structure but retaining the people

Source: Mullins, L.J. (2005) *Management and Organisational Behaviour* (7th edn), Harlow: Financial Times/Prentice Hall, p. 612.

- *Increased competition* – each managerial layer takes time to make decisions and faster decision making is needed as competition intensifies. Hence removing layers should accelerate decision making. Tougher competition may also be raising the complexity of the decisions that are needed. Flatter hierarchies seem more conducive to greater creativity by decision makers compared to a ladder of micromanagers.
- *Better corporate governance* – this may have contributed to the elimination of layers of management
- *Information technology* – if this increases the capacity of middle and junior managers to make decisions then the effective span of control can increase.

Rajan and Wulf conclude that while CEOs are more directly connected 'deeper down' the organization and across more business units (akin to centralization) there is a trend to push decision making authority downwards (akin to decentralization). This is an interesting finding that suggests that centralization and decentralization are not reciprocally related but that they can coexist.

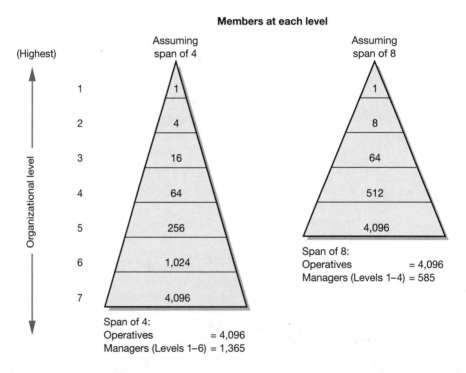

Figure 3.2 Flattening the structure but saving the people

Source: Robbins, S.P. (2003) *Organizational Behavior* (10th edn), Englewood Cliffs, NJ: Pearson Education Limited, pp. 433, 419.

Illustration 3.3

Organigraphs

Uncomfortable with the classic portrayals of structure using organization charts, Henry Mintzberg and colleague Ludo van der Heyden use 'organigraphs' to show how organizations really function.

Organigraphs contain two basic components; sets and chains. Sets are machines or groups of people that rarely interact with each other. Teachers of physics and sociology in a university rarely interact even though they are supported by the same infrastructure. Chains are systems for converting inputs into outputs such as assembly lines; something is processed and passed on to the next link in the chain.

In addition, there are hubs and webs. Hubs are where 'people, things and information' move and they can be buildings, machines or people. Webs show how points in an organization communicate with each other.

Unlike charts, organigraphs show the multiple relationships between components of organizations. There is no single correct organigraph – it is just a matter of how a particular manager sees how the organization works. There is no one way of symbolising the four components either – they can be drawn in many ways. Herein lies a criticism of the idea – if they can be anything then what analytical value do they have? But that is perhaps missing the point that organigraphs are ways of visualising how things work as a prelude to imagining change.

Source: Mintzberg, H. and van der Heyden, L. (1999) 'Organigraphs: drawing how companies really work', *Harvard Business Review*, Sep/Oct, pp. 87–94.

Horizontal differentiation – the departmentalization of work

The decision on which way to departmentalize frequently relies on the characteristics of the work to be done, the size of the organization, the physical locations of activities and the need to maintain a balance between high-level strategic decision making and lower-level operational imperatives. Power struggles also play a part. Some organizations design around functional areas, others departmentalize by product, customer or geographical region. Each method of structuring has its advantages and disadvantages.

Multifunctional structures

Multifunctional structures are a common structural form particularly in the stages of an organization's development when the early entrepreneurial phase gives way to a more settled phase of sustained growth, what Greiner (1972) calls the 'growth through direction' phase (see Figure 2.4 in Chapter 2). Large corporations of the early twentieth century were mostly structured on these lines due to the emphasis in early management theories on specialization, span of control, relationships, authority and responsibility (Cummings and Worley, 2005).

Common functional specialisms are production, marketing, purchasing and finance. Retailers have buying and selling departments, customer services and finance.

A functional structure serves organizations well as they move from what Greiner (1972) termed the 'growth by creativity' stage in a company's development to the 'growth by direction' stage (see Figure 2.4 in Chapter 2). However, as they grow and diversify in customer and product markets they pass through what Greiner calls a 'crisis of autonomy'. This is characterized by demands for greater autonomy on the part of middle managers who frequently possess greater knowledge about markets and operations than top management. As different product groups can experience different market conditions, organizing around products rather than functions can be more efficient. Illustration 3.4 lists advantages and disadvantages of functional structures together with the factors that provide the forces for moving towards this type of structure.

Illustration 3.4

Advantages and disadvantages of functional structures

Advantages
Departmentalization by function has advantages in its logical mirroring of the basic functions of business. Each function has its high-level representative to guard its interests. Tight control is possible at the top. It encourages the development of specialist skills and expertise and provides a career structure within the function. Training can be organized along specialist lines. In organizations where technical skill gives competitive advantage, the functional structure can enhance this.

Disadvantages
As organizations grow and diversify or locate in geographically distributed places, coordination of activities across functions can become more difficult. Functionalism sometimes encourages narrow thinking which works against innovation which requires cooperation across functions. Important market intelligence can be overlooked. Functional structures limit the opportunity for the development of general managers.

Contingency factors
These are based on the factors suggested by Cummings and Worley (2005):

- stable and certain environment
- small to medium size
- routine technology, interdependence with functions
- goals of efficiency and technical quality.

Multidivisional structures

It is not difficult to imagine the problems that the BB Company might have with a multifunctional structure. Its current and hoped-for activities cross at least four product areas (public buildings, industrial buildings, houses/homes, and commercial accommodation). Each of these product areas is governed by different sets of customer expectations, research and design problems and building regulations. Each is prey to different environmental influences. Departmentalizing by product might then be a sensible move for BB. Figure 3.3 shows how it could look if designed around its markets.

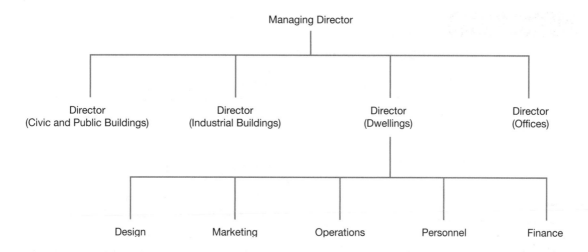

Figure 3.3 The BB Company – departmentalization by product

Multidivisional structures are built around outputs rather than inputs. They overcome the dangers of poor coordination and responsiveness and allow faster responses to market conditions. This was the reason for Unilever's restructuring, which began in 2004 as they clearly saw advantages in restructuring around product markets (see Illustration 3.5).

Departmentalization by product or service has advantages of maximizing the use of employees' skills and specialized market knowledge. There is more opportunity for innovative ideas for new or modified products to flourish. Product differentiation facilitates the use of specialized capital. Product divisions can be made profit centres in their own right thus making them responsible for budgets and sales. Differentiation by product makes it easier to concentrate on different classes of customer, particularly when different products coincide with different customer groupings. Where a product division has its own set of business functions these can be coordinated towards the product's markets. Lastly, this type of structure offers good opportunities for the training of general managers.

Disadvantages are that there can be overlap of functions from one product division to another, that is, duplication of central service and other support activities. Overall administration costs tend to be higher than in pure functional structures. Where business functions are not wholly devolved, product-based divisions are 'top sliced' to provide resources for more centralized functions. This can be felt by product line managers as burdensome overheads, which detract from their overall profits. Top management may have more difficulty in controlling what happens at the product divisional level. Coordinating policy and practice across product areas can be complex.

Illustration 3.5

Structural transformation at Unilever

Unilever, a leading supplier of fast-moving consumer goods known for global brands such as Birds Eye, Flora, Cif, Marmite, Hellmann's and Ben & Jerry's, has recently restructured in response to competition and performance results. Unilever has about 200,000 employees in nearly 100 countries.

Unilever combined three operating companies to create a new and more efficient structure to concentrate on product sales specific to the individual countries in which it operates. The reasoning was to simplify management to enable faster local decision making and improve agility in the marketplace. A 'one Unilever' programme created single operating companies in each country together with outsourcing of support functions such as IT, human resources and finance. Senior

management numbers fell by about 40 per cent. Each operating company is better suited to match its product portfolio to the country it operates in. The rationale for the structural changes was:

● single point responsibility
● faster decision making
● clear accountability for delivery
● leadership close to customer and consumer
● balance between market focus and scale.

But structural change is ongoing and in late 2006 the Foods group further restructured into six Centres of Excellence in Europe. This meant reorganizing 1,160 people in 60 locations into 29 food research and development locations with a loss of about 240 jobs.

Old management structure

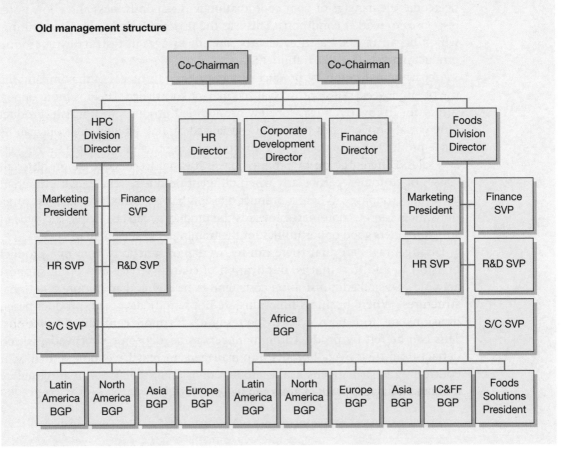

New management structure

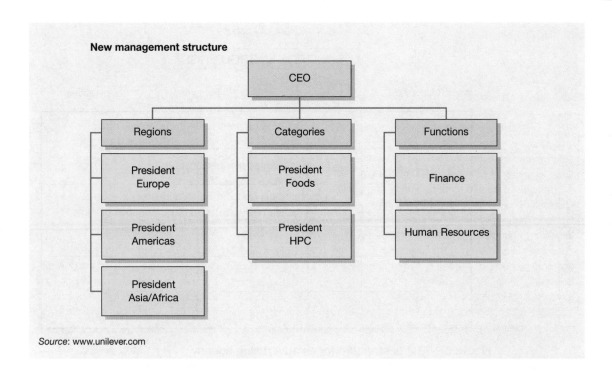

Source: www.unilever.com

Matrix organization

The essence of a matrix design is that a typical vertical hierarchy is overlayed with a horizontal structure commonly designed around big projects. Employees find that they report to different people for different areas of responsibility.

Figure 3.4 shows a hypothetical matrix structure for an advertising agency. In this case, the heads of marketing, finance, personnel, and research and development form the vertical lines of reporting while the different customer bases represent the divisions that operate horizontally across the structure.

Faced with shortening product life cycles Texas Instruments realized that its traditional functional hierarchy would not cope with the need to reduce time to market and introduced a 'Balanced Matrix' structure in one of its divisions. A key finding from the restructuring was that initially performance can fall but improved later on (Bernasco *et al.*, 1999).

Drawing on Davis and Lawrence's (1977) work, Bartol and Martin (1994) maintain that organizations which ultimately adopt a matrix structure usually go through four identifiable stages.

Stage 1 is a *traditional structure*, usually a functional structure, which follows the unity-of-command principle.

Stage 2 is a *temporary overlay*, in which managerial integrator positions are created to take charge of particular projects (e.g. project managers), oversee product launches (e.g. product managers), or handle some other issue of finite duration that involves co-ordination across functional departments. These managers often lead or work with temporary interdepartmental teams created to address the issue.

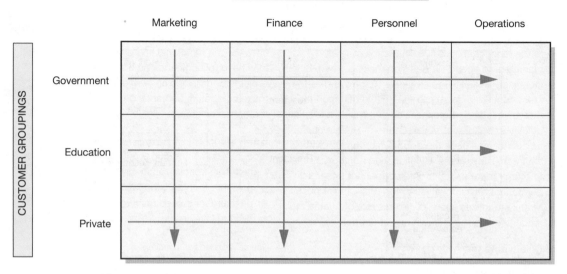

Figure 3.4 Matrix structure for an advertising agency

Stage 3 is a *permanent overlay* in which the managerial integrators operate on a permanent basis (e.g. a brand manager coordinates issues related to a brand on an ongoing basis), often through permanent interdepartmental teams.

Stage 4 is a *mature matrix*, in which matrix bosses have equal power.

(Bartol and Martin, 1994, pp. 321–322)

More recently, Cummings and Worley (2005), also drawing upon Davis and Lawrence (1977), suggest that matrix structures are appropriate under three important conditions. First there needs to be pressure from the external environment for a dual focus such as university lecturers focusing on teaching and research income. Second, a matrix structure is of benefit when an organization must process a large amount of information. This is particularly useful when organizations operate in an environment of unpredictability or need to produce information quickly. Finally, there must be pressures for sharing resources which matrixes support.

Matrix structures rely heavily on teamwork with managers needing high-level people management skills. The focus is on solving problems through team action. In a mature matrix structure, team members are managed simultaneously by two different managers – one is their functional line manager and the other the team or project leader. This type of organizational arrangement, therefore, requires a culture of cooperation, with supporting training programmes to help staff develop their teamworking and conflict-resolution skills. Illustration 3.6 summarizes the advantages and disadvantages of matrix structures, together with the factors that provide the forces for moving towards this type of structure.

Illustration 3.6

Advantages and disadvantages of matrix structures

Advantages

With a matrix design, decisions can be decentralized to the functional and divisional/ project-level managers to speed-up decision making. There is increased flexibility in being able to form and re-form cross-functional teams. These teams can monitor their own localized business environments and move quickly to adapt to changes in them. Staff in one functional area have the opportunity to work with staff from other areas. By allocating functional staff to one or more projects on a permanent or semi-permanent basis, loyalties to the projects are built. Matrix structures allow for flexible use of human resources and the efficient use of support systems.

Disadvantages

Matrix structures are complex and can be administratively expensive. There can be confusion over who is ultimately responsible for staff and project outcomes, particularly if things go wrong. The dual arrangement and need for enhanced communications between the 'arms' of the matrix can increase the potential for conflict, particularly between the functional and project managers. Staff may have to juggle their time between different projects or divisions and project managers may make competing demands on staff who work across more than one team.

Contingencies

- dual focus on unique product demands and technical specialization
- pressure for high information-processing capacity
- pressure for shared resources
- divided loyalties between two or more managers.

Source: Adapted by Cummings, T. and Worley, C. (2005) *Organization Development and Change* (8th edn), Mason, OH: Thomson South-Western, from McCann, J. and Galbraith, J.R. (1981) 'Interdepartmental Relations' in Nystrom, P.C. and Starbuck, W.H. (eds) *Handbook of Organizational Design: Remodelling Organizations and Their Environment*, vol. 2, New York: Oxford University Press.

Activity 3.2

Koontz and Weihrich (1990) say that matrix-type organizations occur frequently in construction, aerospace, marketing and management consulting firms in which professionals work together on a project.

Figure 3.4 shows a matrix structure for an advertising agency, which is a an example of the last of the instances just mentioned. The BB Company, as a building construction company, is an example of the first of Koontz and Weihrich's examples.

Using any general knowledge you may have of the building industry to embellish the description of the BB Company, attempt to design a matrix structure for the way the organization, as a whole, might operate. Then design a matrix structure for a division or department which dealt only with the building of homes.

Compare your results with those of anyone else who can be persuaded to do this. Argue the pros and cons for any differences.

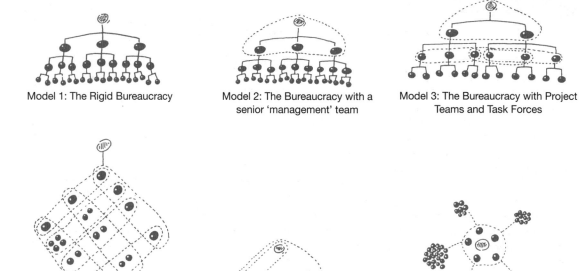

Model 1: The Rigid Bureaucracy

Model 2: The Bureaucracy with a senior 'management' team

Model 3: The Bureaucracy with Project Teams and Task Forces

Model 4: The Matrix Organization

Model 5: The Project Organization

Model 6: The Loosely coupled Organic Network

Figure 3.5 From bureaucracies to matrix, project and network organizations

Source: Reprinted by permission of Sage Publications, Inc. Morgan, G. (1989) *Creative Organization Theory. A Resource Book*, London: Sage, p. 66. Copyright © 1989 by Sage.

Wilson and Rosenfeld (1991) consider that it is usually not worth moving to a matrix structure unless the tasks to be performed are complex, unpredictable and highly interdependent. However, some organizations have gone beyond a matrix structure to devise structures that Morgan (1989) calls 'loosely coupled networks', but which can be (more generally) called 'network organizations' (Snow, Miles and Coleman, 1992).

New organizational forms

The main point about new organizational forms is that they are an attempt to go beyond the classic bureaucratic models. Figure 3.5 illustrates the transition from bureaucracy to what Morgan (1989) calls the 'project organization' and the 'loosely coupled organic network'.

According to Morgan, the project organization carries out most of its activities through project teams. Functional departments exist but they are there only to play a supporting role. The main work of the organization is done wholly through teams that rely for their success on being 'dynamic, innovative, powerful and exciting' and to which senior management tries to give free rein within the strategic direction of the organization. Morgan summarizes the nature of the project organization as follows.

The organization is much more like a network of interaction than a bureaucratic structure. The teams are powerful, exciting, and dynamic entities. Co-ordination is informal. There is frequent cross-fertilization of ideas, and a regular exchange of information, especially between team leaders and the senior management group. Much effort is devoted to creating shared appreciations and understandings of the nature and identity of the organization and its mission, but always within a context that encourages a learning-oriented approach. The organization is constantly trying to find and create the new initiatives, ideas, systems, and processes that will contribute to its success.

(Morgan, 1989, p. 67)

The project organization has overlapping characteristics with what Mintzberg (1983, p. 262) calls 'The Adhocracy'. The adhocracy, as its name suggests, is an *ad hoc* group of people (mainly professionals) who are brought together for a single purpose associated with a particular project. The team is usually short-lived and once the project is complete the team will disband – for example a group of professionals coming together to make a film. Adhocracies are characterized by having few formal rules and regulations or standardized routines. The shape of the organization is flat, but with horizontal differentiation generally high because adhocracies are staffed mainly by professionals, each with their own specialism.

The project organization usually employs its own staff. The adhocracy may also do this but may additionally have staff who work on a contract basis. This contrasts with Morgan's (1989) description of the loosely coupled organic network. In terms of a continuum of organizational forms, this type of network organization might be said to be at the end furthest from the rigid bureaucracy. The loosely coupled organic network describes a form of structure that, rather than employing large numbers of people directly, operates in a subcontracting mode. The small number of permanent staff set the strategic direction and provide the necessary operational support to sustain the network. However, while project teams and adhocracies have limited lives, the loosely coupled network can be a permanent structure. Figure 3.6 depicts three types of network.

Internal networks

According to Snow *et al.* (1992, p. 11), the internal network 'typically arises to capture entrepreneurial and market benefits without having the company engage in much outsourcing'.

Internal networks are typical of situations where an organization owns most or all of the assets associated with its business. However, it has usually created 'businesses within the business' that, although still owned by the organization as a whole, operate independently in terms of the discipline of the market. The argument is that if they are subject to market forces they will constantly seek to improve performance. A typical example would be a training and development unit that, on the one hand, 'sells' its services to its parent organization and, on the other, seeks to sell its services outside. The internal network is not dissimilar to Morgan's (1989) description of a project organization.

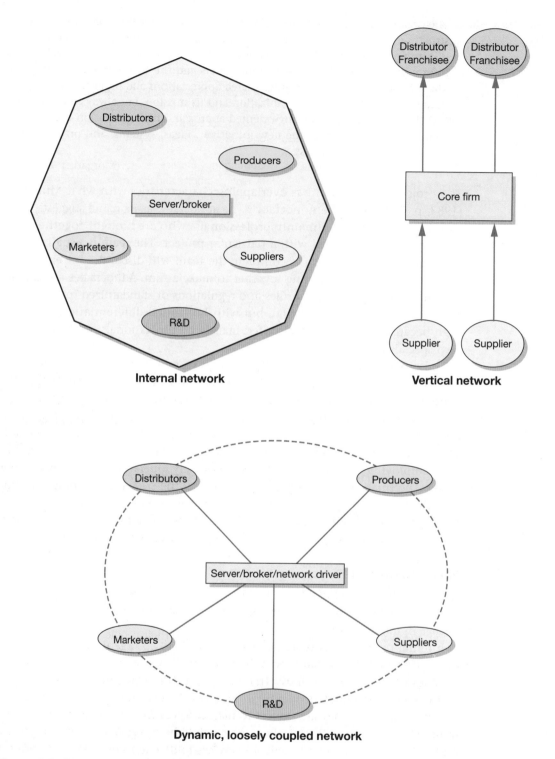

Figure 3.6 Common types of network

Illustration 3.7

Advantages and disadvantages of network organizations

Advantages

They enable a highly flexible and adaptive response to dynamic environments with the potential to create 'the best of the best' organization to focus resources on customer and market needs. Due to the fast pace and flexible nature each organization can leverage a distinctive competency. This structure also allows/permits rapid global expansion if needed. Lastly, they can produce synergistic results.

Disadvantages

Managing lateral relations across autonomous organizations is difficult. It is also difficult motivating members to relinquish autonomy to join the network. There are also issues relating to sustaining membership, and benefits can be problematic. Finally, this structure has the opportunity to give partners access to knowledge and technology that one may not wish to part with.

Contingency factors

- highly complex and uncertain environments
- organizations of all sizes
- goals and organizational specialization and innovation
- highly uncertain technologies
- worldwide operations.

Source: Cummings, T. and Worley, C. (2005) *Organization Development and Change* (8th edn), Mason, OH: Thomson South-Western.

Vertical networks

The vertical network (Hinterhuber and Levin, 1994) is typical of the situation where the assets are owned by several firms but are dedicated to a particular business. This is similar to what Snow *et al.* (1992, p. 13) call a 'stable' network that consists of 'a set of vendors . . . nestled around a large "core" firm, either providing inputs to the firm or distributing its outputs'. Thus the core organization spreads asset ownership and risk across a number of other independent organizations and gains the benefits of dependability of supply and/or distribution.

Toyota could be perceived as the core firm within a stable network of subcontractors, many of which had plants within the production complex surrounding Toyota in Toyota City (Clegg, 1990, referring to Cusamano, 1985). Handy's (1989, p. 110) description of what he terms the 'federal organization' is reminiscent of the Toyota example:

> [Federalism] allows individuals to work in organization villages with the advantages of big city facilities. Organizational cities no longer work unless they are broken down into villages. In their big city mode they cannot cope with the variety needed in their products, their processes, and their people. On the other hand, the villages on their own have not the resources nor the imagination to grow. Some villages, of course, will be content to survive happy in their niche, but global markets need global products and large confederations to make them or do them.

Dynamic, loosely coupled networks

For Snow *et al.* (1992), the dynamic network organization is the one that has 'pushed the network form to the apparent limit of its capabilities' (p. 14). This form operates with a lead firm (sometimes called the 'server', 'broker' or 'network driver') that identifies and assembles assets which are owned by other companies. The lead firm may, itself, provide a core skill such as manufacturing or design. However, in some cases the lead firm may merely act as broker. The dynamic network is probably the form nearest to Morgan's loosely coupled organic network.

Illustration 3.8 describes TFW Images, a communications and image design organization where the lead firm provides the core skill of design and 'brokers' other activities such as photography and illustration, printing, translations into other languages, and marketing.

However, whether dynamic networks operate in a partial or pure broker capacity, they are unlikely to function effectively without good and effective communications between their component parts. This is what is likely to distinguish dynamic or loosely coupled organic networks from the more 'in-house' internal and stable networks. For instance, TFW Images could not operate without fast and effective information technology links to the other organizations. Telecommunications links enable TFW Images' design team to send its output anywhere to be modified, marketed, printed or manufactured. Except for its relatively permanent status, the company might be likened to what some are now calling the 'virtual organization', particularly given its link-up with Omni-Graphics.

Illustration 3.8

TFW Images

TFW Images was formed in 1989 by two former employees of IBM who became the managing director and creative director of the new company and were very soon joined by a sales director. The main business of TFW Images is communications in its widest sense. Examples of its activities are designing corporate brochures such as annual reports as well as advertising material, designing and organizing conferences and all the material that goes with them, creating company logos and other symbols of corporate identity.

TFW Images' main client was IBM. In fact, the rise of the company coincided with the large-scale changes IBM went through as it refocused its efforts away from large scale business computing markets towards personal computers. As technology began to replace people, TFW Images was able to take advantage of the willingness of companies such as IBM to outsource some of their design requirements.

In a volatile market one reason for the company's success is its ability to maintain a flexible structure that could be tailored to the demands of the market. Essentially, TFW Images is an organization that 'brokers' services from other organizations to bring its products to the market. Rather than employing printers, photographers, illustrators, market researchers and additional writers and designers directly, it closely associates with other companies and independent consultants who offer these services. Telecommunications facilitate the transfer of the part-finished products from one sector of the network to another.

Most recently, TFW Images has joined in partnership with Omni-Graphics, a well-established design company operating in publishing and arts. Given the equality of skills and size of the two organizations, the benefits of the partnership come from their complementary activities (TFW Images is business oriented while Omni-Graphics is arts oriented) and the financial advantages that will flow from this. The management of the two partner organizations will remain separate and both will keep their own names. Thus, to clients nothing will have changed. Yet, conceptually and financially, a new overarching organization has been 'virtually' created.

(This is a real example in which the names of the companies have been changed.)

The virtual organization

A virtual organization uses information and communication technology to link people, assets and ideas to create and distribute things without having to rely on conventional organizational boundaries and locations. They are totally dependent on ICT to the point that the people in them seldom if ever meet (Burkhard and Horan, 2006). Illustration 3.9 summarizes the key attributes of the virtual organization.

It seems clear from Illustration 3.9 that network (particularly dynamic network) and virtual organizations are suited to organizational environments that are themselves dynamic. The emphasis in these forms of organization is on horizontal rather than vertical structuring and the concept of partnership rather than command and control. However, organizations structured on these principles have implications for employment and the reward expectations of employees, whether full time, part time, contract or in other kinds of relationships with the organization. Network and virtual organizations are only able to offer stable, secure employment to a few, from whom they expect commitment and loyalty. The idea

Illustration 3.9

Key attributes of the virtual organization

- **Technology.** Informational networks help far-flung companies and entrepreneurs link up and work together from start to finish.
- **Opportunism.** Partnerships will be less permanent, less formal and more opportunistic. Companies will join together to meet all specific market opportunities and, more often than not, fall apart once the need evaporates.
- **No borders.** This new organizational model redefines traditional organizational boundaries. More cooperation among competitors, suppliers and customers makes it harder to determine where one company ends and another begins.

- **Trust.** These relationships make companies far more reliant on each other and require far more trust than ever before. They will share a sense of 'co-destiny', meaning that the fate of each partner is dependent on the other.
- **Excellence.** Because each partner brings its 'core competencies' to the effort, it may be possible to create a 'best-of-everything' organization. Every function and process could be world class – something that no single company could achieve.

Source: Business Week, 'The Virtual Corporation', *Business Week*, 8 February 1993, pp. 98–102.

of the ultra-flexible firm is attractive for the owners and core staff, but can bring a sense of being used to those who are employed on a short-term contract basis, particularly if these people are employed in temporary, perhaps part-time, less skilled, lower-paid jobs. Lack of commitment may not be restricted to the lower paid. More highly paid consultants and contractors will give service as long as it suits them, but may leave as soon as something more attractive comes along.

On the other hand, Geisler (2002) suggests that advances in communication infrastructures globally have dramatically changed the nature of teamwork and, subsequently, organizational structures. Traditional groupings are gradually being replaced with virtual teams, distributed across boundaries of time, space and existing organizational structures.

Luthans (1995) uses the term 'horizontal organizations' to cover the more recent matrix and network type of organizational design. He maintains that, in these organizations, teams are used to manage everything, with team performance, rather than individual performance, being rewarded. Yet teamworking does not come naturally to all people; team building and development are common training activities. The emphasis on empowerment and more democratic ways of working, which come with these 'modern organization designs' (Luthans, 1995, p. 458), does not happen without planned human resource development. What is more, the move away from classical ways of organizing may not suit every organizational situation.

The main issue for organizations is not whether one form of structure is any better than another. It is whether the structure currently adopted is one that is able to facilitate the achievement of the organization's purpose and respond to the need for organizational change in the prevailing environmental circumstances.

Illustration 3.10

Post-bureaucratic organization

A post-bureaucratic model of organizations assumes a 'shifting intra and extra-organizational boundaries, recourse to a contingent labour force, teamwork and consensual decision making' (Briand and Bellemare, 2006, p. 65) but there are serious questions about the extent to which organizations like this actually exist and whether employees are more emancipated.
Briand and Bellemare (2006) review an attempt by a Canadian public scientific research centre to adopt a post-bureaucratic structure. Staff numbers reduced by about 25 per cent, divisions were merged, management levels were reduced and performance indicators introduced. Government funding reduced for the Centre. Sound familiar? In theory the reforms were an attempt to go post-bureaucratic for instance:

- Much greater focus on service consumers not on itself.
- Focus on results above processes.
- Funding linked more closely to performance.

Reforms were far-reaching but led to 'disorder and insecurity' (p. 72). A problem that arose was a clash of values. Post-bureaucratic models are rooted in private sector values (efficiency, teamwork, innovation) and these conflicted with stronger concerns for ethical and democratic values. They found that the new organization, as experienced by employees, intensified surveillance and produced a new structure of domination. The case raises doubts whether anything approaching a post-bureaucratic form was achieved in this instance.

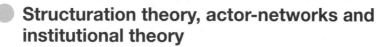

Structuration theory, actor-networks and institutional theory

Structuration theory

So far, the emphasis has been on the tangible side of design and structure. However, structuration theory offers an alternative view of organizational structure. Structuration theorists regard structure, not so much as 'patterned regularity' but, as something that emerges from 'the routine behaviour of people, (which in turn) influences those behaviours' (Cunliffe, 2008, p.37).

Organizations have structure, within which the departments and divisions are used to arrange and contain distinct, but sometimes overlapping, activities. It is in these structures that people (who Giddens terms 'actors') do their work. Saturation theory, developed by Giddens (1984, 1991), focuses on the reciprocal nature of interactions between structures and the actors within them. Organizational structures allow us to do some things but not others; they give certain freedoms but also lay down boundaries in these freedoms are exercised.

As well as departmental and divisional structures, structure can be seen in the rules and operating procedures that have to be followed; job descriptions are an example. These procedures influence what we do and how we do things. Consider what you would do differently at work if you were liberated from the constraints of your organization's structure. However, by abiding by the rules and following procedures, we enforce, reinforce and perpetuate them.

Hence there is a relationship between actions and structure. Giddens (1991, p. 204) explains structuration theory as offering a way of understanding how actors create the social systems in which they work while simultaneously being creations of them. We create structures and then become dependent upon them.

Consequently, actors have to be knowledgeable in relation to the social systems in which they act. They need to know how the systems function and what will be the consequences of actions that they contemplate or enact. Supplementing this general awareness of actions and outcomes is a need to be thoughtful and reflective about oneself. Reflection helps actors to monitor what they are doing and to change and adjust future actions. By virtue of their knowledge and reflection actors are free agents to decide whether they will contribute, or not, to events. Knowledge and reflection give at least limited power to intervene and try to influence what is going on.

According to structuration theory, structures exist only in the sense that actors/agents continue to reinforce them. In a bureaucratic organization it is only by routine referral of decisions to, say, a Director of This and That, that that part of the structure functions. If actors ignore the Director, then that structure would not exist, except in the flesh. So structures only exist in so far as we continue to reinforce them. They do not exist in and by themselves.

Giddens (2001, p. 668) argues that although we are constrained by aspects of society the same aspects 'do not determine what we do'. Drivers can choose to drink and drive albeit at greater risk of accident and punishment. We are not simply unquestioning followers of society's norms and values – people do make choices. Social structures and individual actions are therefore linked and are in a constant state of renewal. We have democratic political processes for electing leaders of nations that have evolved over centuries. The leaders influence government actions and the actions of government agents such as local authorities and the police. If all voters refused to vote, the political structure would have to change.

Sometimes at work you might have thought that 'the structure gets in the way' or 'the structure won't let this good idea happen'. However if we see structures not as a fixed thing that organizations are built upon but as a dynamic thing, a set of rules and procedures that can be changed, then new views open up. Of course, from a practical point of view it may be very sensible to conclude that 'the structure will get in the way' and move on to something more fruitful. But, from a critical point of view, structuration theory provides new vistas on structure; seeing it as a social construction and as a collective consciousness.

Structuration and change

What this means for organizational change is that the paths followed and outcomes achieved are influenced by how actors understand the organization and the social settings that they are in. In similar organizations in terms of size and product/market, facing the same or similar business challenges, it is the actors' pattern and depth of understanding that explain why different strategic paths are followed and why different outcomes are reached.

Sarason (1995) also uses the idea of organizational identity to explain why organizations differ. As well as seeing the outcomes of change initiatives being dependent upon how well actors understand their organizations, outcomes are also shaped by a sense of identity. Do actors see their organization as a dynamic risk-taker not afraid to take bold decisions and learn from mistakes or as a nervous and cautious place? Illustration 3.11 shows how organisational identity can both restrain and catalyse change.

Chu and Smithson (2007) give an account of applying structuration theory to an attempt by a major motor manufacturer to implement e-business claiming that structuration theory was useful:

> in understanding the interaction between the e-business initiative (agency) and the organizational structures. It facilitated the examination of the heterogenous systems of meaning, power relations and norms of the different stakeholder groups. The interaction of agency and structure was easy to apply . . . It also

helped us to understand the complex structures that guide, facilitate and contain peoples' working lives while the notion of duality shows how these structures are themselves constructed, maintained and sometimes changed by the people concerned. (p. 386)

By duality, they mean that 'structure is both the medium and outcome of human interaction, (p. 372).

Illustration 3.11

Changing organizational identity

One of us worked for an organization that provided technical and management consulting to manufacturing and retail supply chains. For about 70 years it provided services to organizations only in high labour cost countries largely in northern Europe, North America and Australasia. For decades this strong organizational identity impacted upon all discussions and decisions and shaped strategic direction. Slowly, however, as new manufacturing capacity in southern Europe and Asia came on stream in the 1970s and new business opportunities were clear and plentiful, organizational identity began to transform. Suddenly it was OK to talk about working with low cost producers and this led to what, for the organization, was a transformational strategic change. For decades, strategic actions reinforced the same identity but then new actions began to signal a new identity.

Giddens introduced the concept of structuration to explain how social structure is made and re-made. Structure and action are intertwined since the constant repetition of action strengthens the constraining structure. Giddens called this the duality of structure: 'all social action presumes the existence of structure. But at the same time structure presumes action because "structure" depends on the regularities of human behaviour' (2001, p. 669). Structuration theory explains therefore how the constant repetition of behaviour perpetuates structures whether they be good, bad or indifferent. It is only through behavioural change that old structures and the constraints that go with them are dismantled and re-made.

Actor-Network Theory (ANT)

The actor-network concept (Latour, 2005) recognizes that actors build networks involving other actors which can be human or non-human (individuals, groups or animals). Non-human actors could be a particular technology or a species around which human actors are manoeuvring. For instance, conservationists dedicated to the reintroduction of the Red Kite in England would see the bird as an actor in the network. Actor-networks can also be seen operating on a global level. The decision to occupy Iraq involved political networks of institutions and key individuals such as presidents and prime ministers, anti-war groups, arms manufacturers and construction companies, among others.

Gao (2005) applied ANT to analyze change in China's telecommunications market. The market was defined as a non-human actor and the public, the state and the operators made up three groups of human actors. Stanforth (2007) applied ANT to help understand the causes of e-government success or failure.

Actors create networks and thus themselves – but these networks are undergoing constant transformation and renewal. At a point in time we can imagine a social entity to be made up of interconnecting networks but 'there is no social order. There are only endless attempts at ordering through the formation and stabilization of networks' (Stanforth, 2007, p. 39). Think of the past few months in your life. Perhaps you have made new friends and contacts who sympathize with what you are trying to achieve. In or out of work, they may open up some of the resources that you need. Perhaps there are one or two actors that you have given up on and who, if you get your way, will not feature in your network much longer.

Van der Duim and van Marwijk (2006) used ANT to explain innovation in the sense that innovation means new 'patterns of coordination between people and organizations, technologies and environmental phenomena' (p. 450). In the case of an organization, for example one trying to implement a new project, ANT helps to explain how the social order is built. It involves the idea of 'translation' which involves explaining things in ways that persuade actors to fit with what a network is trying to achieve. Conservationists would try to persuade farmers to adopt particular land management practices that will raise breeding populations of species. Objections and queries by farmers, perhaps about economics, might be met by rationalizations of species decline and the non-financial value of biodiversity. Successful translation involves four stages:

1 *Problematization*: here the project is 'sold' to actors as a way of tackling their problems if they sign up to it.
2 *Interessement*: this is about translating/projecting the rationale for and the concerns that go with a project onto others involved and then stabilizing a network.
3 *Enrolment*: if interessement occurs then the behaviour of those involved is geared to achieving the outcomes desired by the enrolling actors.
4 *Mobilization*: if enrolment is successful then a new network will exist that works towards outcomes and solutions that fit the initial rationale for project set-up.

One of the features of recent and contemporary business and public management is the growth of networks in getting things done. Public spending constraints, the sheer size and complexity of projects, the specialist knowledge needed and the risks involved have led to much more collaboration between organizations in a sector and/or a region, for example. ANT explains how and why the networks that are initiated are more or less successful. It describes how ways of ordering at time 1 and which are not capable of delivering are altered, so that they are viable at time 2. If the four stages of translation are achieved the outcome is known as a *collectif*. Something that could not be achieved before is achievable through the collectif.

ANT has also been used to study change in a US telecommunications company (Sarker, Sarker and Sidorova, 2006). Examining the failure of change, they observed that while leadership, vision and communication are put forward as key ingredients of change success, top management needs to '(re)define the interests of human and non-human elements in the organization consistent with those of the initiative' (p. 81). It is not just about top management sharing a vision but about making connections between the interests of multiple actors and the global mission held by leadership. It is about persuading others that their interests are best served by connecting up to the global vision.

Dent (2003) explored ANT in relation to a hospital threatened with closure. For instance, a hospital contains networks of professional groups, managers and administrators and it is networked with external organizations under a National Health Service umbrella. For long periods these networks can be fairly stable albeit showing minor reconfiguration as interests evolve. Periodically, something happens to disturb the relative peace such as new legislation or new government edicts and targets, with subsequent disturbance to the roles of professionals and their relationships to managers, noting of course that many professionals are also managers. Dent found that interessment, the coming together of agents into a network, involves 'persuasion, intrigue, calculation and rhetoric' (Miller, 1992) and that these tools were used in the processes of actors reconfiguring to help their network resist the disturbances. Using ANT, Dent was able to 'delineate more clearly the complex configuration of relationships within which a hospital is embedded. In particular, it facilitated the exploration of the changing professional-management relations' (p. 123).

'Translation' helps to understand how the different interests of the several actors become aligned into a sociotechnical arrangement. Even non-human actors are seen to have interests, e.g. the interests of skylarks are appropriated into the interests of human actors in a conservation scheme. Collectively, the interests of other actors are appropriated and translated into the interests of each actor. When interests are internalized by the several actors then an actor-network exists.

Figure 3.7 shows actors in a speed reduction initiative in a particular locality. Double-headed arrows represent alignment of interests of the three initiating actors. This diagram is a simple model to which could be added national government, which has road safety targets, as well as self-styled road safety groups. The model shows drivers as being a target of the actor-network and uninvolved in interest sharing. Of course, one could represent drivers' interests but for simplicity they are not shown.

The socio-political context includes pressure put upon police and local government to reduce accidents and injuries and the general efforts to raise awareness of the dangers of excessive speed. There may be localized pressures, such as the presence of schools or an accident 'black spot'. An additional interest affecting drivers is the punitive regime, that is, what happens to them if they are convicted of speeding. In time, the socio-political contexts change and the interests of the actors change. If drivers' attitudes to speeding changed such that ignoring speed limits became much less common then the need for an actor-network would diminish. If the penalties in the form of fines for speeding were substantially reduced or increased this would impact upon the interests of law enforcement actors.

Actor-network theorists regard structure 'as the process of organizing' people, technology, knowledge and other things into a stable network (Cunliffe, 2008, p. 49).

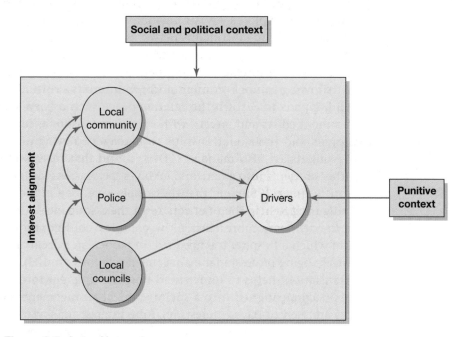

Figure 3.7 Actor Network

Illustration 3.12

Plane Stupid

Protest groups are a feature of our times and in December 2008 one group made the headlines for 'invading' Stansted Airport near London. Stansted is a busy regional airport, so much so that there are plans to build another runway much to the consternation of the locals. Protesters are often well educated and/or middle class people of all ages and associate with a group called Plane Stupid.

What is of interest to us here is the way the group organizes. It is said to be based on the 'rhizome concept' developed by Deleuze and Guatteri as a non-hierarchical way of connecting people to share ideas. Taking the name from the type of plant, the rhizome connects any point in the group to all other points. It is not built around units but around dimensions. It does not have a beginning or end, rather it has a middle from which it keeps growing.

Unlike classic organizational structures which have lines and positions, the rhizome has only lines of connection. Anyone who has planted and then later dug a root of potatoes will know what the rhizome looks like – there are lots of potatoes all connected to each other and to the originating middle seed potato.

The rhizome organization uses horizontal connections and communications unlike the vertical,

horizontal and hierarchical communications found in typical structures that resemble family trees.

Whatever we think of their tactics of disruption, for protest groups this way of organizing seems effective and for students of structure quite interesting.

Source: Deleuze, G. and Guattari, F. (1980) *A Thousand Plateaus: Capitalism and Schizophrenia*, translated by B. Massum, 2004; Gourlay, G. and Montague, B. (2008) 'Meet the Plane Stoppers', *Sunday Times*, 14 December, p.18.

Institutional Theory

The earlier part of this chapter dealt with structures as if they are a rational choice; things that are shaped by internal drives for improvement and by best fit with environmental pressures and opportunities. Institutional theory, which has much in common with structuration theory, emphasizes the cultural influences on decisions about design and structure. The people who decide what organizations should look like are 'suspended in a web of values, norms, rules, beliefs and taken for granted assumptions that are at least partially of their own making' (Barley and Tobert, 1997, p. 93). The combination of these things gives the culture of the organization its unique identity and the culture influences decisions about structure which may be sub-optimal.

Through culture, institutions work within a bounded rationality which restricts the range of responses and which raises the likelihood that certain types of behaviour will occur. Institutional theory is not a theory of change but it is a way of explaining the similarities of arrangements that are often found in a sector. Before going further though we need to distinguish between an organization and an institution. Barley and Tobert (1997, p. 94) describe institutions as 'socially constructed templates for action, generated and maintained through ongoing interactions' and herein lies the similarity to structuration. They go on to define institutions as 'shared rules and typifications that identify categories of social actors and their appropriate activities or relationships' (p. 96).

Although they can be seen as one and the same, an institution may not be an organization. Apartheid in South Africa was an institution, not an organization – although it was something that existed as a result of organizing. Slavery was not an organization but it was institutionalized across several countries that supplied and used the slave trade. Again, there was much organizing underpinning the institution of slavery.

Institutions are created out of action and once created they restrict actions within them. Hence we find institutions inside organizations and the structures that are found in organizations reflect those institutions. A good analogy is with speech and grammar. The sentence, 'The dog ran after the cat' has a particular meaning. If 'cat' and 'dog' are transposed the sentence has a different meaning.

Grammar brings structure to speech and institutions bring structure and meaning to organizations. Another analogy is to the idea of scripts, such that people are playing to scripts in their day-to-day behaviour. For example, we defer to the same people for decisions even though we know they will give us the same scripted answer – perhaps something like, 'It's a good idea but don't bother pushing it because Jim doesn't like it'.

Johnson and colleagues (2000, p. 573) defined scripts as 'the cognitive schema informing behaviour and routines appropriate in particular contexts'. They applied institutional theory to privatization; the deinstitutionalization of public sector templates and the institutionalization of private sector templates. To enact change, the scripts used by actors have to change. New scripts develop through experiences as people move from a familiar set of routines to experimentation with another. Barley and Tobert (1997) also saw scripts as more than cognitive scheme considering them as behavioural regularities, that is, something that can be observed. They suggest that the accreditation processes used by universities are examples of scripts in action as elaborated on in Illustration 3.13.

Institutional theory explains how the principles of organizing are accepted and perpetuated and how conformity to norms leads to particular outcomes. Survival of the main protagonists (typically top managers) and conformance to norms explain actions more so than rational responses in the search for better performance. It is useful to explain why things exist as they do, and stay as they are, but is less informative about how change to institutions occurs (Kondra and Hinings, 1998). One of the reasons for this is the idea of *isomorphism* which refers to the tendency of organizations in the same field to adopt the same or similar

---

Illustration 3.13

The Institutionalization of accreditation

Universities in the UK are very sensitive to league tables and in particular to their position in them. The tables rank universities on a combination of factors like staff/student ratios, research income and the percentage of staff with doctorates. Let's face it, when we know how we are being measured we tend to divert attention into bettering our performance on those measures. One of the accolades that business schools seek is accreditation by bodies such as the Association of MBAs (AMBA) and the European Quality Improvement System (EQUIS). A common accreditation strategy is as follows:

The school applies for accreditation having checked itself against broad criteria set by the accrediting body.

If the application is accepted, the school writes a set of self-assessment documents (SADs) detailing and reflecting on its performance.

A small panel of senior academics drawn from top business schools is despatched to the school who entertain them for several days during which the panel meets and questions a range of groups representing the school's activities (research, teaching, consulting and so on).

The panel writes a report including recommendations and conditions that is considered by the board of the accrediting body.

The actors are playing out a script. As well as scripts operating at a grand level we can also see scripts at individual level and influencing individual participation in the accreditation visits. The school, if it is smart, will be briefing groups before they have meetings with the panel and debriefing them afterwards so that issues can be passed on to the next group. Those in charge bang on with exhortations such as, 'We can be really proud of X so make sure you tell them about it but make sure they never get to know about Y'.

We are not suggesting that the outcomes can be taken for granted or that the processes are not useful; far from it. Useful recommendations and ideas for change usually come out of these rituals and accreditation, if achieved, is a valuable thing. Yet the scripts used lead to similar outcomes. The 'dirty washing' stays hidden and the panel concludes by emphasizing some things the school already knew about and which it could even have discretely guided them towards. The scripts used in these events lead to a bounded and institutionalized level of performance improvement.

structures and ways of thinking and doing which lead to isomorphism of performance. Indeed, performance standards can themselves become institutionalized. Three reasons for this can be put forward (Kondra and Hinings, 1998):

- People who think they can see ways of improving things do not bother to pursue their ideas because compliance with norms is much easier.
- Mimetic behaviour occurs (that is, when organizations copy each other's behaviour) and is perhaps more likely to persist when performance measures are not well defined as is the case with the public sector organizations.
- Mimetic behaviour can also occur because of risk aversion. A dominant coalition (such as a management team) can argue that not implementing what might be a performance enhancing action in the short term is an efficient strategy in the long term when the risks of the actions are considered. If the coalition can be confident of return X in the future, why seek greater than X when there is a risk that the actual returns could be less than X?

Greenwood and Hinings (1996) go further, however, in showing how institutional theory connects to a theory of change. They propose three characteristics of neo-institutional theory (neo-institutional theory includes developments to the original theory).

Institutional context – organizations embed institutions even though these institutions have little or no impact on performance. The professional partnership form of organizing stems from the philosophy that professionals in a business venture should be jointly liable for their professional decisions. Accountants and lawyers, for instance, typically organize as partnerships. Clearly it is an effective way of organizing otherwise they would not keep doing it but this is an institution rather than a rational analysis of the most efficient way to organize.

Templates – pressures from institutions push organizations in the same sector to adopt the same or similar forms and designs, that is, templates for organizing, shaped by underpinning ideas and values. These arise from mimetic behaviour and leads to isomorphism in the sector. Hence institutional theorists focus more on what they term populations of organizations in a particular field, seeing them as networked and interconnected and subject to the institutional pressures in the field. Universities illustrate the point well. There are about 100 universities in the UK which serve different segments of the market but there are, arguably, more similarities between them than there are differences in the way they respond to the institutionalization of higher education.

Resistance to change – templates for organizing cover not just designs and forms but also ways of thinking and thus inertia. Institutional theory therefore emphasizes the stability of arrangements and while accepting that change occurs it sees change a 'reproduction and reinforcement of existing models of thought and organization' (p. 1027). It explains convergent and incremental change much more than radical change which is far more problematic. Greenwood and Hinings (1996) point out the reciprocal nature of the relations between an organization and the field it is in. A university, for instance, does what the field expects of it and behaves in ways that are acceptable to the field. Behaviours manifest as policies on a wide range of issues affecting staff and students (policies that would look very similar if put side by side), similar products delivered to students in similar ways, similar ways of allocating work to employees and similar ways of measuring performance.

To help explain the pace and scope of change two additional concepts are used; tight coupling and sectoral permeability (Greenwood and Hinings, 1996). Tight coupling occurs when a sector exerts a high level of influence and control over the templates that organizations in the sector use. Professional practices and public organizations are subject to high levels of regulation and expectations and are examples of tight coupling. Any new organization entering the field would be subject to such pressures to comply and conform. Contrast this with a new private business venture – let's say to design and manufacture fashion shoes. So long as it complies with the law no-one is concerned about how it is organized or about how it organizes. Similarly, in new sectors that form around a technological breakthrough the institutional pressures will be less well developed so we could expect change to be less impeded by inertia.

Sectoral permeability describes how much a sector is insulated from others. A sector with low permeability experiences a low influx of people from other sectors so the transfer of ideas is within the sector, not across sectors. Where permeability is higher and people come into the sector from other sectors we would expect higher import of ideas and thus higher rates of radical change. Examples of where institutional theory has been used include analyzing change in an accounting and financial system (Tsamenyi, Cullen and Gonzalez, 2006), law firms (Sherer and Lee, 2002) and professional associations (Greenwood, Suddaby and Hinings, 2002).

Activity 3.3

Think of a small part of an organization that you know well and try to identify where the routine actions of people are creating structure and structural relationships.

Then consider why these situations exist, for example individual management styles, dominating personalities and organizational politics.

How amenable are these structures to change?

Influences on structure

Choosing how to structure is not straightforward and choices are closely linked to many factors as Figure 3.8 shows. As identified earlier, one of the most important links is the relationship between strategy and structure – as an organization changes its strategy to respond to environmental triggers, so should its structure change to maintain the strategy–structure relationship. However, apart from technological advances from outside the organization, which may force changes in production methods or in the way that services are delivered, the organization's own use of technology, particularly information technology, will affect the way in which it is structured. The earlier discussion shows also how organizational structure is likely to change as organizational size increases.

What is less tangible are the roles that organizational culture and politics play on structure one way or another. That is why, in Figure 3.8, these two factors are shown as mediating variables rather than as direct influences. There is nothing set, however, in the way all these variables should be regarded. Figure 3.8 is offered as a helpful descriptive device for summarizing the factors that influence organizational forms rather than as a tried and tested model of how they work in practice. Even so, there is a body of literature that helps us understand which organizational structure

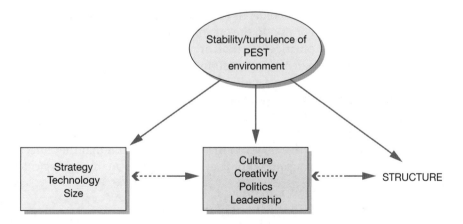

Figure 3.8 The determinants of organizational structure

is most appropriate to which set of circumstances. Before moving to this, it is worth pausing to think why 'good' or appropriate organizational structure is so important to the efficient and effective operation of organizations.

The consequences of deficient organizational structures

The consequences of a deficient organizational structure are shown in Illustration 3.14. What is interesting about this list is that some of the main 'dysfunctions' listed (e.g. 'Motivation and morale may be depressed') could be regarded as having little to do with structure. Yet, as the other points make clear, structural deficiencies could very well be major contributing causes.

Activity 3.4

1 *Considering an organization that you know well, to what extent do any of the five consequences of structural deficiencies listed in Illustration 3.13 apply to it?*

2 *If you think that some of these deficiencies are present what does this imply for the way the organization is structured? What changes for the better could be made?*

Strategy–structure fit

For the purpose of this discussion the definition of strategy given by Johnson, Scholes and Whittington (2008, p. 3) is used.

> Strategy is the *direction* and *scope* of an organisation over the *long term*: which achieves *advantage* for the organization through its configuration of *resources* within a changing *environment*, to meet the needs of *markets* and to fulfil *stakeholder* expectations.

The term 'stakeholder' is taken to represent anyone who has an interest (specifically some level of risk) in the organization such that their interest is affected by the policies and practices of that organization. This includes shareholders, suppliers, unions, financiers and customers and employees. Johnson *et al.* list six characteristics that are associated with strategy and strategic decisions. These characteristics elaborate the notion that strategy and strategic decisions encompass all the organization's activities; that they are concerned with the organization's internal and external environments; that they are influenced by the values and expectations of those who have power in the organization; and that they affect the long-term direction of the organization. They suggest (pp. 3–6) that strategic decisions are likely to:

- be complex in nature
- be made in situations of uncertainty
- affect operational decisions
- require an integrated approach (both inside and outside the organization)
- involve considerable change.

Illustration 3.14

Consequences of deficient organizational structures

There are a number of problems that so often mark the struggling organization and which even at the best of times are potential dangers. John Child suggests the following dangers that structural deficiencies exacerbate.

1 *Motivation and morale may be depressed because*:
   (a) Decisions appear to be inconsistent and arbitrary in the absence of standardized rules.
   (b) People perceive that they have little responsibility, opportunity for achievement and recognition of their worth because there is insufficient delegation of decision making. This may be connected with narrow spans of control.
   (c) There is a lack of clarity as to what is expected of people and how their performance is assessed – perhaps due to inadequate job definition.
   (d) People are subject to competing pressures from different parts of the organization due to absence of clearly defined priorities, decision rules or work programmes.
   (e) People are overloaded because their support systems are not adequate. Supervisors, for instance, have to leave the job to chase up materials and equipment as there is no adequate system for communicating what people need.

2 *Decision making may be delayed and lacking in quality because*:
   (a) Necessary information is not transmitted on time – perhaps due to an over-extended hierarchy.
   (b) Decision makers are too segmented into separate units and inadequately coordinated.
   (c) Decision makers are overloaded due to insufficient delegation on their part.
   (d) There are no adequate procedures for evaluating the results of similar decisions made in the past.

3 *There may be conflict and a lack of coordination because*:

   (a) There are conflicting goals that have not been structured into a single set of objectives and priorities. People are acting at cross-purposes. They may, for example, be put under pressure to follow departmental priorities at the expense of product or project goals.
   (b) People are working out of step with each other because they are not brought together into teams or because liaison mechanisms are poor.
   (c) The people who actually carry out operational work and who are in touch with changing contingencies are excluded from participating in work planning – a breakdown between planning and operations.

4 *An organization may not respond innovatively to changing circumstances because*:
   (a) It has not established specialized jobs concerned with forecasting and scanning the environment.
   (b) There is a failure to ensure that innovation and planning of change are mainstream activities backed up by top management through appropriate procedures to provide them with adequate priority, programming and resources.
   (c) There is inadequate coordination between the people responsible for identifying changing market needs and the people who could provide solutions.

5 *Costs may be rising rapidly, particularly in administration, because*:
   (a) The organization has a tall hierarchy with a high ratio of managers to workers.
   (b) There is an excess of procedure and paperwork distracting people's attention away from productive work and requiring additional staff personnel to administer.
   (c) Some or all of the other organization problems are present.

Source: Child, J. (1988) *Organizations: A Guide to Problems and Practice*, London: Paul Chapman.

Mintzberg, Quinn and James (1988) asked, 'Is strategy a process or the outcome of a process?' and drew attention to the issue of whether strategy should be regarded as being amenable to rational planning or whether it is the emergent result of a social and political process. Mintzberg's (1994) view is that effective strategies are both deliberate and emergent. It is clear that, sometimes, strategy can be thought about and planned prior to being implemented. The organizational changes that follow will be incremental or more radical, depending on implementation process. Such changes most frequently involve changes in the organization's structure, because it is the structure that must provide the framework within which the strategic process to achieve the organization's objectives must operate.

Chandler's strategy–structure thesis

Chandler (1962) found that the owner-managed companies that were predominant during the 1800s usually started with a single product line and a structure where the owner–manager took all major decisions and monitored the activities of employees. Miles and Snow (1984b) refer to this type of organization as having an 'agency' structure, given that key subordinates acted as agents of the owner–manager to ensure their wishes.

As companies grew they became more complex and were more likely to employ professional managers who began the process of dividing the organization into different functional areas. The appearance of the functional organization (around 1900) enabled growth to occur, particularly through acquiring suppliers, to ensure guaranteed inputs, and through market penetration. As strategies led to restructuring this drew Chandler to conclude that structure follows strategy.

The 'structure follows strategy' dictum is widely accepted and the reason why different structures associated with different structures was simple economic efficiency. More recent research has shown that although there is a strategy–structure relationship it is not a simple, one-way path; strategy has a stronger influence on structure than structure has on strategy (Amburgey and Dacin, 1994).

Mintzberg's forces and forms

Mintzberg (1991) offers the concepts of forces and forms that can be loosely translated as strategy and structure although Mintzberg himself uses these terms sparingly. Figure 3.9 illustrates the seven forces, each of which is associated with a particular form.

The seven forces which drive the organization can be described briefly as follows:

● The force for *direction*, which can be likened to having a 'strategic vision'. This gives a sense of where the organization must go as an integrated entity.

- The force for *efficiency*, which balances the costs and benefits – the lower the ratio of costs to benefits the higher the efficiency. The force for efficiency tends to encourage standardization and formalization, focusing on rationalization and restructuring for economy.
- The force for *proficiency*, that is for carrying out tasks with high levels of knowledge and skills.
- The force for *concentration*, which means the opportunity for particular units to concentrate their efforts on serving particular markets. This is necessary in organizations that are diversified in structure.
- The force for *innovation*, which encourages the search for new products or services or for different ways of delivering them. The force for innovation encourages adaptation and learning.
- The forces for *cooperation* and *competition* are the forces Mintzberg calls 'catalytic'. Cooperation describes the pulling together of ideology, that is, the culture of norms, beliefs and values that 'knit a disparate set of people into a

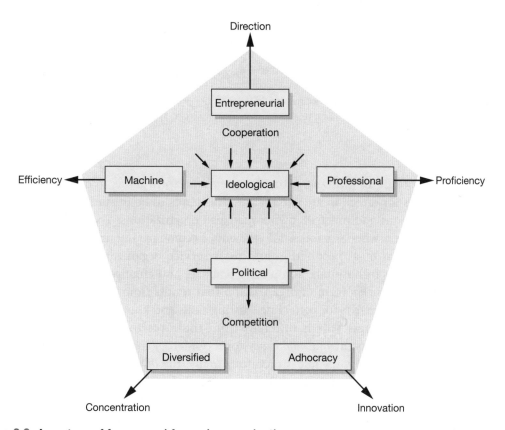

Figure 3.9 A system of forces and forms in organizations

Source: Mintzberg, H. (1991) 'The Effective Organization: Forces and Forms', *Sloan Management Review*, Winter 1991, 32, part 2, p. 55. Copyright © 1991 by Massachusetts Institute of Technology. All rights reserved. Distributed by Tribune Media Services.

harmonious, cooperative entity' (Mintzberg, 1991, p. 55). Competition describes the pulling apart of politics in the sense of politics as the non-legitimate, technically non-sanctioned organizational behaviour. Mintzberg uses the term 'configuration' to describe the form an organization is driven towards by the system of forces (see Illustration 3.15).

Illustration 3.15

Mintzberg's (1979, 1983) organizational forms

- **Entrepreneurial form** – tends to be low in formalization and standardization, but high in centralization with authority located in a single person.
- **Machine form** – high formalization and standardization, centralized authority vested in rules and regulations, functional departments.
- **Professional form** – high in complexity and formalization, but low in centralization; allows the employment of trained specialist staff for the core work of the organization.
- **The adhocracy form** – very low in standardization and formalization, little hierarchy, much use of temporary project teams.

- **Diversified form** – a combination of functions and products, with products dominating; they can be of matrix form or organized as divisions on the basis of products/markets.

These five forms are based on Mintzberg (1979, 1983). His 1991 paper, on which much of this section is based, adds the *ideological* and *political* forms, giving as examples the Israeli kibbutz and a conflictual regulatory agency respectively. However, these two forms are uncommon.

According to Mintzberg, the *entrepreneurial* form tends to dominate when the forces for direction are paramount. This tends to be in start-up and turnaround situations and in small, owner-managed organizations. The *machine* form tends to appear when the forces for efficiency become paramount, for instance in situations of mass production and mass service organizations. Mintzberg gives examples of hospitals, accounting practices and engineering offices to illustrate the *professional* form of organization that results from the force for proficiency. The drive here is for perfecting existing skills and knowledge rather than inventing new ones. This is different from the force for innovation that pushes organizations into an *adhocracy* form, which is characterized by independent project teams with fluid structures. Finally, the *diversified* form arises as a result of the force for an organization to concentrate on more than one distinct product or market. Each division will have a different structure and enjoy considerable autonomy from the small central headquarters.

Mintzberg calls the fit between the forces and forms that organizations take 'configuration'. 'My basic point about configuration is simple: when the form fits, the organization may be well advised to wear it, at least for a time'

(Mintzberg, 1991, p. 58). This argument supports the proposition that organizational structure should align with organizational strategy. The implications of this are that, as an organization's strategy changes, so must its structure if tensions, contradictions and, eventually, crises are not to ensue. However, strategy is not the only factor upon which structure is contingent.

The influence of size on structure

The classic study by Derek Pugh and his associates (1969) mentioned earlier found that size (measured by numbers employed) was positively correlated with overall role specialization and formalization (measured by the amount of paperwork procedures and usage). However, as Pugh (1973) points out, there are organizations whose size suggests particular structural configurations, but which confound the predictions. Even so, the degree of constraint on organizational form imposed by variables such as size and technology is substantial, possibly accounting for some 50 per cent of the variability.

Child (1988) studied the effects of size on organizational performance finding that, for large organizations, the more bureaucratically structured they were, the better they performed. Smaller organizations performed better if they were less bureaucratically structured. In organizations with below about 2,000 people performance was assumed to be better in those that have little formal structure whereas in organizations with more than 2,000 employees the association between more bureaucracy and superior performance was greater.

Both Pugh and Child did their research some time ago and the use of number of employees as a measure of size might not be as useful a measure for organizations with matrix or network structures. Illustration 3.16 (see next page) is an account of the way a division of a medium-sized multinational organization was able to radically change its structure independently of the structure of other divisions in the organization – with good results. What is notable about this change is the very careful way it was planned with the total involvement of the workers, managers and trade union members.

The influence of technology

In this context technology refers to the processes by which an organization transforms inputs into outputs. Two classic studies – by Joan Woodward (1965) and Charles Perrow (1967) are usually referred to in discussions of the relationship of technology to organizational structure. Woodward studied manufacturing firms in England to investigate the relationship between organizational performance and elements of organizational structure such as unity of command and span of control. The companies were divided into three categories according to their production methods; unit or small batch production; large batch and mass production; and process production.

Illustration 3.16

From hierarchy to self-managed teams

In 1994 a factory of some 200 employees, which was part of a division of a US organization manufacturing ceramics, took a deliberate decision to move from a hierarchically structured organization to one based on self-managed teams. The factory, based in Scotland, was one of 74 manufacturing plants employing a total of 8,500 people in 21 countries. As the company started operating new plants, employees were often sent for training or retraining to the Scottish factory, which, by that time, was the oldest in the company. However, the management realized that the factory's status as a 'master plant' could not be taken for granted. In the words of the operations manager: 'Here we are, a successful company in the west of Scotland. But the head office is in Brussels and we have no customers nearer than the north of England and no raw materials nearby.' Having no natural advantages other than themselves, the concern was that, if they were not seen as being as good as the rest they would 'wither on the vine'.

Consequently a change programme was put into place under the banner of what is known as the business excellence model developed by the European Foundation for Quality Management (EFQM). The programme centred on the introduction of self-managed teams. Elements of the programme included the institution of new work practices for which all staff received training. All facilitators gained NVQs at level 3 with all 185 shop floor workers gaining an NVQ level 1. Every employee had an individual development plan linked to team targets, which in turn linked to wider business objectives.

The factory's clocking-in system was removed to symbolize management's trust in the workforce. Consultations and negotiations with trade union representatives overcame their initial resistance, particularly in the context of no loss of jobs.

Over a four year period the differential pay rates for different production jobs were replaced by a single wage structure and complete labour flexibility across jobs and departments. At an average age of 51, the plant's supervisors undertook an extensive development programme designed to equip them for their new roles as facilitators rather than supervisors.

Indicators of the success of the new structure came from the results of employee opinion surveys. These indicated significantly increased levels of overall satisfaction and satisfaction with quality and productivity, company image, employee involvement and career development. Satisfaction with health and safety rose steeply to 90 per cent. At the time of this account (1999), all aspects of the business – including HR, purchasing, accounts and senior management – were self-managing teams. However, the ultimate measure of success comes from the company's results. The plant's turnover rose from £37 million in 1993 to £55 million in 1998 – a result the company attributes to the competitive edge gained from empowering the employees and giving them responsibility for quality. Cost savings amount to £500,000 a year. Most significantly, the company's market share has grown.

Source: Based on Arkin, A. (1999) 'Peak Practice', *People Management*, 11 November, pp. 57–59.

Activity 3.5

1 *Refer back to the discussion of external and internal environment triggers for change. Drawing on your own speculations, as well as what you can glean from the account, consider where you think the triggers for change were coming from for the organization in Illustration 3.16.*

2 *If your organization (or your particular part of it) is structured into self-managing teams, what, if any, are the issues which cause most concern? What benefits are there for managers and others?*

3 If your situation is one of individualized working or managed teams, what benefits and barriers could you envisage in moving to a structure of self-managed teams?

Woodward found a relationship between the types of technology used and aspects of structure – in particular, the number of levels of management authority and the span of control of first-line supervisors. In addition, she concluded that the effectiveness of organizations was related to the 'fit' between technology and structure. In her words, 'not only was the system of production an important variable in the determination of organizational structure, but also that one particular form of organization was most appropriate to each system of production' (p. 69). For instance, firms with large-batch/mass-production were more likely to be successful with a more mechanistic structure (e.g. similar to Mintzberg's machine form). Firms falling into either of the other two categories were more likely to be successful if they adopted a more organic structure (e.g. more flexible, decentralized with low standardization and formalization).

Unlike Woodward who concentrated on production technologies, Perrow (1967) defined technology more generally and he was more concerned with knowledge technology – that is, with both the ends and the means of achieving an output. He suggested that technology could be viewed as a combination of two variables; 'task variability' and 'problem analyzability'. Thus a task that is highly routine would be low in task variability and vice versa; in other words, variability refers to the number of exceptional or unpredictable cases which have to be dealt with. Problem analyzability refers to the extent to which problems are clearly defined and can be solved by using recognized routines and procedures, in other words, whether a task is clearly defined or whether it is ambiguous in terms of the task itself and how it might be completed. Where task completion requires innovative thinking, it is likely to be low on problem analyzability.

Perrow used these two dimensions to construct a two-by-two matrix that provided a continuum of technology ranging from the routine to the non-routine as shown in Figure 3.10. The cells in the matrix represent four types of technology: routine, engineering, craft and non-routine.

In line with Woodward, Perrow argued that each type of technology would produce the best organizational performance if linked to an appropriate structure. Consequently, technologies such as are described in cell 1 are most likely to fit well with mechanistic structures. Cell 2 technologies require mechanistic structures but with aspects of organic organizational forms. Cell 4 technologies link most closely to much 'looser' organic structures (perhaps of the matrix, project or network type) while cell 3 technologies require mainly organic structures with aspects of mechanistic bureaucracies.

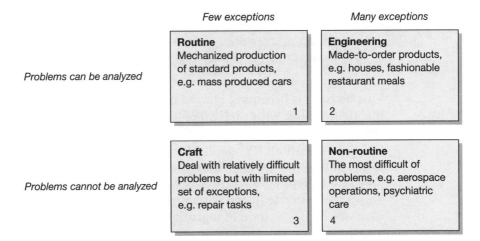

Figure 3.10 Perrow's technology classification

Source: Based on summaries by Robbins, S.P. (2003) *Organizational Behavior* (10th edn), Englewood Cliffs, NJ: Prentice Hall and Mullins, L. (2005) *Management and Organizational Behaviour* (7th edn), Harlow: Financial Times Prentice Hall.

ICT and structure

The advent of information and communication technologies has increased the quality and quantity of information available to people and Day (1999) commented that ICT is proving to be one of the 'levellers' of hierarchy. Managers have the ability to push information closer to the point where it is used and to increase responsibility on employees to use it effectively. ICT has had the following impacts on structure according to Mukherji (2002):

- Supporting decentralization by enabling communication and control from a distance, and assisting matrix and network structures.
- Increasing the routinization of some jobs.
- Reducing hierarchy.
- Creating much closer links across supply chains.
- Making the boundaries between divisions in an organization and even between organizations more fuzzy and less relevant.
- Revolutionizing how small businesses can operate, e.g., by Internet businesses.

Robbins (2003) talks of the 'boundaryless' organization where both internal and external boundaries are eliminated. He refers to Lucas's (1996) use of the term 'the T-form (or technology-based) organization'. The removal of internal vertical boundaries flattens the hierarchy with status and rank minimized. This type of organization uses cross-hierarchical teams, which are used to coordinating their own work. The removal of external barriers against suppliers has been mentioned already. With regard to customers, the increasing use of what Hollinger (2000) refers to as 'e-tailing' makes the buying of goods from a wide range of producers and retailers much easier for those linked up to the Internet.

The breaking down of organizational barriers extends also to the home/work boundary. Lyons (2000, p. 60) says: 'For many people, the division between work and life is becoming blurred . . . people now live and work in the post-farm, post-factory setting. They travel, they work at home. They even work while they travel – in hotels, planes, cyber cafés, and at "touch down spaces".' This division is becoming blurred mainly because of the ability of workers to maintain contact with their offices and organizations through the use of email and mobile phones, which can also be used to send and accept emails and other telecommunications. Cooper (2000, p. 32) remarks, 'The future of employment seems to lie either in small and medium-sized businesses or in outsourced and portfolio working for virtual organizations.'

Illustration 3.17

ICT and retail banking

One of the most vivid examples of how technology impacts on structural change at sector and organization level is found in retail banking (Consoli, 2005). The main breakthroughs were:

1965	Automated bank statements are produced
1966	The first credit card in the UK
1967	Database management systems automate money transfer
1970s	Microprocessors enable branches to become fully automated
1970s	Automatic teller machines spread ('holes in the wall')
1982	Microchips in cards enable direct debiting
1990s	Internet banking enables services from anywhere

In conjunction with changes to the ways retail banking is regulated, technology has reshaped the speed and convenience of transactions. It has also increased consumers' exposure to fraud and for investors with e-accounts their ability to get money out relies upon the operating system working. Given recent events in financial markets it is easy to imagine a bank shutting down its e-banking systems in order to keep your money in times of emergency! Consoli (2005, p. 472) argues that technological change 'triggers the emergence and/or demise of activities, competences, processes and services at the firm level. At industry level the pace of change is driven by the amount of interaction between organizations, suppliers, consumers and regulators.'

He found that the disappearance of competition between branches had led to the decline of the vertically integrated structures that had been commonplace. In their place there was much more need to coordinate a bigger range of services, some of which were outsourced. ICT was at the root of 'radical transformation' by incumbent organizations and enabled the entry of new organizations which reshaped the boundaries and structure of the industry.

We might wonder though in light of the credit crisis of 2008 how much these structural changes enabled the creation of very high-risk (toxic) products that, coupled with a failure of corporate social responsibility, created the conditions for the crisis in the first place.

The influence of the external environment

Environmental stability and turbulence

One of the best-known studies on the effects of the environment on organizational structure was by Burns and Stalker (1961). In studying some 20 British industrial organizations they concluded that organizations had different structures depending on whether they operated in stable environments that changed little over time or in dynamic, changeable environments. They identified two main structural types – mechanistic structures that were more suited to stable unchanging environments and organic structures which were more suited to the unpredictable, more dynamic environments.

Mechanistic structures conform to Morgan's models 1 and 2, shown in Figure 3.5 (rigid bureaucracies and bureaucracies with a senior management team) and Mintzberg's 'machine' form of organization (see Illustration 3.14). Organic structures resemble Morgan's models 4, 5 and 6 and Mintzberg's 'adhocracy' and 'diversified' forms of organization.

Key characteristics of organic forms are the harnessing of knowledge and experience upon tasks rather than specialized task definitions, emphasis on communication across the organization (not just up and down), fast changes to how tasks are defined compared to slow, and procedural changes. While the organic form is generally thought best for large organizations in complex environments, Sine *et al.* (2006) argue that the theory breaks down with new ventures in turbulent environments. They found that new ventures, which are by nature very flexible, can lack the benefits of structure such as role clarity and higher efficiency. New ventures with more role clarity and specialization in the founding management teams outperformed others.

Waldersee *et al.* (2003) in a study of major changes in Australian organizations, found that mechanistic organizations could implement technological and structural change successfully but were not so good at implementing social change, e.g., attidudinal, behavioural and cultural. Organic organizations were good at both technical, structural and social change.

Lawrence and Lorsch (1967) went further than Burns and Stalker in suggesting that different departments within organizations face different environments and that, in successful organizations, each department would structure itself in line with its specific sub-environment. However, to ensure success, organizations operating in highly uncertain environments would need to differentiate those departments most exposed to the environment from those that were less exposed. In addition, where differentiation of departments was required, an organization would need to ensure appropriate integrating mechanisms between departments to avoid the negative effects of different structures and operating procedures for different departments.

Robbins (2003) also addresses the issue of environments specific to different parts of organizations. Drawing on other research (see Robbins, p. 472), he suggests that environments can be characterized in terms of three key dimensions.

The first is the *capacity* of the environment, which refers to the degree to which it can support growth. The second is the degree of *stability* in the environment; stable environments are low in volatility whereas unstable environments are characterized by a high degree of unpredictable change. The third is environmental *complexity*, that is the degree of homogeneity or heterogeneity among environmental elements. Given this three-dimensional definition of environment, Robbins concludes that the scarcer the capacity and the greater the degree of instability and complexity, the more organic a structure should be; the more abundant, stable and simple the environment, the more mechanistic a structure should be.

Socio-cultural influences

The discussion so far has concentrated on macro influences on organizational structure; size, technology and environment. Increasing size pushes organizations towards increasingly bureaucratic structures, which Robbins (2001, pp. 443–444) concludes is still the most efficient way to organize large-scale activities. By the same token, the desire of employees for more flexible ways of organizing their home/leisure/work relationships, coupled with the opportunities for self-employment and/or virtual forms of working, may force organizational structures into forms that are less well understood.

Regardless of the size of organizations and type of technology used, more flexible working patterns and ways of structuring the work appear to be increasing. An interesting issue, however, is whether this trend is a result of initiatives taken by employers for the sole benefit of business or in response to the changing expectations of the labour force. For instance, Cooper (2000, p. 32) says:

> The future of employment seems to lie either in small and medium-sized businesses or in outsourced and portfolio working for virtual organizations. Since the industrial revolution, managerial and professional workers have not experienced high levels of job insecurity, so will people be able to cope with permanent job insecurity without the security of organizational structure?

In contrast, Bevan (2000, p. 20) reporting on work/life balance found that employees who have benefited from more flexible work arrangements imply few difficulties as they choose arrangements to suit their particular home and life circumstances. The benefits to employers and businesses seem to outweigh the disadvantages.

It is difficult to know whether most people who work on production lines and supermarket checkouts would prefer to do something else. Work serves many purposes besides being a source of income. According to Robbins (2003), however: 'While more people today are undoubtedly turned off by overly specialized jobs than were their parents and grandparents, it would be naïve to ignore the reality that there is still a segment of the workforce that prefers the routine and repetitiveness of highly specialized jobs.' Not everyone is suited to working in highly organic or loosely structured networks, let alone working in virtual organizations.

People choose organizations as much as organizations choose people. Those working in organizations are more likely to remain in organizations whose structures, with their particular degrees of centralization, formalization, specialization and traditionalism, suit their individual and group preferences and needs. Designing organizational structures that satisfy the needs of those working in and associated with them is not straightforward. Indeed, designing organizational structures for change, while at the same time ensuring that the needs of the market and of employees are met, is as much an art as a science.

Organizational structure and change

There is no one best way to design organizational structures or any particular form that will guarantee successful performance. Depending on factors such as strategy, size, technology used, the degree of predictability of the environment and the expectations and lifestyle of employees, an organization could well be successful and respond to the need for change whether it was structured along bureaucratic, mechanistic lines or as one of the newer network forms.

Care must be taken, however, not to assume that these contingency relationships are straightforward and that, provided the 'formula' is learned and applied, success will result. Robbins (1993, p. 528), drawing on the work of Child (1972) and Pugh (1973), states that: 'Strategy, size, technology and environment – even when combined – can at best explain only fifty per cent of the variability in structure.' In addition, the idea that there is a one-way causal relationship between an organization's environment and its structure is questionable.

Illustration 3.18

Beyond hierarchy?

Oxman and Smith (2003) argue that structure is increasingly irrelevant to how work is done. They observe that the regularity of restructuring is testimony to how ineffective it is.

- Information technology cuts across the old boundaries.
- Performance management is often shaped by more than one party, i.e., it is not the old style of boss on subordinate – performance on projects cuts across this.
- Layoffs contribute to alienation of employees to an 'organization' and reduced relevance of what the 'organization' is.

- Networking in the managerial and professional classes supplements whatever the old structure is contributing and networking fills roles once taken by the organization.
- Knowledge management, storing and sharing of organizational learning and knowledge saps some of the power from traditional hierarchies in which it could be stored.
- Cross-unit cooperation is important to ensure that the best brains are attached to a project.

While organizations are influenced by their environments some are able to exert some control over them – for example, oil producers by cutting or increasing production. The political environment can be influenced by lobbying, customers influenced through advertising and people's expectations of employment influenced by the way organizations design jobs. Organizations in monopoly markets are well placed to influence their environments. In times of high unemployment, the introduction of technology that significantly changes working practices will be easier.

If organizations are able, to some extent, to manipulate their environments to suit their strategies and structures, this will enable them to preserve existing structures and operational arrangements. The pressure to do this is evident from Mullins' (2005, p. 648) statement that: 'Developing organizations cannot, without difficulty, change their formal structure at too frequent an interval. There must be a significant change in contingency factors before an organization will respond.' This implies a considerable time lag between situational change and changes in structure. Therefore, even if changes in strategy, size, technology and environmental factors do build forces for changes in organizational structure, there are other factors that may accelerate or, more likely, impede this process.

Illustration 3.19

Resisting arrest?

The first decade of the 21st century saw new forms of terrorism and in 2008 three men were convicted in the UK of offences relating to planning to bring down aircraft with 'liquid' bombs. Yet according to a former senior police officer, the structure of policing in the UK could impede the fight against terrorism (Hayman, 2008).

Policing in England and Wales is still substantially organized around counties which are themselves largely administrative districts dating from medieval times. While adequate for local policing, coordination across county forces could get in the way of a long and at times fast-moving surveillance operation where targets are moving around. Communication systems do not always line-up and 'the lines of command and control become

stretched'. Local resources may not be sufficient to provide what a particular operation needs.

Plans to reduce the 43 police forces and create fewer but larger forces each with a more strategic capability struggle to gain favour. Hayman implies that this is due to an inability to resolve 'competing interests' in policing and to placate egos. Presumably these are the egos of senior officers who could see their forces disappear in mergers and perhaps see their posts eliminated. Structural change in policing and the creation of a national counter-terrorist force appear to be compromised by structural inertia and police politics.

Source: Based on Hayman, A (2008) 'Police Politics are Stalling our War On Terror', *The Times*, 10 September, p. 28.

One of these factors is associated with the concept of 'strategic choice' (Child, 1972) and draws attention to the power of senior managers to choose which criteria they will use in assessing what organizational changes should take place. Managers who may lose power and/or position are unlikely to choose those alternatives that, from a logical–rational point of view, maximize the organization's interest. Robbins (1993, p. 528) summarizes this view of structure as the 'power–control' explanation of organizational structure, that is, 'an organization's structure is the result of a power struggle by internal constituencies who are seeking to further their interests'. Thus, given the discretion available to management, rather than changes in organizational structure being logically planned and implemented, what results will be a structure that 'emerges' to satisfy not only the imperatives of the internal and external environments, but the personalities and power needs of dominant stakeholders.

Organizational politics and the issue of power balance are not the only factors influencing structural change in organizations. Neither does the mere process of changing an organization's structure necessarily bring about permanent change in management strategy, style of operating and other employees' attitudes and behaviour. The pervasiveness of organizational and national cultures can be strong enough to work against change. Thus the mechanisms for managing any kind of organizational change must take account of what French and Bell (1990) call the informal, 'covert' aspects of organizational life such as people's values and feelings, the informal, as opposed to formal, groupings and the norms of behaviour that become part of any organization but which are rarely 'spelt out'. Johnson (1990) puts emphasis on the role of symbols, rituals, stories and myths as being important parts of an organization's culture. He says that organizational change cannot be brought about simply by changing strategy and structure. The organizational culture has a significant and maybe even dominant role to play if anything more than incremental change is to happen and this is explored in the next chapter.

Structural inertia and population ecology

As we have emphasized, organizations and subunits of organizations scan their environments and change their organizational structures accordingly. Good managers can be seen as those who can adapt their structures smoothly in ways that have little impact on operations. From this perspective organizations are *adapting* to their environments using a form of 'social Darwinism' (Hannan and Freeman, 1979, p. 930). In what has become a classic paper in its field, Michael Hannan and John Freeman suggested, however, that not all of the variation that we can observe in the way organizations are structured can be explained by adaptation.

They introduced the idea that there exists in organizations pressures and processes that bring about a level of structural inertia as illustration 3.19 shows. Adaptive flexibility decreases with increasing inertia such that when inertia is high the organization is more likely to fall victim to the forces of natural selection – that is, cease operating. Internal forces creating inertia include:

● Past investment in plant, technology and people that is not easily switched into other tasks.

- Decision makers having to work with incomplete information about environments.
- Structural change means disturbance to the 'political equilibria' that exist at any point in time. Some departments and some people come off better than others after reorganization which means that proposals are resisted. Resistance can be big enough to put-off future reorganization.
- Organizational history leads to ways of operating that become embedded.

External forces include:

- The barriers to exiting one industry and entering another such as regulation, capital investment and market knowledge.
- The costs of acquiring specialist knowledge about unfamiliar markets.
- Organizations acquire a certain public legitimacy from their past actions which can act as an asset. Attempts to move into new areas can be compromised by lack of legitimacy in those areas. Failing shoe factories do not change into hospitals. Fundamental structural change of this magnitude simply does not happen.
- A successful adaptive strategy for one organization may not lead to successful adaptation by another – there is no general strategy that organizations can follow.

Inertia theory suggests that because older organizations have more stable and standardized routines they will have higher inertia. Likewise as size increases so does predictability and inflexibility and thus inertia. Hence both age and size should increase resistance to change (Kelly and Amburgey, 1991). Organizational complexity is also assumed to raise inertia and hence increase the duration of reorganization and the risk of failure. Complexity in this context is not the number of departments but the links between them. If a unit can reorganize without affecting others then complexity is low. If changes in one unit require responses in other units, which in turn require further changes in the initiating unit, then complexity is high (Hannan and Freeman, 1984).

To better understand the links between organizations and environments Hannan and Freeman borrowed ideas from biology and in particular ideas about how populations of species survive. Although it is true that every organization has a distinctive structure (in terms of rules, processes and activities) groups of organizations share a 'blueprint' that allows them to be considered similar enough to consider them as a species. Although there are many owls, for instance, each type of owl is a separate species adapted to survive in a particular environment. Organizations with similar blueprints are similar in terms of their vulnerability to the environment and constitute a population of organizations in the same sense that there is a population of tawny owls.

Although broad structural types are found (multifunctional, for instance) from looking at exactly how organizations function, it is clear that organizations with the same general structure are uniquely different. In the same way as we can ask why there are so many different plants and animals we can ask why there are so many types of organizations (blueprints). In answer to this:

> In each distinguishable environmental configuration one finds, in equilibrium, only that organizational form optimally adapted to the demands of the environment.
>
> (Hannan and Freeman, 1979, p. 939)

Forms that are not optimally adapted are 'selected out' of business. Yet we can see that organizations have to adapt and this calls for a certain level of slack in the structure. Slack can be seen as resources that are not committed and which can be used – some might call it waste or less than optimum efficiency.

While adaptation explains to some extent whether organizations survive or not, it is not the only explanation. Hannan and Freeman (1979) argued that selection rather than adaptation is important. Structural inertia impedes adaptation such that organizations drift away from their environment and are replaced by others that are better equipped to survive. A powerful fact in favour of this argument is that lists of the top 100 or top 500 companies in a country change over time. What proportion of the organizations in business 50 years ago are still trading? How many companies in the top 100 list of 1980, 1990 and 2000 are still in business? There are no exact answers to these questions but it is likely that the attrition rate is quite high. Failure is common. Selection rather than adaptation is a strong argument here. Inertia also explains why it seems many organizations need to experience a 'survival-threatening crisis' before they embark on meaningful change processes (Schaefer, 1998).

Conclusions

We have seen that design is not the same as structure, which has a stronger social action perspective. Design change is influenced by strategy, size, production technology, ICT and environment. Different organizational forms have been described and of particular interest are the newer and network and virtual forms of organization along with the consequences of flattening. Defective designs and structures have serious consequences for organizational performance. Redesigning an organization's structure has to be carefully planned with change taking place as current business performance has to be sustained. This implies a mixture of incremental and transformational change.

Chapter 1 showed how organizations are, to some extent, a product of their history. In addition, organizations have existing structures, workforces (who are used to working in them), existing cultures, current businesses to sustain and, in many cases, trades unions to satisfy. Given this context, it is interesting to see how organizations have managed to adapt their formalized structures and developed matrix and virtual organizations layered over their existing structures to ensure responsiveness in fast-moving operating environments.

Small businesses with less that 200 people make up the majority of organizations worldwide and the traditional approaches to structure will need adapting to fit. Managers need to be vigilant about changes in the environment and respond to them but if restructuring is to make a difference it has to change what people do – not just how they are grouped and who they report to. Without an alteration in behaviour changes to design do not have much impact on the 'real' structure. People push their own interests and networks of aligned interests are continually forming and dissolving.

The next two chapters extend this discussion by addressing the more informal, covert cultural and political aspects of organizational life.

Discussion questions and assignments

1 Consider the following statement:

Starting from scratch underplays the fact that significant redesign has to be planned and implemented in a real-life context that won't go away. Hospitals' re-engineering projects run into the problems of physician power. Government projects are often stifled by a context where people can't see the need for fundamental change. In manufacturing and service organizations, plans to implement a new way of doing business are often undermined by the thinking and mindsets of the old way. These realities have to be actively managed and changed if new initiatives are to succeed. (Morgan, 1994)

To what extent do these or similar issues apply to your own organization or one you know well? How can the issues be managed?

2 'In spite of the talk about network and virtual organizations, most organizations conform to more traditional structure types.' Why is this?

Case example ●●●

Mitsubishi Motors revises organization

Mitsubishi Motors Corporation (MMC) announced plans to revise its organizational structure. The changes will see the company's structure slim down from 230 departments to 131, which will hopefully speed up the decision-making process and clarify responsibilities.

The MMC affirms the guiding principles below in conducting business, which are the same since the company began in the 1930s. It has recognized that there have been dramatic shifts in values, the structure of society and environment since its first values were announced, and therefore some revisions are necessary to bring it up to date.

'Shoki Hoko' – Strive to enrich society, both materially and spiritually, while contributing towards the preservation of the global environment.

'Shoji Komei' – Maintain principles of transparency and openness, conducting business with integrity and fairness.

'Ritsugyo Boeki' – Expand business, based on an all-encompassing global perspective.

To support its desire to restore consumer trust in the company and a belief in how employees should be treated, MMC has created a number of restructuring initiatives.

Case example *continued*

Restoring trust, implementing reform

- A Business Ethics Committee consisting mainly of experts from outside the company will be established to supervise the company's efforts to comply with its pledge to place the utmost importance on customers, safety and quality.
- A new Quality Affairs Office will handle issues related to quality assurance and management, while a new Corporate Social Responsibility (CSR) Promotion Office, directly under the CEO, will promote and improve quality auditing and compliance issues throughout the company.
- A Corporate Restructuring Committee (CRC), headed by a Corporate Restructuring Office appointed from among outside investors, will be set up directly under the CEO for one year and cross-functional teams created for all issues related to the revitalization plan. The teams will reach through the entire organization and make bold proposals to the CRC.

Organizations directly under the CEO (Chief Executive Officer) and COO (Chief Operating Officer)

- The CEO will supervise departments related to overall management while the COO will supervise departments involved in executing business operations. Newly established departments reporting to the CEO include the CSR Promotion Office, Finance Group Headquarters, Group Corporate Strategy Office and the secretariat of the CRC.

- Newly established departments reporting directly to the COO include the Quality Affairs Office, Corporate Staff Office, Product Operations Group Headquarters, Domestic Operations Controlling and Accounting Department, and Produce Controlling and Accounting Department.

Other departments to be set or reorganized

- CSR Promotion Office, which also includes the Business Ethics Committee
- Finance Group Headquarters will include the Group, Overseas, Domestic and product Controlling and Accounting Departments
- Group Corporate Strategy Office
- Quality Affairs Office
- Corporate Staff Office
- Product Operations Group Headquarters
- Production and Logistics Office
- Global Aftersales Office
- Domestic Operations Group Headquarters
- Overseas Operations Group Headquarters.

In short, all functions will fall under the CEO or the COO. The aim is to clarify the roles and responsibilities for each part of the business. More detailed information can be found at:

> http://media.mitsubishi-motors.com/pressrelease/e/corporate/detail1069.html.

(This case dates from 22 June 2004.)

Case exercise

1 How would you categorize these changes in terms of the types of change discussed in Chapter 2?

2 Attempt to match the proposals to the types of organizational structure discussed in this chapter.

3 What might be the advantages and disadvantages of Mitsubishi's proposed structural changes?

●●●● Indicative resources

Watson, T. (2002) *Organising and Managing Work*, Harlow: Pearson Education. The aim of this text is to provide a resource for understanding present-day work activities and how they are managed, and Chapters 7 and 8 relating to structure and culture are particularly relevant.

Huczynksi, A.A. and Buchanan, D. (2007) *Organizational Behaviour*, (6th edn), FT Prentice Hall has a good coverage of structure and design in Chapters 14 to 16.

Useful websites

www.istheory.yorku.ca/structurationtheory.htm
www.lancs.ac.uk/fass/centres/css/ant/antres.htm

To click straight to these links and for other resources go to
www.pearsoned.co.uk/senior

References

Amburgey, T.L. and Dacin, T. (1994) 'As the Left Foot Follows the Right? The dynamics of strategic and structural change, *Academy of Management Journal*, 37(6), pp. 1427–1452.

Ansoff, I. H. and McDonnell, E. J. (1990) *Implanting Strategic Management*, Englewood Cliffs, NJ: Prentice-Hall.

Arkin, A. (1999) 'Peak practice', *People Management*, 11 November, pp. 57–59.

Barley, S.R. and Tobert, P.S. (1997) 'Institutionalisation and Structuration: Studying the Links between Action and Institution', *Organization Studies*, 18, (1), pp. 93–117.

Bartol, K.M. and Martin, D.C. (1994) *Management* (2nd edn), Maidenhead: McGraw-Hill.

Bate, P. (1995) *Strategies for Cultural Change*, Oxford: Butterworth-Heinemann.

Bate, P., Khan, R. and Pyle, A.J. (2000) 'Culturally Sensitive Restructuring: An Action Research-Based Approach to Organization Development and Design, *Public Administration Quarterly*, 23(4), pp. 445–470.

BBC News (2005) 'Unilever Shakeup as Profit Slips', www.bbc.co.uk, 10 February.

Bernasco, W., Weerd-Nederhof, P.C., Tillema, H. and Boer, H. (1999) 'Balanced Matrix Structure and New Product Development Processes at Texas Instruments', *R&D Management*, 29(2), pp. 121–131.

Bevan, S. (2000) 'Flexible Designs on Domestic Harmony', *Financial Times*, 5 October, p. 5.

Briand, L. and Bellemare, G. (2006) 'A Structurationist Analysis of Post-bureaucracy in Modernity and Late Modernity', *Journal of Organizational Change Management*, 19(1), pp. 65–79.

Burkhard, R.J. and Horan, T.J. (2006), 'The Virtual Organization: Evidence of Academic Structuration in Business Programs and Implications for Information Science', *Communications of AIS*, 17, Article 11, pp. 2–48.

Burnes, B. (2004) *Managing Change* (4th edn), Harlow: Pearson Education.

Burns, T. and Stalker, G. M. (1961) *The Management of Innovation*, London: Tavistock.

Business Week (1993) 'The virtual corporation', 8 February, pp. 98–102.

Butler, R. (1991) *Designing Organizations: A Decision-making Perspective*, London: Routledge.

Chandler, A. D. (1962) *Strategy and Structure: Chapters in the History of the Industrial Enterprise*, Cambridge, MA: MIT Press.

Child, J. (1972) 'Organization Structure, Environment and Performance: the role of strategic choice', *Sociology*, January, pp. 1–22.

Child, J. (1988) *Organizations: A Guide to Problems and Practice* (2nd edn), London: Paul Chapman.

Chu, C. and Smithson, S. (2007) 'E-business and Organizational Change: a structurational approach', *Information Systems Journal*, 17, pp. 369–389.

Clegg, S.R. (1990) *Modern Organizations: Organization Studies in the Postmodern World*, London: Sage.

Clegg, S., Kornberger, M. and Pitsis, T. (2008) *Managing and Organizations: An Introduction to Theory and Practice* (2nd edn), London: Sage.

Consoli, D. (2005) 'The Dynamics of Technological Change in the UK Retail Banking Services: an evolutionary perspective', *Research Policy*, 34, pp. 461–480.

Cooper, C. (2000) 'Rolling With It', *People Management*, 28 September, pp. 32–34.

Cummings, T. and Worley, C. (2005) *Organization Development and Change* (8th edn), Mason, OH: Thomson South-Western.

Cunliffe, A.L. (2008) *Organization Theory*, London: Sage.

Cusamano, M. (1985) *The Japanese Automobile Industry: technology and management at Nissan and Toyota*, Cambridge, MA: Harvard Industry Press.

Davidow, W.H. and Malone, M.S. (1992) *The Virtual Corporation*, New York: Harper Business.

Davis, S.M. and Lawrence, P.R. (1977) *Matrix*, Reading, MA: Addison-Wesley.

Day, G. (1999) 'Aligning Organizational Structures to the Market', *Business Strategy Review*, 10(3), pp. 33–46.

Dent, M. (2003) 'Managing Doctors and Saving a Hospital: rhetoric and actor networks', *Organization*, 10(1), pp. 107–126.

Drucker, P.F. (1999) *The Practice of Management*, Oxford: Butterworth Heinemann.

French, W.L. and Bell, C.H. (1999) *Organization Development: Behavioral Science Interventions for Organization Improvement*, Englewood Cliffs, NJ: Prentice-Hall.

Gao, P. (2005) Using Actor-network Theory to Analyse Strategy Formulation, *Information Systems Journal*, 15, pp. 255–275.

Geisler, B. (2002) *Virtual Teams*, Newfoundations.com.

Giddens, A. (1984) *The Constitution of Society*, University of California Press: Berkeley.

Giddens, A. (1991) *Modernity and Self-Identity*, Cambridge: Polity Press.

Giddens, A. (2001) *Sociology* (4th edn), Cambridge: Polity Press.

Greenwood, R. and Hinings, C.R. (1996) 'Understanding Radical Organizational Change: bringing together the old and new institutionalism', *Academy of Management Journal*, 21(4), pp. 1022–1054.

Greenwood, R., Suddaby, R. and Hinings, C.R. (2002) 'Theorising Change: the role of professional associations in the transformation of institutionalised fields', *Academy of Management Journal*, 45(1), pp. 58–80.

Greiner, L. (1972) 'Evolution and Revolution as Organizations Grow', *Harvard Business Review*, July–August, pp. 37–46.

Hammer, M. and Champy, J. (1993) *Reengineering the Corporation: A Manifesto for Business Revolution*, New York: Harper Business.

Handy, C.B. (1989) *The Age of Unreason*, London: Business Books.

Hannan, M.T. and Freeman, J. (1979) The Population Ecology of Organizations, *American Journal of Sociology*, 82(5), pp. 929–964.

Hannan, M.T. and Freeman, J. (1984) 'Structural Inertia and Organizational Change', *American Sociological Review*, 49, April, pp. 149–164.

Hayman, A. (2008) Police Politics are Stalling our War on Terror, *The Times*, 10 September, p. 28.

Hinterhuber, H.H. and Levin, B.M. (1994) 'Strategic Networks: the organization of the future', *Long Range Planning*, 27(3), pp. 43–53.

Hollinger, P. (2000) 'Festive Internet Rush May Surprise Retailers', *Financial Times*, 30 October, p. 6.

Jackson, N. and Carter, P. (2000) *Rethinking Organisational Behaviour*, Harlow: Financial Times Prentice Hall: Pearson Education.

Johnson, G. (1990) 'Managing Strategic Action: the role of symbolic action', *British Journal of Management*, 1, pp. 183–200.

Johnson, G., Scholes, K. and Whittington, R. (2005) *Exploring Corporate Strategy* (7th edn), Harlow: Pearson Education.

Johnson, G., Scholes, K. and Whittington, R. (2008) *Exploring Strategic Change: Texts and Cases* (8th edn), Harlow: Pearson Education.

Johnson, G., Smith, S. and Codling, B. (2000) 'Microprocesses of Institutional Change in the Context of Privatisation', *Academy of Management Review*, 25(3), pp. 572–580.

Kelly, D. and Amburgey, T. (1991) 'Organizational Inertia and Momentum: a dynamic model of strategic change', *Academy of Management Journal*, 34(3), 591–612.

Kondra, A.Z. and Hinings, C.R. (1998) 'Organizational Diversity and Change in Institutional Theory', *Organization Studies*, 19(5), pp. 743–767.

Latour, B. (2005) *Reassembling the Social: An Introduction to Actor-Network Theory*, Oxford: Oxford University Press.

Lawrence, P.R. and Lorsch, J.W. (1967) *Organization and Environment: Managing Differentiation and Integration*, Boston, MA: Harvard Business School.

Lucas, H.C., Jr (1996) *The T-Form Organization: Using Technology to Design Organizations for the 21st Century*, San Francisco, CA: Jossey-Bass.

Luthans, F. (1995) *Organizational Behavior* (7th edn), New York: McGraw-Hill.

Lyons, L. (2000) 'Management is Dead', *People Management*, 26 October, pp. 60–64.

McCann, J. and Galbraith, J.R. (1981) 'Interdepartmental Relations' in Nystrom, P.C. and Starbuck, W.H. (eds) *Handbook of Organizational Design: Remodelling Organizations and Their Environment*, vol. 2, New York: Oxford University Press.

McHugh, M. and Bennett, H. (1999) 'Introducing Teamwork Within a Bureaucratic Maze', *The Leadership and Organization Development Journal*, 20(2), pp. 81–93.

Miles, R.E. and Snow, C.C. (1984a) 'Fit, Failure and the

Hall of Fame', *California Management Review*, 26(3), pp. 10–28.

Miles, R.E. and Snow, C.C. (1984b) 'Designing Strategic Human Resource Systems', *Organisational Dynamics*, 13(8), pp. 36–52.

Miller, P. (1992) 'Accounting and Objectivity: the invention of calculating selves and calculable spaces', *Annals of Scholarship*, 9, pp. 61–86.

Mills, M. (2000) 'Coming to a Screen Near You …', *Office Hours*, the *Guardian*, 18 September, p. 2.

Mintzberg, H. (1979) *The Structuring of Organizations*, Englewood Cliffs, NJ: Prentice-Hall.

Mintzberg, H. (1983) *Structure in Fives: Designing Effective Organizations*, Englewood Cliffs, NJ: Prentice-Hall.

Mintzberg, H. (1991) 'The Effective Organization Forces and Forms', *Sloan Management Review*, winter, 32(2), pp. 54–67.

Mintzberg, H. (1994) 'Rethinking Strategic Planning. Part I: pitfalls and fallacies', *Long Range Planning*, 27(3), pp. 12–21.

Mintzberg, H., Quinn, J.B. and James, R.M. (1988) *The Strategy Process: Concepts, Contexts and Cases*, Hemel Hempstead: Prentice Hall.

Mintzberg, H. and van der Heyden, L. (1999) Organigraphs: drawing how companies really work, *Harvard Business Review*, Sep/Oct, pp. 87–94.

Morgan, G. (1989) *Creative Organization Theory: A Resource Book*, London: Sage.

Morgan, G. (1994) 'Quantum Leaps . . . Step by Step', *The Globe and Mail* (Canada's national newspaper), 28 June. Also available at http://www.imaginiz.com/leaps.html.

Mukherji, A. (2002) 'The Evolution of Information Systems: their impact on organizations and structures', *Management Decision*, 40(5), pp. 497–507.

Mullins, L. (2005) *Management and Organizational Behaviour* (7th edn), Harlow: Financial Times Prentice Hall.

Ody, P. (2000) 'Working Towards a Total, Visible Network', *Financial Times* Survey, *Supply Chain Management*, 25 October, p. 1.

Oxman, J.A. and Smith, B.D. (2003) 'The Limits of Structural Change', *MIT Sloan Management Review*, 45(1), pp. 77–83.

Perrow, C. (1967) *Organizational Analysis: A Sociological View*, London: Tavistock.

Pugh, D.S. (1973) 'The Measurement of Organisation Structures: does context determine form?' *Organisational Dynamics*, Spring, pp. 19–34.

Pugh, D. (1990) *Organization Theory: Selected Readings*, Harmondsworth: Penguin.

Pugh, D.S., Hickson, D.J., Hinings, C.R. and Turner, C. (1969) 'Dimensions of Organization Structure', *Administrative Science Quarterly*, 17, pp. 163–176.

Rajan, R.G. and Wulf, J. (2006) 'The Flattening Firm: evidence from panel data on the changing nature of corporate hierarchies', *Review of Economics and Statistics*, 88(4), pp. 759–773.

Robbins, S.P. (1993) *Organizational Behavior*, Englewood Cliffs, NJ: Prentice-Hall.

Robbins, S.P. (2001) *Organizational Behavior: Concepts, Controversies, Applications* (9th edn), Englewood Cliffs, NJ: Prentice-Hall.

Robbins, S.P. (2003) *Organizational Behavior* (10th edn), Englewood Cliffs, NJ: Prentice Hall.

Sarason, Y. (1995) 'A Model of Organizational Transformation: the incorporation of organizational identity in a structuration theory framework', *Academy of Management Proceedings*, pp. 47–51.

Sarker, S., Sarker, S. and Sidorova, A. (2006) 'Understanding Business Process Change Failure: an actor-network perspective', *Journal of Management Information Systems*, 23(1), pp. 51–86.

Schaefer, S. (1998) 'Influence Costs, Structural Inertia, and Organizational Change', *Journal of Economics & Management Strategy*, 7(2), pp. 237–263.

Sherer, P.D. and Lee, K. (2002) 'Institutional Change in Large Law Firms: a resource dependency and institutional perspective', *Academy of Management Journal*, 45(1), pp. 102–119.

Sine, W.D., Mitsuhashi, H. and Kirsch, D.A. (2006) 'Revisiting Burns and Stalker: formal structure and new venture performance in emerging economic sectors', *Academy of Management Journal*, 49(1), pp. 121–132.

Snow, C.C., Miles, R.E. and Coleman, H.J., Jr (1992) 'Managing 21st Century Network Organizations', *Organizational Dynamics*, winter, pp. 5–19.

Stanforth, C. (2007) 'Using Actor-Network Theory to Analyse E-government Implementation in Developing Countries', *Information Technologies and International Development*, 3(3), pp. 35–60.

Swailes, S. (2008) *Organizational Structure*, in Brooks, I., *Organizational Behaviour* (4th edn) pp. 189–231, London: FT Prentice Hall.

Thompson, J.D. (1967) *Organizations in Action*, New York: McGraw-Hill.

Van der Duim, R. and van Marwijk, R. (2006) 'The Implemenation of an Environmental System for Dutch Tour Operators: an actor-network perspective', *Journal of Sustainable Tourism*, 14(5), pp. 449–472.

Waldersee, R., Griffiths, A. and Lai, J. (2003) 'Predicting Organizational Change Success: matching organization types, change types and capabilities', *Journal of Applied Management and Entrepreneurship*, (8)1, pp. 66–81.

Weber, M. (1947) *The Theory of Social and Economic Organization*, Free Press, trans. and ed. by Henderson, A.M. and Parsons, T., in Pugh, D.S. (1990), *Organization Theory: Selected Readings*,

Harmondsworth: Penguin. (German original published in 1924.)

Willamott, H. (1981) The Structuring of Organizational Structure: a note, *Administrative Science Quarterly*, 26, pp. 470–474.

Wilson, D.C. and Rosenfeld, R.H. (1990) *Managing Organizations: Text, Readings and Cases*, Maidenhead: McGraw-Hill.

Wilson, D.C. and Rosenfeld, R.H. (1991) *Managing Organizations: Text, Readings and Cases*, Instructor's Resource Book, Maidenhead: McGraw-Hill.

Woodward, J. (1965) *Industrial Organization: Theory and Practice*, London: Oxford University Press.

Chapter 4

Culture and change

This chapter begins the process of addressing the informal aspects of organizational functioning with an exploration of the concept of culture as it influences organizational life and organizational change processes. The meaning of culture at both the organizational and national levels is discussed and different models and typologies are compared. Methods for diagnosing and identifying organizational culture are discussed together with the different sources from which organizational culture derives. The links between organizational strategy, structure and culture are explored in order to understand the issues associated with and possibilities for changing organizational culture.

Learning objectives

By the end of this chapter you will be able to:

- recognize the importance of the informal organization and its role in relation to organizations and change;

- explain the meaning of culture;

- compare and contrast different cultural models and typologies;

- identify the origins of organizational culture and appreciate how culture pervades all aspects of organizational life;

- examine how cultural differences impact upon organizational change.

The informal organization

Organizations are made up of formal, tangible elements such as structure, strategy and technology, goals and financial resources. These more formal organizational features are, in the main, susceptible to the process of *planned* change (see Chapter 2). However, as Chapter 2 showed, organizational life is not as neat and tidy as this implies. This was captured by French and Bell (1990, 1999) in their use of the concept of the formal and informal organization and the metaphor of the 'organizational iceberg' (see Figure 4.1). This metaphor depicts two contrasting aspects of organizational life. The part visible above water is composed of the more easy-to-see and formal aspects of an organization, that is, those issues that are based on agreed, measurable ouputs/outcomes relating to how organizational goals and objectives will be met. The second, the hidden part of the iceberg, is composed of the more covert aspects of organizational life. These include the values, beliefs and attitudes held by management and other employees, the emergent informal groupings that occur, the norms of behaviour which are rarely talked about but which influence how things are done and the politics of organizational life that drive decisions and actions.

The iceberg metaphor not only points to the overt and covert aspects of organizations but draws attention to the proposition that the informal systems, as well as being out of sight, are the greater part of the organization. Like icebergs, the biggest and most dangerous part lies hidden. French and Bell (1990, p. 18) considered that: 'Traditionally, this hidden domain either is not examined

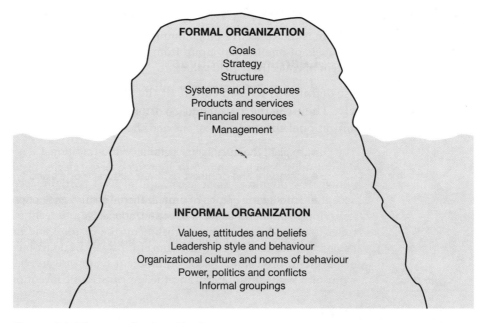

FORMAL ORGANIZATION

Goals
Strategy
Structure
Systems and procedures
Products and services
Financial resources
Management

INFORMAL ORGANIZATION

Values, attitudes and beliefs
Leadership style and behaviour
Organizational culture and norms of behaviour
Power, politics and conflicts
Informal groupings

Figure 4.1 The organizational iceberg

at all or is only partially examined.' However, recognition that the informal organization exists and that it has a powerful influence on organizational activity is reason enough to examine how it impacts upon the extent to which organizations can deal with change.

Culture, politics and power represent much of what is included in the informal organization. What is more, they play an important role in helping or hindering the process of change, as Morgan (1989) observes: 'The culture and politics of many organizations constrain the degree of change and transformation in which they can successfully engage, even though such change may be highly desirable for meeting the challenges and demands of the wider environment.' Regardless of how well change might be planned in terms of the more formal organizational characteristics, it is the hidden and informal aspects of organizational life that will ultimately help or hinder an organization's success.

The meaning of culture

Kroeber and Kluckhohn (1952, p. 181) examined over 100 definitions of culture and offered this summary definition:

> Culture consists in patterned ways of thinking, feeling and reacting, acquired and transmitted mainly by symbols, constituting the distinctive achievements of human groups, including their embodiment in artifacts; the essential core of culture consists of traditional (i.e. historically derived and selected) ideas and especially their attached values.

Another much quoted definition by Hofstede (1981, p. 24) is that:

> Culture is the collective programming of the human mind that distinguishes the members of one human group from those of another. Culture in this sense is a system of collectively held values.

These definitions refer to culture at the level of society and the nation respectively. They can be compared to those used more specifically to describe organizational cultures.

> The culture of the factory is its customary and traditional way of thinking and of doing things, which is shared to a greater or lesser degree by all its members, and which new members must learn, and at least partially accept, in order to be accepted into service in the firm. Culture in this sense covers a wide range of behaviour: the methods of production; job skills and technical knowledge; attitudes towards discipline and punishment; the customs and habits of managerial behaviour; the objectives of the concern; its way of doing business; the methods of payment; the values placed on different types of work; beliefs in democratic living and joint consultation; and the less conscious conventions and taboos.
>
> (Jaques, 1952, p. 251)

> A set of understandings or meanings shared by a group of people. The meanings are largely tacit among members, are clearly relevant to the particular group, and are distinctive to the group. Meanings are passed on to new group members.
>
> (Louis, 1980)

> Culture is 'how things are done around here'. It is what is typical of the organization, the habits, the prevailing attitudes, the grown-up pattern of accepted and expected behaviour.
>
> (Drennan, 1992, p. 3)

These definitions imply that culture can be identified and that it delineates and differentiates one human grouping from another. It is clear that culture has cognitive (to do with thinking), affective (to do with feeling) and behavioural characteristics. However, this does not imply that different cultures are easily identified and, on the whole, this is not so. Schein (1992, p. 6) sums this up by referring to organizational culture as:

> The deeper level of basic assumptions and beliefs that are shared by members of an organization, that operate unconsciously and define in a basic 'taken for granted' fashion an organization's view of its self and its environment.

Also implicit in the iceberg metaphor and these definitions is that culture is 'deep-seated' and is, therefore, likely to be resistant to change. However, as Bate (1996, p. 28) points out: 'Culture can be changed, in fact it is changing all the time.' The issue is the degree of change to which culture can be subjected over the short and long term and the process for changing it. Much depends on the perspective adopted and the type of change proposed. Three perspectives can be identified: that culture *can* be managed; that culture *may* be manipulated; and that culture *cannot* be consciously changed (Ogbonna and Harris, 1998). Most of the research concerned with culture change subscribes to the first two perspectives. The third, if true, presents problems for change agents who will perhaps need some external and perhaps unpredictable forces to make it happen. Recent events in finance may catalyze change to the reward/risk culture that characterized banks, for instance. This discussion, therefore, concentrates on issues associated with the first two perspectives on the assumption that much of what is said would apply if culture change occurs spontaneously rather than as a result of a more planned process.

Advice on how to *plan* culture change is plentiful (for examples see Eccles, 1994; Carnall, 2003; Bate, 1996; Ogbonna and Harris, 1998). There is general agreement that there is a need to:

(i)   assess the current situation;
(ii) have some idea of what the aimed-for situation looks like;
(iii) work out the 'what' and 'how' of moving the organization, or part of it, away from its current culture to what is perceived to be a more desirable one;

(iv) intervene to bring about cultural change; and

(v) monitor outcomes and adjust as needed.

All very logical/rational and, as we will see, very simplistic.

The ingredients of culture

At the most basic level we can list some characteristics of culture and descriptions of culture can be framed in terms of these characteristics. For instance, Brown (1995, p. 8) lists the following:

- artefacts
- language in the form of jokes, metaphors, stories, myths and legends
- behaviour patterns in the form of rites, rituals, ceremonies and celebrations
- norms of behaviour
- heroes (past and present employees who do great things)
- symbols and symbolic action
- beliefs, values and attitudes
- ethical codes
- basic assumptions about what is important
- history.

Robbins (2003, p. 525 – see Illustration 4.1) gives more insight into how these characteristics can take shape. Have a look at this and then attempt Activity 4.1.

Illustration 4.1

The characteristics of organizational culture

1 **Innovation and risk taking**. The degree to which employees are encouraged to be innovative and take risks.

2 **Attention to detail**. The degree to which employees are expected to exhibit precision, analysis and attention to detail.

3 **Outcome orientation**. The degree to which management focuses on results or outcomes rather than on the techniques and processes used to achieve those outcomes.

4 **People orientation**. The degree to which management decisions take into consideration the effect of outcomes on people within the organization.

5 **Team orientation**. The degree to which work activities are organized around groups rather than individuals.

6 **Aggression**. The degree to which people are aggressive and competitive rather than easygoing.

7 **Stability**. The degree to which organizational activities emphasize maintaining the *status quo* in contrast to growth.

Source: Robbins, S.P. (2005) *Organizational Behaviour* (11th edn), New Jersey: Pearson Education, p. 485.

Activity 4.1 *Appraising your own organization*

The scales relate to the organizational culture characteristics listed in Illustration 4.1. Indicate on each scale showing how you rate your own organization (or one you know). If possible, ask others who know the organization to do the same. You could find some different views of the culture emerging.

Organizational culture characteristics

- Innovation and risk taking   High ⟵⟶ Low
- Attention to detail   High ⟵⟶ Low
- Outcome orientation   High ⟵⟶ Low
- People orientation   High ⟵⟶ Low
- Team orientation   High ⟵⟶ Low
- Aggressiveness   High ⟵⟶ Low
- Stability   High ⟵⟶ Low

Analyze how your views and your colleagues' views differ. Consider why their views differ to yours.

The listing approach is useful but does not tell us how these features may be related or ordered. Figure 4.2 illustrates ideas from Hofstede *et al.* (1990) about 'levels' of culture and that culture manifests itself at the deepest level through people's values and at the shallowest level in terms of the things that symbolize those values.

Schein (2004) suggests three levels that are, from the shallowest to the deepest: the *artefacts* level (the visible organizational structures and processes such as language, environment, rituals, ceremonies, myths and stories); the *espoused values* level (the organization's strategies, goals, philosophies); and the *basic underlying assumptions* level (the unconscious, taken-for-granted beliefs, perceptions, thoughts and feelings that are the ultimate source of values and actions). Thus the rituals, heroes and symbols of Hofstede *et al.* equate with Schein's artefacts level. However, Hofstede's values level is, apparently, split into two levels by Schein, who distinguishes between the beliefs, values and attitudes associated with the espoused values level and the deeper level of basic assumptions. Dyer's (1985) four level model proposes *artefacts, perspectives, values* and *tacit assumptions*.

Robbins' list is amenable to being *used* to describe culture in practical terms. However, the levels model can be used in similar fashion. In this case, the process requires interpretation of signs and symbols, as well as language used, to assess the prevailing values and underlying assumptions about how the organization operates. Illustration 4.2 shows how a combination of Schein's and Dyer's models might be applied to the Beautiful Buildings Company described in Chapter 3.

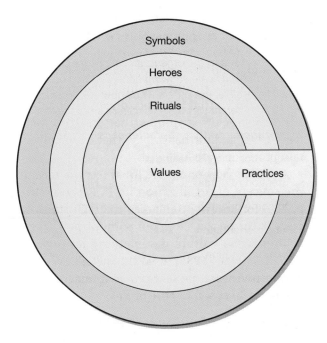

Figure 4.2 **Different levels of culture**

Source: Hofstede, G., Neuijen, B., Ohayv, D.D. and Sanders, G. (1990) 'Measuring Organizational Cultures: a qualitative and quantitative study across twenty cases', *Administrative Science Quarterly*, 35, p. 291.

Illustration 4.2

Levels of culture in the BB Company

1 **Artefacts**. The annual report of the company includes policies concerned with employees as well as customers and shareholders. Building sites have well-kept, clean facilities for the workers. Safety is top priority. Gillian Lambeth is frequently referred to by her first name.

2 **Perspective**. It is acceptable for trade union representatives to know what volume of work is expected in the future, but the directors are not expected to talk about details of the proposed expansion until it becomes well-established.

3 **Values**. Although there is a clear distinction between directors/managers and site workers, pay and conditions for workers should be fair and their views taken into account on matters that affect them. However, gaining contracts and satisfying customers is a priority.

4 **Basic/tacit assumptions**. All people should be treated with dignity whatever their level and function.

Objectivist and interpretive views of culture

List and levels models emphasize the issue of how to bring meaning to the concept of culture. Alvesson (1993), Bate (1996) and Brown (1995) all draw attention to the distinction between two classifications of culture. The first, of which Robbins' list and the levels models might be considered examples, treat culture as a critical variable that forms a partial explanation for differences in organizational operations. This can be termed the objectivist or functional view of culture (Alvesson, 1993). Alternatively, culture can be defined as a set of behavioural and/or cognitive characteristics (Brown, 1995). This view places culture alongside structure, technology and the environment (for instance) as one of the variables that influence organizational life and performance. In summary, this view of culture implies that organizations *have* cultures (see Brooks and Bate, 1994) and further implies that changing cultures is not that difficult if certain procedures are followed.

A second view of culture interprets the meaning of culture as a metaphor for the concept of organization itself. Pacanowsky and O'Donnell-Trujillo (1982, p. 126) for instance, remarked that: 'Organizational culture is not just another piece of the puzzle. From our point of view, a culture is not something an organization *has;* a culture is something an organization *is*' [authors' emphasis]. Gareth Morgan (1986), used the metaphor 'organizations as cultures' in a range of metaphors that present different images of organization. Morgan's definition of culture gives some sense of this:

> Shared meaning, shared understanding and shared sense making are all different ways of describing culture. In talking about culture we are really talking about a process of reality construction that allows people to see and understand particular events, actions, objects, utterances, or situations in distinctive ways. These patterns of understanding also provide a basis for making one's own behaviour sensible and meaningful.
>
> (p. 128)

Morgan maintains that, in doing this, members of organizations are creating the organization itself. In essence this means that organizations are *socially* constructed realities and that, rather than being defined by their structures, rules and regulations, they are constructed as much in the heads and minds of their members and are strongly related to members' self-concepts and identity. Taking this view of culture implies that, if understanding of an organization's culture is to be reached, it is necessary to look at the routine aspects of everyday life as well as at the more obvious and more public signs, symbols and ceremonies, which are more frequently associated with organizational leaders. It also implies a requirement to examine how culture is created and sustained. This means recognizing that culture is part of a much bigger historical pattern, and therefore that 'more often it is a *recurrence* rather than just an occurrence' (see Bate, 1996, p. 29). A model of organizational culture which brings together the idea of culture as congruent with everything that happens in an organization is the cultural web (Johnson, Scholes and Whittington, 2008) described in Illustration 4.3.

The cultural web

It can be seen from Illustration 4.3 that the cultural web is all-encompassing in the organizational elements that it includes. Johnson *et al*. (2008) draw attention to the influence of prevailing organizational paradigms (i.e. the beliefs and assumptions of the people making up the organization) in any attempt to bring about strategic change. They do not go as far as Morgan in equating culture fully with organization, but neither do they completely objectify culture as separate from other aspects of organizational life. In addition, the subtitle of Johnson's (1990) article, 'the role of symbolic action', illustrates the emphasis put upon the rituals or routines, stories or myths, and symbols elements of the cultural web in any attempt to bring about change resulting in a shift in the organizational paradigm.

Illustration 4.3

The cultural web

Johnson *et al.* (2008) explain the different elements of the cultural web as follows:

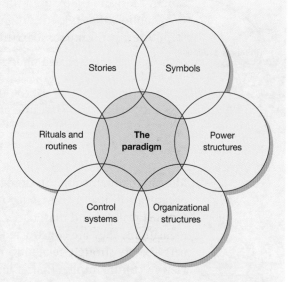

- The *routine* ways that members of the organization behave towards each other and that link different parts of the organization make up 'the way we do things around here', which at their best lubricate the working of the organization and may provide a distinctive and beneficial organizational competency. However, they can also represent a taken-for-granted approach to how things should happen that is extremely difficult to change and highly protective of core assumptions (and people) in the paradigm.
- The *rituals* of organizational life, such as training programmes, promotion and appraisal procedures, point to what is important in the organization and reinforce 'the way we do things around here'. They signal what is important and valued.
- The *stories* told by members of the organization to each other, to new recruits and to outsiders embed the history in the present and flag up important events and personalities, as well as mavericks who 'deviate from the norm'.
- The more *symbolic* aspects of organizations, such as logos, office furnishings, titles, status differentials and the type of language and terminology commonly used become a shorthand representation of the nature of the organization.
- The *control systems*, what gets measured and the reward systems emphasize what it is

important to monitor in the organization and to focus attention on.
- *Power structures*: the most powerful managerial groupings in the organization are likely to be the ones most associated with core assumptions and beliefs about what is important.
- The *formal organizational structure* or the more informal ways in which the organizations work are likely to reflect power structures and, again, to delineate important relationships and emphasize what is important in the organization.

Source: Based on Johnson, G., Scholes, K. and Whittington, R. (2008) *Exploring Corporate Strategy: Texts and Cases* (8th edn), Harlow: Pearson Education.

Illustration 4.4

A cultural web of Paper Unlimited, a large UK-based paper distributor

Stories
- Son of the founder (recently deceased) and his influence on the company policies and practices – a people-oriented company
- Frequent need to expand paper stacking space as example of continuing success

Symbols
- New building and warehouses
- Swimming pool and leisure facilities for employees and families
- IIP award
- Quality award
- Award for excellence in the use of IT

Paradigm
Dedicated to the philosophy laid down by the recently deceased original owner's son, who ran the company for over 40 years. This implies being:
- A people-oriented organization also dedicated to high task performance
- Provider of long-term employment
- Aware of success while also aware of the need continuously to analyze the environment to detect new markets
- Committed to incremental rather than radical changes

Rituals and routines
- Walk-about management – always available to employees
- Management can be interrupted
- Lots of talking
- Yearly employee/family outing

Power structures
- Long-serving managers and workforce
- Can 'work your way up'
- Positions based on expertise in the business rather than on qualifications
- Paternalistic style of management
- Emphasis on continuity
- Relaxed attitudes
- Cooperation at head office, competition between the branches where selling occurs

Controls
- IT controls most operations
- Error measurement
- Help given to improve

Organization structure
- Hierarchical at head office – bureaucracy with a human face
- Teamworking in the branches with team-based rewards
- Profit-related pay
- Responsibilities clearly defined

Activity 4.2 Creating a cultural web for your organization

Illustration 4.4 shows the cultural web for an organization involved in buying paper in bulk and then cutting and preparing it for sale to large-scale paper users.* Using this as a guide, construct a cultural web for an organization you know well.

If you wanted to initiate change at strategic level, what features of the web are barriers to change and how would you go about changing them?

*Additional examples of the use of the cultural web can be found in Johnson, Scholes and Whittington (2008, p. 200).

The cultural web has been applied mainly to organizational cultures. In contrast, Morgan's proposal that organizations *are* cultures discusses (among other things) differences in national cultures, including the way these have formed through historical processes. The notion of culture as a metaphor for organization also encompasses the concept of sub-cultures. This is reinforced by Alvesson (1993), who recommends combining perspectives at three levels. These are:

1 the organization as a culture (unitary and unique);
2 the organization as a meeting place for great cultures (which includes national ethnic and class cultures);
3 local perspectives on organizational sub-cultures.

A cultural compass

Hall (1995) offers a model that appears to accommodate descriptions of culture at the three levels put forward by Alvesson (1993). Hall's compass model of culture and its associated culture typologies have been developed through an apparent interest in cultural differences in 'partnerships', by which she means inter-company relationships typically in the form of alliances, mergers or acquisitions. Hall claims to have identified two components of behaviour. The first of these is *assertiveness*, which is the degree to which a company's behaviours are seen by others as being forceful or directive:

> Companies which behave in high assertive ways are seen to be decisive, quick and firm. There is little hesitation in their action. If they introduce a new product or enter a new market they do so with full force ... Low assertive companies behave in more slow and steady ways. They are careful to consider what they do before they take firm action. They introduce a new product or enter a new market step by step, keeping their options open. Unlike the one-track mind of the high assertive company, the low assertive company has a 'multi-track mind'.
>
> (Hall, 1995, p. 52)

The second behavioural component of culture is *responsiveness*, which is the degree to which a company's behaviours are seen by others as being emotionally expressed. Thus:

> Companies which behave in high responsive ways are seen to be employee friendly, relaxed or spontaneous. These companies give the impression that they compete on feelings more than on facts. In industry gatherings, high responsive companies tend to be very 'likeable'. They seem more open than other companies. Low responsive companies behave in more reserved or closed ways. They are not so much liked as 'respected'. They tend to be more rigid, their employees serious. Low responsive companies compete more on facts than on feelings.
>
> (Hall, 1995, pp. 54–55)

Illustration 4.5 lists behaviour that indicates high and low assertiveness and responsiveness. An example of a moderately assertive but more highly responsive organization is given in Illustration 4.6.

Illustration 4.5

Assertive and responsive behaviours

Behaviours that indicate high and (low) assertiveness are:

- individualistic
- demanding rather than obliging
- taking control
- pushy
- authoritative
- charging ahead
- challenging
- hardworking
- quick moving
- cautious and indecisive (low).

Behaviours that indicate high and (low) responsiveness are:

- sensitive
- loyal
- compromising
- trusting
- team players
- value harmony
- unpredictable
- (low) quantitative rather than qualitative
- (low) factual rather than emotional
- (low) precise rather than inexact
- (low) task rather than people oriented
- (low) consistent (methodological).

Source: Hall, W. (1995) *Managing Cultures: Making Strategic Relationships Work*, Chichester: Wiley, pp. 54–55.

Hall maintains that the four different combinations of the two behavioural components result in four different cultural styles. Figure 4.3 illustrates the compass model; so-called because each of the four styles is labelled as one of the four points of the compass.

Illustration 4.6

RS Components – moderately assertive but highly responsive

RS Components supplies, from a mail order catalogue, a range of components varying from capacitors, bearings, bushes and seals to cleaning agents, fastenings and power tools to trade organizations and the public. However, as one of the product buyers says: 'The company sells just one thing and that is service to the customer.'

Visiting the company, one is struck by the quiet efficiency with which orders are taken by around 100 staff, working in specially designed open-plan environments. Orders are taken at the rate of some 20,000 a day and a customer service standard of answering any telephone call within 5 seconds is maintained. In the order-taking areas overhead displays give continuous information on the number of orders taken that day, the number of customers waiting and the number of staff available and waiting to take calls.

Within 15 minutes of an order being taken it is received in the huge warehouse where product-collecting containers travel on rail-type tracks around the shelves holding the products to take the quickest route past 'pickers' who fill them to satisfy the order, before continuing to the packing and despatch areas. The company guarantees delivery the day after the order is taken or the same day if required. The complete operation, from a customer requesting a product to its despatch, is computer controlled. At any time, computer displays give up-to-the-second information about any part of the process.

RS Components is not, however, just a distributor of products that are required in a hurry. It also offers technical advice and support on the range of products it sells, thus increasing the probability of achieving nearly 100 per cent satisfied customers.

Through its large, on-the-road sales staff and other market intelligence-gathering activities, it is successful in keeping up with projected market demands. Yet it does not act hastily in offering a full service for the latest emerging products. If a new product appears to fit the company's selling policy, buyers will hold small stocks of the item until the demand can be more clearly gauged. If demand becomes more established the item will be stocked in quantities appropriate to meet customers' needs and the 'boast' to be able to supply the day after order.

Given the high level of computerization that also allows almost every employee to be monitored, it might be thought that care for employees comes some distance after attention to the task. However, care for employees is important. Every employee is identified by name, either by a name 'tag' attached to their computer (if one of the staff taking orders) or attached to their workstation (if in the 'pick and pack' warehouse). With a fairly large workforce, this enables everyone, whether known to each other or not, to address others by their name. The majority of staff work in teams that, although led by a team leader, are to a large extent self-managing.

Wages are slightly above the average for the type of work and pleasant restaurant facilities are available. The site the company occupies includes garden areas where staff can sit or walk in break times. A series of different start and finish times are available to suit the demands of the business, but these also provide flexible working hours to suit the different needs of different employees.

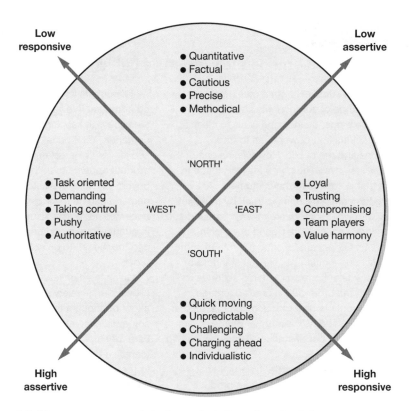

Figure 4.3 The compass model: characteristics of each style

Source: Reprinted by permission of John Wiley and Sons Ltd. Hall, W. (1995) *Managing Cultures: Making Strategic Relationships Work*, Chichester: Wiley, p. 58.

While the compass model is a useful schematic to help us understand cultural differences there are some reservations about its validity. Results were based on 211 responses from executives with experience of living and working in seven countries – in light of the complex nature of what is being analyzed this is a very small sample. The views were mainly those of executives who had, through their own work across national boundaries, experience of managers from the countries in the sample. In addition, the research sampled executives from two industries only – automobiles and high-technology. Given these reservations, Hall's typology attempts to link Alvesson's (1993) three levels of culture and it highlights one of the influences on organizational culture through its focus on differences between national cultures.

Competing values framework

Quinn and Rohrbaugh (1983) proposed a competing values model as a way of understanding variations in organizational effectiveness. The model represents a framework or cognitive map used by people when they describe organizations and it has since been adapted to interpret culture (Cameron and Quinn, 2005; Kwan and Walker, 2004; Howard, 1998; Igo and Skitmore, 2005).

The framework is a familiar 2 × 2 matrix built on two axes. The vertical axis represents flexibility and change versus stability and control. The horizontal axis represents an internal, person-centred focus versus an external, organization-centred focus. Each of the four quadrants represents one of four types or cultures as shown in Figure 4.4.

The human relations model embodies flexibility and a focus on people. Morale, cohesion, team spirit and training and development are valued with the end focus being on well-being and personal development. The open systems model embodies flexibility with an external focus. It is about being adaptable, looking for growth and acquiring resources, with the focus being more on the organization than the people in it. The rational system model embodies an external focus and control. Managers will emphasize planning, goals, target setting and monitoring in the pursuit of efficiency and productivity. The internal process model embodies a people focus with control. Information management and communication are valued in the pursuit of stability and control (Quinn and Rohrbaugh, 1983).

The two diagonals connect models that lie in stark contrast to each other, e.g. human relations and rational systems. The four models illustrate the ongoing conflicts, i.e. the competing values, of life in organizations. The competing

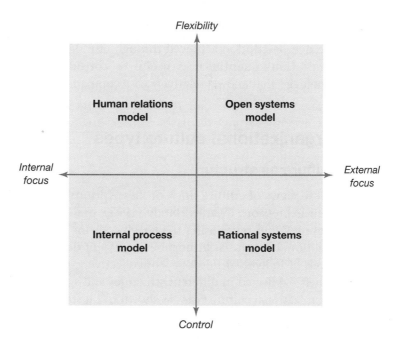

Figure 4.4 Competing values framework

Source: Adapted from Quinn, R.E. (1991) 'A Competing Values Framework for Analysing Presentational Communication in Management Contexts', *Journal of Business Communication*, 28(3), pp. 213–232.

values framework does not suggest that organizations fit into one of the four types nor does it suggest that one model is better than another. What it emphasizes is that these tensions coexist. Managers seek growth but there are forces for stability. They seek high productivity but also want high levels of cooperation between employees. Although any attempt to reduce the undeniable complexity and uniqueness of culture to models like this oversimplifies, they are useful in cutting through the fuzzy haze that is culture.

It is worth noting that the competing values framework did not come out of research with organizations, rather it came out of ordering and making sense of the criteria that organizational researchers use to evaluate them.

Activity 4.3 *Competing values?*

Thirty years have passed since the competing values framework was introduced. Perhaps management has changed since then. To what extent do you think that the four values are in competition? For instance, can organizations focus both on their employees and on the organization? Can we have flexible approaches to work with an overlay of managerial control and centralization?

So far we have seen some attempts to objectify and describe, even measure, culture. This is useful in helping us understand cultures even if they do not capture the rich description achieved through ethnographic studies in single organizations. Consequently, it is useful to consider other organizational culture typologies that allow a relatively easy comparison of one culture with another.

Organizational culture types

Culture as structure

These views of culture draw on descriptions of different structural forms for their expression. Charles Handy (1993), drawing on Harrison's (1972) studies, proposed four types using the Greek gods for inspiration. Handy refers to organizational culture as atmosphere, ways of doing things, levels of energy and levels of individual freedom – or collectively, the 'sets of values and norms and beliefs – reflected in different structures and systems' (p. 180). He suggested four organizational culture types as shown in Illustration 4.7.

Illustration 4.7

A structural view of organizational culture

The power culture

Power cultures are those in which a single person or group dominates. Handy refers to this culture as a web in the sense that a spider in the middle of its web senses and is connected to all movement elsewhere in the web. Decision making is centralized. This type of culture is seen as, essentially, political in that decisions are taken on the basis of influence rather than through a logical rational process. Power is held by the centre by virtue of personal charisma or the control of resources. Family businesses, small entrepreneurial companies and occasionally trade unions are likely to have this type of culture. The strength of the culture depends on the strength of the centre and the willingness of other organizational members to defer to this power source. Handy likens this culture to the Greek god Zeus who ruled by whim and impulse, by thunderbolt and shower of gold from Mount Olympus.

The role culture

Handy likens role cultures to a *Greek temple*. The patron god here is Apollo, the god of reason, the argument being that role cultures work by logic and rationality. The pillars of the temple are strong in their own right and activity is controlled more by rules and regulations than by personal directive from the top. The pediment of the temple is seen as coordinating activity rather than overtly controlling it. Emphasis is on defined roles and occupants are expected to fulfil these roles but not overstep them. Role cultures flourish in stable situations and are the least conducive to change.

The task culture

The task culture is represented by a *net*. The dominant concept in a task culture is project work associated with matrix-type structures. Handy pushes the Greek mythology association somewhat here in suggesting Athena, whose emphasis was on getting the job done. The task culture, therefore, is not particularly concerned with personal power or hierarchy, but with marshalling the required resources to complete work efficiently and effectively. People are connected via networks. Decision making is devolved to the project groups to enhance flexibility of working method and speed the outcomes. The task culture is said to flourish where creativity and innovation are needed particularly in organizations concerned with research and development, marketing, advertising and new ventures.

The person culture

According to Handy, this culture is unusual as it exists only to service the needs of the participating members. It does not have an overarching objective such as is found in more conventionally structured organizations. Examples of person cultures are barristers' chambers, doctors' centres, hippy communes and small consultancy firms. Person cultures have minimal structures and can be likened to a cluster or galaxy of individual stars. Handy proposes Dionysus as its patron deity – the god of the self-oriented individual.

Source: Based on Handy, C. (1993) *Understanding Organizations*, London: Penguin, pp. 183–191.

Pheysey (1993) builds on Handy's typology to propose a categorization of role, power, support and achievement cultures. The definitions of role and power cultures are those used by Handy, with support and achievement cultures having similar characteristics to Handy's task and person cultures. However Pheysey goes beyond Handy in linking her four types of culture not only to organizational structure (i.e. the design of organizations) but also to control systems, employee motivation, leadership styles and organization development.

Activity 4.4

Consider your own organization in terms of Handy's four cultural types. Which description best matches the culture as you see it?

Culture, strategy and environment

Activity 4.4 asks you to think about the internal environment of an organization. By contrast, Deal and Kennedy's (1982) proposed four generic cultures – the tough-guy, macho culture, the work-hard/play-hard culture, the bet-your-company culture and the process culture – link more closely to the external environment (the marketplace) of the organization (see Illustration 4.8).

Illustration 4.8

Deal and Kennedy's typology

The tough-guy, macho culture
People in these organizations regularly take high risks and receive rapid feedback on what they do. Examples cited are police departments, publishing, sports and entertainment. In tough-guy, macho cultures the stakes are high and there is a focus on speed rather than endurance. Staff tend to be young and financial rewards come early, but failure is punished harshly. Burnout, internal competition and conflict are normal. This means tantrums are tolerated and people try to score points off each other. However, while tough-guy cultures can be highly successful in high-risk, quick-return environments they are less suited to making long-term investments. Being unable to benefit from

cooperative activity, these organizations tend to have a high turnover of staff and thus often fail to develop a strong and cohesive culture.

The work-hard/play-hard culture
This culture exists where there is low risk but quick feedback on actions such as sales organizations that incorporate hard work and fun. Persistence, keeping at it and working to recognized procedures are typical of work-hard/play-hard cultures. The risks are small because an individual sale is unlikely to severely damage the salesperson. In addition production systems are built to withstand temporary hitches. However, being selling oriented, all employees gain quick feedback on their

performance. Heroes in these organizations are the super salespeople who turn in volume sales. Contests, conventions and other means of encouraging intense selling are used. Yet the culture emphasizes the team because it is the team that makes the difference, not the achievements of single individuals. However, although work/play cultures can achieve sales volumes, this can be at the expense of quality – they frequently forget that success may be 'one shot' only.

Bet-your-company culture

These cultures are typical of organizations where the risks are high and the feedback on actions and decisions takes a long time. Bet-your-company organizations are those that invest heavily in projects which take years to come to fruition. Examples include aircraft manufacturers and oil companies. In contrast to tough-guy cultures, people in bet-your-company cultures bet the company rather than themselves. Consequently there is a sense of deliberateness that manifests itself in ritualized business meetings. All decisions are carefully thought through. Decision making tends to be top down, reflecting the hierarchical nature of the organization. The survivors in these organizations respect authority and technical competence and have the stamina to endure long-term ambiguity with limited feedback. They will act cooperatively, and have proved themselves over a number of years – immaturity is not tolerated in this culture. Bet-your-company cultures lead to high-quality inventions and major scientific breakthroughs, but their slow

response times make them vulnerable to short-term economic fluctuations in the economy. However, these companies may be those that the economy most needs.

The process culture

This culture is typical of organizations where there is low risk and slow feedback on actions and decisions. Examples (at the time of the research 30 years ago) were banks, insurance companies, public and government organizations and heavily regulated industries. (Banks, as we have discovered to our cost, were deregulated). Working with little feedback, employees have no sense of their own effectiveness or otherwise.

Consequently they tend to concentrate on the means by which things are done rather than what should be done. Values tend to focus on technical perfection, working out the risks and getting the process right. Protecting one's back is what most employees do, so the people who prosper are those who are orderly and punctual and who attend to detail. The ability to weather political storms and changes becomes a desirable trait. In process cultures there is considerable emphasis on job titles and status and the signs that symbolize them, such as style of office furniture. Position power is desired. Staying with the organization is revered by the institution through long-service awards. Process cultures are effective when dealing with a stable and predictable environment, but find it difficult to react quickly to changing circumstances.

Deal and Kennedy's typology dates from the early 1980s. While the cultural types may still be relevant, it is questionable in light of political and regulatory changes whether the examples of each type given are still valid. Deal and Kennedy (2000, p. 169) agreed that previous assumptions needed revising. For instance, banks (as examples of process cultures) have evolved more into sales-type organizations but do not, perhaps, yet fit the work-hard/play-hard culture suggested for sales-oriented companies. Figure 4.5 shows Trompenaars and Prud'homme's (2004, p. 67) depiction of these four types with more up-to-date examples of each culture. Even this recent update raises questions about the placement of banks in the process culture category. Given their more recent behaviour, a 'bet your company' category would seem more fitting.

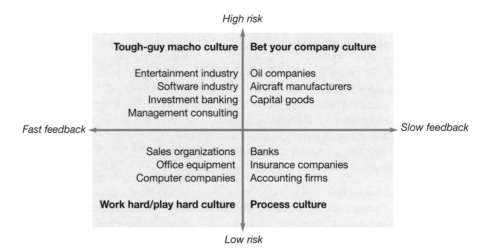

Figure 4.5 Deal and Kennedy model for corporate culture

Source: Reprinted by permission of John Wiley & Sons Ltd on behalf of Capstone Publishing Ltd. Trompenaars, F. and Prud'homme, P. (2004) *Managing Change Across Corporate Cultures*, Chichester: Capstone Publishing.

In contrast to previous emphases on links between culture and, either the internal, or the external environment, Scholtz (1987) brought these together, using three dimensions. The external-induced dimension of organizational culture draws on the work of Deal and Kennedy's four culture types. The internal-induced dimension identifies three culture types (production, bureaucratic and professional) that derive from organizational structure characteristics. The evolution-induced dimension goes beyond earlier models in its relationship to the strategic orientation of the organization and its environment. From these, five culture types are identified:

1 *Stable,* with a time orientation towards the past and an aversion to risk.
2 *Reactive,* with a time orientation towards the present and an acceptance of 'minimum' risk.
3 *Anticipating,* also oriented towards the present but more accepting of 'familiar' risks.
4 *Exploring,* with a time orientation towards the present and the future and an acceptance of increasing risk.
5 *Creative,* looking forward to the future and accepting risk as normal.

Thus far we have seen how culture is expressed and have noted the influences of dominant personalities, professional norms and market economics, among others, on shaping organizational culture. Organizational history also plays a part. Another important overlay comes from national cultural differences.

The influence of national culture

The literature on cultural similarities and differences between nations identifies a long-standing debate known as the convergence–divergence debate. In summary, those who support the convergence view argue that the forces of industrialization as well as increasing size will push organizations, whatever their location, towards particular configurations with respect to strategy, structure and management. In addition, the growth of international organizations increases the need for 'international managers' who bring common management practices to all parts of their organizations wherever they are in the world. In support of this view, Ohmae (1991) puts forward the concept of the 'global organization', which has no national allegiance, only an international common purpose. Furthermore, Ohmae argues for 'getting rid of the headquarters mentality', implying the possibility that an organization's national cultural base will have no influence on the culture of the organization itself. Illustration 4.9 shows how Ford attempted to eliminate the regional fiefdoms built up over a long period of time. Ohmae speaks of the markets valuing a global approach to business – 'an approach in which a company's units, divisions, teams, functions, and regions are all tightly integrated and synchronized across borders' (p. 78).

Opposing this view is the notion that differences in language, religion, social organization, laws, politics, education systems, and values and attitudes (Hofstede, 1980; Tayeb, 1989; Wilson, 1992) will, of necessity, mean that national cultures will not converge but continue to remain distinct.

Illustration 4.9

Driving change at Ford

In an interview for the *Harvard Business Review* (1999) Jacques Nasser, Chief Executive Officer of Ford Motor Company, spoke of his attempt to bring about radical change in the company 'mind-set' of everyone working there. According to the interview account, Nasser asked his employees in 200 countries 'to think and act as if they own the company'. 'To adopt, in other words, the capital markets' view of Ford – to look at the company in its entirety, as shareholders do.' Nasser says that this is 'a radically different mentality for Ford'. This mentality (or culture as it might be termed in the context of this discussion) is very different from the one that has, apparently, prevailed for much of the time since the company was formed over 100 years

ago – one Nasser describes as: 'A collection of fiercely independent fiefdoms united under the flag of their functional or regional expertise'. Each division in this 'collection' appears to have its own organizational sub-culture for which, as Nasser comments, there were 'legitimate historical reasons'.

Elaborating on this he says: 'Think about Ford's history in three chunks: from its founding in 1905 to the early 1920s, the late 1920s through to the 1950s, and the 1960s through the 1980s.' The first period was one of 'colonization' and the opening of assembly plants (which were smaller versions of the original company in Detroit) in other countries, but with very little competition from other automotive companies. The second period was one of 'intense

Illustration 4.9 *continued*

nationalism' with large automotive companies growing up in the United Kingdom, France, Germany, Australia, all making their own vehicles and exporting them to others – but in their own regions. The third period saw the rise of regionalism and the emergence of the European Union and the North American Free Trade Association (NAFTA). It was this period that saw the entrenchment of the regional and functional fiefdoms.

Nasser comments that, given the prevailing environment at that time, this arrangement worked very well: squeezing 'every last ounce of efficiency out of the regional model'. However, he goes on to say that this model does not work any more in the current environment of increasing globalization of capital, communications, economic policy, trade policy, human resources, marketing, advertising, brands – and so on. Consequently there is a perceived need to 'reinvent' Ford as a global organization with a single focus on consumers and shareholder value.

Nasser talks of striving for some kind of DNA that drives how Ford does things everywhere. This includes a global mind-set, an intuitive knowledge of customers and a strong belief in leaders as

teachers. However, this does not mean that the same products are produced and sold everywhere. What it does mean is that, although Ford cars have many common systems that bring scale efficiencies, they can also be tailored to individual local markets. What is more, although Ford would like to see common reward systems for staff wherever they work, Nasser recognizes that different cultures have different attitudes to pay and rewards, for instance about the balance between fixed and variable rewards. What is also clear is that different tax laws require different attitudes to employment, stock purchase and so on.

Having said all this, it is clear that Nasser was looking for a significant cultural shift. The article describes, in some detail, the approach taken to help this to happen – an approach based on a multi-faceted teaching initiative, led by senior and middle managers and aimed, eventually, at all Ford employees wherever they are located. Nasser said: 'The Ford you see today has no resemblance to the Ford of five years ago. If you dissected us and inspected every blood vessel, we're different; our DNA has changed. I don't think we'll go back.'

Source: Based on Nasser, J. and Wetlaufer, S. (1999) 'Driving Change: an interview with Ford Motor Company's Jacques Nasser', *Harvard Business Review*, March–April, pp. 76–88.

The diversity of national cultures

Illustration 4.10 summarizes a frequently referenced framework by Kluckhohn and Strodtbeck (1961), who claim that the cultural orientation of societies can be described using six basic dimensions.

Illustration 4.10

Six different cultural orientations of societies

1 *People's qualities as individuals in terms of whether people are seen as basically good or basically bad*. Societies that consider people good tend to trust people, while those that consider people bad tend to start from a premise of mistrust and suspicion.

2 *People's relationship to their world*. Some societies believe they can dominate their environment while others believe the environment and themselves to be inseparable and, therefore, that they must live in harmony with it.

3 *People's personal relationships in terms of individualism or collectivism*. Some societies encourage individualism and the notion of being self-supporting with achievement being based on individual worth, while others are more group-oriented, where people define themselves as members of clans or communities (which might be the work organization) and consider the group's welfare to be more important than the individual.

4 *An orientation to either doing or being*. Societies that are doing- and action-oriented stress accomplishments which are measurable by standards believed to be external to the individual; societies oriented to being are more passive, believing that work should be enjoyed and they should live more for the moment.

5 *People's orientation to time*. Some societies are past-oriented, believing that current plans and actions should fit with the customs and traditions of the past, while future-oriented societies justify innovation and change in terms of future pay-offs, believing radical change to be desirable as well as acceptable.

6 *People's use of space*. Societies differ on such matters as offices in relation to status, the designation of public space compared to private space, the separation of managers from subordinates.

Both Adler (1997) and Robbins (1996) draw on Kluckhohn and Strodtbeck's framework in their discussions of societal and national cultures. Regarding the good–evil dimension or trust–mistrust dimension, the way one group of people regards another will differ according to whether they set off with the assumption that people are trustworthy or that all people will cheat if given the opportunity. This translates, for instance, into whether information is freely available, the extent of surveillance and how one group's actions are interpreted by another. Adler contrasts the North Americans and Chinese with the Navaho in terms of the former's belief that they can dominate nature and the latter's belief that they must live in harmony with nature.

Adler describes the strong individualistic tendencies of Americans as evidenced in their language, such as 'trounced the opposition', and their recruitment and promotion practices based on criteria relating to individual knowledge and skills. This contrasts with more group-oriented societies such as Japan, China, Indonesia and Malaysia that put more stress on assignments, responsibilities and reporting relationships in collective terms. People in these societies are more likely to gain employment through personal contacts who can vouch for their trustworthiness and ability to work with others. Favouring family friends when making appointments or making decisions is not seen as unusual as it would be in more individualistic societies.

Adler points out that different time orientations impact significantly on attitudes to timekeeping and punctuality. Different time orientations influence the length of time someone might be given to show their worth in a job; the focus on short-term or long-term results. Finally, Adler uses the examples of North

Americans and Japanese to contrast different attitudes to the use of space. The former prefer closed offices and meetings behind closed doors while the latter prefer open-plan working areas that include managers as well as subordinates. Other interesting differences can be seen in how close one desk is to another and whether an office can be entered without ceremony or whether people must wait outside for permission to enter.

Figure 4.6 is based on Robbins's summary of the Kluckhohn–Strodtbeck framework showing a profile for the US. Influential research by Geert Hofstede (1980, 1981, 1993, 1994a) and Hofstede, Neuijen, Ohayv and Sanders (1990) supports the concept of geographically identifiable, culturally differentiated regions based on national boundaries. Hofstede's initial research was carried out in IBM and involved the analysis of questionnaires from some 116,000 employees in 50 different countries. This analysis resulted in the identification of four dimensions which were used to differentiate national cultural groups. A fifth dimension based on Confucian philosophy (which Hofstede categorized as virtue versus truth or, more simply, long-term versus short-term orientation) was added later (Chinese Culture Connection, 1987). See Illustration 4.11.

Dimensions	Variations		
Nature of people	Good	Mixed	Bad
Relationship to the environment	Domination	Harmony	Subjugation
Focus of responsibility	Individualistic	Group	Hierarchical
Activity orientation	Being	Controlling	Doing
Time orientation	Past	Present	Future
Conception of space	Private	Mixed	Public

Figure 4.6 Variations in Kluckhohn and Strodtbeck's cultural dimensions

Source: Based on Robbins, S.P. (1996) *Organizational Behavior: Concepts, Controversies, Applications*, Englewood Cliffs, NJ: Prentice Hall, p. 56.

Illustration 4.11

Hofstede's dimensions of national culture

Power distance

Power distance refers to how a society deals with the fact that people are unequal, for instance in physical and intellectual abilities. Some societies let these inequalities grow over time into inequalities in power and wealth whereas others try to play down inequalities. In high power distance societies, inequalities of power and wealth are accepted not only by the leaders but also by those at the bottom of the power hierarchy, with corresponding large differences in status and salaries. In low power distance societies, inequalities among people will tend to be minimized, with subordinates expecting to be consulted by superiors over decisions that affect them, and to be treated more as equals of those with the power. Status differentials vary according to power distance.

Individualism/collectivism

Individualism/collectivism refers to relationships between an individual and their fellow individuals. In an individualistic society, the ties between individuals are very loose. Everybody is expected to look after self-interest and perhaps that of their immediate family. Individuals in these societies have high freedom of action. In collectivist societies the ties between individuals are very tight. The concept of the extended family is important and can reach out to work groups and organizations. Everybody is supposed to look after the interests of their in-group, which will protect them when they are in trouble.

Masculinity/femininity

Masculinity/femininity refers to the degree to which social gender roles are clearly distinct. In high-masculinity societies, the social division between the sexes is maximized, with traditional masculine social values permeating the society. These values include the importance of showing off, of making money and of 'big is beautiful'. In more feminine societies, the dominant values – for both men and women – are those more traditionally associated with the feminine role of nurturing and caring, putting relationships before money, minding the quality of life and 'small is beautiful'.

Uncertainty avoidance

Uncertaintly avoidance refers to how a society deals with the fact that time runs only one way – from the past to the future – and that the future is unknown and, therefore, uncertain. Some societies are more comfortable with uncertainty than others. Uncertainty avoidance manifests, for example, in the creation of rules, systems and procedures to cope with events. People in low uncertainty avoidance societies tend to accept each day as it comes and are comfortable with a higher degree of risk taking. Societies demonstrating strong uncertainty avoidance characteristics socialize their people into trying to beat the future. Precision and punctuality are important in a context of fear of ambiguous situations and unfamiliar risks.

Long-term/short-term orientation

This dimension is about virtue versus truth. Societies with a long-term orientation look to the past and present for their value systems. People living in these societies have a respect for traditions and fulfilling social obligations. It is important that they 'save face'. They do not believe in absolute truths. Societies with a short-term orientation look towards the future, cultivating habits of thrift and perseverance. People living in these societies value analytical thinking and the search for truths.

Based on information given by Hofstede (1993) and elaborated by Burnes (2004, p. 175), Table 4.1 illustrates how several countries vary on these dimensions.

Table 4.1 Culture dimension scores for ten countries

Country	Power distance	Individualism*	Masculine**	Uncertainty avoidance	Long-term orientation***
China	High	Low	Moderate	Moderate	High
France	High	High	Moderate	High	Low
Germany	Low	High	High	Moderate	Moderate
Hong Kong	High	Low	High	Low	High
Indonesia	High	Low	Moderate	Low	Low
Japan	Moderate	Moderate	High	High	High
Netherlands	Low	High	Low	Moderate	Moderate
Russia	High	Moderate	Low	Low	Low
United States	Low	High	High	Low	Low
West Africa	High	Low	Moderate	Moderate	Low

* A low score implies collectivism. ** A low score implies feminine. *** A low score implies short-term orientation.

Source: Adapted with permission from Hofstede, G. (1993) 'Cultural Constraints in Management Theories', *Academy of Management Executive*, February, p. 91. Copyright © Geert Hofstede.

Figure 4.7 illustrates four possible organizational models that, according to Hofstede (1991), refer to empirically derived relationships between a country's position on the power distance/uncertainty avoidance matrix and models of organizations implicit in the minds of people from the countries concerned. Hofstede uses the metaphors of a village market, a well-oiled machine, a pyramid and a family to describe different approaches to organizing. Thus, people from countries with a 'village market' culture do not have the same need for hierarchy and certainty as those from a pyramid type culture. These contrast with people from cultures reminiscent of 'well-oiled machines' – such as Germany – where hierarchy is not particularly required because there are established procedures and rules to which everyone works. People who live in countries located in the 'family' quadrant – such as India, West Africa and Malaysia – are said to have an implicit model of organization that resembles a family in which the owner–manager is the omnipotent (father) figure.

It is clear that if, as Hofstede maintains, these differences between cultural groupings exist and any convergence across them will be very slow, then there is a good chance that they will influence organizational cultures in correspondingly different ways. It should not be forgotten, however, that Hofstede's research was carried out some time ago and mainly within a single multinational organization. The clustering of countries into the four models depicted in Figure 4.7 is a gross simplification of the complexity of distinguishing one country's culture from another, let alone differences within countries.

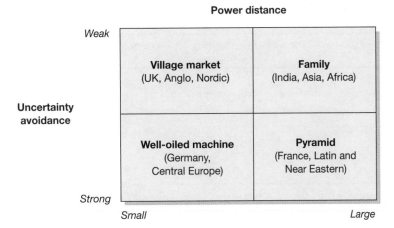

Figure 4.7 Implicit models of organization

Source: Adapted with permission from Hofstede, G. (1991) *Cultures and Organizations*, Maidenhead: McGraw-Hill. Copyright © Geert Hofstede.

However, while there are arguments against attempts to quantify and compare things as complex as national cultures other research on this topic has supported Hofstede's basic propositions. Laurent (1983), for instance, focused on the views of upper- and middle-level managers in a large number of different organizations, spread across nine European countries and the US. Laurent's hypothesis was that the national origin of managers significantly affects their views of what proper management should be. The focus was, perhaps, slightly narrower than that of Hofstede, but had the advantage of sampling across several different organizations.

From his survey of 817 managers across ten countries, Laurent identified four dimensions, which he labelled – organizations as political systems, organizations as authority systems, organizations as role-formalization systems and organizations as hierarchical-relationship systems. Table 4.2 summarizes the relative position of the ten countries on each of Laurent's dimensions. The results show France and Italy at the high end of the scores for all dimensions – meaning that they were politicized, hierarchical, had high degrees of role formalization and believed in the authority of individuals. Denmark and the UK are positioned similarly to each other with low levels of hierarchy and politicization, moderate degrees of belief in individual authority and high levels of role formalization. Sweden had the lowest score in terms of hierarchical relationships with moderate scores on the other three dimensions. Other similarities and differences can be seen from the table.

Table 4.2 Summary of Laurent's findings

Dimension	Denmark	UK	The Netherlands	Germany	Sweden	US	Switzerland	France	Italy	Belgium
Organizations as:										
Political systems	26	32	36	36	42	43	51	62	66	missing
Authority systems	46	48	49	34	46	30	32	65	61	61
Role-formalization systems	80	80	67	85	57	66	85	81	84	81
Hierarchical-relationship systems	37	36	33	47	25	28	43	50	66	50

Source: Summarized from Laurent, A. (1983) 'The Cultural Diversity of Western Conceptions of Management', *International Studies of Management and Organisation*, XIII (1–2), pp. 75–96.

The GLOBE framework

The GLOBE (Global Leadership and Organization Behaviour Effectiveness) study attempted to extend Hofstede's earlier work (House *et al.*, 2004), again using very large samples spanning 62 countries but taken from a much wider range of organizations and sectors. GLOBE tried to understand how cultural values connected to organizational behaviour.

The study found nine dimensions as shown in Table 4.3. These show similarities to Hofstede's typology with the main differences, at least linguistically, being the addition of dimensions relating to concern for performance and concern for gender equality. Hofstede (2006) argues that after allowing for 'data reduction' the nine dimensions are a strong reflection of his earlier work and thus further validation of it.

Table 4.3 Dimensions of national culture from the GLOBE study

GLOBE Dimension	Summary	Code
Achievement, performance orientation	Focus on performance improvement and rewarding it	ACH
Future orientation	Focus on short-term or long-term results	FUT
Assertiveness	Focus on dominating others	ASS
Collectivism	Use of groups in society and organizations	COLL1
Gender egalitarianism	Concern for gender equality	GEN
Humane orientation	Desire and concern for fairness & tolerance	HUM
Power distance	The extent to which power is unequally distributed	POW
Family collectivism	The integration of people into the family	COLL2
Uncertainty avoidance	Focus on alleviating unpredictable outcomes, trying to minimise uncertainty	UNC

Source: Adapted from Koopman *et al.* (1999) 'National Culture and Leadership Profiles in Europe: some results from the GLOBE study', *European Journal of Work and Organizational Psychology*, 8(4), pp. 503–520.

Table 4.4 Selected country ranks from the GLOBE study

	ACH	FUT	ASS	COLL1	GEN	HUM	POW	COLL2	UNC
Switzerland	1	2	36	37	53	53	46	56	1
Sweden	48	9	1	1	9	30	50	59	2
England	34	11	32	30	14	48	36	53	13
Italy	55	56	28	56	37	51	20	41	42
Hungary	58	58	54	60	3	58	12	37	60

Source: Adapted from Koopman *et al.* (1999) 'National Culture and Leadership Profiles in Europe: some results from the GLOBE study', *European Journal of Work and Organizational Psychology*, 8(4), pp. 503–520.

In a paper summarizing differences among European countries, Koopman *et al.* (1999) ranked the 62 countries on each dimension and an extract is shown in Table 4.4.

Based on these rankings GLOBE data suggest the following for the countries shown (partly tongue in cheek). The Swiss are exercised by achievement, future planning and minimizing uncertainty. The Swedes are exercised by assertiveness and group collectivism. The English seem relatively average although they are relatively short termist in their outlook. The Italians seem relaxed about most things but do like a bit of power distance. Hungarians seem most of all to be concerned with gender equality. Koopman *et al.* (1999) concluded that European countries do fit in 'culture clusters' and cautioned against the idea of a European culture. Culture clusters were explained by differences in language roots (e.g. Germanic versus Latin), geographic proximity, post-war Soviet expansion, religion (e.g., Protestant versus Catholic) and political/economic systems, amongst other things.

Some of the cultural dimensions found in studies of this type correlate with national prosperity (or poverty) which poses an important question of whether some dimensions are proxies for levels of economic development rather than true cultural differences.

In contrast to the 'culture as numbers' approach, Illustration 4.12 describes Danish managers and how to do business with them.

Illustration 4.12

On a wavelength with the Danes

At first sight, doing business in Denmark may seem straightforward. The country is prosperous and integrated into the European Union. Its people communicate in a friendly and direct way. Negotiators tend to be to the point, relaxed and informal. And the whole process is accompanied with a sense of humour. But do not fall into the trap of thinking you need only be yourself.

Throughout Scandinavia, communication is characterised by calmness and understatement.

This applies to Danes, too, although they are known for being more temperamental than Swedes and Norwegians and are sometimes described as the 'Italians of the north'.

That does not make Copenhagen the same as Rome. Extrovert rhetoric and exaggeration are poorly regarded in Denmark. The body language of Danes underlines this – especially on a first meeting. To touch someone's arm or to pat someone on the back while shaking hands is not appropriate when dealing

Illustration 4.12 *continued*

with a Danish business partner. You should also keep enough distance from your counterpart for him or her to feel comfortable.

Danes tend to be open-minded when they deal with foreign business partners. A formal introduction from an international bank or sales representative, for example, is not absolutely necessary. Most Danish people speak and read English fluently.

At the start of the negotiations, your Danish counterpart will tend to understate his or her own achievements, much as the English would. It is good to be punctual and to structure the agenda. To display the sort of self-confidence that would strike extrovert cultures as quite normal would be inappropriate in Denmark.

One general principle of communication applies throughout Scandinavia: less is more. It is in your interest to provide a realistic initial offer with enough room for concessions. You should also avoid giving the impression that you think you are more successful than other people.

It is unwise to 'oversell' yourself and to reveal everything about yourself and your company. Instead, try to let your Danish business partner seek out the relevant information about a potential match with your company, your products and services. The same applies for presentations: a properly documented presentation aligned with a consistent argument goes down better than a hard sell.

Your Danish counterparts will be open, polite, flexible and ready to provide you with insights into their point of view. In brainstorming sessions they will be prepared to think up imaginative solutions and to evaluate them with you afterwards. In all this you should deploy humour, especially of the understated English variety.

However, you should be cautious in some respects. Danes do not start negotiations as quickly as, for example, Americans. They consider it rude for anyone to be interrupted in mid-sentence, especially if it is not to clarify something that has just been said. Be patient with the decision-making process: Danish executives do not like to be rushed.

The notion of 'fair play' counts for a lot in Denmark. It is reflected in social welfare and culture. Thus, your partner will usually try to find win–win solutions where both parties will receive a fair amount of profit – though Danes can drive a hard bargain.

The concern for fair play can be seen in Danish management culture: managers do not place much emphasis on hierarchy. Women have done well in Denmark too as there is a high percentage of women in business.

Most Danes are friendly, generous hosts. Entertaining is done at lunch or dinner, mostly in restaurants. An invitation to someone's home is a great honour. Wherever you are dining, you should arrive on time. Evening meals take place early but, unlike many east Asian business people, your Danish counterpart will expect you to stay and chat at the hotel bar.

Source: from 'On a Wavelength with the Danes', *Financial Times*, 23 October 2005, 15 (Frank, S.), reprinted with permission of Sergey Frank, International Management Consultant

Activity 4.5

Compare and contrast the account in Illustration 4.12 with Laurent's findings with respect to the orientations of Danish managers in Table 4.2. Hofstede's results, in Table 4.1, show Danish workers as having low power distance, low uncertainty avoidance, high feminine values, and moderately high individualist characteristics and British managers as having low power distance, low uncertainty avoidance, high masculine values and very high individualism characteristics. Does this accord with what is said about Danish managers and implied about British managers in the account in Illustration 4.13?

Hofstede's and Laurent's approaches exemplify the way large questionnaire surveys can be used to demonstrate national cultural similarities and differences. Their methods of course can be criticized in terms of their attempts to 'objectivize' culture compared to more qualitative methods. This criticism can, however, be balanced by other studies (e.g. Maurice, Sorge and Warner, 1980; d'Iribarne, 1989) that have found differences between national cultures, but which were based on in-depth, comprehensive examinations of similar organizations in a limited number of countries.

A third method was employed by Calori and De Woot (1994) who used non-directive interviews with 51 human resource directors in 40 large international companies with headquarters or major operating units in Europe. They claim to have found country clusters that suggest a typology of management systems (see Figure 4.8). Illustration 4.13 summarizes their conclusions on the characteristics typical of the first two levels of segmentation, that is the Anglo-Saxon, Latin and Northern European (using the German model as an example) groupings.

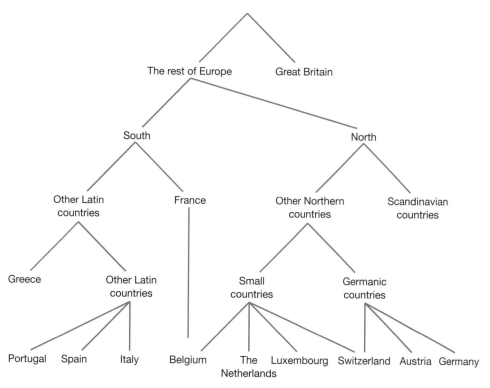

Figure 4.8 Typology of management systems in Europe

Source: Calori, R. and De Woot, P. (1994) *A European Management Model Beyond Diversity*, Hemel Hempstead: Prentice Hall, p. 20.

Illustration 4.13

Differences between the United Kingdom, Southern Europe and Northern Europe

The United Kingdom, an exception in Europe

Management in the United Kingdom has more in common with the United States than the rest of Europe. It has:

- a short-term orientation (more than continental Europe);
- a shareholder orientation (whereas the rest of Europe has more of a stakeholder orientation);
- an orientation towards trading and finance (the importance of the stock market was more developed than in continental Europe);
- a higher turnover of managers;
- a greater liberalism towards foreigners (e.g. the Japanese);
- more freedom for top management vis-à-vis the workers and government;
- more direct and pragmatic relationships between people;
- more variable remuneration.

However, different from the United States, it additionally has:

- adversarial relationships with labour*;
- the tradition of the manager as a 'gifted amateur' (as opposed to the professionalism of US managers);
- the influence of class differences in the firm.

The Latin way of doing business

Southern Europe (including France) differs from the rest of Europe in that it has:

- more state intervention;
- more protectionism;
- more hierarchy in the firm;
- more intuitive management;
- more family business (especially in Italy);
- more reliance on an elite (especially in France).

The German model

Characteristic of Germany, Austria and, to some extent, Switzerland and the Benelux countries, the German model is based on three cultural and structural characteristics:

- strong links between banks and industry;
- a balance between a sense of national collectivity and the *Länder* (regional) system;
- a system of training and development of managers.

It has the following five components:

- the system of co-determination with workers' representatives present on the board;
- the loyalty of managers (and employees in general) who spend their career in a single firm, which then gives priority to in-house training;
- the collective orientation of the workforce, which includes dedication to the company, team spirit and a sense of discipline;
- the long-term orientation that appears in planning, in the seriousness and stability of supplier–client relationships and in the priority of industrial goals over short-term financial objectives;
- the reliability and stability of shareholders, influenced by a strong involvement of banks in industry.

*Since the late 1980s employee relations in the UK have been generally good and this description probably reflects the high levels of unrest seen in the 1970s and early 1980s.

Source: Based on Calori, R. and De Woot, P. (1994) *A European Management Model Beyond Diversity*, Hemel Hempstead: Prentice Hall, pp. 22–29.

Activity 4.6

Compare and contrast Calori and De Woot's country groupings and characteristics with the same countries' positions on Laurent's cultural dimensions and the models presented in Figure 4.7. To what extent do any of these characterizations agree with your own experience, either through business or tourism?

World Values Survey

In addition to Hofstede and GLOBE, the World Values Survey is another attempt to understand national cultures and how they are changing. Inglehart and Baker (2000) offer some revealing finding about the convergence-divergence debate from their longitudinal analysis of 65 societies. They found evidence for both 'massive cultural change and the persistence of distinctive cultural traditions' (p. 19). They found that economic development promotes a shift away from traditional values to less religious values such that if economic development continues then institutionalized religious systems will decline. (Consider the fall in religious observance in Protestant industrialized Europe.)

Societies that enter a post-industrialist era see a departure from absolute norms. However, the historic cultural roots, e.g. Protestantism, Islam or Confucianism persist in shaping societies. So, rather than converge, societies are changing but moving in parallel 'shaped by their cultural heritage' (p. 49). Inglehart and Baker also caution against seeing cultural change as 'Americanization'. As antidote to this they found that the Nordic countries (Denmark, Finland, Norway, Sweden) best illustrate the culture that others are moving towards.

National culture and organizational culture

Activity 4.6 shows how difficult it is to fit national culture into categories yet it would be hard to argue that these differences do not exist. In addition, the evidence points to close relationships between national culture and organizational culture. For instance, Furnham and Gunter (1993) provide examples of organizations in Australia, Israel and Denmark (low scores on Hofstede's power distance dimension) having common organizational structures. Their structures incorporated low centralization of decision making and flatter pyramids of control, reminiscent of Handy's task organizational culture. These structures contrasted with those in countries such as the Philippines, Mexico and India, which scored highly on Hofstede's power distance dimension. Here, organizations were typified by strict hierarchical structures and centralized decision making, reminiscent of Handy's role culture.

National cultures overlay principles, practices and assumptions that affect management practices such as selection, development and reward and as such influence interpersonal relationships and individual performance. Indeed, one of the GLOBE dimensions relates to performance orientation. However, variations between organizational cultures in the same country (within-country variations) are more influential than national cultural differences (Gerhart and Fang, 2005). Put another way, in a cross-border merger the two organizational cultures have more bearing on outcomes that the two national cultures. In a study of international alliances, differences in professional cultures had the most disruptive effect on outcomes followed by organizational culture which was more disruptive than differences in national cultures (Sirmon and Lane, 2004). Professional cultures exist in groups of people in similar occupations and develop through education, training, the ways knowledge is generated and the ways competence is demonstrated – consider differences in engineering, science and accounting for instance. In a study of organizations in the US, Brazil and India, Nelson and Gopalan (2003) found clusters of organizations with cultures matching the national culture (isomorphism) and clusters that rejected national values (rejective). This led them to suggest that debates about *either* convergence or divergence are unhelpful and that it would be better to talk about how forces for convergence interact with forces for divergence in the local setting.

Activity 4.7

Look back at Figure 4.7 which positions four models of organization on Hofstede's power distance and uncertainty avoidance dimensions. Consider Deal and Kennedy's four culture types described in Illustraton 4.8 and consider how far each can be related to one or more of Hofstede's organizational models. What conclusions can you derive from this?

Both Hofstede (1994b) and Adler (1991) draw attention to the way organizational theory (as it relates to motivation, decision making and leadership) is culturally determined. Because most management and organizational theory derives from research in western universities caution is advised before extending it uncritically elsewhere. For instance, cultures that value adherence to participative styles of leadership and decision making may not be welcomed in societies that see consultation on the part of leaders as a weakness and where workers would be embarrassed if consulted by their managers.

Organizational culture and change

Defending and supporting change

Figure 4.9 depicts the way elements of organizational culture can support and/or defend against change. Burns and Stalker's (1961) classic research is a good

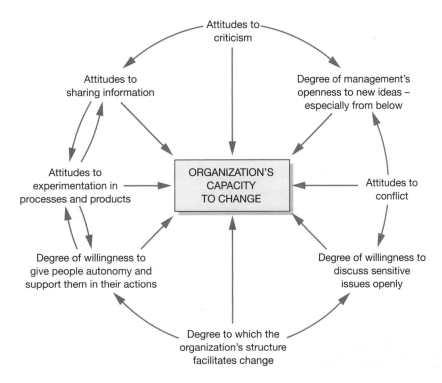

Figure 4.9 Organizational culture and change

example of the merger of the concepts of structure and culture as organic types of organization are much more likely to be able to respond to the need for change than mechanistic forms. However, this is not to say that mechanistic-type organizations *defend* against change but they are less open to it. They are, however, unlikely to support, without serious trauma, the frame-breaking, transformational or revolutionary types of change discussed in Chapter 2. Structural characteristics as well as attitudes, beliefs and values are more likely to act as barriers.

Kanter (1983) describes two extremes of organizational culture that are not only different in structural characteristics but also differ in the underlying attitudes and beliefs of the people working in them. The first she calls a 'segmentalist' culture and the other an 'integrative' culture (see Illustration 4.14).

In addition, Kanter (1983, p. 101) offer ten 'rules for stifling innovation':

1 Regard any new idea from below with suspicion – because it is new, and because it is from below.
2 Insist that people who need your approval to act first go through several other levels of management to get their signatures.
3 Ask departments or individuals to challenge and criticize each other's proposals. (That saves you the task of deciding; you just pick the survivor.)

4 Express your criticisms freely and withhold your praise. (That keeps people on their toes.) Let them know they can be fired at any time.

5 Treat identification of problems as signs of failure, to discourage people from letting you know when something in their area isn't working.

6 Control everything carefully. Make sure people count anything that can be counted, frequently.

7 Make decisions to reorganize or change policies in secret, and spring them on people unexpectedly. (That also keeps people on their toes.)

8 Make sure that requests for information are fully justified and make sure that it is not given out to managers freely. (You don't want data to fall into the wrong hands.)

9 Assign to lower-level managers, in the name of delegation and participation, responsibility for figuring out how to cut back, lay off, move people around or otherwise implement threatening decisions you have made. And get them to do it quickly.

10 And above all, never forget that you, the 'higher-ups', already know everything important about this business.

Illustration 4.14

Segmentalist and integrative cultures

Segmentalist cultures:
- compartmentalize actions, events and problems;
- see problems as narrowly as possible;
- have segmented structures with large numbers of departments walled off from one another;
- assume problems can be solved by carving them up into pieces that are then assigned to specialists who work in isolation;
- divide resources up among the many departments;
- avoid experimentation;
- avoid conflict and confrontation;
- have weak coordinating mechanisms;
- stress precedent and procedures.

Integrative cultures:
- are willing to move beyond received wisdom;
- combine ideas from unconnected sources;
- see problems as wholes, related to larger wholes;
- challenge established practices;
- operate at the edge of competencies;
- measure themselves by looking to visions of the future rather than by referring to the standards of the past;
- create mechanisms for exchange of information and new ideas;
- recognize and even encourage differences, but then are prepared to cooperate;
- are outward looking;
- look for novel solutions to problems.

Source: Based on Kanter, R.M. (1983) *The Change Masters*, London: Routledge, chapter 1.

Organizational learning and types of change

Argyris (1964) pointed to the difference between two kinds of learning. *Single-loop learning* is indicative of a situation where an objective or goal is defined and a person works out the most favoured way of reaching the goal. In single-loop learning, while many different possibilities for achieving personal or organizational goals might be considered, the goal itself is not questioned. Single-loop learning is also referred to as individual learning, that is, learning which an individual achieves but that seldom passes throughout the organization in any coherent way.

In contrast, with *double-loop learning* questions are asked not only about the *means* by which goals can be achieved, but about the *ends*, that is, the goals themselves. Johnson (1990) refers to this type of learning as *organizational relearning*, which he says is a 'process in which that which is taken for granted and which is the basis of strategic direction – the paradigm – is re-formulated' (p. 189). Given that the organizational paradigm contains all the elements of Johnson *et al.*'s (2008) cultural web, this implies change throughout the organization in all aspects of its behaviour.

Individual or single-loop learning is most likely to be the dominant form to occur in a segmentalist or defensive culture. The characteristics of this type of culture militate significantly against the sharing of information and openness that are required for organizational learning to take place. Therefore, while it could be sufficient for the types of change which Dunphy and Stace (1993) define as 'fine-tuning' and 'incremental adjustment', it will be blind to the need for the kind of radical thinking required to bring about change in the organization's direction – strategic change. In addition, the inability of an organization to operate double-loop learning contributes to the process of 'strategic drift' (Johnson *et al.*, 2008) which can lead to change being forced upon organizations.

People can learn but can an organization learn over and above what its people learn? Organizations can of course store knowledge in databases and systems that capture past learning. Furthermore, an organization's culture does capture and express accumulated learning – recall the blunter definitions of culture as 'the way we do things around here' and the way cultures perpetuate stories and recipes. The idea of organizational memory was explored by van der Bent *et al.* (1999) in a Dutch electronics firm. They identified four 'memory carriers'; culture, structure, systems and procedures. After following a major change programme attempted by the firm over several years they concluded:

1 Change managers must become intimate with the memory carriers at the start of a change intervention. Organizational memory while a force for stability is also a barrier to change. Which carriers can impede the change?
2 Memory carriers are not isolated rather they are interconnected. Efforts to change one carrier must appreciate how they will touch upon others. Both the carriers and their relationships need attention.
3 Not all carriers lead to organizational learning. Memories led to learning where the changes were more complex and hard to achieve. Use of memories operated at a deep level and influenced change issues that employees felt were important to the organization. Remembering was more likely in relation to important organizational issues.

4 Outcomes of change are influenced by the spirit in which they are pursued as much as the intended changes *per se*. Organizational memory is part of that spirit.

According to Brown (1995, p. 74), 'Organizational cultures differ markedly in terms of their relative strengths'. Whether defensive or supportive, a strong culture implies a commonly understood perspective on how organizational life should happen, with most organizational members subscribing to it. Conversely, a weak culture is made up of many different cultures, some of which are in conflict with each other. Payne (1990) has suggested that the strength of an organization's culture can be measured by, first, the degree to which it is shared by all members and, second, by the intensity with which organizational members believe in it. The greater the intensity the more it pervades all levels at which culture manifests in influencing attitudes, values, basic assumptions and beliefs. Strong cultures facilitate the following functions at the organizational level (Brown, 1995):

● Conflict resolution.
● Coordination and control in a common direction.
● Reduction of uncertainty and complexity.
● Motivation over and above motivation from extrinsic rewards.
● Competitive advantage.

This last point is perhaps the most contentious. For instance, Kotter and Heskett (1992) identified ten large and well-known organizations (including Sears, Procter & Gamble and Goodyear), all of which had exceptionally strong cultures, but all of which had weak performance.

Cultural change

Culture is, by definition, a dominant influence on organizational life. It follows then that in order to bring about significant organizational change organizational culture must be managed accordingly. But can culture be managed?

Assessing cultural risk

Schwartz and Davis (1981) thought culture could be changed and devised a way of measuring culture in terms of descriptions of the way management tasks are typically handled in company-wide, boss–subordinate, peer and interdepartmental relationships as a way of assessing the degree of cultural compatibility with any proposed strategic change. Figure 4.10 is an example of their corporate culture matrix designed to carry out the first part of this process. It has been completed for the UK-based division of a company in the computer services industry.

At this stage we ask readers to carry out Activity 4.8 as this gives a way of making judgments about how the culture fits with required changes. The

Tasks	Relationships				Summary of culture in relation to tasks
	Companywide	Boss-subordinate	Peer	Inter-department	
Innovating	Innovation if part of the mission	Bosses open to suggestions	Teamwork	Teamwork	Encourage creativity and innovation
Decision making	Has to fit in with strategy	Input from subordinates encouraged – boss has final word	Collective decisions	Work together to produce an integrated package	Collaborative decision making but boss has the final word; corporate strategy rules
Communicating	Easy, use of email and phone	Friendly	Face to face and open	Easy, use of email and phone	Easy, informal and friendly communications
Organizing	Market focus	Democratic	Professional relationships	Collaborative	Organized on the basis of skills and professional relationships
Monitoring	Shareholder-led organization	Meet short-term profit targets and deadlines	Project management	Project management	Need to meet short-term profit goals
Appraising and rewarding	Encourage performers	Hard work = good rewards	Results important	Results important	Meritocracy
Summary of culture in relation to relationships	Allow freedom to managers as long as they operate within the strategy and meet profit targets; output-oriented	Friendly, rely on each other for success	Highly skilled professionals who help each other out	Work together	Overall performance and profit matter in a culture that welcomes dynamic and performance-related individuals

Figure 4.10 Corporate culture matrix

Source: Matrix adapted from Schwartz, H. and Davis, S.M. (1981) 'Matching Corporate Strategy and Business Strategy', *Organizational Dynamics,* Summer, p. 36; example from the author's own experience. Copyright (1981), with permission from Elsevier.

Activity 4.8

For an organization you know well use the basic matrix in Figure 4.10 to do the following:

1 *Write in the cells of the main part of the matrix, words and/or phrases that encapsulate the different relationships (listed horizontally) according to the management of the tasks (listed vertically).*

2 *In the final column on the right, summarize the corporate culture for each task.*

3 *In the bottom row, summarize the corporate culture for each of the relationships.*

What do the summaries tell you about this organization's overall culture?

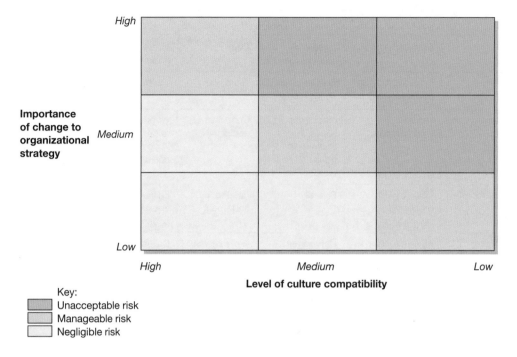

Key:

■ Unacceptable risk
■ Manageable risk
□ Negligible risk

Figure 4.11 Assessing cultural risk

Source: Matrix adapted from Schwartz, H. and Davis, S.M. (1981) 'Matching Corporate Strategy and Business Strategy', *Organizational Dynamics*, Summer, p. 41. Copyright (1981), with permission from Elsevier.

framework for this comparative assessment is shown in Figure 4.11 as a matrix that allows elements of the proposed strategy changes to be positioned against their importance to the strategy and the degree to which they are compatible with the culture. For instance, if a change to a matrix structure is needed yet the culture resembles Handy's (1993) role culture, the need for a matrix structure would be positioned in the top right cell of the matrix in Figure 4.11 (high importance but low cultural compatibility). Other elements of the changes might be low in level of culture compatibility but if they are of low importance in the overall change strategy they would be positioned towards the lower right-hand part of the matrix.

The relevance of culture change to organizational change

Assessing cultural risk helps management pinpoint where resistance to change could occur because of incompatibility between strategy and culture. This allows managers to make choices regarding whether to:

(a) ignore the culture;
(b) manage around the culture;

(c) try to change the culture to fit the strategy; or

(d) change the strategy to fit the culture, perhaps by reducing performance expectations.

Ignoring the culture

Ignoring the culture is dangerous unless the organization has sufficient resources to draw on to weather the subsequent storm and the possibility of an initial downturn in business.

Managing around the culture

The second option – managing around the culture – is a real possibility given that there are, in most cases, more ways than one of achieving desired goals. Figure 4.12 reproduces Schwartz and Davis's (1981) example of how to manage around an organization's culture. This outlines four typical strategies that companies might pursue and what Schwartz and Davis call the 'right' organizational approaches to implement them. The two columns on the right set out the cultural barriers to these 'right' approaches and the alternative approaches that could, therefore, be used.

	Strategy	'Right' approach	Cultural barriers	Alternative approaches
Company A	Diversify product and market	Divisionalize	Centralized power One-person rule Functional focus Hierarchical structure	Use business teams Use explicit strategic planning Change business measures
Company B	Focus marketing on most profitable segments	Fine-tune reward system. Adjust management information system	Diffused power Highly individualized operations	Dedicate full-time personnel to each key market
Company C	Extend technology to new markets	Set up matrix organization	Multiple power centres Functional focus	Use programme coordinators Set up planning committees Get top management more involved
Company D	Withdraw gradually from declining market and maximize cash throw-offs	Focus organization specifically Fine-tune rewards Ensure top management visibility	New-business driven Innovators rewarded State-of-the-art operation	Sell out

Figure 4.12 How to manage around company culture

Source: Matrix adapted from Schwartz, H. and Davis, S.M. (1981) 'Matching Corporate Strategy and Business Strategy', *Organizational Dynamics*, Summer, p. 44. Copyright (1981), with permission from Elsevier.

Changing the culture

The third option, deliberately changing the culture to fit the desired strategic changes, is also a possibility and, according to Ogbonna and Harris (2002, p. 33) is still a popular form of management intervention. However, as much of the literature cautions, this can be an extremely difficult and lengthy process, particularly if culture is strong (Scholz, 1987; Furnham and Gunter, 1993). Furthermore, there are strong arguments (e.g. Hope and Hendry, 1995) against cultural change given what they describe as the move away from the large-scale hierarchies characteristic of the multinationals of the 1970s and 1980s towards the leaner and more focused units of today.

This move has been accompanied by an increase in the employment of professional and knowledge workers and for some workers an erosion of security of employment and predictable career paths. Two problems arise from this. The first is that the knowledge workers who are likely to flourish in these new types of organization are least likely to be open to cultural manipulation. Second, where there are histories of downsizing or delayering some cynicism seems inevitable, at least in the short term. As a consequence, 'employees in general may be less receptive to evangelical calls for shared cultural values' (Hope and Hendry, 1995, p. 62).

Beer, Eisenstat and Spector's (1993) view that trying to change attitudes and values directly is futile is still relevant; particularly their comment that the way to bring about organizational change is first to change behaviour. The behavioural change will then lead to the desired changes in attitudes and values. Thus Beer *et al.* argue for changing the organizational context (people's roles, responsibilities and the relationships between them) first, in an effort to achieve changed behaviour and attitudes. This view of change rests on the assumption that changing organizational structures, systems and role relationships, which comprise, in the main, the formal aspects of organizational life, will bring about desired cultural changes incorporating organizational members' attitudes and beliefs. Many (arguably uncritical) models of planned change subscribe to this view such as the 'Six steps to effective change' shown in Illustration 4.15.

Beer *et al.* and Hope and Hendry are supported by Bem (1970, p. 60 cited in Hofstede, 1981, p. 26): 'One of the most effective ways of changing mental programmes of individuals is changing behavior first.' He continues: 'That value change has to precede behavior change is a naive (idealistic) assumption that neglects the contribution of the *situation* to actual behaviour.'

Supporters of the culture can/cannot be changed camps can both find support in the literature. Some methods of attempting culture change call upon education and persuasion or, in some cases, coercion, to help bring about changes in attitudes (Anthony, 1994). Others rely more on changing recruitment, selection, promotion, reward and redundancy policies to alter the composition of the workforce and so retain those who have the desired beliefs, values and attitudes associated with the desired culture.

Illustration 4.15

Six steps to effective change

1 Mobilize commitment to change through joint diagnosis of business problems.

2 Develop a shared vision of how to organize and manage for competitiveness.

3 Foster consensus for the new vision, competence to enact it and cohesion to move it along.

4 Spread revitalization to all departments without pushing it from the top.

5 Institutionalize revitalization through formal policies, systems and structures.

6 Monitor and adjust strategies in response to problems in the revitalization process.

Source: Beer, M., Eisenstat, R. A. and Spector, B. (1993) 'Why Change Programs Don't Produce Change', in Mabey, C. and Mayon-White, B. (eds) *Managing Change*, London: PCP, pp. 99–107.

Illustration 4.16 portrays an example of a company that was able to manage around its culture for a number of years and during that time still succeeded in growing and developing in the global market. However, to achieve longer-term success, the company decided to create a strategy that would ultimately attempt to change the culture.

Illustration 4.16

Cultural change at the BBC

Now almost 90, Auntie Beeb (the BBC) is a strong yet vulnerable institution. Funded out of TV licence fees it enjoys a guaranteed income yet following an explosion of new TV channels the BBC is exposed. After all, when viewers can choose the satellite packages they want why should UK residents be forced to pay the BBC an annual licence fee just to own a television?

While it is a producer of outstanding drama and documentary programmes it is naïve enough to fall victim to the infantile behaviour of its 'stars'. In October 2008 two of its presenters conspired to make what many licence payers felt were offensive telephone calls and then broadcast the 'show' on air. The BBC's management had approved the airing demonstrating at best gross misjudgement.

By the 1990s the belief in the supremacy of market forces in the UK had extended to include the creation of quasi or internal markets in some public organizations. In the BBC this was attempted by separating the people who commissioned programmes (the purchasers) from those who produced them (the providers). This change was aimed at transforming the organization away from a highly bureaucratic outfit ill-suited to change to a market-driven organization better placed to respond and compete.

According to an account written by BBC insiders the first phase of the BBC's change programme dealt with restructuring and faster decision making (Grossman and Smith, 2002). The second phase aimed at changing the culture. Top management decided upon four priorities:

Clarifying purpose and vision.

Changing culture by altering how employees behaved.

Illustration 4.16 *continued*

Developing leadership to reflect and articulate a new culture.

Shifting internal and external perceptions of the Corporation.

The new vision emphasized being 'the most creative organization in the world'. Quite a challenge! Communication was a big part of the cultural change programme and this included listening to how employees felt about the organization. Employees said they were concerned about lack of leadership, feeling undervalued, lack of rewards for creativity and a risk-averse culture. Constructive criticism was encouraged. Staff expressing concerns and ideas were asked to put forward solutions and take ownership of them. Change had to be positive and all staff had a responsibility to play their part. Key principles were: 'just do it', make workspaces better for all, live the values of the BBC, understand what leadership is and demonstrate it, value people, inspire creativity everywhere and stay in touch with viewers and listeners.

This summary account is not untypical of management-led change. Indeed, if a management group decides to try and change organizational culture then these are the sort of things that are

usually attempted. But did it work? Harris and Wegg-Prosser (2007) offer a revealing account of change in the BBC from 1991–2002 and are rather doubtful.

Staff attitude surveys showed improvements but were these merely reflecting employees' feelgood ratings while they thought someone was showing interest in them? The sight of a Chief Executive brandishing a 'Cut the crap – make it happen' card would probably be welcome in many workplaces and may well have enthused staff to think and act differently. But how sustainable was it? In short, several years later the producer choice initiative had not brought about the behavioural and cultural changes intended according to Harris and Wegg-Prosser (2007). The crap-cutting chief executive left in 2004. The strong bureaucracy that prevailed had evolved and absorbed the narratives of strategic change and the new mechanisms within it. The point of this illustration is that major initiatives run over several years can struggle. Rather than being a story of decisive organizational changes the BBC story can be seen as 'surges of managerial control' overlaying periods of creative autonomy (Harris and Wegg-Prosser, 2007, p. 299).

Conclusions

The concept of culture is complex given its application to societies, organizations and groups, all of which interact one with another. Efforts to describe national culture typically produce a set of bipolar dimensions on which cultures vary. Different studies have produced similar schema. Managers working across international borders need to appreciate cultural differences and in particular their implications for the way work is organized and the behavioural expectations of employees.

Organizations can be seen *as* cultures rather than as *having* them. Cultures are unique yet numerous typologies have been produced in efforts to describe and classify the common variants found. Within an organization different sub-cultures can exist, reflecting different histories, personalities and professional norms. When people join and work in an organization they learn how to act according to expectations and norms even though outside the organization they may behave rather differently. Selection processes often look for cultural fit in prospective employees. Given that the more organic and integrative organizational cultures are said to support change and, in particular, the increasing requirement for creativity and innovation in order for organizations to remain forward looking and competitive, it seems reasonable for many organizations to attempt to change their cultures in these directions. However, attempts to change culture are frequently problematic.

Consequently, if attempting to change culture is too risky then ways of managing around the culture or even changing the strategy to take account of the culture are needed. Organizational politics and the politics of change are both a part of culture and we examine the issues of power, politics, conflict and change in the next chapter.

Discussion questions and assignments

1 Drawing on your experience consider how realistic it is for managers to try and change organizational culture.

2 To what extent does an organization's structure influence its culture and its capacity to work with change?

3 Review the evidence for and against the notion that national cultures are converging.

4 Drawing on typologies of culture, prepare a presentation to demonstrate how cultural types relate to different types of organizational change.

Case example ●●●

Daimler and Chrysler: lessons from a merger

The auto industry has a long history of domestic and cross-border mergers and acquisitions activity. One high profile merger took place in 1998 between German company Daimler-Benz (best known for Mercedes perhaps) and US car producer Chrysler. At the time Daimler wanted to push existing business into new markets and develop new products. As the company stood however, executives felt that this would not be achieved through Mercedes alone and that a tie-up with another auto producer was needed. Chrysler, although the most profitable vehicle producer at the time, was aware of big over-capacity in the industry and executives felt that there had to be a shake-out of manufacturers. To compete, Chrysler felt it needed a partner. After full due diligence investigations focusing on the assets and financial structures of the organizations a decision to merge was made.

During negotiations by the merger teams some sociocultural issues came to the surface. First,

Case example *continued*

Daimler was never going to be seen as the junior partner but was happy with the idea of 'a merger of equals'. Would the merged organization be German or American? There was no way that Daimler could end up as American so it was agreed that the new company would be German. A new name, DaimlerChrysler, was agreed upon, again reflecting the strength of the German position.

When the two companies were being integrated further sociocultural issues came out. Rewards for the top American executives were much higher than their counterparts in Germany. Daimler employees flew first class ostensibly because this fitted the company's market position. Only the top Chrysler executives flew first class and reconciling travel policies took six months to resolve. Working patterns differed. There were differences in dress codes, informal versus formal behaviour in business meetings, the ways decisions were made and the hours worked, for instance. Financial reporting in the US was geared to quarterly reporting unlike the annual cycle seen in Germany.

Another problem was the culture surrounding the two brands. One was a luxury brand built around superior engineering and the other much more associated with a brash American image and 'blue collar' purchasers. The two companies 'didn't just make cars differently; they lived in different worlds' (p. 310).

The upshot of this was that the merger quickly began to falter. Financial performance collapsed and in 2001 the company announced big job losses and closure of plants to turn around a loss-making situation. Chrysler had benefited from Mercedes, e.g. through the use of shared production systems and components but benefits to Daimler were harder to find. In 2007 Daimler sold 80 per cent of its stake in Chrysler for $7.4 billion – far less than it had invested in the venture.

Mergers and acquisitions only make sense if they add to the sum of what the two partners were already achieving. On this measure, this particular partnership was a failure. Analyzing the causes of failure in a case like this could rely on economic, market and technical explanations and they cannot be overlooked. However, it does seem that cultural clashes were inevitable in this case and that they were not sufficiently accounted for in pre-merger analysis.

Source: Based on Badrtalei, J. and Bates, D.L. (2007) 'Effect of Organizational Cultures on Mergers and Acquisitions: the case of DaimlerChrysler', *International Journal of Management*, 24(2), pp. 303–317.

Case exercise

Keeping the Daimler Chrysler illustration in mind, Riad (2007) cautions us against seeing cultures in terms of, say, 'similar' or 'different' and then of taking managerialist views about whether they fit or not. She points out that cultural tension in society, as might arise from fundamentally different religious beliefs or views about gender (in)equality, can coexist if points of common ground are recognized and appreciated.

1 From your understanding of Diamler and Chrysler how could the two different organization cultures be described?

2 How could organizations that are moving towards a merger or acquisition begin to carry out a cultural audit? In particular, how could they assess the compatibility of their respective cultures to identify possible problem areas that could impede integration?

Indicative resources

Hofstede, G.H. (2005) *Cultures and Organizations: Software of the Mind* (2nd edn), London: McGraw-Hill. This book is an essential read for any student or manager interested in work relating to culture, both at national and organizational level.

Schein, H.E. (2004) *Organizational Culture and Leadership* (3rd edn), San Francisco, CA: Jossey-Bass. This book does not focus on the basic details in relation to culture; it assumes the reader has this knowledge already. It goes into more depth in relation to national and organizational culture. There are also useful case examples of Schein's work with organizations that add insight into this area.

Trompenaars, F. and Prud'homme, P. (2004) *Managing Change Across Corporate Cultures*, Chichester: Capstone Publishing. This book focuses on culture at company, national and international levels. It offers theoretical perspectives relating to corporate culture, and includes case studies and research conducted by the authors.

Useful websites

www.thtconsulting.com This site presents the ideas of Trompenaars and Hampden-Turner in relation to cross-cultural issues. A 'culture compass' that explores intercultural issues is demonstrated.

www.new-paradigm.co.uk/resources.htm This site provides a link to various organizational activities including culture.

www.geert-hofstede.com This site explains dimensions of national culture and gives information on how different countries compare.

To click straight to these links and for other resources go to
www.pearsoned.co.uk/senior

References

Adler, N.J. (1991) *International Dimensions of Organizational Behavior* (2nd edn), Belmont, CA: Wadsworth Publishing Company.

Adler, N.J. (1997) *International Dimensions of Organizational Behavior* (3rd edn), Cincinnati, OH: South Western College Publishing, ITP.

Alvesson, M. (1993) *Cultural Perspectives on Organizations*, Cambridge: Cambridge University Press.

Anthony, P. (1994) *Managing Culture*, Milton Keynes: Open University Press.

Argyris, C. (1964) *Integrating the Individual and the Organization*, New York: Wiley.

Bate, S.P. (1996) 'Towards a Strategic Framework for Changing Corporate Culture', *Strategic Change*, 5, pp. 27–42.

Beer, M., Eisenstat, R.A. and Spector, B. (1993) 'Why Change Programs Don't Produce Change', in Mabey, C. and Mayon-White, B. (eds) *Managing Change* (2nd edn), London: PCP.

Bem, D.J. (1970) *Beliefs, Attitudes and Human Affairs*, Belmont, CA: Brooks/Cole.

Brooks, I. and Bate, S.P. (1994) 'The Problems of Effecting Change within the British Civil Service: a cultural perspective', *British Journal of Management*, 5, pp. 177–190.

Brown, A. (1995) *Organisational Culture*, London: Pitman.

Burnes, B. (2004) *Managing Change* (4th edn), Harlow: Financial Times Prentice Hall.

Burns, T. and Stalker, G.M. (1961) *The Management of Innovation*, London: Tavistock.

Calori, R. and De Woot, P. (1994) *A European Management Model Beyond Diversity*, Hemel Hempstead: Prentice Hall.

Cameron, K.S. and Quinn, R.E. (2005) *Diagnosing and Changing Organizational Culture: based on the Competing Values Framework,* San Francisco: Jossey-Bass.

Carnall, C. (2003) *Managing Change in Organizations* (4th edn), Harlow: Financial Times Prentice Hall.

Chinese Culture Connection (1987) 'Chinese Values and the Search for Culture-free Dimensions of Culture', *Journal of Cross-Cultural Psychology*, 18(2), pp. 143–164.

Deal, T.E. and Kennedy, A.A. (1982) *Corporate Cultures: The Rites and Rituals of Corporate Life*, Reading, MA: Addison-Wesley.

Deal, T.E. and Kennedy, A.A. (2000) *The New Corporate Cultures*, London: Perseus Books.

D'Iribarne, P. (1989) *La Logique de l'Honneur: gestion des entreprises et traditions nationales,* Paris: Seuil.

Drennan, D. (1992) *Transforming Company Culture*, London: McGraw-Hill.

Dunphy, D. and Stace, D. (1993) 'The Strategic Management of Corporate Change', *Human Relations*, 46(8), pp. 905–920.

Dyer, W. (1985) 'The Cycle of Cultural Evolution in Organizations', in Kilmann, R.H., Saxton, M.J. and Serpa, R. (eds) *Gaining Control of the Corporate Culture*, San Francisco, CA: Jossey-Bass.

Eccles, T. (1994) *Succeeding with Change Implementing Action-driven Strategies*, Maidenhead: McGraw-Hill.

Frank, S. (2000) 'On a Wavelength with the Danes', *Financial Times*, 23 October, p. 15.

French, W.L. and Bell, C.H., Jr (1990) *Organization Development: Behavioral Science Interventions for Organization Improvement* (4th edn), Englewood Cliffs, NJ: Prentice-Hall.

French, W.L. and Bell, C.H., Jr (1999) *Organizational Development* (6th edn), Englewood Cliffs, NJ: Prentice-Hall.

Furnham, A. and Gunter, B. (1993) 'Corporate Culture: diagnosis and change', in Cooper, C.L. (ed.) *International Review of Industrial and Organisational Psychology*, Chichester: Wiley.

Gerhart, B. and Fang, M. (2005) 'National Culture and Human Resource Management: assumptions and evidence', *International Journal of Human Resource Management*, 16(6), pp. 971–986.

Grossman, R. and Smith, P. (2002) 'Humanizing Cultural Change at the BBC', *Strategic Communication Management,* 7(1), pp. 28–32.

Hall, W. (1995) *Managing Cultures: Making Strategic Relationships Work*, Chichester: Wiley.

Handy, C. (1993) *Understanding Organizations*, Hamondsworth: Penguin.

Harris, M. and Wegg-Prosser, V. (2007) 'Post-bureaucracy and the Politics of Forgetting: management of change at the BBC 1991–2002', *Journal of Organizational Change Management*, 20(3), pp. 290–303.

Harrison, R. (1972) 'How to Describe Your Organization', *Harvard Business Review*, September–October, pp. 119–128.

Hill, S. and McNulty, D. (1998) 'Overcoming Cultural Barriers to Change', *Health Manpower Mangement*, 24(1), pp. 6–12.

Hofstede, G. (1980) *Culture's Consequences: International Differences in Work-related Values,* London and Beverly Hills, CA: Sage, pp. 4–10.

Hofstede, G. (1981) 'Culture and Organizations', *International Studies of Management and Organizations*, X(4), pp. 15–41.

Hofstede, G. (1991) *Cultures and Organizations: Software of the Mind*, Maidenhead: McGraw-Hill.

Hofstede, G. (1993) 'Cultural Constraints in Management Theories', *Academy of Management Executive*, February, pp. 81–94.

Hofstede, G. (1994a) *Cultures and Organizations*, London: McGraw-Hill.

Hofstede, G. (1994b) 'Management Scientists are Human', *Management Science*, 40(1), pp. 4–13.

Hofstede, G. (2006) 'What did GLOBE Really Measure? Researchers' minds versus respondents' minds', *Journal of International Business Studies*, 37, pp. 882–896.

Hofstede, G., Neuijen, B., Ohayv, D. and Sanders, G. (1990) 'Measuring Organizational Cultures: a qualitative and quantitative study across twenty cases', *Administrative Science Quarterly*, 35, pp. 286–316.

Hope, V. and Hendry, J. (1995) 'Corporate Cultural Change: is it relevant for the organisations of the 1990s?', *Human Resource Management Journal*, 5(4), Summer, pp. 61–73.

House, R., Hanges, P.J., Javidan, M. Dorfman, P.W. and Gupta, V. (2004) *Culture, Leadership and Organizations: The GLOBE Study of 62 societies*, Thousand Oaks, CA: Sage.

Howard, L.W. (1998) 'Validating the Competing Values Model as a Representation of Organizational Cultures', *International Journal of Organizational Analysis*, 6(3), pp. 231–250.

Igo, T. and Skitmore, M. (2005) 'Diagnosing the Organizational Culture of an Australian Engineering Company using the Competing Values Framework', *Construction Innovation*, 6, pp. 121–139.

Inglehart, R. and Baker, W.E. (2000) 'Modernization, Cultural Change and the Persistence of Traditional Values', *American Sociological Review*, 65(1), pp. 19–51.

Jaques, E. (1952) *The Changing Culture of a Factory*, New York: Dryden.

Johnson, G. (1987) *Strategic Change and the Management Process*, Oxford: Blackwell.

Johnson, G. (1990) 'Managing Strategic Action: the role of symbolic action', *British Journal of Management,* 1, pp. 183–200.

Johnson, G., Scholes, K. and Whittington, R. (2008) *Exploring Strategic Change: Texts and Cases* (8th edn), Harlow: Pearson Education.

Kanter, R.M. (1983) *The Change Masters*, London: Routledge.

Kluckhohn, F. and Strodtbeck, F.L. (1961) *Variations in Value Orientations*, Evanston, IL: Row, Peterson.

Koopman, R., den Hartog, D.N. and Konrad, E. (1999) 'National Culture and Leadership Profiles in Europe: some results from the GLOBE study', *European Journal of Work and Organizational Psychology*, 8(4), pp. 503–520.

Kotter, J.P. and Heskett, J.L. (1992) *Corporate Culture and Performance*, New York: Free Press.

Kroeber, A.L. and Kluckhohn, F. (1952) *Culture: A Critical Review of Concepts and Definitions*, New York: Vintage Books.

Kwan, P. and Walker, A. (2004) 'Validating the Competing Values Model as a Representation of Organizational Culture through Inter-Institutional Comparisons', *Organizational Analysis*, 12(1), pp. 21–37.

Laurent, A. (1983) 'The Cultural Diversity of Western Conceptions of Management', *International Studies of Management and Organisation*, XIII (1–2), pp. 75–96.

Louis, M.R. (1980) 'Organizations as Culture-bearing Milieux', in Pondy, L.R. *et al.* (eds) *Organizational Symbolism*, Greenwich, CT: JAI.

Maurice, M., Sorge, A. and Warner, M. (1980) 'Societal Differences in Organizing Manufacturing Units', *Organization Studies*, 1, pp. 63–91.

Morgan, G. (1986) *Images of Organization*, London: Sage.

Morgan, G. (1989) *Creative Organization Theory: A Resource Book*, London: Sage.

Nasser, J. and Wetlaufer, S. (1999) 'Driving Change: an interview with Jacques Nasser', *Harvard Business Review*, March–April, pp. 76–88.

Nelson, R.E. and Gopalan, S. (2003) 'Do Organizational Cultures Replicate National Cultures? Isomorphic, rejective and reciprocal opposition in the corporate values of three countries', *Organization Studies*, 24(7), pp. 1115–1151.

Ogbonna, E. and Harris, L.C. (1998) 'Managing Organizational Culture: compliance or genuine change', *British Journal of Management*, 9, pp. 273–288.

Ogbonna, E. and Harris, L.C. (2002) 'Managing Organisational Culture: insights from the hospitality industry', *Human Resource Management Journal*, 12(1), pp. 33–51.

Ohmae, K. (1991) 'Getting Rid of Headquarters Mentality', in *The Borderless World: Power and Strategy in the Interlinked Economy*, London: Fontana, pp. 101–124.

Pacanowsky, M.E. and O'Donnell-Trujillo, N. (1982) 'Communication and Organizational Culture', *The Western Journal of Speech Communication*, 46, Spring, pp. 115–130.

Payne, R.L. (1990) 'The Concepts of Culture and Climate', Working Paper 202, Manchester Business School.

Peters, T.J. and Waterman, R.H. (1982) *In Search of Excellence*, New York: Harper & Row.

Pettigrew, A.M. (1990) 'Is Corporate Culture Manageable?', in Wilson, D.C. and Rosenfeld, R.H. (eds) *Managing Organizations: Text, Readings and Cases*, Maidenhead: McGraw-Hill, pp. 266–272.

Pheysey, D.C. (1993) *Organizational Cultures: Types and Transformations*, London: Routledge.

Quinn, R.E. (1991) 'A Competing Values Framework for Analysing Presentational Communication in Management Contexts', *Journal of Business Communication*, 28(3), pp. 213–232.

Quinn, R.E. and Rohrbaugh, J. (1983) 'A Spatial Model of Effectiveness Criteria: towards a competing values approach to organizational analysis', *Management Science*, 29(3), pp. 363–377.

Riad, S. (2007) 'Of Mergers and Cultures: "What happened to shared values and joint assumptions?"', *Journal of Organizational Change Management*, 20(1), pp. 26–43.

Robbins, S.P. (1996) *Organizational Behavior: Concepts, Controversies, Applications* (7th edn), Englewood Cliffs, NJ: Prentice-Hall.

Robbins, S.P. (2001) *Organizational Behavior: Concepts, Controversies, Applications* (9th edn), Englewood Cliffs, NJ: Prentice-Hall.

Robbins, S.P. (2003) *Organizational Behaviour* (10th edn), Englewood Cliffs, NJ: Pearson Education.

Robbins, S.P (2005) *Organizational Behaviour* (11th edn), Englewood Cliffs, NJ: Pearson Education.

Schein, E.H. (1992) *Organizational Culture and Leadership* (2nd edn), San Francisco, CA: Jossey-Bass.

Schein, E.H. (2004) *Organizational Culture and Leadership* (3rd edn), San Francisco, CA: Jossey-Bass.

Scholz, C. (1987) 'Corporate Culture and Strategy: the problem of strategic fit', *Long Range Planning,* 20(4), pp. 78–87.

Schwartz, H. and Davis, S.M. (1981) 'Matching Corporate Strategy and Business Strategy', *Organizational Dynamics*, Summer, pp. 30–48.

Sirmon, D.G. and Lane, P.J. (2004) 'A Model of Cultural Differences and International Alliance Performance', *Journal of International Business Studies*, 35, pp. 306–319.

Tayeb, M. (1989) *Organizations and National Culture: A Comparative Analysis*, London: Sage.

Trompenaars, F. and Prud'homme, P. (2004) *Managing Change across Corporate Cultures*, Chichester: Capstone Publishing.

Van der Bent, J., Paauwe, J. and Williams, R. (1999) 'Organizational Learning: an exploration of organizational memory and its role in organizational change processes', *Journal of Organizational Change Management*, 12(5), pp. 377–404.

Wilson, D.C. (1992) *A Strategy of Change: Concepts and Controversies in the Management of Change,* London: Routledge.

Chapter 5

The politics of change

Power and conflict and the issues they generate are part of the politics of life in organizations. Their importance is recognized in this chapter through a discussion of the sources of power and the way political action, as an expression of power, is used in the management of change. The concept of powerlessness is discussed, particularly in relation to the position of women and minorities in organizations. The dysfunctional and functional sides of conflict are explored.

Learning objectives

By the end of this chapter, you will be able to:

- explain what is meant by organizational politics;
- distinguish between different sources of power and ways of using power to influence change;
- define and discuss the links between power, politics and conflict;
- identify different ways of resolving conflict and the situations they can be applied to.

●●●●● **Organizational politics**

> Politics is the act of preventing people from taking part in affairs which properly concern them.
>
> (Paul Valéry, 1943)

In the previous chapter we noted that organizational culture is rather like a sleeping giant that stirs when it is awakened by episodes of change. The same might be said about the political processes in organizations. Yet the concepts of politics, power and conflict, particularly in the context of resistance to change, frequently appear in the role of the more undesirable aspects of organizational life. For instance, Robbins (2005, p. 390), drawing on Kanter (1979), says: 'Power has been described as the last dirty word ... People who have it deny it, people who want it try not to appear to be seeking it, and those who are good at getting it are secretive about how they got it.'

English managers surveyed on their attitudes towards change management and organizational politics reported that politics was a distracting side issue compared to the issue of organizational performance (see Buchanan and Badham, 1999, p. 19). In the survey, 53 per cent agreed (24 per cent disagreed) that organizational politics is usually damaging, is a sign of incompetent management and that it should be eradicated wherever possible. Although we might sympathize with the first sentiments we will see that the idea of eradicating it is a rather naïve wish.

In contrast, 72 per cent agreed that 'the more complex and wide-reaching the change, the more intense the politics become', with most agreeing that change agents (those facilitating or managing change) needed to be politically skilled. This survey suggests that many managers would like to manage without resort to political behaviour yet acknowledge the reality of it particularly in the context of organizational change.

Defining power and politics

These two concepts are relatively slippery and we can take our pick of definitions. Huczynski and Buchanan (2007, p. 797) suggest that:

> Power concerns the capacity of individuals to exert their will over others, while political behaviour is the practical domain of power in action, worked out through the use of techniques of influence and other (more or less extreme) tactics.

Power is thus an ability to make things happen and to overcome resistance in order to achieve desired objectives or results. Political behaviour according to Huczynski and Buchanan is 'the observable, but often covert, actions by which executives (and others) enhance their power to influence decisions'.

The concept of 'power in action' is echoed by Robbins (2005, p. 390) who maintains that this happens whenever people get together in groups and where an individual or group seeks to influence the thoughts, attitudes or behaviours of another individual or group. Acting politically is also a part of negotiation as a means to overcoming resistance and of resolving conflict. It can, however, be the cause of conflict in that an individual or group seeks to affect, negatively, another individual or group. However, as Hardy (1994) points out, although power can be used to overcome conflict it can also be used to avert it.

Robbins divides politics into 'legitimate' and 'illegitimate' political behaviour, the former being normal everyday politics such as bypassing the chain of command, forming coalitions, obstructing organization policies and so on; the latter being deliberate sabotage, whistle-blowing and groups of employees reporting sick. Robbins' viewpoint is expressed in his formal definition of political behaviour: _notes_

> ... political behaviour in organizations [is defined as] those activities that are not required as part of one's formal role in the organization, but that influence, or attempt to influence, the distribution of advantages and disadvantages within the organization (pp. 400–401).

These definitions view political behaviour an aspect of organizational behaviour which mirrors the 'objectivist' view of culture discussed in Chapter 4. Given Morgan's (1997) opposing views on organizational culture, it is not surprising that he poses organizations as political systems displaying different types of political rule as summarized in Illustration 5.1.

Illustration 5.1

Organizations and modes of political rule

- **Autocracy**. Absolute government where power is held by an individual or small group and supported by control of critical resources, property or ownership rights, tradition, charisma and other claims to personal privilege.
- **Bureaucracy**. Rule exercised through use of the written word, which provides the basis for a rational–legal type of authority or 'rule of law'.
- **Technocracy**. Rule exercised through use of knowledge, expert power and the ability to solve relevant problems.
- **Codetermination**. The form of rule where opposing parties combine in the joint management of mutual interests, as in coalition government or corporatism, each party drawing on a specific power base.

- **Representative democracy**. Rule exercised through the election of officers mandated to act on behalf of the electorate and who hold office for a specified time period or so long as they command the support of the electorate, as in parliamentary government and forms of worker control and shareholder control in industry.
- **Direct democracy**. The system where everyone has an equal right to rule and is involved in all decision making, as in many communal organizations such as cooperatives and kibbutzim. This political principle encourages self-organization as a key mode of organizing.

Source: Morgan, G. (1997) *Images of Organizations*, London: Sage, p. 157.

In his discussion of different types of political rule, Morgan draws attention to how the suffix -*cracy*, which appears in these terms, is derived from *kratia* – a Greek term meaning power or rule. Thus the word *autocracy* implies the rule of one person, that is, the use of dictatorial power; the term *bureaucracy* is associated with people who sit at bureaux or desks, making and administering rules; a *technocracy* is associated with the power of those with technical knowledge and skills; and *democracy* draws on the meaning of the prefix *demos* or 'populace', so that in democratic forms of organization power rests with the people as a whole or through their representatives. Like culture, politics surrounds us but it is the form that differs. In order to understand the relationship between the politics of organizations and their ability to cope with change we need to understand more about power, conflict and resistance.

Power in organizations

What is power?

Consider these definitions of power.

Power influences who gets what, when and how.   (Morgan, 1997, p. 170)

. . . power is the probability that one actor within a social relationship will be in a position to carry out his own will, despite resistance and regardless of the basis on which this probability rests.

(Weber, 1947, p. 47)

Power is the potential or actual ability to influence others in a desired direction. An individual, group, or other social unit has power if it controls information, knowledge, or resources desired by another individual, group, or social unit.

(Gordon, 1993, p. 392)

Power is defined as the potential ability to influence behaviour, to change the course of events, to overcome resistance, and to get people to do things that they would otherwise not do.

(Pfeffer, 1993, pp. 204–205)

These definitions emphasize one thing – power means being able to influence the behaviour of others, sometimes in a direction which the person or group would not, otherwise, have chosen. Power is a function of relationships. It is not something a person has regardless of what other people are thinking or doing; it only manifests when one person has something that the other values such as a manager's ability to recommend a subordinate for promotion.

Power also derives from differences between people and groups. Some people have more knowledge, expertise or resources than others do and, if these are scarce and desired, that person or group will have more power than others. This can be referred to as the 'elasticity of power'. In universities, lecturers with good research records usually have more job mobility than those without. They are thus often better placed to negotiate favourable outcomes for themselves if the university wants to keep them.

Furthermore, power to some extent is bestowed upon people by others; it is partly in the eye of the beholder. While resources or knowledge can give some-one power so can the belief by A that B can exercise power over them. Handy (1993, p. 125) refers to the 'relativity of power' to describe the situation where one person or group perceives another to have power while a second person or group believes otherwise: 'The group that overawes one person with its prestige and renown looks ludicrous to another.' Handy also notes that power is rarely one-sided. Hitting back or saying no is an option open to those who are seem-ingly powerless although doing so may not be in their interest.

In summary, power is about the potential to influence as well as the actual use of influence. It is a function of relationships and differences between people, their beliefs about each other and how much one person has in relation to another.

Sources of power

French and Raven (1959) identified five sources of power and their ideas have had a big influence on research on social power (Frost and Stahelski, 2006; Peiro and Melia, 2003).

1 Positional (legitimate) power – power invested in a person's formal position in a hierarchy, for example the power to issue a formal performance warning. This is perhaps the most obvious source of power that we are used to. We give our boss some power simply because they are our boss and they have rights to ask us to do things.
2 Expert power – this derives from a person's skills and knowledge and was rec-ognized by Francis Bacon (1597) in his observation 'knowledge itself is power'. For instance, we credit doctors with expert power when we see them in surgery.
3 Referent power – this is power deriving from charisma, i.e., the ability to attract others to a cause. It is about liking and identifying with another. Referent power can cut across hierarchy – a well-liked person at the bottom of an organization may develop referent power perhaps as a spokesperson in communications with higher management.
4 Reward power – the ability to give some sort of reward, for example, salary, promotion, time off or access to a resource.
5 Coercive power – the power of forcing someone to do something that they would not want to do. It is negative and based on the use of punishment for non-compliance.

Power and influence can be seen as separate things – see Handy's (1993) separa-tion shown in Illustration 5.2. This classification of power and influence is useful but life is not always as clear-cut as is suggested. For instance, a particular method of influence could be used in conjunction with several sources of power. In addition, the distinction between power and influence may, to some extent, be artificial – one shades into another. Morgan's (1997) chapter on 'Organizations as political systems', does not differentiate between power and influence but discusses a list of 14 sources of power (see Illustration 5.3).

Paton (1994) discusses the power sources in Illustration 5.3 but divides them into 'visible' and 'invisible' sources. Many of these categorizations overlap with Hardy's (1994) identification of four dimensions of power – decision-making power, non-decision-making power, symbolic power and the power of the system.

Illustration 5.2

Power and influence

The possible sources of individual power that give one the ability to influence others are as follows:

- *Physical power*: the power of superior force.
- *Resource power*: the possession of valued resources; the control of rewards.
- *Position power*: legitimate power; comes as a result of the role or position held in the organization.
- *Expert power*: vested in someone because of their acknowledged expertise.
- *Personal power*: charisma, popularity; resides in the person and in their personality.
- *Negative power*: illegitimate power; the ability to disrupt or stop things happening.

Methods of influence

Different types of power are used in different ways. Particular methods of influence attach themselves (more or less) to particular types of power:

- *Force*: derived from having physical power; bullying, hold-ups, loss of temper.
- *Rules and procedures*: derived from having position power, backed by resource power; devising rules and procedures to result in particular outcomes.
- *Exchange*: derived from having resource power; bargaining, negotiating, bribing.
- *Persuasion*: derived from having personal power; use of logic, the power of argument, evidence of facts.
- *Ecology*: derived from different power sources; manipulating the physical and psychological environment to achieve certain purposes.
- *Magnetism*: derives from personal and sometimes expert power; inspiring trust, respect; using charm, infectious enthusiasm.

Source: Based on Handy, C. (1993) *Understanding Organizations*, London: Penguin, pp. 126–141.

Illustration 5.3

Morgan's sources of power in organizations

1 Formal authority.

2 Control of scarce resources.

3 Use of organizational structure, rules and regulations.

4 Control of decision processes.

5 Control of knowledge and information.

6 Control of boundaries.

7 Ability to cope with uncertainty.

8 Control of technology.

9 Interpersonal alliances, networks, and control of 'informal organization'.

10 Control of counterorganizations.

11 Symbolism and the management of meaning.

12 Gender and the management of gender relations.

13 Structural factors that define the stage of action.

14 The power one already has.

Source: Morgan, G. (1997) *Images of Organizations*, London: Sage, p. 171.

Robbins (2005) drawing on French and Raven's ideas suggests two broad categories of power; formal power and personal power. Formal power relates to the position of the individual within the organization and incorporates coercive, reward, legitimate and information power, all of which are particularly important in times of uncertainty and change. Personal power derives from the 'unique characteristics' of individuals such as their skills and expertise, their personalities and their favoured association with others from whom they gain status and other desirable resources.

In the summaries of power above a common theme is recognition that power comes with position and the ability to control resources.

Activity 5.1

1 *In relation to French and Raven's sources of power, identify individuals in your own organization who you consider 'fit' each of the five categories.*

2 *Repeat the activity above but this time thinking of people outside your organization. They might be in the media, government or entertainment and use one or more sources of power to influence opinions and actions – even your own!*

Power sources and change

Weber (1947) drew attention to three types of authority. The first derives from tradition, that is, authority legitimized by custom and practice and a belief in the right of certain individuals to rule others. The second is charismatic authority, which is legitimized through the leader's particular qualities being valued and an inspiration to others. The third type of authority Weber called 'rational–legal authority'. This type of authority characterizes the power held by people because of their position in some formal or understood hierarchy that has some independent standing with regard to the rules and procedures sustaining it. Position power bestows certain rights on those who have it, for instance the right to order others to do things or to refuse other people's requests. Position power or formal authority is a distinctive source of power in organizations and is distributed asymmetrically – a few people have a lot, most have little and even perceptions of vertical differences influence the judgement of power (Schubert, 2005).

Resource power

Resource power stems from the power associated with being able to distribute or withhold valued rewards. Both 'push' and 'pull' strategies can be used to exercise it, as illustration 5.4 shows..

Illustration 5.4

Influencing others through push and pull strategies

'Push' strategies

Push strategies attempt to influence people by imposing or threatening to impose 'costs' on the people or groups concerned if they do not do what is desired. This may be done either by *withdrawing* something that the 'target' of influence values, for example your cooperation and support, or by threatening a sanction if the target does not comply, for example disciplinary action, a poor appraisal, removal of a bonus or perk, or perhaps public criticism. The ability to impose such costs will depend largely on a person's *position* and the *resources* that they control.

'Pull' or 'reward' strategies

If push strategies are the stick, then 'pull' or 'reward' strategies are the carrot. They are the content theories motivation that emphasize material, social and other extrinsic rewards. Rewards are often used to influence people by a process of *exchange*. Pull strategies may follow from any of the power bases. Resources, such as extra pay or extra staff, may be offered, expertise or information may be traded, increased status may be conferred or access to valuable contacts given. Less obvious, but perhaps more common, there are friendship and favour, approval and inclusion in a group.

Source: Based on Handy, C. (1993) *Understanding Organizations*, London: Penguin, pp. 126–141.

Activity 5.2

Think about some occasions at work when you have tried to achieve something that you wanted. To what extent were 'push' strategy or 'pull' strategies used?

Were the strategies successful? If so, why do you think they worked?

If any of the strategies were not successful, why was this?

Invisible power

Control over resources such as budgets or promotions are examples of *visible assets* of the power holder but we can also 'see' invisible assets (Paton, 1994). These are, first, the power to control information. Handy (1993, p. 129) observed:

> A flow of information often belongs as of right to a 'position' in the organization. If it does not already belong it can often be originated as a necessary input to that position. This can be horizontal information, i.e. information, often of a technical nature, from the same level of the organization; vertical information, from above or from below but potentially trapped in the particular 'position' and to be dispersed with the agreement of the occupant.

Morgan (1997, p. 179) echoes this by saying:

> These (people) are often known as 'gatekeepers' who open and close channels of communication and filtering, summarizing, analyzing, and thus shaping knowledge in accordance with a view of the world that favours their interests.

The ability to slow down or accelerate the flow of information gives power to many people who probably do not occupy 'high' positions but who simply act as messengers or copiers of information from one part of the organization to another. A second type of invisible asset is that of right of access, for example, to alliances and the informal organization:

> The skilled organizational politician systematically builds and cultivates such informal alliances and networks, incorporating whenever possible the help and influence of all those with an important stake in the domain in which he or she is operating.
>
> (Morgan, 1997, p. 186)

The right to organize which goes with position power is another invisible asset. This fits with Morgan's (1997) statement that a source of power is being able to use the organization's structure, rules and regulations to suit one's own purposes. An example is the power to say who gets the best offices or to waive certain rules according to convenience.

Controlling decisions

Position power includes the right to make certain decisions and this is a frequently visible and unquestioned because of the position. However, issues that are not, strictly speaking, directly concerned with the decision itself can be presented in such a way as to influence the outcome (see Illustration 5.5).

Illustration 5.5

Controlling the decision agenda

The marketing manager of an insurance company was on the brink of launching a large product development campaign. At the next management meeting it had been decided to discuss poor profit performance in the previous two quarters. At issue was whether to deploy resources into expanding sales or into cutting costs by increasing automation. He knew that if this issue was raised at the meeting he would be outvoted by a small minority of peers who leaned toward investing in automation. However, he was convinced that automation did not sell insurance! Therefore he needed to find an issue that would rearrange the coalition structure currently against him. He realized that the key issue he would prefer to have discussed was market share and not profits, so he did three things. First, he sent a report to all the management committee members that showed how losses in market share could be regained by his proposal. Second, he sent to all members of the management committee a memo asking them to consider ways in which his proposed product development programme could be carried out effectively and at a lower cost. Third, he persuaded the chief executive to place his project proposal first on the agenda. When the meeting started, the issue was not whether the product launch should take place or not, but what funds would be required to launch the product. The automation proposal was postponed because some marginal members of the automation coalition had become committed to the market share issue.

Source: Paton, R. (1994) 'Power in Organizations', in Arson, R. and Paton, R., *Organizations, Cases, Issues, Concepts*, London: PCP, p. 194.

Wilson (1992, p. 54) refers to the type of power described in Illustration 5.5 as 'covert' power, saying: 'Here power is exercised through "non-decision making" rather than by means of attempts to influence readily identifiable (and commonly known) decision topics.' Invisible or covert power associated with decision making takes many forms. For instance, Illustration 5.5 shows it may take the form of the power to 'set' the agenda under which something will be discussed, limiting who may or may not take part in the discussion or defining the scope of the discussion – so-called safe agendas where some issues do not even get discussed (Hardy, 1994). Some topics and people are deliberately excluded from the decision-making process and exclusion from this process can also come about because participants do not have the knowledge or expertise to take part in any meaningful debate. The role of the 'expert' appears in many guises.

Expert or knowledge power

On some issues we rely on and accept the judgements of people who possess a particular know-how or understanding. Those who have specialist knowledge or expertise in scarce supply have a particular kind of resource power.

The middle-ranking research chemist who calmly says 'it just can't be done' can stop the marketing director of a chemical firm dead in his or her tracks. If the director is unwise enough to press the point he or she simply invites a lecture on, say, some finer points of polymer chemistry, whereupon – whether he or she pretends to understand and agree, or instead admits to not understanding and refuses to agree – the point is irretrievably lost.

(Paton, 1994, p. 191)

However, as Handy (1993, p. 130) observed, 'expert power is hedged about by one major qualification; it can only be given by those over whom it will be exercised'. Only when someone's claim to expertise is recognized can it become a power source. The IT technician who can decide when to fix a computer has, albeit temporarily, power over someone who may be much more senior.

Illustration 5.6

Political skulduggery

Consider this recent episode that was written by one of the actors in the performance. One of the managers of a strategic business unit (SBU) of about 150 people wanted to push through changes to the unit's product offering. The stimulus for this was largely due to recommendations made by assessors for external quality schemes that, if awarded, are seen as an important boost to status and which boost competitive position of the organization.

There are five fairly autonomous product groups in the SBU each with their own staff. What happens in one group by and large does not impact on the other areas. The management of the SBU like to think it is democratic and inclusive and so a 'working group' was formed to look at alternative ways of changing the portfolio before recommending to the top management team (TMT). The working group consisted of a 'director' in the chair and one representative from each of the five areas. Previous 'rationalization' had already hit one of the groups – let's call it Consulting as it provided products and services in that general area. The Consulting representative was a new member of staff unused to a) the complexity of product offerings and b) organizational politics.

After several meetings a proposal emerged which met the working group's initial remit and which would streamline the product offering. The Consulting group

was a clear loser in the proposals, seeing a substantial cut in its services if the recommendations were implemented. The chair of the working party said that 'the mood of the meeting' was that the proposals were the best overall for the SBU. Translated, that means that the Consulting group representative's voice was downplayed and the more experienced representatives from other areas all convinced themselves that their interests would be protected. They didn't really care about recommendations that hit areas other than their own.

The working group's proposals were put before a full meeting of the Consulting group at which strong and considered objections were made. Surprisingly, the head of the group did not speak against the objections which raises speculation as to why. Objections were minuted but to no avail. The TMT, on which the working group chair sits, rejected the objections and so accepted the proposals. Further rationalization of the Consulting group's services went ahead.

So what does this tell us? First, that the chair's grasp of the minutiae of the total product offerings (i.e., information) was a source of power used to favour certain points of view and disfavour counter points. Second, that membership of the working party could be (and was) engineered to minimize the arguments against what many believed had been

Illustration 5.6 *continued*

thought out by one or two TMT members in the first place. The working party can be seen simply an illusion of democracy giving legitimacy to pre-planned intentions and not as a democratic exercise at all.

Third, that filtering of the objections raised by the Consulting group took place. They were downplayed in the final group meeting. When others heard of the proposals and objected their views were also downplayed as they were being raised outside the formal processes. The minutes of the Consulting group's meeting to discuss the proposals did not convey the intensity of feeling that had arisen over concerns about jobs and careers as well as alternative views of viable changes. Fourth, it shows how one person's knowledge of organizational systems and access to others allows them to manoeuvre for outcomes in their interest.

The case is a microcosm of organizational politics. In the eyes of the TMT the working party chair responsible led a democratic process that came to a clear decision that doubtless reflected upon their abilities. Others see it as a stage-managed political process rooted in self-interest and self-promotion that was rigged from the outset. This is one explanation for the lack of fight and engagement shown by the group head – had she already been 'nobbled'?

Although small fry in the grand scheme of things, this short case is a good reminder of Vera Brittain's quote (1964): 'Politics are usually the executive expression of human immaturity'.

This case is one account of a real and recent change event.

Symbolic power

Symbolic power is widespread in political systems, for instance statues of 'great leaders', the use of violence by police or security forces and surveillance. Individual managers and politicians use it to hold on to their positions (Bourdieu, 1991). The power that comes from the ability to manipulate symbols comes from their capacity to signal to others the meaning, not of the symbol itself, but of what they stand for. This is implicit in Morgan's (1997) reference to symbolism as the management of meaning. Artefacts can also be seen as possessing three dimensions (Vilnai-Yavetz and Rafaeli, 2006):

- *Symbolic* – what meaning does the artefact carry for the beholder?
- *Aesthetic* – what emotions are aroused by the artefact?
- *Instrumental* – how does the artefact influence performance?

Symbolic power is, therefore, the power to manipulate and use symbols to create organizational environments and the beliefs and understandings of others to suit one's own purposes. Hardy includes the use of language, rituals and myths as examples of symbolic power. The use of phrases such as, 'all pulling in the same direction', 'we are a happy team', or 'flatten the opposition' all give their own specific, covert messages about expected behaviour. The use of phrases such as 'we are a happy team' negates the need to say that conflict and disagreement are not expected in this organization. Rituals involving who sits where at meetings and how people greet each other are indications of who holds power in relation to whom. Leaving the chair at the head of the table free symbolizes that the person about to occupy it has a power base. Addressing someone as 'boss' symbolizes their power in relation to another. If, like us, you work in organizations then you can probably see how people in powerful positions align with selected others, thus symbolizing the chosen person's favourable standing in relation to them. (They are sometimes rather cynically referred to as 'the chosen ones'.) We can also see how 'organizational climbers' try to position themselves in relation to bosses in attempts to gain a little power for themselves simply by virtue of the associations they are making.

Morgan (1997) uses the term 'theatre' to describe the physical settings, appearances and styles of behaviour that can add to someone's power. He says of those who seek to add to their power in this way: 'Many deserve organizational Oscars for their performances' (p. 189). Examples of the use of theatre are the size and furnishing of offices, the seating of visitors and the often unspoken rules of dress. Morgan says (p. 190):

> Style also counts. It's amazing how you can symbolize power by being a couple of minutes late for that all-important meeting where everyone depends on your presence, or how visibility in certain situations can enhance your status.

He gives an example of how some people visiting the US president in the White House turn up early so as to be seen by as many people as possible while waiting for their appointment, thus dramatizing their supposed importance.

Organizational change often requires change to symbols and symbolic actions, for example changing the time spent on things, reinterpreting things that happened in the past or which are happening in the present. In all but the smaller organizations most employees do not interact much with people in leadership positions. Symbolic action is what most employees see and maybe it is all they need to see to begin to appreciate changes needed (Das, 1988).

Symbols of power are inevitably intertwined with an organization's culture and are frequently an outward expression of it. Any analysis of power in organizations must take account of not only the types of power which are exercised over the content of decisions, but also the types of power that influence attitudes and behaviour, frequently in ways that those influenced are hardly aware of. Activity 5.3 helps to show how symbolic power is used in a particular organization.

Activity 5.3

This activity will help identify the routines, rituals and symbols prevalent in an organization and who uses them. Think of your own organization or one you are familiar with.

1 *Which routines and rituals are most emphasized? How are they enforced (think of the people and systems behind them).*

2 *How do the organization's leaders use language to perpetuate their own values and keep power to themselves and their chosen followers? What does this tell you about the topics that can be debated and which are out of bounds?*

3 *Who, in the organization, has the most impressive 'trappings' of office (office, furnishings, car, expense account etc.)? What kind of power do they symbolize?*

4 *Give examples of two people who use gamesmanship to get their own way: (a) one who does so through aggressive means; and (b) one who does so through operating craftily and with an apparently low profile. Consider just what it is they are manipulating in these processes.*

Individual power

In addition to power sources deriving from how an organization is structured and the roles played by people working in them there is another source of power – that which derives from the personal characteristics of those wielding power (Pfeffer, 1992 in Huczynski and Buchanan, 2007, p. 799). These include:

- energy, endurance and physical stamina;
- ability to focus energy and to avoid wasteful effort;
- sensitivity and an ability to read and understand others;
- flexibility and selecting varied means to achieve goals;
- personal toughness; willingness to engage in conflict and confrontation;
- able to 'play the subordinate' and 'team member' to enlist the support of others.

In a way, power derived from these sources is potentially available to anyone given its non-dependence on position, status or control of knowledge or resources. However, the use of power is unlikely to succeed unless used in conjunction with these. This leads to the issue of those who lack power – in other words the issue of powerlessness.

The politics of powerlessness

If there is one thing that symbols of power are intended to do, it is to make others who do not control these symbols feel their own lack of power.

Conversely, many people are relatively powerless because of the way particular organizational factors affect them. In addition, some groups of people, for instance women and those from some ethnic minorities, appear powerless in relation to the majority groups, for example although not always, white males. People with physical disabilities may be excluded from positions of status and decision making because of prejudice or simply a lack of physical access to the spaces and places where the exercise of power takes place.

Gender and powerlessness

Several writers have discussed the relative powerlessness of women (Kanter, 1979; Gordon, 1993; Handy, 1993). Morgan (1997) argues that formal organizations typically mirror what, in the West, has been (and to a large extent still is) a patriarchal society. 'Strategic' jobs such as marketing, production or finance are generally done by men and jobs that involve caring, supporting and helping others tend to be done by women. This gender segregation across occupations goes some way to explaining why in spite of 'equal pay for equal work' legislation and much greater parity of women in educational systems women earn less than men on average, why they occupy a much greater proportion of jobs at the lower levels of organizations and why many women's jobs are part-time and/or temporary (Wilson, 1995). A similar picture is seen on an international scale. In many sectors the higher the ladder the fewer women are found and the percentage of women in top jobs in big corporations is very small (ILO, 2009).

Maitland (2000a, 2000b) reported that, although women held a 54 per cent share of banking, finance and insurance jobs their presence in the top jobs in the City of London (Britain's financial centre) was low. A 'macho culture of long hours and big bucks' was said to discriminate against women becoming managers. The same report commented, 'The City is about ten years behind business . . . There's a lot of open discrimination, but there's also a lot of covert and very subtle discrimination, in running down women's confidence. *We're not talking about sexual issues but about power*' [author's emphasis].

The *Female FTSE Report, 2008* showed that in the UK the percentage of women directors rose from 6.9 in 1999 to 11.7 in 2008 and that there were five female chief executives in the FTSE top 100. Some top UK companies had no women on the board (Sealy, Vinnicombe and Singh, 2008). Illustration 5.7 demonstrates the slow progress made by women entering the higher levels of management.

There are several explanations of why women, on average, do less well than men and, if they have achieved professional status, still do not rise in similar proportions to the higher levels in their profession or the higher levels of management. They include:

Illustration 5.7

Women in the boardroom

Looking across Europe there is a north–south divide reflected in the make-up of the boardrooms of big business. In the far north, women directors are starting to make their presence felt, occupying 44 per cent of board seats in the largest companies in Norway and 27 per cent in Sweden. Boards in Spain and Portugal, however, remain almost exclusively male. The split is revealed by a survey indicating that across Europe women hold just 9.7 per cent of the directorships in the top 300 companies up from 8 per cent in 2004. Between the extremes of Norway and Portugal lies the UK where women have 1,1 per cent of seats, the Netherlands with 12 per cent and France with 8 per cent.

Greater representation of women in top management in Scandinavia can be explained by a traditional acceptance of feminine values in society (see the discussion of national culture in Chapter 4) coupled with a more radical understanding of gender equality together with professionalization of gender equality work (Wahl and Hook, 2007). Furthermore, Norway tops the list because it introduced quotas to increase women's representation in the boardroom. However, across Europe only a handful of women have achieved the top job. Although women's representation in Scandinavia has grown steadily in the past few years, outside the region change has been slow.

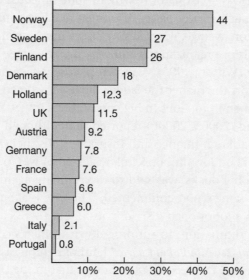

Source: European PWN BoardWomen Monitor 2008, European Professional Women's Network.

- Perceptions of the social roles that men and women should perform although social attitudes are changing to lessen these distinctions.
- Placement of women in non-strategic roles from which it is harder to progress to the top and which bring exclusion from networks that are important in underpinning career advancement.
- Child-bearing and child-care, which limit the amount of time available for work given that progress to the top often calls for long working hours.

Perceptions of the 'visible' commitment of women, i.e. being present at work, can be compromised by this factor.

Structuralist theorists argue that the structure of jobs affects the job holder's ability to exercise power. Kanter, for instance, argues that women are typically shepherded into powerless jobs and hence find themselves in positions without much influence. Entry to a succession of powerless jobs perpetuates the situation. In contrast, socialization theory argues that it is learned behaviour, i.e. the behaviour that girls and young women are socialized into in the family and at school, that makes them less effective users of power in the workplace. Hence there is a big question around whether the behaviours of men and women at work are a result of their situations or a result of more stable differences between men and women.

O'Neill (2004) explored whether men and women use different forms of upward influence at work. Upward influence concerns the ways that people try to influence the attitudes of people above them in their favour. Tactics include:

- *Rationality* – using facts and figures to support arguments and thinking.
- *Coalition* – claiming that lots of other people support you.
- *Ingratiation* – managing the impressions of others and flattering them.
- *Exchange* – using the exchange of benefits to gain favour.
- *Assertiveness* – being forceful in pushing for your way of thinking.
- *Upward appeal* – getting support of higher levels of managers for one's ideas and plans.

O'Neill's research was inconclusive and suggested that the differences in upward influence that were observed were not explained by gender but by different sources of power. Mainiero (1986) questioned whether women used different coping strategies at work, i.e. is there a gender effect on ways of influencing others that they depend upon? She found that women were more likely to use an acquiescence strategy of accepting the power imbalance and acting in a dependent manner than men.

Another reason put forward for relative lack of power is that the prevailing structures and power balances in organizations, which are predominantly based on a male model of what organization and management is about, conspire indirectly to reduce the power sources of women (Kanter, 1979; Morgan, 1997). Access to power structures in organizations is an important part of the explanation of wage inequalities. In Sweden, women working in power structures populated by men earned less than women in power structures with more women in them (Hultin and Szulkin, 1999, 2003). This was explained through differential access to networks which determine rewards in labour markets. 'Women are less central than men in those networks in which organizational power is located and important decisions on organizational policies are made.

Hence women may receive less support for their arguments and their claims' (1999, p. 459). Their research shows that it is not individual discrimination against women that is occurring but attitudes towards typically female jobs and barriers to higher paid positions.

Another take on powerlessness comes from the gendered nature of workplace behaviour and the norms surrounding the behaviour associated with promotability. McKenna (1997) (in Buchanan and Badham, 1999, p. 123) refers to the world of male politics in which 'Sitting back and hoping for recognition is seen as passivity, a lack of fire, guts and ambition. Essential for success is self-promotion, and conformity to the "unwritten rules of success"'. McKenna (1997, p. 51) says: '[Success is about] maintaining silence in the face of politics and backstabbing . . . It has little to do with performing good work or being productive and everything to do with pecking order and egos.' We do not intend to imply here that women cannot display the political behaviour to get ahead – indeed some are very effective at it and can be just as talented or just as devious and self-promoting in organizational politics as men. But on balance there is a body of thinking that suggests they are less likely to display such behaviour – hence the imbalance.

Research published by Catalyst, a US company organisation that works for women's advancement in business, suggests investors should be worried about the lack of women in top jobs. In assessing the gender make-up of top management and the financial performance of 353 Fortune 500 companies between 1996 and 2000, it found that, on average, the quartile with the largest proportion of women had a return on equity 35.1 per cent higher, and a total return to shareholders 34 per cent higher, than the quartile with the lowest female representation. The link worked the other way too; on average, top-performing companies had more women in their leadership teams (Maitland, 2004).

Other studies have linked women in the boardroom to improved corporate performance (Stevenson, 2004), decreased likelihood of going bust (*The Times*, 2009) and enhanced corporate reputation in sectors in close contact with consumers (Brammer *et al.*, 2009). Reasons put forward include:

● That men and women bring complementary skills to corporate management.
● Women may be more risk averse.
● Women who make it to the top are better managers than men because they had to perform much better than men to get there.
● Assessors of corporate reputation believe that women contribute distinctively to boards.

Activity 5.4

Some studies have shown that organizations with women in the boardroom outperform men-only boards. The same reports imply that gender diversity is a causal factor in explaining better performance. If this is true, then how would you explain the causal mechanism? Would an all-women board perform less well than a mixed board?

In the UK the number of women in management is rising steadily. In 2005 about one third of management roles, across all levels, were held by women, having trebled since the mid-1990s (CMI, 2005). It seems certain that the numbers of women in senior management positions will continue to increase and it looks as if this will alter the typical structures of organizational politics and power. However, given the continuing situation it is too soon to say that feminization of the workplace will make a difference to the endemic organizational issues of power imbalances and the nature of organizational politics. After all, meta-analyses (aggregates of many smaller studies) show that, at work, men and women are more similar than they are different (Dindia and Allen, 1992).

Activity 5.5

Think of someone whom you consider does their job very well, but has been passed over for promotion. Assuming there is no reason why this person could not do the higher-level job (given time and training if necessary), why do you think they have not progressed?

In your analysis, draw on the concepts of power and political activity discussed above in relation to the possible lack of power of the person concerned.

National culture and powerlessness

Lien (2005) gives an interesting account of powerlessness among Taiwanese women employees and how this links directly to prevailing national culture. Feelings of powerlessness came from:

- Structural barriers such as assumptions that women leave work when married so why bother giving them opportunities to develop. Due to lack of seniority they lacked position power.
- Behavioural barriers such as bosses not 'letting go' of work and giving younger women a chance, prescribing how to do things and insisting that orders and procedures are followed without deviation. Women's talents were not called upon and bosses gave credit to others, overlooking the roles that women had played in achieving things.
- Accommodation and rationalization – this sums-up the Darwinian idea of adaptation in that to survive women tended to adapt to their work environment because if they did not they could not survive in it. However, adaptation meant surviving in a powerless niche.

Since national cultural differences influence many aspects of organizational life care must be taken not to assume that practices in one culture, for instance Taiwan (see above), can be transferred, without question, to another. For instance, it would be unwise to assume that motivating or leadership styles that work well in a western culture will be effective in other countries – although they might be.

The implications of these cultural differences for a discussion of power and powerlessness hinge on the very issue of difference. People from different cultures behave differently and bring different values and attitudes to the workplace. People from cultures scoring high on Hofstede's (1981) high power distance dimension will expect managers to make most workplace decisions. However, in Western cultures, which characteristically score low on power distance, people who defer to others to make decisions may well be seen as lacking ambition and not ready to take responsibility. This, in turn, does not encourage people to gain power sources such as 'control of decision processes' and 'formal authority' (Morgan, 1997). Morgan also cites 'ability to cope with uncertainty' as another source of power. This relates directly to another of Hofstede's cultural dimensions – uncertainty avoidance. Consequently, if a minority group's cultural upbringing is one where ambiguity must be controlled they are less likely to demonstrate the attitudes and behaviour which could win them power of this kind.

Another example is the difference in orientation towards others that is found between different cultural groupings. The perspective of power in Western society is based mainly on the power of the individual, yet in many societies (particularly in East Asian countries) group loyalty is a virtue; it is the performance of the group that matters. Power is linked to the power of the group. Yuet-Ha (1996) points this out in her discussion of the differences between Western and East Asian work-related values and their relationship to work-related competencies. Her findings suggest that, for people from an East Asian culture, it is relatively easy to implement teamworking and shared responsibility and support. However, it is relatively difficult to implement open communication, participation, decisiveness, delegation of authority and taking leadership responsibility. Given that most of these competencies are valued in Western societies, people from minority groups that value other competencies are less likely to progress when working in the UK, the US and some European countries unless they can change others' perceptions of their differences. Their lack of power in the first place makes this difficult to achieve.

Position and powerlessness

Legislation has certainly helped to eliminate the more overt prejudices that have prevented women and minority groups from enjoying the benefits given to others, even if certain organizational and covert processes still contrive to reduce their access to power sources and influence. However, we should not simply focus on equality group membership since many employees in majority groups find themselves relatively powerless due to their position. These groups are not, as might be expected, simply those working at the lowest levels of the organization. They are powerless because of the particular positions they occupy. People near the bottom of hierarchies do not have much access to resources, information and support to get a task done or the cooperation of others to do what is necessary (Kanter, 1979).

Kanter identified three 'lines' of organizational power: (1) lines of supply; (2) lines of information; (3) lines of support. These have been discussed already as being basically related to resource and position power but of additional relevance here is the power that comes from *connections* with other parts of the organizational system. Kanter identifies this as deriving from two sources – job activities and political alliances. She says (pp. 65–66):

1 Power is most easily accumulated when one has a job that is designed and located to allow *discretion* (non-routinized action permitting flexible, adaptive and creative contributions), *recognition* (visibility and notice), and *relevance* (being central to pressing organizational problems).

2 Power also comes when one has relatively close contact with *sponsors* (high level people who confer approval, prestige, or backing), *peer networks* (circles of acquaintanceship that provide reputation and information, the grapevine often being faster than formal communication channels), and *subordinates* (who can be developed to relieve managers of some of the burdens and to represent the manager's point of view).

When people are in situations where they have strong lines of supply, information and support, their job allows them discretion and their work is recognized as being relevant to the organization's purposes, they can more easily relinquish some control and, thereby, develop their staff more effectively. In contrast to this situation, Kanter (1979, p. 67) says:

> The powerless live in a different world. Lacking the supplies, information, or support to make things happen easily, they may turn instead to the ultimate weapon of those who lack productive power – oppressive power: holding others back and punishing with whatever threats they can muster.

This situation is frequently that of the first-line supervisor. Illustration 5.8 shows how multiple causes combine to influence the attitudes and behaviour of first-line supervisors and people in similar positions and increase their feelings of powerlessness.

Kanter also discusses the position of staff professionals, that is, those people who act as 'advisers behind the scenes'. These are people who must 'sell' their knowledge and expertise and bargain for resources but who, quite often, do not have power to bargain with – they have few favours to offer in exchange. People working in human resource departments are frequently in this situation. They often have little line experience and, therefore, are not involved in the mainstream organizational power networks. Being specialists, their ability to cross functions or undertake general management positions is restricted. They are, therefore, likely to get 'stuck' in a limited career structure. Having little power themselves, they cannot pass it on to others. In addition, they are prey to having their work contracted to agencies or consultants outside the organization. The effect of this relative powerlessness is that they tend to become 'turf-minded', protecting their patches, drawing strict boundaries between themselves and other functional managers. These various aspects of powerlessness, collectively, lead to conservative attitudes that are resistant to change. Activity 5.6 asks you to assess a job in terms of its capacity to generate power for its occupant.

Illustration 5.8

First-line supervisors and powerlessness

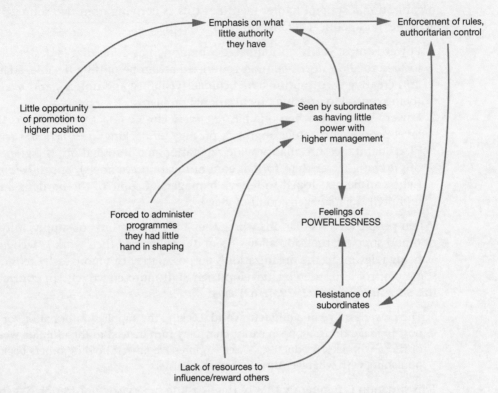

Source: Based on the description in Kanter, R.M. (1979) 'Power Failure in Management Circuits', *Harvard Business Review*, July–August, pp. 65–75.

Politics, power and conflict

Earlier in this chapter politics was described as the use of power. Political behaviour extends beyond formal roles and is observed in activities that are not part of someone's formal organizational role. Even in organizations which have a strong culture the experience of that culture will vary for individuals and groups who operate within their own sub-cultures. What is more, a dominant culture will not solve one of the perennial issues in all organizations – the existence of scarce resources and so people more disposed towards political behaviour will use their skills to satisfy their needs at the expense of others.

Activity 5.6

The following factors contribute to power or powerlessness. For your own job, or one you know well, take each factor in turn and tick the middle or last column as appropriate.

Factor	Generates power when factor is:	Generates powerlessness when factor is:
Rules in the job	☐ Few	☐ Many
Predecessors in the job	☐ Few	☐ Many
Established routines	☐ Few	☐ Many
Centralized resources	☐ Few	☐ Many
Communications	☐ Extensive	☐ Limited
Task variety	☐ High	☐ Low
Physical location	☐ Central	☐ Distant
Relation of tasks to current problem areas	☐ Central	☐ Peripheral
Competitive pressures	☐ High	☐ Low
Net-forming opportunities	☐ High	☐ Low
Contact with senior management	☐ High	☐ Low
Advancement prospects of subordinates	☐ High	☐ Low
Authority/discretion in decision making	☐ High	☐ Low
Meaningful goals/tasks	☐ High	☐ Low
Participation in programmes, meetings, conferences	☐ High	☐ Low

Consider the overall picture obtained of the job. How powerful might the person occupying it be?

Source: Based on factors suggested by Kanter, R.M. (1979) 'Power Failure in Management Circuits', *Harvard Business Review*, July–August, pp. 65–75; and Gordon, J.R. (1993) *A Diagnostic Approach to Organizational Behavior*, Needham Heights, MA: Allyn & Bacon, p. 425.

As we have seen, resource power stems from scarcity and additional resource power is frequently being fought over. The issue then becomes one of whether competition for resources is helpful to the achievement of organizational performance or whether it becomes dysfunctional. Handy (1993, p. 298) appears in no doubt about this – 'competition for power nearly always turns to conflict', – with the implication that, while competition is not necessarily undesirable, conflict is. However, whereas Handy's discussion of conflict implies some disapproval, Morgan (1997) takes a more pragmatic view pointing out that conflict is a familiar feature of life in an organizational society. His argument rests on the assumption that, because organizations are designed as systems which, at the same time, promote competition as well as cooperation, one of their outputs will, inevitably, be conflict.

This view emphasizes the plural nature of interests, conflicts and sources of power and has become known as the 'pluralist' frame of reference (Morgan, 1997, p. 199). This stands in contrast to the 'unitary' frame of reference that emphasizes the philosophy that organizations have goals to which all organizational members subscribe, with all working towards their attainment. Whereas managers holding a pluralist view of the way organizations should operate stress the idea of a coalition of divergent interests that will sometimes result in conflict, managers subscribing to a unitary philosophy consider conflict as an aberration from the normal state of affairs which recognizes only formal authority as the legitimate source of power. Thus, from a unitary frame of reference, managers are considered as the only people with the 'right to manage' while others are expected to subordinate their own personal interests to the good of the organization. From this point of view, the only type of power recognized is formal position power. Expert power might be recognized but, in the main, only as a facet of position power.

Robbins (2005, p. 423) prefers the term 'traditional' to describe this view which assumes that all conflict is bad. He says: 'The traditional approach treats conflict synonymously with such terms as violence, destruction, and irrationality. Consonant with this perspective, one of management's major responsibilities is to try to ensure that conflicts don't arise and, if they do, to act quickly to resolve them.' The idea, still to be heard, that all industrial action by workers is wrong stems from this view. The difficulty in accepting a unitary view of organizational life, as the human relations theorists showed (e.g. Mayo, 1933; Barnard, 1938; McGregor, 1960), is that it leaves no room for dealing with the multiplicity of interests which are now accepted as part of a democratic way of doing things; hence the formulation of the concept of 'pluralism'. Illustration 5.9 summarizes these two different views.

Consideration of the unitary frame of reference portrayed in Illustration 5.9 shows that organizational politics, in the well-ordered world of the unitarist, should not exist. However, this view sits uncomfortably not only with the notion of a pluralist society, but also with the increasingly chaotic circumstances that organizations deal with. In such times political behaviour is to be expected, with its associated tendency to generate both competition and cooperation (of which conflict is a part). To ignore the role of conflict as a positive force as well as a negative force in the context of organizations and change is to ignore the realities of human nature. Therefore a more detailed understanding of the nature and sources of conflict and how to manage in situations of conflict is important for anyone involved in organizational change.

Conflict in organizations

The previous section established a link between power, politics and conflict but the concept of conflict itself is by no means uncontentious. What one person calls conflict another might call bargaining or competition. Definitions of conflict include:

> . . . as a process that begins when one party perceives that another party has negatively affected, or is about to negatively affect, something that the first party cares about.

> (Robbins, 2005, p. 422)

Illustration 5.9

The unitary and pluralist views of interests, conflict and power

	The unitary view	The pluralist view
Interests	Places emphasis upon the achievement of common objectives. The organization is viewed as being united under the umbrella of common goals, and striving towards their achievement in the manner of a well-integrated team.	Places emphasis upon the individual and group interests. The organization is regarded as a loose coalition that has but a remote interest in the formal goals of the organization.
Conflict	Regards conflict as a rare and transient phenomenon that can be removed through appropriate managerial action. Where it does arise it is usually attributed to the activities of deviants and troublemakers.	Regards conflict as an inherent and ineradicable characteristic of organizational affairs and stresses its potentially positive and functional aspects.
Power	Largely ignores the role of power in organizational life. Concepts such as authority, leadership and control tend to be preferred means of describing the managerial prerogative of guiding the organization towards the achievement of common interests.	Regards power as a variable crucial to the understanding of the activities of an organization. Power is the medium through which conflicts of interest are alleviated and resolved. The organization is viewed as a plurality of power holders drawing their power from a plurality of sources.

Source: Burrell, G. and Morgan, G. (1979) *Sociological Paradigms and Organisational Analysis*, London: Heinemann Educational Books Ltd, p. 204.

> Conflict is best viewed as a process that begins when an individual or group perceives differences and opposition between him/herself and another individual or group about interests, beliefs or values that matter to him or her.
>
> (De Dreu and Beersma, 2005)

Conflict must be perceived by the parties to it otherwise it does not exist. Second, one party to the conflict must be seen as about to do or be doing something that the other party (or parties) does not want – in other words there must be opposition. Third, some kind of interaction must take place. In addition, conflict can take place at a number of levels; between individuals, between groups or between organizations. We can of course, as individuals, experience conflict within ourselves when we are wrestling with choices and decisions.

Conflict might arise because of the incompatibility of goals set for people or a confusion over the roles they are asked to play. Conflict, however, is not a unidimensional concept. It comes in different guises according to its degree of seriousness and its capacity to disrupt or, in some cases, improve a difficult situation. Thus a further definition that captures the possibilities of conflict is offered by Martin (2005, p. 746):

Conflict can be considered as something that disrupts the normal and desirable states of stability and harmony within an organization. Under this definition it is something to be avoided and if possible eliminated from the operation. However, it is also possible to consider conflict as an inevitable feature of human interaction and perhaps something that if managed constructively could offer positive value in ensuring an effective performance within the organization.

The nature of conflict

Illustration 5.10 shows different levels and causes of organizational conflict.

Illustration 5.10

The 'layers' of organizational conflict

Misunderstandings
These are 'getting the wrong end of the stick' – genuine misconceptions about what was said or done and which have the capacity for speedy resolution.

Differences of values
Value differences are the other end of the scale to misunderstandings. Conflicting values lead to the most serious disagreements. The values involved may be based on ethical considerations such as whether to take bribes to win contracts; the level at which safety should be set; whether to deal with regimes that condone particular ways of behaving (e.g. imprisoning those who disagree with them). Differences of values may also involve disagreements about the purpose of the organization, i.e. the ends for which it exists. Thus differences of values are almost always about ends or goals or objectives.

Differences of viewpoint
Different parties may share the same values but have different views on how particular goals or purposes should be met. Thus differences of viewpoint are disagreements on the means by which particular ends should be achieved. For example, two parties may agree on a goal but disagree on how to reach it. One may argue for increasing prices, the other may argue for cost cutting and redundancies.

Differences of interest
Status, resources, advancement are all desirable outcomes that most people want and, if they have them, they want to keep hold of them. The distribution of these outcomes is not a once and for all process; it is constantly being adjusted through budget setting, organizational restructuring, strategic planning and so on. Therefore, competition between individuals and, particularly, departments is ever present.

Interpersonal differences
Some people find it difficult to work with others – what most people would refer to as personality clashes. This might be because of differences of temperament, style or ways of behaving. Care should be taken, however, not to mistake other types of differences for personality clashes. Accounting for conflict under this heading is often used as an excuse for not facing up to differences that might be occurring for other reasons.

Source: Based on Open University (1985), Units 9–10 'Conflict' course T244, *Managing in Organizations*, Milton Keynes: Open University, p. 57.

Handy (1993) argues that all conflicts start from two types of difference; differences over goals and ideologies and differences over territory. Other writers suggest the sources of organizational conflict below (Pfeffer, 1981; Tosi *et al.*, 1994; Mullins, 2005; Robbins, 2005).

Interdependence

Different organizational groups depend upon each other to a greater or lesser extent. A marketing department depends on the production department to produce and deliver goods to specifications. Production is dependent on marketing for winning customers who want the products that it makes. At other times, the dependence is more one-way. The direction of dependence is related to power balances between groupings. Most line-staff relations are based on one-way task dependence (Robbins, 2005).

Organizational structures

Conflict is likely because of the power imbalances that prevail in hierarchical structures. Lawrence and Lorsch (1969) demonstrated how research, sales and production departments all had different orientations towards formality of structure, interpersonal relationships and timescales. Increased differentiation between departments, with each becoming more specialized in its activities, has the potential to lead to increased conflict between them.

Rules and regulations

On one hand, high formalization (i.e. standardized ways for people and units to interact with each other) creates fewer opportunities for disputes about who does what and when. Conversely, where there is low formalization, the degree of ambiguity is such that the potential for jurisdictional disputes increases. Robbins (2005) maintains that conflict is more likely to be less subversive in highly formalized situations as in instances where the rules are vague the opportunity to compete for resources increases. On the other hand, in situations of over-regulation, people can become frustrated by their lack of autonomy and see rules and regulations as an expression of low trust by management.

Limited resources

In times when resources are plentiful, the potential for conflict through competition for resources is reduced. In conditions of falling profits and revenues or when redundancies are occurring the potential for conflict over resources rises. Resource conflict can also knock-on to influence levels of individual satisfaction and commitment.

Cultural differences

Conflict can arise through misunderstandings or through inappropriate behaviour when working across national cultures. In addition, we can expect different national cultures to display different approaches to conflict resolution. For instance, people who come from a collectivist culture, such as Japan, are more likely to avoid outright confrontation than people who come from more individualistic cultures such as the US. People used to a high power distance culture are more likely to appeal to a higher authority and use bureaucratic rules and regulations to resolve conflict than people from cultures that score low on power distance.

Environmental change

Shifts in demand, increased competition, government intervention, new technology and changing social values are possible causes of conflict (Mullins, 2005).

The relationship between sources of conflict to the layers of conflict identified above is complex. Many situations involve more than one layer, for instance, most types of conflict will include elements of misunderstanding and differences of values are often entwined with interpersonal differences. In addition, differences of viewpoint are closely linked to differences of interest. For example, the means thought appropriate to gain particular goals (for instance the formulation of rules and procedures) are intimately related to issues about control, status and resources. The relationship between interests and views is well summarized below.

> Interests are not only shaped by our views, they are also masked by them. The pursuit of personal or departmental advantage is a largely covert affair. Interests are modest to the point of prudishness; they do not walk naked through the corridors of organizations but go heavily clothed, preferably in a fashionable attire woven from the latest ideas about the best way to achieve organizational goals.
>
> (Open University, 1985, p. 59)

This quotation shows how conflict can be bubbling away underneath a calm exterior and shows how political behaviour is frequently the outcome of differences that result in conflict.

Managing conflict

Strategies for managing conflict will vary according to the managers' frame of reference. The orientation of managers subscribing to a unitary philosophy of organization will be to suppress conflict whenever possible. Conflict is likely to be seen as the work of agitators and the dominant strategy will, therefore, be one of denigrating those thought to be the cause or dismissing them from the organization. The paradox is, however, that, in a democratic society, this strategy may either cause further, more extreme, conflict behaviour or drive the expression of conflict underground. The suppression of conflict within a unitary frame of reference will be successful so long as those without power fear the consequences of conflict (e.g. lockouts, dismissal, unemployment) sufficiently to avoid it. However, as soon as acceptable alternatives to the prevailing situation are available (e.g. alternative employment, successful industrial action), then conflict will again manifest itself, thus reinforcing the view that organizations cannot, in general, be managed as unitary wholes. Recognition of their pluralist characteristics is required if conflict is to be managed successfully.

Resolving conflict has attracted a big following. An influential starting point is the Conflict Management Grid (Blake and Mouton, 1970) which has been the basis of much subsequent research. They suggested that techniques of conflict management can be mapped on two dimensions, concern for production and concern for people. On each dimension an individual can score from low to high. The five styles are:

- Accomodating (high concern for people, low for production).
- Avoiding (low/low).
- Competing (high production, low people).
- Collaborating (problem solving) – a more constructive approach of information sharing, trying to meet both sides, represented by high scores on both dimensions.
- Compromising (moderate scores on both dimensions).

The same terminology occurs in the conflict resolution behaviour put forward by Thomas (1976) and shown in Figure 5.1. Here, however, each style is mapped in terms of assertiveness (a concern to satisfy one's own needs) and cooperativeness (a concern to satisfy the other party's needs). Illustration 5.11 identifies situations when it would be most appropriate to use each conflict-handling style.

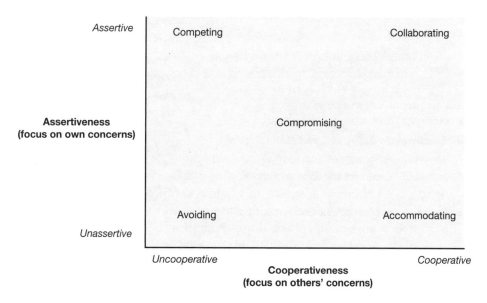

Figure 5.1 A model of conflict-handling styles

Source: Adapted from Thomas, K.W. (1976) 'Conflict and Conflict Management', in Dunnette, M.D. (ed.) *Handbook of Industrial and Organizational Psychology,* Chicago: Rand McNally, p. 900.

Illustration 5.11

Conflict resolution and situational appropriateness

Competing

1 When quick, decisive action is vital – e.g. emergencies.

2 On important issues where unpopular actions need implementing – e.g. cost cutting, enforcing unpopular rules, discipline.

3 On issues vital to company welfare when you know you are right.

4 Against people who take advantage of non-competitive behaviour.

Collaborating

1 To find an integrative solution when both sets of concerns are too important to be compromised.

2 When your objective is to learn.

3 To merge insights from people with different perspectives.

4 To gain commitment by incorporating concerns into a consensus.

5 To work through feelings that have interfered with a relationship.

Compromising

1 When goals are important, but not worth the effort or potential disruption of more assertive modes.

2 When opponents with equal power are committed to mutually exclusive goals.

3 To achieve temporary settlements of complex issues.

4 To arrive at expedient solutions to complex issues.

5 As a back-up when collaboration or competition is unsuccessful.

Avoiding

1 When an issue is trivial or more important issues are pressing.

2 When you perceive no chance of satisfying your concerns.

3 When potential disruption outweighs the benefits of resolution.

4 To let people cool down and regain perspective.

5 When gathering information supersedes immediate decision.

6 When others can resolve the conflict more effectively.

7 When issues seem tangential or symptomatic of other issues.

Accommodating

1 When you find you are wrong – to allow a better position to be heard, to learn and to show your reasonableness.

2 When issues are more important to others than to yourself – to satisfy others and maintain cooperation.

3 To build social credits for later issues.

4 To minimize loss when you are outmatched and losing.

5 When harmony and stability are especially important.

6 To allow subordinates to develop by learning from mistakes.

Source: Thomas, K.W. (1977) 'Toward Multi-dimensional Values in Teaching: the example of conflict behaviors', *Academy of Management Review*, 12, p. 487.

Each conflict-handling style has an outcome in terms of its capacity to tackle the content of the conflict and the relationship with the other party as follows:

1 *Competing.* This creates a win/lose situation and so the conflict will be resolved to suit one party only. The win/lose situation can lead to negative feelings on the part of the loser and damage the relationship.

2 *Collaborating.* This creates a win/win outcome, where both parties gain. It frequently brings a high quality solution through the results of the inputs of both parties. Win/win outcomes result in both sides being reasonably satisfied. They require openness and trust and a flexibility of approach.

3 *Compromising.* The needs of both parties are partially satisfied. It requires a trading of resources. Openness and trust may not be as great as for collaboration but compromise might set up a relationship that, in the future, could move to collaboration.

4 *Avoiding.* This does not tackle the problem. It creates a no-win situation. It does, however, allow a cooling-off period and allows the parties to (perhaps) gather more information to begin negotiations afresh or decide there is no conflict after all. It can give rise to frustration on one side if they think the issue is important while the other side do not.

5 *Accommodating.* This can create a lose/win situation, but retains a good relationship between the parties. It involves recognizing when the other party might have a better solution than oneself. It is used when relationships are more important than the problem. It builds goodwill.

Most people will have a preferred conflict-handling style, depending on their personality, culture, socialization and organizational experiences. However, effective management of conflict can call upon the use of any of these styles, depending on the circumstances.

Activity 5.7

Analyze a conflict from your own organizational experience to identify which one or more of the layers of conflict described in Illustration 5.10 apply to it.

If the conflict has already been resolved, which of Thomas's approaches identified in Illustration 5.11 were used?

If it is still happening, which of Thomas's approaches do you think is best suited to resolving it?

Sometimes, however, conflict is of a different kind altogether. Rather than having a philosophy of pluralism, some organizations are 'radicalized' to the extent that divisions between managers and other employees are almost irreconcilable

(Morgan, 1997). Thus the radical frame of reference that characterizes these organizations derives from a view of society as comprising antagonistic class interests which will only be reconciled when the differences between the owners of production and the workers have disappeared. Based on a Marxist perspective, this view does not usually prevail in the West to the extent that behaviour in conflict situations goes so far as to cause the downfall of organizations and the social structures that support them. While occasionally, as a result of industrial action on the part of workers and management, organizations may close down, in the long run the power of the owners tends to prevail.

Activity 5.8

Please read the following scenario.

Raheel and Veronica both worked at the same level in the sales department of Keen Machine, a large importer of motorcycles that held the sole rights to sell one of the leading Japanese brands in Europe. They each managed a team of salespeople responsible for a different geographical area. Although the teams operated independently of each other they shared the services of two female administrators who dealt with orders, invoicing, etc. The administrators also carried out typing and other administrative work for Raheel and Veronica. This work was done by whoever was available at a particular time.

Every year, all the salespeople had to undergo performance appraisals, which were performed by their manager (either Raheel or Veronica). However, the two administrators had been excluded from this process and the sales director decided that they also should be appraised as well and, to be fair to both, by the same person (either Raheel or Veronica).

Raheel's sales team had faced some difficulties on their territory recently and Raheel was having to work hard to recoup their previous good performance. The sales director, not wanting to
distract Raheel from this task, asked Veronica to carry out the administrative staff appraisals.

Up to this time, Raheel had always had a good relationship with both administrators and had no complaint about their work for him. However, recently he began to notice that, if both he and Veronica gave work to the administrators at the same time, Veronica's work seemed to get done first – this was in spite of the fact that he had always thought he had a better relationship with them than Veronica. He complained to the administrators, who both declared they did not show any 'favouritism' to either himself or Veronica. He was still not satisfied but could think of no reason why their behaviour towards him should have changed.

Attempt to explain this situation using concepts and ideas related to issues of power and conflict.

Power, conflict and change

Power, politics and conflict are indisputable aspects of social systems and organizational change. On the issue of power, French and Bell (1990, p. 280) take an upbeat view saying: 'The phenomenon of power is ubiquitous. Without influence (power) there would be no cooperation and no society.' Yet, as we have seen, power, conflict and politics can have negative effects. The issue for managers of organizational change, therefore, is to use power and conflict as constructively as possible. This is, however, easier said than done.

The two faces of power

The idea that power has two faces was put forward by McClelland (1970) to explain its positive and negative aspects. In their discussion of McClelland's theories, French and Bell (1990, p. 280) remarked: 'The negative face of power is characterized by a primitive, unsocialized need to have dominance over submissive others.' Positive power derives from a more socialized need to initiate, influence and lead and recognizes other people's needs to achieve their own goals as well as those of the organization. Negative power is about domination and control of others; positive power seeks to empower not only the self, but also others.

The terms 'constructive and destructive' can also be used in relation to different types of conflict and are clearly linked to the concepts of positive and negative power. The use of negative power almost inevitably results in destructive conflict, with the attendant breakdown in communications and unwillingness to contemplate any view but one's own. Discontent such as this tends to multiply in conditions of uncertainty that often exist when change is attempted. It is in such situations that power balances are upset and disagreements that might, normally, have been settled by compromise, escalate into destructive win–lose situations. Organizations facing conditions of change are, in many respects, at their most vulnerable to the political actions of those who stand to gain from the change as well as those who stand to lose.

The use of power

Among the cast of actors in a change process we find the 'change agent'. This person has a 'special responsibility for planning, implementation and outcome of strategic change' (Lines, 2007, p. 144). Lines found that power does play a role in influencing the success of strategic implementation but the relationship between power and success is complex. Different types of power are enacted in different ways and the effects of power are mediated by the different implementation processes used.

Organizational life is full of occasions when people try to influence how others see the world around them. The term used to describe this is 'sensegiving' and it captures the processes that are used in efforts to help others make sense of what is going on around them (sensemaking) in an effort to reach some new, redefined, position (see Maitlis and Lawrence, 2007). Change agents with power derived from expertise are more likely to involve people and use sensegiving than change agents with low expert power (Lines, 2007). An implication is that in organizations where participation is a strong part of the culture then expert power should be a characteristic of change agents if resistance is to be minimized.

Cynthia Hardy argues that power 'can provide the energy needed to drive the organization and its members through the strategic change process' (1996, p. S4). In addition to resource power (rewards and punishment) and process power (control of agendas and decisions) she identifies:

- *Power over meaning*: that is, attempting to alter values and norms. This involves the contemporary phenomenon of 'spin', for example, giving a set of reasons for change steeped in greater efficiency, modernization and cost savings when the real reason is to reorganize certain people out of a structure and away from positions of influence – possibly so that others more acceptable to the ruling class can be slotted-in to positions of influence.
- *System power*: this is not a source that can be grasped and manipulated, rather it is a power source lying within the organization and existing by virtue of its particular culture and structure. It is the power embedded in people's acceptance of the social conditions they work in. It is hard to change and is a backdrop to the exercise of the three other dimensions below (see Table 5.1).

Hardy argues that strategic change needs to utilize the range of dimensions to stand much chance of success. Drawing on one or two sources only will not provide the breadth of approach that is needed.

Table 5.1 Mobilizing the dimensions of power

	Power of resources	Power of processes	Power of meaning
Impact on actions	Principles of behaviour modification are used to influence specific actions	Confusion – focus on process without the support of resource power to direct behaviour	Confusion – focus on meaning without supporting resource power makes it difficult to influence specific behaviour
Impact on awareness	Inertia – resource power is inadequate to influence awareness	New awareness is created by the introduction of new participants, agendas and processes	Confusion – focus on meaning without the support of process power makes it difficult to translate awareness into behaviour
Impact on values	Inertia – resource power is inadequate to influence values	Inertia – process power is inadequate to influence values	Strategic change is given new meaning by influencing values and norms

Source: Hardy, C. (1996) 'Understanding Power: bringing about strategic change', *British Journal of Management*, 7 (special issue), S3–S16.

Some types of change are less problematic than others. Radical, frame-breaking change, for instance, is more likely to bring the greatest conditions of fear and uncertainty. Even so, small-scale, incremental change can upset the balance of power through small but significant redistributions of resources or changes in structure that make the skills or experience of some people more desirable than those of others. However, regardless of the content of any change it is the process that the organization must go through to get from one state to another that brings the most problems. Nadler (1988) suggests three major problems associated with this transition process. First is the problem of resistance to change, second is the problem of organizational control and third is the problem of power.

Figure 5.2 builds on these ideas to illustrate some interconnections between power, conflict, change and political action. It also shows some possible implications for attitudes and behaviour during periods of change. Thus the transition process from one organizational state to another (desired) state, rather than being merely a series of mechanistically designed steps, is fraught with possibilities of conflict and political action.

Some types of change challenge the values and beliefs of some of the people involved and induce an internal state of conflict that, in turn, raises their resistance to change. In addition, because values and beliefs are involved, this resistance will have a moral imperative attached to it. Confusion about the means of organizational control – that is, who and what is being monitored and how – is closely associated with disturbances in the power balance which will most frequently be linked to position and resource power. During times of confusion like this opportunities present themselves for taking political action using invisible sources of power. In this context conflict, viewed as a problem, is likely to be resolved by the use of win–lose strategies.

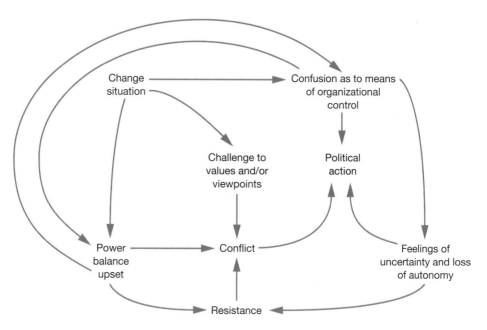

Figure 5.2 The problems of change

We discuss the role of symbolic action in the next chapter but of interest here is the fact that, during periods of relative stability, symbols such as stories, myths, rituals and routines and the more physical manifestations of status and power play a major part in sustaining that stability. Consequently, in periods of organizational change, these same symbols (and their relationship with symbolic power) can be used in the process of resisting change. What is more, this argument holds whether the change is incremental or concerned with a shift in the organizational paradigm. In addition resistance, as a general term, to other than marginal changes incurs strategic drift (see Chapter 2). The process of strategic drift, if it continues without check, leads to confusion about organizational goals and the means of achieving them. This in turn lays down the conditions for conflict and political action.

Covert political action

Covert political action is a phrase used to describe actions of the most extreme kind witnessed during episodes of change. It embraces four interrelated themes – contestation of power and authority, 'perceptions of collective injury', 'social occlusion' and officially forbidden forms of dissent – each of which helps to explain change in organizations (Morrill, Zald and Rao, 2003). Covert political action is often not seen as organizational politics and is seen instead as criminal or deviant behaviour. But this overlooks the underlying tensions that are causing it since it is used by subordinated groups to display resistance and non-conformity in political struggles. Morrill and colleagues see covert political action as follows. First, it manifests in both material and symbolic forms. Sabotage and theft are explicit forms of covert action and this includes sabotage of ideas and goals, not just of machines or systems. Products can be badly assembled, production lines disrupted, machines broken or viruses released into computer systems. Some instances of whistle-blowing can be seen as attempts to sabotage an organization. Theft and misappropriation can be used to redress perceived imbalances in relations between employees and organizations.

Second, covert political action carries an element of social visibility. Organized union resistance to management plans is an example of a highly visible interest. At other times, the interests of parties to conflict may be in the open but the time and place of actions are hidden (e.g., sabotage). Here, covert political action is occurring behind a veneer of conformity.

Third, covert political action can be conducted by an individual acting alone but is often undertaken in a collective and organized way, for example, workplace stoppages or refusing to cover for colleagues away sick. Fourth, covert action connects to change in that it challenges routines and practices that individuals or groups see as unfair. In wider society covert political action impacts on political change with an extreme example being changes won through civil disobedience or sustained terrorist activity. So why does it occur? Morrill *et al.* (2003) give the following reasons:

- *Declining control* – if control held by organizations or groups falls below a threshold level then action is taken to restore control to an acceptable level.
- *Identity* – people who identify with and who try to influence powerful groups are much less likely to engage in covert action than, say, employees who identify with each other far more strongly than they identify with the organization that is pushing for change.
- *Social networks* – the extent of social networks in an organization influences the extent of covert action since an individual is less likely to take action against a target if a friend is connected to the target. Hence the more extensive networks are, the less the climate for covert action.
- *Organization structures* – in particular how well they allow employee voice (speaking out). If people feel unable to say what they are feeling there is greater likelihood of covert action. Lack of voice is likely to foster the conditions in which grievances become long standing and eventually covert actions begin to take shape.

Covert actions should not simply be dismissed as deviant but should be recognized as a means through which individuals and groups who feel disenfranchised 'defend their dignity' and regain a level of control. It acts as a check against institutional authority.

The problems of change sometimes appear overwhelming. However, power, conflict and political action have both a positive and a negative aspect in the context of organizational change (De Dreu and van de Vliert, 1997).

Activity 5.9

Thinking of places where you have worked, can you identify any examples of employee behaviour that could be classed as covert political action?

The positive use of conflict and power

Robbins (2005) uses the terms functional and dysfunctional and constructive and destructive conflict respectively. Indeed, he regards functional conflict as, not only a positive a force, but also one that is absolutely necessary for effective performance. In similar vein, DeDreu and Beersma (2005) maintain that, between low conflict (a climate of complacency and apathy) and high conflict (a climate of hostility and mistrust), there is an optimal level of conflict that engenders self-criticism and innovation to increase unit performance. These theories are shown in Figure 5.3 and are expressed as a curvilinear or inverted U-shaped relationship.

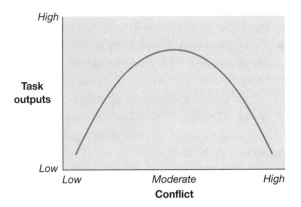

Figure 5.3 Curvilinear relationship between conflict and performance

Figure 5.4 illustrates the mechanisms that are assumed to be operating. It depicts a five-stage process of moving from an initial conflict situation through to alternative positive or negative outcomes. Note stage III 'Intentions' uses Thomas's (1976) model of conflict-handling styles shown in Figure 5.1.

These theories are not without criticism (De Dreu and Beersma, 2005). On the other hand, many organizations continue to function effectively in spite of conflicting relationships within them. Mills and Murgatroyd (1991, p. 159) talk about conflict and consent 'being in tension' depending on the methods of control used to achieve organizational purposes. Studies of relationship between job stress and performance (stress would be a logical outcome of conflict) frequently assume a curvilinear relationship although not all studies support it (Muse, Harris and Field, 2003; Onyemah, 2008).

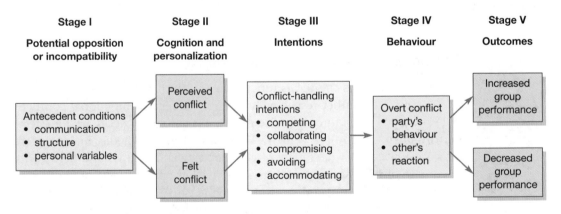

Figure 5.4 The conflict process

Source: Robbins, S.P. (2005) *Organizational Behavior: Concepts, Controversies, Applications* (11th edn), Englewood Cliffs, NJ: Prentice Hall, p. 424.

Furze and Gale (1996) take an optimistic view of conflict and Illustration 5.12 lists some of their guidelines. The conflict guidelines are general and may result in what Thomas (see Figure 5.1) called collaboration, where both parties stand to win.

Based on their work as change consultants, Lehman and Linsky (2008) offer the following advice. Given that 'deep' change almost always throws up conflict, those leading change are encouraged to see it as a healthy sign that a journey is underway. To harness conflict to change they recommend the following practices.

Illustration 5.12

Guidelines for dealing with conflict

1 *Encourage openness*. This refers to the need to explore objectives, facts, views and the assumptions that surround the issues. Openness requires statements of who benefits and how. It assumes that conflicts cannot be resolved if issues associated with them remain hidden.

2 *Model appropriate responses*. The issue here is one of role modelling. If one party is prepared to make positive responses to contention, rather than being defensive or dismissive, this acts to encourage the other party to do likewise.

3 *Provide summaries and restatements of the position*. This helps to keep communication going and helpfully slows down the process when it becomes heated and when points that are made are in danger of being ignored and lost.

4 *Bring in people who are not directly involved*. Outsiders can act as additional information providers or take on the more process-oriented role of mediator or arbitrator. A mediator can facilitate a negotiated solution while an arbitrator can dictate one. Other possibilities are conciliators who act as communicators between the two parties (particularly if they will not communicate directly) and consultants. Instead of putting forward specific solutions, the consultant tries to help the parties learn to understand and work with each other.

5 *Encourage people to take time to think and reassess*. This means building in time for reflection. It may mean 'shelving' the problem for a while but not as a means of avoiding it.

6 *Use the strengths of the group*. This refers to taking advantage of opportunities to use non-combative members of the group to which the combatants belong. Doing this brings others into the conflict, not to take sides but to play a positive and creative role.

7 *Focus on shared goals*. Rather than concentrating from the start on differences, seek instead to identify where agreements exist – even if these are very small. These form a useful base from which to move outwards to assess just where differences exist. Parties to a conflict are often surprised at the amount of agreement present but of which they were unaware.

8 *Use directions and interests to develop areas of new gain*. Concentrating on other people's ideas can identify areas of potential gain. Then using guideline 2, summarize ideas in order to move forward.

9 *Try to build objectivity into the process*. Objectivity can be encouraged by asking those involved to express both the strengths and weaknesses of their position. What must be recognized, however, is that objectivity will always be tempered by people's value systems.

10 *Adopt an enquiring approach to managing*. This means probing through what appear to be the symptoms of conflict to understand the actual causes. Unless the fundamental cause is identified, the conflict will continue to flare up at regular intervals.

Source: Based on Furze, D. and Gale, C. (1996) *Interpreting Management. Exploring Change and Complexity,* London: Thompson International Press, pp. 312–317.

- *Build a container.* The container metaphor represents a space (a padded cell perhaps) where people can 'vent their spleen'. Such a space could be off-site and allow a 'no-holds barred' approach with guarantees that there will be no repercussions for speaking out.
- *Leverage dissident voices.* Angry voices may be making some serious, if unpopular, points. Leaders of change should be open-minded about what dissidents say and not let other parties, with their peculiar political interests, suppress them.
- *Let others resolve the conflicts.* Leaders are often expected to intervene and make rulings to resolve a conflict situation. While this is something that is often needed there are times when the disputants have to be told to sort out their differences and report back to the top. Warring parties can be asked to put solutions to top management and when objections are out in the open they can be opportunities for learning.
- *Raise the heat.* Whereas leaders are often expected to maintain a climate of calm it is sometimes necessary to turn up the heat on a group to force fresh thinking. This might come from confronting a group with extensive information about its performance in an effort to force them to confront change issues.

Action on power, conflict and change

Nadler (1988) proposed four action steps for shaping the political dynamics of change. These actions are proposed in response to what he perceives as one of the problems of change mentioned earlier – the problem of power. The first of these is to ensure or develop the support of key power groups. This involves identifying those individuals and groups who have the power either to assist change or to block it although not all power groups have to be intimately involved in the change. However, some groups will need to be included in the planning of change to guard against them ultimately blocking it, not because it might affect them adversely, but because they had been ignored.

The second action step is using leader behaviour to generate energy in support of the change. The guidelines for dealing with conflict listed in Illustration 5.12 could very well be guiding principles here. In addition, sets of leaders working in coordination can significantly influence the informal aspects of organizational life. The third action step is using symbols and language to create energy. Lastly, the fourth action step for shaping the political dynamics of change is the need to build in stability. This is the use of power to ensure some things remain the same. These might be physical locations, group members, even hours of work. It is helpful to provide sources of stability like these to provide 'anchors' for people to hold on to during the turbulence of change. In addition, there is a need to let people know what will remain stable and what is likely to change.

Indicators of power to help or hinder change	Individual Group A*	Individual Group B*	Individual Group C*
Position 1 Status to hierarchy/formal authority 2 Power to change organizational structure, rules and regulations 3 Control of strategic decision processes 4 Control of operational decision processes			
Resources 5 Control of scarce resources 6 Control of budgets 7 Control of technology 8 Ability to reward or punish staff			
Personal characteristics 9 Involvement in interpersonal alliances and networks, with links to the informal organization 10 Able to exert 'charismatic' leadership to get others to follow 11 Able to cope with uncertainty			
Knowledge and expertise 12 Information specific to the change situation 13 Skills specific to the change situation 14 Knowledge and expertise unique to situation concerned			
Symbols 15 Quality of accommodation 16 Use of expenses budget 17 Membership of high-level decision-making committees 18 Receipt of company 'perks' 19 Unchallenged right to deal with those outside the organization 20 Access to the 'ear' of top management			

* Indicate against each indicator, the degree of power for each individual or group, according to whether it is high (H), medium (M) or low (L).

Figure 5.5 Assessing power

This chapter set out to show the importance of power and conflict as elements in the politics of change. Managers who, in times of change, can reasonably assess how power is distributed and the way in which it will be used – with possible consequences for potential and actual conflict – have a good chance of implementing the change they seek. The chapter concludes, therefore, with a description of one way of analyzing the potential for action of individuals and groups according to their power to block change and their motivation to do so.

A first step in analyzing the potential for action, in favour of or against change, is to identify who holds sufficient power to assist change or, alternatively, to work against it – that is, to carry out a 'power audit'. This can be done by using a framework such as that shown in Figure 5.5 based on the descriptions of the characteristics and sources of power discussed earlier. The framework should be used for each individual or group that is considered to be significant for the success or otherwise of any change process.

The second step is to compare the power of any individual or group to block change with their desire or motivation to do so. Assessing motivation to block change is not straightforward. It can be gauged, however, by considering whether the changes proposed will alter the degree of power held. As a general rule, if this is likely to be lowered then resistance to change can be expected. Figure 5.6 allows individuals or groups to be categorized according to their power to block change and their motivation to do so.

Each cell of the matrix shown in Figure 5.6 represents a different situation and strategy to deal with it. Thus, if an individual or group has little power to block change and, in addition, little motivation to do so (as represented by cell C) then no immediate action needs to be taken. However, if there is both power to block change and the motivation to do so (cell B) this represents a serious situation in terms of the need to negotiate with those concerned and, if possible, to reach a collaborative agreement.

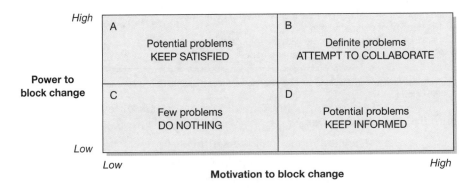

Figure 5.6 The power and motivation to block changes

A potential threat to change is represented by those who fall into cell A of the matrix – those with a high degree of power but little motivation to challenge it. This is because if the situation itself changes their interest could be increased and this might then move them into cell B. A strategy towards these groups should be one of 'keeping them satisfied'. This means maintaining their awareness of how the change might benefit them.

Cell D of the matrix represents a different kind of problem. It might be tempting to ignore these people but, because change situations are dynamic – particularly situations of incremental change – the people categorized in cell D might begin to gain power and thus move into the more contentious group represented by cell B. Consequently, they should be kept informed of change developments with some effort made to understand their motivations and concerns. However, people in cell D may in any radical restructuring face serious consequences, even job loss. Containment in the short term might, therefore, be the most appropriate strategy.

The axes of the matrix in Figure 5.6 are presented in negative terms in relation to organizational change. It is equally possible to label the axes 'power to facilitate change' and 'motivation to facilitate change'. The categorization of individuals and groups according to this framework would not necessarily be the converse of that used in Figure 5.5. Therefore, it is worth completing two matrices for a more complete analysis of power, conflict and change.

The capacity for organizations to change, both incrementally and radically, depends on the multiplicity of different interests and values that are present. Power and conflict can be used to further the aims of change as well as resist them. People and groups in organizations will share some common interests and also have some conflicting ones. The style and function of leadership in the sharing or withholding of power and the management of conflict are crucial for change and we consider this in the next chapter.

Conclusions

Power and politics are driven by human differences and until relatively recently they were a neglected area of study in organizational behaviour and change. They are in fact relatively difficult to research given that they rely on qualitative and ethnographic approaches to capture the rich details of organizational life. Their importance in explaining much of what really happens in organizations is now beginning to be understood although we suggest that managers often, because it is the easiest option, overlook power and politics and rely on rational arguments to explain the behaviour of others. Managers need to be aware of their own sources and levels of power and recognize the power and powerlessness of others. Managing change usually invokes a need for political actions to keep the interests of individuals and groups in balance.

Power is a *property of individuals*, a *property of relationships* and an *embedded property* of the structures, regulations, relationships and norms of the organization perpetuating existing routines and power inequalities (Buchanan and Badham, 1999, p. 56). Power is won and lost during change and change agents have to appreciate how and where it is being redistributed if they are to obtain a deep understanding of what they are attempting. Managers and others working with change ignore the politics of change at their peril.

Discussion questions and assignments

1 Think of people in your organization and give examples of the sources of power that they enjoy.
2 How are power relations expressed and managed, overtly and covertly, in your organization?
3 Discuss the proposition: 'In times of change, conflict between individuals and groups is inevitable.'
4 Discuss the following statement: 'If it is managed well, conflict can add substantial value to change processes'
5 What are the main symbols of power in your organization?

Indicative resources

Brooks, I. (2009) *Organizational Behaviour* (4th edn), Harlow: Pearson Education. Ian Brooks' chapter on power, politics and conflict is a useful introduction to this topic.

Clegg, S., Courpasson, D. and Phillips, N. (2006) *Power and Organizations*, Sage. A comprehensive and advanced text analyzing power in organizational, social and political theory.

Vigoda-Gadot, E. and Drory, A. (2006) *Handbook of Organizational Politics*, Edward Elgar. This text contains a collection of theoretical and empirical papers on politics and power. Perspectives covered include leadership, emotions, fairness and stress.

Robbins, S.P. (2005) *Organizational Behaviour* (11th edn), Englewood Cliffs, NJ: Prentice Hall. This book has an excellent section on conflict and negotiation and it focuses mostly on these topics in relation to organizations, groups and teams.

Useful websites

www.acas.org.uk The Advisory, Conciliation and Arbitration Service (ACAS) provides advice and mediation to employers and employees. The website identifies common areas of conflict in employee relations.

www.cipd.co.uk The website of the professional body for human resource managers (Chartered Institute of Personnel and Development) contains guidance on conflict management including a substantial downloadable guide.

www.catalyst.org Contains facts and information on women in leadership.

To click straight to these links and for other resources go to **www.pearsoned.co.uk/senior**

References

Barnard, C. I. (1938) *The Functions of the Executive*, Cambridge, MA: Harvard University Press.

Blake, R.R. and Mouton, J.S. (1970) 'The Fifth Achievement', *Journal of Applied Behavioral Science*, 6, pp. 414–426.

Bourdieu, P. (1991) *Language and Symbolic Power*, Cambridge Mass: Harvard University Press.

Brammer, S., Milington, A. and Pavelin, S. (2009) 'Corporate Reputation and Women on the Board', *British Journal of Management*, 20(1), pp. 17–29.

Brooks, I. (2009) *Organizational Behaviour* (4th edn), Harlow: Pearson Education.

Buchanan, D. and Badham, R. (1999) *Power, Politics and Organizational Change*, London: Sage.

Burrell, G. and Morgan, G. (1979) *Sociological Paradigms and Organisational Analysis*, London: Heinemann Educational.

CMI (2005) *National Management Salary Survey*, Chartered Management Institute, London.

Das, H. (1988) 'Relevance of Symbolic Interactionist Approach in Understanding Power: a preliminary analysis', *Journal of Management Studies*, 25(3), pp. 251–267.

De Dreu, C. and Beersma, B. (2005) 'Conflict in Organizations: beyond effectiveness and performance', *European Journal of Work and Organizational Psychology*, 14(2), pp. 105–117.

De Dreu, C. and van de Vliert, E. (1997) *Using Conflict in Organizations*, Thousand Oaks, CA: Sage.

Dindia, K. and Allen, M. (1992) 'Sex Differences in Self-disclosure: a meta-analysis', *Psychological Bulletin*, 112(1), pp. 774–791.

French, W.L. and Bell, C.H. (1990) *Organization Development: Behavioral Science Interventions for Organization Improvement*, Englewood Cliffs, NJ: Prentice-Hall.

French, J.R.P. and Raven, B.H. (1959) 'The Bases of Social Power', In Cartwright, D. (ed.) *Studies in Social Power* Ann Arbor: University of Michigan, pp. 150–167.

Frost, D.E. and Stahelski, A.J. (2006) 'The Systematic Measurement of French and Raven's Bases of Social Power in Work Groups', *Journal of Applied Social Psychology*, 18(5), pp. 375–389.

Furze, D. and Gale, C. (1996) *Interpreting Management: Exploring Change and Complexity*, London: Thompson International.

Gordon, J.R. (1993) *A Diagnostic Approach to Organizational Behavior*, Needham Heights, MA: Allyn & Bacon.

Handy, C. (1993) *Understanding Organizations*, Harmondsworth: Penguin.

Hardy, C. (1994) *Managing Strategic Action: Mobilizing Change: Concepts, Readings and Cases*, London: Sage.

Hardy, C. (1996) 'Understanding Power: bringing about strategic change', *British Journal of Management*, 7 (special issue), S3–S16.

Hofstede, G. (1981) 'Culture and Organizations', *International Studies of Management and Organizations*, X(4), pp. 15–41.

Huczynski, A. and Buchanan, D. (2007) *Organizational Behaviour* (6th edn), Harlow: Financial Times Prentice Hall.

Hultin, M. and Szulkin, R. (1999) 'Wages and Unequal Access to Organizational Power: an empirical test of gender discrimination', *Administrative Science Quarterly*, 44, pp. 453–472.

Hultin, M. and Szulkin, R. (2003) 'Mechanisms of Inequality: unequal access to organizational power and the gender wage gap', *European Sociological Review*, 19, pp. 143–159.

ILO (2009) *Global Trends for Women*, Geneva: International Labour Office.

Kanter, R.M. (1979) 'Power Failure in Management Circuits', *Harvard Business Review*, July–August, pp. 65–75.

Lawrence, P.R. and Lorsch, J.W. (1969) *Organization and Environment: Managing Differentiation and Integration*, Homewood, IL: R.D. Irwin.

Lehman, K. and Linsky, M. (2008) 'Using Conflict as a Catalyst for Change', *Harvard Management Update*, April, pp. 3–5.

Lien, B.Y. (2005) 'Gender, Power and Office Politics', *Human Resource Development International*, 8(3), pp. 293–309.

Lines, R. (2007) 'Using Power to Install Strategy: the relationship between expert power, position power, influence tactics and implementation success', *Journal of Change Management*, 7(2), pp. 143–170.

Mainiero, L. (1986) 'Coping with Powerlessness: the relationship of gender and job dependency to empowerment-strategy usage', *Administrative Science Quarterly*, 31, pp. 633–653.

Maitland, A. (2000a) 'Sexual Incrimination: management women in the city: the macho culture of long hours and big bucks has been highlighted by two bankers' discrimination cases, but there are signs of change', *Financial Times*, 20 January.

Maitland, A. (2000b) 'Wanted: More Uppity Women: boardroom appointments: Alison Maitland looks at the reasons why only 5 per cent of the directors of FTSE 100 companies are female', *Financial Times*, 7 November.

Maitland, A. (2004) 'The north–south divide in Europe Inc.', *Financial Times*, 14 June, p. 9.

Maitlis, S. and Lawrence, T.B. (2007) 'Triggers and Enablers of Sensegiving in Organizations', *Academy of Management Journal*, 50(1), pp. 57–84.

Martin, J. (2005) *Organizational Behaviour and Management* (3rd edn), London: Thomson.

Mayo, E. (1933) *The Human Problems of Industrial Civilization*, New York: Macmillan.

McClelland, D.C. (1970) 'The Two Faces of Power', *Journal of International Affairs*, 24(1), pp. 29–47.

McGregor, D. (1960) *The Human Side of Enterprise*, New York: McGraw-Hill.

McKenna, E.P. (1997) *When Work Doesn't Work Anymore: Women, Work and Identity*, New York: Hodder & Stoughton.

Morgan, G. (1997) *Images of Organizations*, London: Sage.

Morrill, C., Zald, M.N. and Rao, H. (2003) 'Covert Political Conflict in Organizations: challenges from below', *Annual Review of Sociology*, 29(1), pp. 391–415.

Mullins, L.J. (2005) *Management and Organizational Behaviour* (7th edn), Harlow: Pearson Education.

Muse, L.A., Harris, S.G. and Field, H.S. (2003) 'Has the inverted-U Shape Theory of Stress and Job Performance had a Fair Test?' *Human Performance*, 16(4), pp. 349–364.

Nadler, D.A. (1988) 'Concepts for the Management of Organizational Change', in Tushman, M.L. and Moore, W.L. (eds) *Readings in the Management of Innovation* (7th edn), New York: Ballinger, pp. 718–732.

O'Neill, J. (2004) 'Effects of Gender and Power on PR Managers' Upward Influence', *Journal of Managerial Issues*, XVI(1), pp. 127–144.

Onyemah, V. (2008) 'Role Ambiguity, Role Conflict and Performance: empirical evidence of an inverted-U relationship', *Journal of Personal Selling and Sales Management*, XXVIII(3), pp. 299–313.

Open University (1985) Units 9–10, 'Conflict', Course T244, *Managing in Organizations*, Milton Keynes: Open University.

Paton, R. (1994) 'Power in Organizations', in Arson, R. and Paton, R., *Organizations, Cases, Issues, Concepts*, London: PCP.

Peiro, J.M. and Melia, J.L. (2003) 'Formal and Interpersonal Power in Organizations: testing a bifactorial model of power in role sets', *Applied Psychology: An International Review*, 52(1), pp. 14–35.

Pfeffer, J. (1981) *Power in Organizations*, Marchfield, MA: Pitman.

Pfeffer, J. (1992) *Managing with Power: Politics and Influence in Organization*, Boston, MA: Harvard Business Press.

Pfeffer, J. (1993) 'Understanding Power in Organizations', in Mabey, C. and Mayon-White, B. (eds), *Managing Change* (2nd edn), London: PCP.

Robbins, S.P. (1974) *Managing Organizational Conflict: A Nontraditional Approach*, Upper Saddle River, NJ: Prentice-Hall.

Robbins, S.P. (1990) *Organization Theory: Structure, Design and Applications*, Englewood Cliffs, NJ: Prentice-Hall.

Robbins, S.P. (2005) *Organizational Behavior* (11th edn), Englewood Cliffs, NJ: Prentice Hall.

Schubert, T.W. (2005) 'Your Highness: vertical position as perceptual symbols of power', *Journal of Personality and Social Psychology*, 89(1), pp. 1–21.

Sealy, R., Vinnicombe, S. and Singh, V. (2008) *The Female FTSE Report, 2008*, Cranfield University.

Stevenson, R. (2004) 'The Secret of Success: women in the boardroom improve performance', *The Independent*, 8 December.

Thomas, K.W. (1976) 'Conflict and Conflict Management', in Dunnette, M.D. (ed.) *Handbook of Industrial and Organizational Psychology*, Chicago, IL: Rand McNally, pp. 889–935.

Thomas, K.W. (1977) 'Toward Multi-dimensional Values in Teaching: the example of conflict behaviors', *Academy of Management Review*, 12, pp. 484–490.

Thompson, P. and McHugh, D. (2002) *Work Organisations* (3rd edn), London: Palgrave.

The Times (2009) 'Women in the Boardroom Help Companies Succeed', 19 March.

Tosi, H.L., Rizzo, J.R. and Carroll, S.J. (1994) *Managing Organizational Behavior*, Oxford: Blackwell.

Vilnai-Yavetz, I. and Rafaeli, A. (2006) 'Managing Artifacts to Avoid Artifact Myopia', in Rafaeli, A. and Pratt, M.G. (eds), *Artifacts and Organizations: Beyond Mere Symbolism*, Mahwah, NJ: Lawrence Erlbaum Associates.

Wahl, A. and Hook, P. (2007) 'Changes in Working with Gender Equality Management in Sweden', *Equal Opportunities International*, 26(5), pp. 435–448.

Weber, M. (1947) *The Theory of Social and Economic Organization*, London: Oxford University Press.

Wilson, D.C. (1992) *A Strategy of Change*, London: Routledge.

Wilson, F.M. (1995) *Organizational Behaviour and Gender*, Maidenhead: McGraw-Hill.

Yuet-Ha, M. (1996) 'Orientating Values with Eastern Ways', *People Management*, 25 July, pp. 28–30.

Chapter 6

Leadership and change

One of the major debates in organizational change relates to the contributions made by those who lead it. Different theories of leadership are introduced in this chapter together with a look at the classic portrayals of organizational leaders. Then a critical look at these portrayals is taken to see how they can be interpreted from alternative perspectives. Issues regarding resistance to change and the identification of strategies for managing it are also recognized.

Learning objectives

By the end of this chapter, you will be able to:

- explain the differences between leaders and managers;

- discuss whether there is 'one best way' of leading or whether leadership style and behaviour should vary according to the circumstances;

- take a critical stance in relation to conventional portrayals of organizational leaders;

- assess the compatibility of different leadership approaches with different types of change situations;

- identify sources and causes of resistance to change and discuss ways of countering it.

Management and leadership

> The art of leadership is saying no, not yes. It is very easy to say yes.
>
> (Tony Blair, 1994)

One of the earliest writers on management, the French engineer Henri Fayol, who died in 1925, was among the first to describe management as a set of processes; planning and forecasting, organizing, coordinating, commanding and controlling. Some of these labels are somewhat unfashionable now but around the time of World War I they were not out of place and are still a fair description of what many managers do. Around the same time as Fayol, Frederick Taylor introduced his principles of 'scientific management' and catalyzed interest in productivity and production methods and hence in organizing. Interest in understanding how to improve the performance of managers grew strongly in the interwar and post-war periods, particularly in the US as management theory kept pace with the industrial and economic growth of the early to mid twentieth century. Indeed, advances in production methods and the huge scale of some industrial enterprises increased the pressure for a new way of looking at organizations and understanding leadership was a part of this.

Studies of what managers and leaders actually do, however, are less common than one might think. One of the best known studies of managers is Watson's (1994) ethnographic account of his time in a UK manufacturing company. He defined management as, '. . . organizing, pulling things together and along in a general direction to bring about long-term organizational survival' (1994, p. 33). The charm of Watson's book is that it does not just describe from a distance what managers do, it portrays a lived experience. It reveals how managers struggle to make sense of what was happening around them and it reveals management to be a search for meaning in a world of ambiguity.

One of the leading contemporary writers on management, Henry Mintzberg, studied chief executives in large and small organizations and grouped managerial roles into three sets: interpersonal roles (figurehead, leader, liaison); informational roles (monitor, disseminator, spokesman); decisional roles (entrepreneur, disturbance handler, resource allocator, negotiator) (Mintzberg, 1979). These roles (see Illustration 6.1) highlight the ambiguity of the relationship between management and leadership; leadership appears as just one aspect of a top manager's job.

Illustration 6.1

Mintzberg's managerial roles

Figurehead

In the figurehead role, the manager acts as the representative or symbol of the organization. Examples of this role are attending meetings on behalf of the organization, meeting and greeting or appearing on platforms as a representative of local business.

Leader

The manager, as leader, is concerned with interpersonal relationships, what motivates their staff and what needs they might have.

Liaison

The liaison role emphasizes the network of contacts with others in and outside the organization. Liaising with others allows managers to collect information and may come through involvement in professional networks.

Monitor

Monitoring the environment to keep informed of competitors' activities, new legislation, changes in the market, and so on, are all examples of a manager's monitoring role.

Disseminator

The role of disseminator includes keeping staff and others within the organization informed. This could be done in a variety of written and spoken forms and may be on a one-to-one basis or through group meetings.

Spokesperson

As spokesperson, the manager gives information to others outside the organization. They speak on behalf of the organization, for instance on the organization's policies and activities.

Entrepreneur

The role of entrepreneur is associated with innovation and change. It includes the design and implementation of different types of change, from small-scale job redesign to large-scale organizational restructuring depending on the level of the manager concerned.

Disturbance handler

The manager in this role acts to solve problems that arise, often unexpectedly. Managing to intervene in a conflict situation or find a solution to a machine breakdown are examples of this role.

Resource allocator

The majority of managers control some kind of resource (e.g. money, labour, time) that they can use, or allocate, at their discretion. Allocating money according to budgets is one aspect of this role. Other possibilities are the scheduling of subordinates' work and allocating equipment.

Negotiator

All managers have to play the role of negotiator when they debate who will do some things and who will do others. Coming to agreements on the scope of people's jobs and their pay are examples of negotiating.

Source: Based on Mintzberg, H. (1979) *The Nature of Managerial Work*, Englewood Cliffs, NJ: Prentice Hall.

The differences between leading and managing (Kotter, 1990) are shown in Illustration 6.2 and highlight that management is more about what goes on within the formal structure of the organization while leadership focuses more on interpersonal behaviour in a broader context.

Illustration 6.2

Comparing management and leadership

	Management	Leadership
Creating an agenda	Planning and Budgeting – establishing detailed steps and timetables for achieving needed results, and then allocating the resources necessary to make that happen	Establishing Direction – developing a vision of the future, often the distant future, and strategies for producing the changes needed to achieve that vision
Developing a human network for achieving the agenda	Organizing and Staffing – establishing some structure for accomplishing plan requirements, staffing that structure with individuals, delegating responsibility and authority for carrying out the plan, providing policies and procedures to help guide people, and creating methods or systems to monitor implementation	Aligning People – communicating the direction by words and deeds to all those whose cooperation may be needed so as to influence the creation of teams and coalitions that understand the vision and strategies, and accept their validity
Execution	Controlling and Problem Solving – monitoring results vs. plan in some detail, identifying deviations, and then planning and organizing to solve these problems	Motivating and Inspiring – energizing people to overcome major political, bureaucratic, and resource barriers to change by satisfying very basic, but often unfulfilled, human needs
Outcomes	Produces a degree of predictability and order, and has the potential of consistently producing key results expected by various stakeholders (e.g. for customers, always being on time; for stakeholders, being on budget)	Produces change, often to a dramatic degree, and has the potential of producing extremely useful change (e.g. new products that customers want, new approaches to labor relations that help make a firm more competitive)

Source: Adapted with the permission of The Free Press, a division of Simon & Schuster Adult Publishing Group, from *A Force for Change: How Leadership Differs from Management* by John P. Kotter. Copyright © 1990 by John P. Kotter Inc. All rights reserved.

Approaches to leadership theory

Looking back over the past 100 years or so it is possible to see how leadership theory has steadily evolved. The earliest approach was to look for the traits (innate qualities) of man (leaders were almost invariably men) that marked the good leader from the rest.

The 'one best way' to lead

Trait theory

Trait theory underpins the idea that leaders are born not made, yet Stodgill (1948) and Mann (1959) came to the conclusion that there were few relationships between the traits possessed by leaders and their performance. The notion of some people being born to lead did not hold up under scrutiny and, as a result, by the 1950s trait research fell by the wayside (Zaccaro, 2007). Despite falling out of fashion, however, trait research clings on and studies continue to appear that propose identifiable sets of personality and cognitive traits that are said to characterize successful leaders. Six traits of successful leaders were put forward by Lord, De Vader and Alliger (1986); intelligence, an extrovert personality, dominance, masculinity, conservatism and being better adjusted than non-leaders.

A few years later, Kirkpatrick and Locke (1991) surveyed existing leadership studies and suggested six leadership traits:

- drive (achievement, ambition, energy, tenacity, initiative)
- leadership motivation (personalized or socialized)
- honesty and integrity
- self-confidence (including emotional stability)
- cognitive ability (the ability to marshal and interpret a wide variety of information)
- knowledge of the business.

Kanter (1991, p. 54) claimed to have discovered the skills of change masters (by which she means those successfully bringing about change) 'by researching hundreds of managers across more than a half-dozen industries. I put change-master skills in two categories: first, the personal or individual skills and second, the interpersonal ones, how the person manages others.' She goes on to identify what she calls 'kaleidoscope thinking' as well as the ability to communicate visions, and be persistent. Coalition building and working through teams are aspects of her second skills category.

Dulewicz and Herbert (1996) reported on managers who had been identified as either 'high-flyers or low-flyers'. (Surely some subjective distinctions there!) High-flyers scored higher than the low-flyers on the following and also showed exceptional managerial skills in planning and organizing, managing staff and motivating others:

- risk-taking
- assertiveness and decisiveness
- achievement
- motivation
- competitiveness.

Activity 6.1

Bring to mind one or two people in leadership positions that you think show leadership qualities. Write your own list of the traits and characteristics that these people show that mark them out as leaders compared to non-leaders. How does your list of traits compare to that above?

A study of the traits of chief executives in South Korea (Shin, 1999), however, reveals a sobering contrast to the traits typically proposed for Anglo-American leaders shown above. In descending order they were:

- Management respect for employees; caring for people and trying to develop them.
- Initiator attitudes; solving problems visibly in the workplace, showing leadership, 'mucking-in' to get things done.
- Tenacity and spirit; not wavering in the face of adversity.
- Network-building ability; relations with employees outside the organization such as government officials and financiers.
- Emphasis on competency; endless development of technology and people.

Top of the list we find leaders showing a refreshing interest in the people they are leading in contrast to the far more ego-centred traits typically identified in US/UK studies.

Activity 6.2

Think of two leaders you know or have known well. One should be a person whom you judged to be successful as a leader and the other quite the opposite – unsuccessful. On the following scales, indicate the extent to which each person possesses the particular trait.

If possible, ask some other colleagues to carry out the same activity.

	Very high	High	Average	Low	Very low
Need to achieve					
Need for power					
Leadership motivation					
Self-confidence					
Honesty and integrity					
Intelligence					
Knowledge of the business					

	Very high	High	Average	Low	Very low
Assertiveness and decisiveness					
Competitiveness					
Emotional stability					
Extrovert personality					
Willingness to take risks					
Intuition and use of tacit knowledge					
Self-awareness					
Self-regulation					
Empathy					
Social skills					

From your results, what conclusions can you form as to whether successful leaders possess different traits to unsuccessful leaders? Compare your results with the literature and with other people's views.

Leadership styles and behaviour

When trait research struggles to explain successful leaders, researchers began to turn to studying the behaviour (the styles) that leaders use. Wright (1996, p. 36) groups different leadership behaviours into four main leadership styles:

1 *Concern for task*. The extent to which the leader emphasizes high levels of productivity, organizes and defines group activities in relation to the group's task objectives and so on. (Also called concern for production, production-centred, task-oriented and task-centred leadership.)

2 *Concern for people*. The extent to which the leader is concerned about their subordinates as people – their needs, interests, problems, development, etc. – rather than simply treating them as units of production. (Also called person-centred, person-oriented and employee-centred leadership.)

3 *Directive leadership*. The extent to which the leader makes all the decisions concerning group activities themselves and expects subordinates simply to follow instructions. (Also called authoritarian or autocratic leadership.)

4 *Participative leadership*. The extent to which the leader shares decision making concerning group activities with subordinates. (Also called democratic leadership.)

Given this classification of leadership styles, it might be supposed that there are differences in the effects of using one style rather than another. However,

Wright's review of a range of studies attempting to link leadership style with high performance and subordinate satisfaction found little evidence of differences. Consequently, no one style emerged as the most appropriate in all situations and where, for instance, a participative leadership style was related to high performance and satisfaction of subordinates, it was not clear whether the leader's style was the causal variable or vice versa. Perhaps high satisfaction was a causal factor in enabling a participative style.

The Michigan and Ohio studies

Given the above, it is interesting to note that two famous studies of leadership (Stodgill and Coons, 1957; Likert, 1961), known respectively as the University of Michigan studies and the Ohio State studies, separately identified two independent dimensions of leadership which were, in essence, a combination of the four types of behaviour described earlier. The Ohio researchers named these 'consideration' and 'initiating structure'.

Consideration is the degree to which a leader builds trust and mutual respect with subordinates, shows respect for their ideas and concern for their well-being. This dimension is linked to a participative, human relations approach to leadership. It therefore combines the 'concern for people' and 'participative leadership' styles identified by Wright.

Initiating structure is the degree to which a leader defines and structures their role and the interactions within the group towards the attainment of formal goals. It has elements of both the 'directive leadership' and 'concern for tasks' styles described above.

The Michigan researchers used the terms 'employee-centered' and 'production-centered' leadership for these dimensions but they were virtually the same as the Ohio descriptions. The main point about these dimensions is that, because they are deemed to be independent of each other, a leader's behaviour can be categorized in four different ways. Leaders can be:

● high on consideration and high on initiating structure
● high on consideration and low on initiating structure
● low on consideration and low on initiating structure
● low on consideration and high on initiating structure.

The Leadership Grid®

Building on the Ohio and Michigan studies Blake and Mouton (1964) proposed that the most effective leadership style is one which is high on both person and job dimensions. Figure 6.1 gives the positions of five different leadership styles on a later version of Blake and Mouton's managerial grid – now called the 'Leadership Grid®' (Blake and McCanse, 1991). The different combinations of concern for people and concern for production set out in Figure 6.1 result in different combinations of leadership characteristics as follows.

The 9,1 Authority–Compliance leader has a high concern for the task and little concern for people, emphasizing efficiency and the organization's needs at the expense of the needs of people. There is a belief that production can only be achieved if people are closely supervised and controlled. According to Blake and McCanse (1991, p. 55): 'A Grid style like 9,1 is unlikely to elicit the cooperation, involvement, or commitment of those who are expected to complete the task.'

The 1,9 Country Club leadership style is based on the assumption that productivity will follow if the needs of people are satisfied. These leaders believe that people cannot be pressured into doing things – they need to be well treated to get them to perform well. According to Blake and McCanse, however, this leadership style, although encouraging friendly and pleasant relationships, produces results where productivity suffers. Creativity and innovation are undermined because of the possible conflict that might surface as a result of challenges to existing ways of doing things.

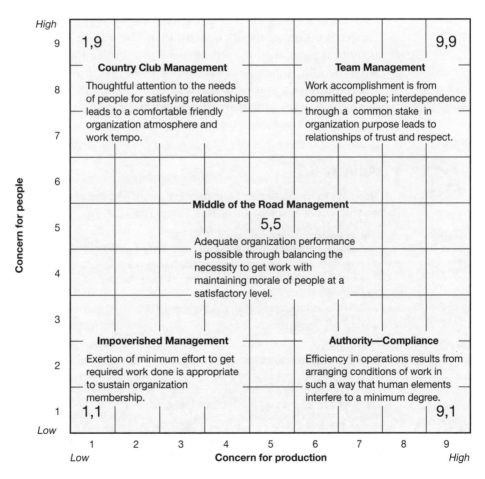

Figure 6.1 The Leadership Grid®

Source: Blake, R. and McCanse, A.A. (1991) *Leadership Dilemmas: Grid Solutions*, Houston, TX: Gulf Publishing, p. 29. Copyright © 1991 by Robert R. Blake and the Estate of Jane S. Mouton, Austin, Texas. Used with permission. All rights reserved. The Grid® designation is the property of Scientific Methods Inc. and is used here with permission.

The 1,1 Impoverished Management or laissez-faire *leadership style* is characterized by minimum concern for both production and the needs of people. The 1,1 leader's desire is to remain as uninvolved as possible with other people, compatible with fulfilling the requirements of the job and sustaining organization membership. Conflict is deliberately avoided by remaining neutral on most contentious issues.

The 5,5 Middle of the Road leadership style is concerned with moderate rather than high performance. This results from a desire to balance the contradiction between production and people's needs through compromising in the face of conflict. It includes a willingness to yield on some points in order to gain on others. This is a team-oriented style, but because negativity is not tolerated complacency can set in and the team can lose sight of reality.

The 9,9 style of Team Management incorporates high concern for production with a high concern for people. In contrast to the 5,5 leadership style, which assumes an inherent contradiction between production and people, the 9,9 leadership style assumes that concern for both is necessary and that the two concerns do not contradict each other. There is an emphasis on working as a team that recognizes the interdependence of people with each other, together with the task to be done. Relationships between people are based on mutual trust and respect, and work is assumed to be accomplished only if employees are committed to the task, team and organization.

Activity 6.3

Read the following extract from an article about Mrs Isabella Beeton, famous for her book on household management written in 1859.

Mrs Beeton: management guru
Mrs Beeton's approach can be summarized in three principles, which would certainly appear in most modern management texts: setting an example and giving clear guidance to staff; controlling the finances; applying the benefits of order and method in all management activities.

An example to staff
(In her own words.)
'Early rising is one of the most essential qualities . . . as it is not only the parent of health but of other innumerable advantages. Indeed when a mistress is an early riser, it is almost certain that her house will be orderly and well managed. On the contrary, if she remain in bed till a late hour, then the domestics, who . . . invariably partake somewhat of their mistress's character, will surely become sluggards.'

'Good Temper should be cultivated . . . Every head of a household should strive to be cheerful, and should never fail to show a deep interest in all that appertains to the well-being of those who claim the protection of her roof.'

'The Treatment of Servants is of the highest possible moment. ... If they perceive that the mistress's conduct is regulated by high and correct principles, they will not fail to respect her. If, also, a benevolent desire is shown to promote their comfort, at the same time that a steady performance of their duty is enacted, then their respect will not be unmingled with affection, and they will be still more solicitous to continue to deserve her favour.'

Source: Wensley, R. (1996), 'Mrs Beeton: management guru', *Financial Times*, 26 April, p. 15.

The article continues to quote from Mrs Beeton's book on the need to keep 'a house-keeping account-book ... punctually and precisely'. On the issue of order and method she says: 'Cleanliness, punctuality, order and method are essentials in the character of a good housekeeper.'

Where would you place Mrs Beeton on the Leadership Grid®? Support your positioning.

The Leadership Grid® assumes that there is one best style of leadership, namely 9,9 'Team Management' style – regardless of the situation. It is a simplified way of categorizing different aspects of leadership behaviour. Other studies of leadership behaviour have generated longer lists such as Useem (1996) who suggested challenging the process, searching for opportunities, experimenting, inspiring a shared vision, envisioning a future, enlisting others, enabling others to act, strengthening others, fostering collaboration, modelling the way, setting an example, celebrating accomplishments and recognizing contributions.

In addition, Useem, drawing on a study of 48 firms among the Fortune 500 largest US manufacturers, gives the following behaviour as characterizing the most successful chief executive officers:

● being visionary;
● showing strong confidence in self and others;
● communicating high-performance expectations and standards;
● personally exemplifying the firm's vision, values and standards;
● demonstrating personal sacrifice, determination, persistence and courage.

Visionary leadership

These five characteristics are not unlike 'charismatic-visionary' leadership (Robbins and Coulter, 2005, pp. 433–436). This focuses on the personality of the leader and the influence they have to get others to behave in certain ways. They suggest that this form of leadership offers clear and compelling imagery that taps into people's emotions and inspires enthusiasm to pursue the organization's goals. Charismatic-visionary leaders exhibit the following characteristics:

● the ability to explain the vision to others;
● the ability to express the vision, not just verbally, but through behaviour and symbols that reinforce the vision;
● the ability to extend or apply the vision to different leadership contexts.

Contingency approaches to leadership

Although trait and style theories of leadership have some support there are many things that can influence a leader's effectiveness over and above a leader's qualities and behaviour. Researchers began to appreciate that effective leader behaviour cannot be separated entirely from the situation that the leader is working with. Effective behaviour therefore is contingent upon situational variables (see Figure 6.2).

Behaviour along a continuum

One of the best-known theories that takes situational factors into account (Tannenbaum and Schmidt, 1973) arranges leadership behaviour along a continuum not unlike the 'directive' and 'participative' leadership styles discussed previously. One end of the continuum represents 'boss-centred leadership' which assumes a high level of authoritarian leader power and that leaders *tell* subordinates what to do. At the other end, 'subordinate-centred leadership', leaders and subordinates *jointly* make decisions in a participative climate.

Tannenbaum and Schmidt suggest that a leader should move along the continuum, selecting the style that is most appropriate to the situation prevailing. They identify 'forces' that determine the style of leadership to use.

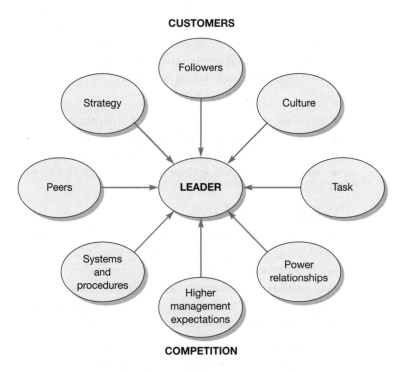

Figure 6.2 Situational influences on leadership effectiveness

- *Forces in the manager*. Each manager will have their own combination of personality characteristics, skills and knowledge, values and attitudes that predisposes the adoption of one particular style of leadership or another.
- *Forces in the subordinate*. Subordinates vary in their characteristics such as the degree of support needed, their experience in and knowledge of the work, commitment to organizational goals, expectations as to how leaders will behave, and previous experience of different leadership styles.
- *Forces in the situation*. These divide into two categories; first, the nature of the task or problem itself and, second, the general context in which the leadership activity takes place. This can include the immediacy and severity of the problem, the time available to make a decision, the organizational culture and power balances between the different participants in the situation and general opportunities and constraints arising from organizational structures and processes as well as environmental and societal influences.

When changes in the organizational environment are sudden and severe then a more authoritative leadership style may be called for. In other cases, the prevailing organizational structure and culture may force a more participative style of leadership. Illustration 6.3 is an example of the application of these concepts to leadership in a situation facing the Beautiful Buildings Company in one of its ventures to build luxury apartments in Japan.

Illustration 6.3

Little room to manoeuvre

Jayne was pleased that she had been put in charge of BB Company's latest building venture, the second of its kind in Japan. She had limited experience of working in this country but had spent some time talking to staff working on the other Japanese site about how to approach the management of those employed on the building works. She knew, therefore, that there were a number of factors she would need to take into account when deciding on her own leadership approach.

The figure below illustrates the situation Jayne faced.

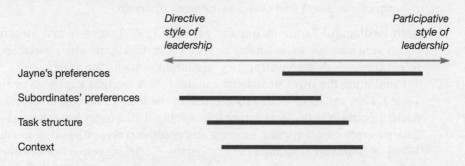

The lengths of rules on the diagram indicate the degrees of freedom available to Jayne in the situation facing her. The line indicating her own leadership style shows her preferences were for a more

Illustration 6.3 *continued*

consultative/participative style that she had been accustomed to using with staff in Britain. However, most of the Japanese employees were accustomed to a more formal management–subordinate relationship and were likely to work in this type of relationship, given the fact that Jayne was a woman. The task of building the apartments was complex but, in many ways, defined. Much of what was required had been worked out beforehand. However, as with all building works, unknown factors such as the weather and possible unexpected problems with the ground, let alone any labour relations problems that could arise, contributed to there being certain unstructured elements to the situation. If any two of these factors combined, some extensive negotiations might need to be held between management and workers or their representatives. The BB Company prided itself on its care for its workers, so the organizational context was one that veered more towards a human relations type of approach than an authoritarian one. Even so, profit was profit and the industry was very competitive. The organization did not want anything to go wrong.

What the figure shows is that Jayne has not much room for manoeuvre in deciding what approach to take as a leader in this situation. The overlap between all the forces is not large. If she cannot influence any of the factors associated with the subordinates, the task and the context, she must make sure to adopt a leadership style that tends towards the directive end of her preferences.

Fiedler's contingency model of leadership

The task-oriented/people-oriented continuum of leadership styles is also the centrepiece of Fiedler's (1967) contingency theory of leadership. In this case, however, the three situational variables said to determine the style of leadership to be adopted are:

- *Leader–member relations:* the extent to which a leader has the support of their group members. This is related to the willingness of group members to do what the leader asks, the degree of trust existing between leader and followers and the extent to which followers will support the leader's decisions.
- *Task structure:* the extent to which the task or purpose of a group is well defined and the work outcomes can be judged clearly as a success or failure. This is influenced by the subjective versus objective nature of the outcomes.
- *Position power:* the amount of power (particularly reward power) the leader has over followers. Low position power means that the leader has little authority to direct and evaluate the work of others.

Both Fiedler and Tannenbaum and Schmidt (1973) identify task structure as a contingent variable to be similar in both cases. While the other variables are different the underlying 'contingency' argument remains the same.

Combining the three situational variables leads to eight situations as shown in Table 6.1. In situation 1, all variables are in the leader's favour. In situation 8 the leader's position is the least favourable. Table 6.1 illustrates how the variations in leader–member relations, task structure and position power influence leadership style. When situations are favourable or unfavourable Fiedler suggests a task-orientation.

Fiedler's contingency theory implies that leaders can adapt their leadership styles to the prevailing situation although Fiedler believes this is difficult and suggests either that leaders should be chosen so that their management style fits the situation or that elements of the situation need to be modified.

Table 6.1 Fiedler's contingency theory of leadership

	Leader–member relationships	Task structure	Position power	Leadership style
1	Good	Structured	High	Task-oriented style recommended
2	Good	Structured	Low	
3	Good	Unstructured	High	
4	Good	Unstructured	Low	Person-oriented style recommended
5	Poor	Structured	High	
6	Poor	Structured	Low	
7	Poor	Unstructured	High	Task-oriented style recommended
8	Poor	Unstructured	Low	

Activity 6.4

Think of someone in a leadership role and think about the leadership behaviour that they display. If they were removed from this role and parachuted into a very different organizational situation would their leadership behaviour and approach to leadership differ?

Hersey and Blanchard's situational theory

Another difficulty with contingency theories is the question of how much importance should be attached to each contingency factor. Clearly the task and the amount of power held by the leader are important, but it seems logical that the characteristics and expectations of group members or subordinates are more important in deciding what style of leadership to adopt – after all, it is they who must carry out the task.

This is the point of Hersey and Blanchard's (1993) situational leadership theory which puts greatest stress on one major situational factor – the readiness of the followers. According to this theory, a leader's behaviour should depend on the maturity and readiness of followers to accept responsibility and make their own decisions. Task and relationship behavior again feature such that a leader could be low on both task and relationship behaviour, high on both or high on one and low on another. As a result a leader's behaviour falls into one of four quadrants – from 'telling' through 'selling' and 'participating' to 'delegating'. The readiness of followers also falls into four categories, each of which, in an ideal world, should trigger one of the four types of leadership behaviour. Gordon (1999, pp. 234–236) refers to this theory as a 'life-cycle' model of leadership, presumably because the followers move from being both unable and unwilling (or too insecure) to take on responsibility for their own actions, to being either unable but willing (or confident) or willing but unable, to the highest state of readiness where they are both able and willing to take responsibility for decisions and actions.

Figure 6.3 shows how a leader's behaviour should change according to the quadrant into which the followers' readiness falls and is similar to the four quadrants of the Leadership Grid® (Blake and McCanse, 1991). This is not surprising given the two leadership styles and the combinations available.

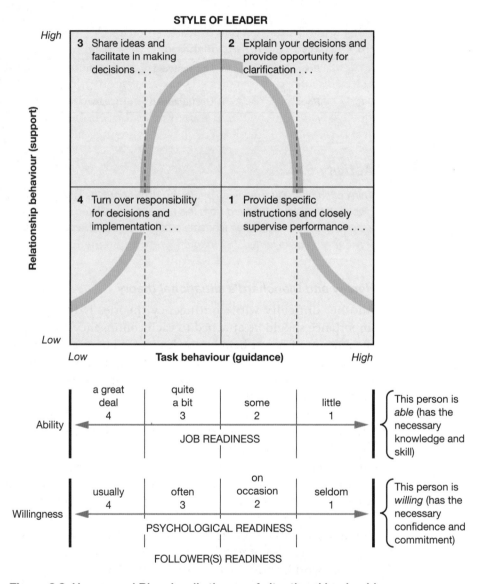

Figure 6.3 Hersey and Blanchard's theory of situational leadership

Source: Hersey, P. and Blanchard, K.H. (1993) *Management of Organizational Behavior: Utilizing Human Resources* (6th edn), Englewood Cliffs, NJ: Prentice Hall, p. 197.

However, while Blake and McCanse argue for a 'one best way' of leading for all occasions (the 9,9 way), Hersey and Blanchard argue that a leader's style should be contingent upon the characteristics and attitudes of those who are led. In contrast to Fiedler, for instance, both theories assume a leader's style is flexible enough to change according to the prevailing situation and, in Hersey and Blanchard's case, that it can presumably change in the presence of different groups and as the followers 'mature' through the cycle (Gordon, 1999).

Path–goal theory of leadership

Originally developed by House (1971), path–goal theory maintains that the leader should use the style of leadership that is most effective in influencing subordinates' perceptions of the goals they need to achieve and the way (or path) in which they should be achieved (Woffard and Liska, 1993). The theory relates directly to expectancy theories of motivation in that a leader will be judged successful if they can help subordinates reach their goals. In other words effective leadership will help subordinates turn effort into appropriate and high-level performance. Four leader behaviours are suggested by path–goal theory:

- *Directive behaviour* – laying down standards, telling what to do and how to do it.
- *Supportive behaviour* – showing concern for followers in an open and approachable manner.
- *Participative behaviour* – inviting opinions and ideas from followers.
- *Achievement-oriented behaviour* – setting challenging objectives that stress improvements over what was once acceptable and showing confidence that followers can achieve.

Two dominant situational factors are relevant to this theory. These are the characteristics of followers and the nature of the task or job and the immediate context in which it takes place. The challenge to the leader is to use a style that is congruent with the skills, motivation and expectations of followers and with the goals to be achieved, the design of the jobs and the resources and time available. Figure 6.4 shows the factors that are presumed to intervene between the effort put into doing a job and the subsequent performance.

The subordinate characteristic of 'locus of control' (see Figure 6.4) is of interest as it has not appeared in the other leadership theories considered so far. It recognizes that people have preferences for the way they are managed and this is influenced by their locus of control, that is, their beliefs about who and what controls their lives. Smith (1991, p. 220) describes the concept of locus of control as follows:

> The locus of control concerns a person's beliefs about who controls their life. People with an internal locus of control believe that they control their own lives. People with an external locus of control believe other people control their lives. According to path–goal theory of leadership non-directive styles of leadership should be used with 'internals' and a directive style should be used with externals. Internals like to be asked, externals like to be told.

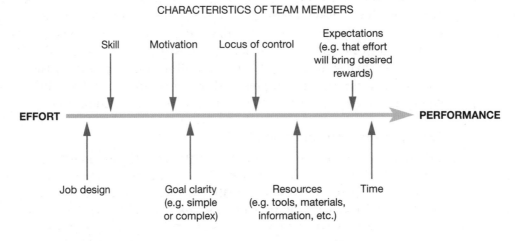

Figure 6.4 Factors intervening between effort and performance

The four leadership behaviours are used, as needed, to fit the context. If followers lack confidence then supportive behaviour is called for. If the nature of the work is vague then directive leadership is needed to clarify a way forward. If work is seen as not challenging enough then achievement-oriented behaviour can be used to raise the goals for followers. If reward strategies are poor then participative leadership can help clarify what followers are seeking and change how rewards are distributed.

Matching organizational models and leadership roles

An organization's strategic focus together with preferred forms of control will determine many situational variables and influence the particular leadership style employed. Two different pieces of research pick up on these ideas to suggest links between different organizational models and different approaches to leadership. Quinn (1988) proposed four organizational models distinguished on the basis of two bipolar dimensions (see Table 6.2). These are:

(a) adaptability and flexibility versus the desire for stability and control;
(b) whether organizations are outward looking (towards the environment and the competition) or internally focused towards the maintenance of systems and procedures.

Table 6.2 summarizes the different characteristics of the four organizational models that result from combining these four different organizational orientations (see also Figure 6.5). Quinn uses the terms 'the hierarchy', 'the firm', 'the adhocracy' and 'the team' as a shorthand way of describing the internal process, rational goal, open systems and human relations organizational models respectively.

Table 6.2 Summary of Quinn's four organizational models

Human relations model (adaptable and internally focused)	Open systems model (adaptable and externally focused)	Rational goal model (stable and externally focused)	Internal process model (stable and internally focused)
Towards: • Flexibility • Decentralization • Differentiation • Maintenance of the socio-technical system	Towards: • Flexibility • Decentralization • Differentiation • Expansion • Competitive position of overall system	Towards: • Centralization • Integration • Maximizing output • Competitive position of overall system	Towards: • Centralization • Integration • Consolidation • Continuity • Maintenance of socio-technical systems
Values: • Human resources • Training • Cohesion • Morale	Values: • Adaptability • Readiness • Growth/acquisition • External support	Values: • Productivity • Efficiency • Planning • Goal setting	Values: • Information • Management • Communication • Stability • Control
THE TEAM	THE ADHOCRACY	THE FIRM	THE HIERARCHY

Source: Based on Quinn, R.E. (1988) *Beyond Rational Management: Mastering the Paradoxes and Competing Demands of High Performance*, San Francisco: Jossey-Bass, p. 48.

What is interesting about the framework in Figure 6.5 is Quinn's linking of different dimensional positions with leadership style and the roles leaders should play. Different leadership styles and behaviour 'fit' different organizational models.

Farkas and Wetlaufer (1996) came to similar conclusions to Quinn about the dependence of leadership style and behaviour on the needs of the organization and the business situation at hand. On the basis of interviews with 160 chief executives they found five distinctive approaches to leadership, each of which was associated with different emphases in terms of strategic planning, research and development (R&D), recruitment and selection practices, matters internal to the organization or matters external to it and with whom, and how, they spent their time. According to Farkas and Wetlaufer (p. 111) the leadership approach to be adopted depends on answering questions such as: 'Is the industry growing explosively or is it mature? How many competitors exist and how strong are they? Does technology matter and, if so, where is it going? What are the organization's capital and human assets? What constitutes sustainable competitive advantage and how close is the organization to achieving it?' To these questions one could also add: 'What kind of changes is the organization facing and what do these mean for the role of leadership?'

Problems with contingency theory

Although it was widely researched, over time it became clear that contingency theory has some serious limitations (Parry and Bryman, 2006). These are:

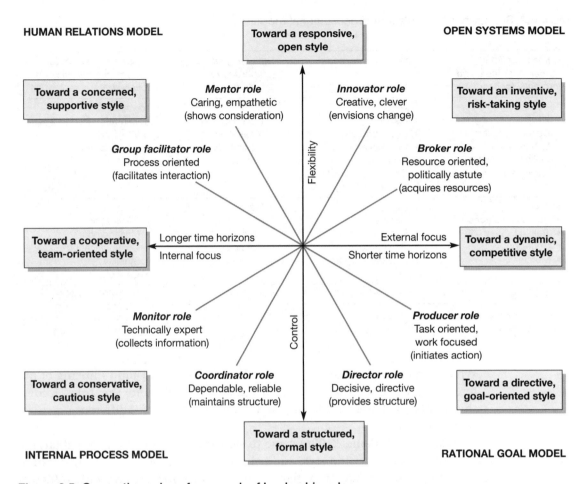

Figure 6.5 Competing values framework of leadership roles

Source: Quinn, R.E. (1988) *Beyond Rational Management: Mastering the Paradoxes and Competing Demands of High Performance*, San Francisco: Jossey-Bass, p. 86.

- There are just too many contingent variables that the theory has to account for;
- Studies struggled to justify why some situational variables should be included and others excluded;
- Leader behaviour was not always situationally contingent;
- Most research was cross-sectional which means that it is impossible to separate cause (leadership behaviour) from effect (performance).

The contribution of contingency theory is the message that there is not one best way of leading regardless of situation. From the 1980s onwards interest moved away from contingency models towards fresh explanations and a key concept in what Parry and Bryman call the 'New Leadership Approach' is charisma.

New leadership theories

Charismatic leadership

The idea of charisma and charismatic leaders is prominent in leadership theory and its links to change. But what is charisma? The concept is not new and originated with Max Weber who contrasted charisma with bureaucratic systems of control. Charisma is about people leading not by virtue of sets of rules and procedures but through creating a following for their mission. Charisma comes from within – its sets its own boundaries. Weber's original ideas illustrate it beautifully:

> The continued existence of charismatic authority is, by its very nature, characteristically unstable; the bearer may lose his charisma . . . and show himself to his followers as 'bereft of his power', and then his mission is dead, and his followers must hopefully await and search out a new charismatic leader. He himself, however, is abandoned by his following, for pure charisma recognises no 'legitimacy' other than that conferred by personal power, which must be constantly re-confirmed. The charismatic hero does not derive his authority from ordinances and statutes, as if it were an official 'competence', nor from customary usage or feudal fealty, as with patrimonial power: rather, he acquires it and retains it only by proving his powers in real life. He must perform miracles if he wants to be a prophet, acts of heroism if he wants to be a leader in war. Above all, however, his divine mission must 'prove' itself in that those who entrust themselves to him must prosper. If they do not, then he is obviously not the master sent by the Gods.
>
> (Runciman and Matthews, 1978, p. 229)

Failure is to charisma as Kryptonite is to Superman. Failure shows the charismatic leader's mortality and punctures their superhero image. Weber described the charismatic figure as one who will blame themselves when missions fail. If things still do not improve then, as history shows, some leaders have chosen banishment or even death. Recognition of the personal mission by followers relies upon their submission, through their faith, to the leader's extraordinariness and their desire to abandon past rules and traditions. Belief in charismatic power revolutionizes people and channels their energies into shaping organizations. Charisma changes the hearts of those it rules. In time, however, bureaucracy follows it and replaces charisma with rules which are followed as if sacred. Even charisma becomes institutionalized eventually. High charisma rejects the sacred practices (or at least many of them). Charisma is mission incarnate.

Although we can describe what a charismatic leader does we have a weaker understanding of the processes and interactions between leaders and followers and which lead to social change. Research on US presidents suggests that charismatic leaders uses 'consistent common strategies for breaking down, moving and re-aligning the norms of their followers'. (Fiol, Harris and House, 1999, p. 450). Fiol and colleagues see change as being about changing values; championing and prioritizing one thing over and above another. It is the 'contrary of conventions' (p. 458) such that the more conventional a leader is the less charismatic they will appear. They use Lewin's three stage model to show how values can be changed, as shown in Illustration 6.4.

Illustration 6.4

How charisma works

Frame breaking (unfreezing)

The charismatic leader has the job of reducing the strength of ties to existing conventions. Whatever the conventions are, the leader has to create a state of 'non-desire' for them. Non-desire can be created by arguing that adherence to convention is dysfunctional. Following the attacks on the World Trade Centre in 2001 legislation was introduced in the UK that redefined terrorism and all things connected to it and increased police powers. The government's justification (under the UK Prime Minister Blair who many though fitted the model of a charismatic leader) was that new legislation was essential to protect national security. Despite little evidence that existing legislation was inadequate the message hammeredout was that only greater power could protect citizens and that arguments to the contrary were dysfunctional and put the nation at risk.

As well as tackling a desire for convention the charismatic leader may encounter a fear of innovation and this is tackled by creating a 'no fear' scenario. Continuing with the terrorism illustration, the government used a 'trust me' approach in response to critics who argued that longer detention without charge amounted to internment and that the new legislation was so broad that anyone possessing a computer or chemistry book could be arrested for having materials that could be used in support of terrorism. 'Trust me' was the reply – we have secret information that we cannot tell you, but do not fear, only the bad guys will be arrested. The other strategy is to convince followers that non-innovation is not a viable future. Doing nothing is not an option; we have to act to protect society from evil doers – and similar exhortations.

Frame moving

In stage 1, communication strategies attempt to move personal and social values from defensive positions to neutral positions (fear of change to non-fear). In stage 2, the neutral values need to be moved on to active states of desires for things. So having moved people away from wanting convention to states of not wanting convention the next step is to create a desire for non-convention, a desire for change and a fear of not changing.

Frame realignment (refreezing)

This phrase requires acceptance (freezing) of new personal and social values which are then tapped by the leader. It should be more straightforward than stages 1 and 2 because while they tackle opposing forces, this phase gives meaning to new values. Keeping followers on-board can require additional communications from leader figures. To support new terror legislation it was not enough to rely on discrediting old conventions. Military occupation of foreign lands as part of a 'war on terror' (a phrase since dropped by those who spun it) was an integral part of the communication strategy that aimed to cement values around state involvement in people's lives.

Charismatic authority is bolstered by four additional dimensions that facilitate change (Conger, 1993, p. 279). First, charisma, being a personal characteristic, bestows on those who posses it a source of power and influence quite different to position power. Second, charismatic leadership glorifies the leader figure and their qualities and breaks with traditions. Challenges to existing social order occur since the leader's heroic attributes are championed above historic and traditional ways of doing. Third, charismatic leadership is short lived compared to rational-legal authority. In an organizational setting it exists for as long as a charismatic leader figure is present but after they have departed the changes they set in play become embedded in rational-legal structures. 'As a revolutionary force, its purpose is to bridge the transition from one existing order to the next. Its role is to create and institutionalize new order. After accomplishing this task, charisma fades or is routinized. Rules, traditions and institutions grow up to stabilize and guide the new social arrangements and to replace the charismatic leader who has departed' (p. 279). Fourth, the commitment of followers to change is a consequence of their emotional ties with the leader figure and not through allegiance to a set of rules and structures that represent the 'organization'.

While we may look at others and think they have a certain charisma, there is an important question about how much context and charisma are interrelated. Are charismatic people charismatic wherever they find themselves or does context bring out their charismatic qualities? Conger (1993) observes that at a moment in time, a group of employees (followers) have concerns for their work situations. If these concerns are shared and if an individual says and does things that resonate with these concerns in a positive way then they can be bestowed with 'followers' attribution of charisma to leaders' (p. 285).

We can also speculate that certain organizational conditions and climate will provide opportunities for would-be charismatic leaders to display their vision and their ways of changing. Then there are further questions about what the psychological ingredients are that are necessary if charisma is to be tapped by contexts and displayed. Conversely, are some people doomed to be uncharismatic if they lack these ingredients?

Landrum, Howell and Paris (2000) point out that while many writers claim that 'strong' charismatic leadership is required for strategic and 'turnaround' change, there is also a 'dark side' to charismatic leaders. They comment that charismatic leaders can lead followers in directions unhelpful to society and organizations. They also point out a possible propensity for narcissism and quote Post (1986, p. 679) who states that the charismatic leader: 'Requires a continuing flow of admiration from his audience in order to nourish his famished self. Central to his ability to elicit that admiration is his ability to convey a sense of grandeur, omnipotence, and strength.' Landrum *et al.* (2000) refer to *unethical* charismatic leaders who are controlling, manipulative and self-promoting – characteristics that can jeopardize and even sabotage the turnaround efforts of the organization. To mitigate these possibilities and overcome the difficulties of leaders being all things to all people and situations, Landrum *et al.* argue for a team approach to designing and implementing strategic change (see below on team and distributed leadership).

Emotional intelligence

According to Goleman (1998, p. 93), who developed the concept, '*Emotional intelligence* is the *sine qua non* of leadership' [author's italics]. On the basis of an examination of competency models in 188 mostly large global companies, Goleman claims to have found the personal capabilities that drive outstanding performance. He grouped the capabilities into three categories: purely technical skills, cognitive abilities and competencies demonstrating emotional intelligence (EI), which he defines as having the five components of:

- self-awareness;
- self-regulation;
- motivation;
- empathy;
- social skills.

While not decrying the need for leaders to have technical skills (such as accounting and business planning) and cognitive capabilities (such as analytical reasoning) he claims these are 'threshold capabilities', that is, while being *necessary* for successful leadership they are not *sufficient* without the addition of emotional intelligence. Cote and Miners (2006) describe emotional intelligence as seeing your own emotions and those of others and using these insights to lead. Bar-On (1997, p. 14, cited in Dries and Pepermans, 2007) described it as 'an array of non cognitive capabilities, competences and skills that influence one's ability to succeed in coping with environmental demands and pressures'. Higgs and Dulewicz (2004, p. 175) suggested that EI is concerned with achieving one's goals through the capabilities to:

1 manage one's own feelings and emotions;
2 be sensitive to the needs of others and influence key people; and
3 balance one's own motives and drives with conscientious and ethical behaviour.

Since different leadership roles have different emotional demands it follows that jobs with high emotional content should be performed better by leaders with high emotional intelligence. Martin (2008) found a moderately strong link between EI and job performance but other studies have produced more mixed results (see Cote, S. and Miners, 2006). To explain the mixed findings, Cote, S. and Miners proposed that the relationship between EI and job performance increases as cognitive intelligence decreases. Cognitive intelligence is usually related to performance in jobs (the smarter the person, the better the performance) because smarter people have a better grasp of information and procedures relating to the core technical work. Emotional intelligence may therefore be a compensator for lower cognitive (general) intelligence. Their proposition is supported for organizational citizenship behaviour (doing positive things over and above what the core job requires) and task performance.

However, do the components of emotional intelligence add anything new to what we already know about the psychological and social characteristics of individuals? Woodruffe (2000) thinks not and rejects the claim that emotional intelligence adds anything new to what is already known about the behaviour and competencies of leaders and others. What Woodruffe does concede, however, is that EI has popularized the need for leaders to exhibit these capabilities in the service of bringing greater effectiveness to their management of people and the tasks they are involved in. All this may be no bad thing if it encourages managers and leaders at all levels in organizations to pay attention to the need to use what Beer and Nohria (2000) call 'soft' *as well as* 'hard' approaches to leading organizational change.

Several models of emotional intelligence exist and each is assessed through a questionnaire approach. The concept has attracted a good following from consultants but a more mixed reaction from academics – some like it; others do not (Murphy, 2006).

Transactional and transformational leadership

Organizations responding to the tightening market conditions that started in the late 1970s often attempted big changes – changes that transformed structures and markets. We began to see 'hero' leaders emerge who were credited with transformational changes; transformational leaders in contrast to the less visionary *transactional* leadership style (see Illustration 6.5). These two concepts were introduced by Burns (1978) and have been influential in leadership theory and research. Transactional leadership is based on giving people rewards for doing what the leader wants. Transformational leadership which borrows much from Weber's ideas about charisma relies on giving followers a purpose, a vision of something to aim for and on creating follower identification with the leader. Transactional leaders make minor adjustments to mission and the ways people are managed. Transformational leaders make big changes to mission and culture and so in theory make bigger impacts upon change.

Illustration 6.5

How charisma works

Three dimensions of transactional leadership

- *Contingent reward:* to what extent are meaningful reward exchanges set up – exchange of rewards for effort, promise of rewards for good performance and recognition of accomplishments?
- *Management by exception (active)*: to what extent do leaders anticipate problems and intervene with corrective action before problems arise?
- *Management by exception (passive)*: to what extent do leaders wait for problems to arise before intervening?

▶

Illustration 6.5 *continued*

Four dimensions of transformational leadership

- *Charisma*: provides vision and sense of mission for followers to follow, instils pride, gains respect and trust.
- *Inspiration*: communicates high expectations and standards, uses symbols to focus efforts, expresses important purposes in simple ways, optimistic about the future.
- *Intellectual stimulation*: challenges assumptions with fresh ideas and solicits ideas from followers.
- *Individualized consideration*: showing interest in individual followers and their development, helping them to develop. Treats employees individually, coaches, advises.

Source: Bass, B.M. (1990) 'From Transactional to Transformational Leadership: learning to share the vision', *Organizational Dynamics*, Winter, p. 22.

Figure 6.6 presents a model of transformational leadership that includes not only the leader's characteristics, attitudes and behaviour but also the reactions of followers.

Transformational leadership behaviours add to the two dimensions of leadership identified in both the Ohio State and Michigan University studies. To summarise, in much of the leadership literature there is a general assumption now that transformational leadership is the way ahead and that where radical

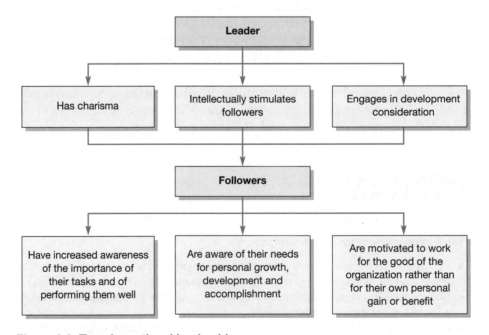

Figure 6.6 Transformational leadership

Source: Adapted from Bass, B.M. (1990) by George, J. and Jones, G. *Understanding and Managing Organizational Behaviour* (4th edn), Harlow: Pearson Prentice Hall, p. 394.

changes are called for it is more likely to be effective. Bass (1990, p. 20) goes so far as to say that transactional leadership is, in many instances, 'a prescription for mediocrity', arguing that only transformational leadership can make a difference in an organization's performance at all levels.

These two leadership styles are not mutually exclusive; transformational leadership is thought to compliment transactional leadership to leverage higher performance by followers (Bass and Avolio, 1993). Transactional leadership on its own will deliver a certain performance but if an overlay of transformational leadership is present then performance can be enhanced. Judge and Piccolo (2004, p. 765) found that the two styles 'are valid concepts but that they are so highly related that it makes it difficult to separate their unique effects' in studies linking leadership to performance. There is a little evidence that women display more transformational behaviours than men but the differences are small (Eagly *et al.*, 2003). However, these results are encouraging for those working to see more women in top management roles.

Researchers have looked for connections between personality traits and transformational leadership but the results are 'generally weak' (Bono and Judge, 2004). Of the 'big five' personality factors only extroversion appears to predict it. This makes sense because extroverts are characterized by positive emotions, enthusiasm, confidence and good communication skills. The results suggest that personality (in so far as it can be assessed through questionnaires) does not predict much leadership behaviour. Given that personality is a stable trait of individuals this evidence supports the idea that much leadership behaviour can be learned.

Activity 6.5

Read the account in Illustration 6.6 of the leadership profile of the head of Ryanair.

Assess Michael O'Leary's leadership style in terms of the discussion above on transactional and transformational leadership and the model of transformational leadership in Figure 6.6.

Illustration 6.6

Portrait of a 'high flyer'

As CEO of Ryanair since 1994, Michael O'Leary has employed a low fares business model that was based on Southwest Airlines (a low-cost US airline company). He felt that he should be able to copy the model and use it in Europe and achieve equal success. In fact O'Leary has pushed the boundaries of what seemed possible in cutting costs and maintaining profitability. His strategy is simple, he says: 'Our strategy is like Wal-Mart: we pile it high and sell it cheap' (*Business Week*, 2004). That

Illustration 6.6 *continued*

means using small airports, where planes can get back in the air in just 20 minutes. Free meals; forget about it. Under the leadership of Michael O'Leary, cost cutting has become the prime objective:

- Online bookings – Ryanair secures most of its bookings online, eliminating travel agents and others who might otherwise gain commission.
- One-class travel – all passengers fly the same class offered by the company.
- In early 2009 the press reported that Ryanair was considering introducing charges for using toilets in-flight.
- Ticketless boarding – Ryanair does not issue tickets. The only cost is to the customer when they print their own ticket from the Internet.
- Unallocated seats – first come first served, which speeds up the boarding process.
- Flying to secondary airports – this lowers operating expenses when Ryanair flies to cheaper, quieter locations, where airport taxes are lower and landing fees usually reduced.
- Point-to-point flying – one-way tickets are booked, therefore the company takes no responsibility for flight connections.
- In-house marketing – by eliminating advertising agencies, the strategy is to spend as little as possible on marketing and benefit as much as possible from free publicity (good or bad).
- No refund policy – unless the flight has been cancelled before the date of travel, there is no circumstance where you would expect a refund.
- Additional charges – for changing a booking, overweight luggage, in-flight service.

From this overview of company practice the developments in the Ryanair strategy led by O'Leary are clear. He has no problem with attacking competitors through the media, there is no union recognition within the company and staff relations have been strained to say the least at times.

His leadership trademarks are varied. He portrays for the media a brash, controversial, larger than life character. He bought taxi plates for his company car so that it could use bus lanes in cities to beat congestion. He rushes around in a rugby shirt and jeans as he has dispensed with the old look of an accountant. He is passionate about his role and rarely apologetic for his behaviour, colourful language and decisions – a no-nonsense manager. He has expressed little concern for carbon emissions and has criticized airport security arrangements.

O'Leary's strategies redefined what no-frills flying meant. The leadership issues are important to assess. Articles about the company (www.ryan-be-fair.org) show that penny-pinching seems to be even worse for the employees. Their mobile phone chargers have been banned from the workplace to save money, staff pay for their own selection and training and their uniforms, and are not paid any sick leave in their probationary time with the company. Michael O'Leary has shown he is very effective at leading at stripping costs out of a business ... while the profits are high he is deemed to be a success.

Source: www.ryanair.com; 'The Guardian Profile: Michael O'Leary', *The Guardian*, 24 June 2005; 'Michael O'Leary: Cheap and Cheerful', *The Independent*, 17 August 2008.

Michael O'Leary (see Illustration 6.6) appears to have a well-defined leadership style that for Ryanair, at least, correlates with strong business performance, but to what extent is the style transferable to other organizations? Would he be effective in the Diplomatic Service? We may never know – but it seems clear that different leadership styles are needed to connect with different organizational situations.

Although transformational leadership has captured the imagination of researchers and executives there are a few problems with it (Parry and Bryman, 2006). First, it was usually studied in the context of top managers only. The second problem relates to the motives of those credited with being transformational. Doubts arise about the integrity of what is happening in some leadership situations with some leaders appearing to be shameless self-promoters manufacturing situations for their own benefit.

Team and distributed leadership

Reich (1991) warns against the idea of reifying the leader as hero, and Landrum, Howell and Paris (2000) argue for a team approach to designing and implementing change. Team and distributed leadership theory moves away from the single heroic figure and recognizes that leadership can be shown by people throughout the organization. Robbins and Coulter (2005, p. 435) echo this view, suggesting that one of the cutting-edge approaches to leadership is team leadership. They maintain that the attributes of leaders discussed in much of the literature need to be adapted when managing in a team setting. For instance, 'they (leaders) have to learn skills such as having the patience to share information, being able to trust others and to give up authority, and understanding when to intervene.' These authors propose four key areas that distinguish team leadership from the leader as heroic individual:

1 the ability to act as a liaison with people and departments external to the team;
2 the ability to act as troubleshooters to try and resolve issues/problems at team level;
3 the ability to resolve conflicts at team level;
4 the ability to act as coach ensuring that all team members develop to their full potential.

These abilities go some way to meeting what Kotter (1996, p. 172) says twenty-first century organizations need:

- fewer bureaucratic structures with fewer rules and employees;
- fewer hierarchical levels;
- management training and support systems for all;
- a culture that is externally oriented, empowering, quick to make decisions, open and candid, more risk tolerant.

Having said this, moving from operating bureaucratically to a team-based structure is not easy as Illustration 6.7 shows.

Illustration 6.7

From bureaucracy to teamwork

By means of a questionnaire survey of 346 employees of a large social services-type organization, McHugh and Bennett (1999) examined the feasibility of carrying out a large-scale transformational change from a structure based on strict bureaucratic principles to one which favoured self-managed teamworking. The proposed change was in response to government initiatives to make such organizations more market-oriented, responsive to clients, flexible in the way staff worked and generally to act more like a commercial company. They questioned the staff on: the degree to which they interacted with others in their day-to-day job; whether they considered themselves as working in teams; and what they thought was meant by teamworking. Having established that most respondents (96 per cent) could define teamworking, that the majority (89 per cent) indicated their job required them to work as part of a team, but that only 66 per cent preferred to work together with others (31 per cent preferring to work independently), they examined a range of attitudes towards teamworking in the light of management's known views that this was the way forward.

The results showed a sizeable percentage (between 35 and 42 per cent) believing that management within the organization did not understand the meaning of teamwork and that managers would find it difficult to give up their control in order to encourage workforce democracy and empower others to make decisions. In spite of this a large majority thought that the organization should move towards teamworking but only, it seemed, because top management had decreed it, even though the infrastructure required to make it work had not been given sufficient attention.

From the research, a number of factors emerged that either facilitated or impeded teamwork. Facilitating factors included: having managers and staff committed to communication, the freedom to make decisions, greater staff enthusiasm, training people to help them understand the concept of teamworking, and having team rewards. Impeding factors included: low staff motivation, lack of management and staff commitment, a reward system that supported competition rather than cooperation, no management and staff understanding of the concept, no acceptance of devolved responsibility, bureaucratic management styles, and adherence by management to the old ways of doing things.

It was evident that a number of 'trip wires', as defined by Hackman (1994), existed within the organization that highlighted the strength of the impeding factors against the facilitating factors in terms of the changes required for teamworking to become established as the preferred way of working.

Source: Based on McHugh, M. and Bennett, H. (1999) 'Introducing Teamwork Within a Bureaucratic Maze', *The Leadership and Organization Development Journal*, 20(2), pp. 81–93.

Activity 6.6

Based on your knowledge of organizations in the public sector, list the trip wires you can see in changing such organizations to permit 'enhanced delegation, empowerment of staff and, among those who occupy managerial roles, a commitment to the concept of team player as opposed to manager'. What stands in the way of achieving these outcomes?

Teamwork emphasizes concepts such as interacting or coordinating, shared leadership roles, individual and mutual accountability, collective work products and decisions by consensus (Baker and Salas, 1997; Katzenbach and Smith, 1993; Senior and Swailes, 2007). Much of this reflects the ideas of democratic or participative leadership but leadership models often focus on the leader as an individual. An alternative view of 'distributive' leadership was expressed by Yukl (2002, p. 432) as follows:

> An alternative perspective (to the heroic single leader), that is slowly gaining more adherents, is to define leadership as a shared purpose of enhancing the individual and collective capacity of people to accomplish their work effectively . . . Instead of a heroic leader who can perform all essential leadership functions, the functions are distributed among different members of the team or organization.

Distributed leadership places leadership 'in the context of participative, shared decision making, which stimulates and leads to more effective organizational change' (Anderson *et al.* 2003, p. 29). It captures the idea of enabling followers to become leaders and benefits of distributed leadership to senior management and others are (Storey, 2004, p. 253):

- avoiding the overloading of senior staff;
- offering growth and development opportunities across the workforce;
- allowing individuals and groups with the most appropriate capabilities to make decisions;
- building motivation and commitment.

Yukl goes on to say, 'Another argument is that, as the environment becomes more complex, uncertain and subject to rapid change, so must organizations adapt. This is usually inferred as requiring leaders at every level, and most notably perhaps in "customer-facing" roles where responsiveness is at a premium.'

Bottery (2004, p. 20) refers to this as 'exciting stuff' with the appeal and attraction of distributed leadership appearing self-evident. Nevertheless, a number of caveats are needed. First, visions of distributed leadership must take account of the asymmetry of power, particularly the accumulation of resources power attaching to some formal positions. Senior managers and others might not wish to share the status and symbols that attach to their positions. However egalitarian an organization is, power and influence in decision taking are hardly ever shared equally. Second, not everyone will subscribe to the idea of being a leader, even if this is an informal one. As Storey (2004, p. 254) says: 'some organizational members may in reality be rather attached to the relative comfort and lack of exposure that may derive from operating under the dominant leader mode'. Third, distributive leadership is concerned not only with matters internal to an organization but also with something that extends outside. However, it is not certain how customers, shareholders and external policy makers will react to dealing with what might appear to be 'weak' senior managers and multiple points of decision making.

Authentic leadership

As we have noted above, although charismatic and transformational leadership attracted a big following, they have a shadow side reflecting concerns about the leader's real motives and where they have led and where they are leading some organizations. Corporate scandals, mismanagement and the disastrous leadership of financial institutions in the recent past should be enough to make the point.

Authentic leadership theories offer some antidote to this dark side, being based on the idea that leaders should know themselves (hence the term 'authentic') and know how their experiences in life have made them what they are (Shamir and Eilam, 2005). The authentic leader knows who and what they are and does not try to copy and mimic some other person or model. They are true to themselves and are acutely aware of their values and beliefs (Avolio and Gardner, 2005) and they are aware of strong moral implications for how their leadership is affecting the organization and their followers. Attributes of authentic leaders (recall the traits approach at the start of this chapter) include:

- Being true to themselves (see Ilies *et al.*, 2005 and their discussion of authentic leaders working in a state of eudaemonia; being self-aware, being unbiased, and behaving authentically).
- Humility and modesty (Treviño *et al.*, 2003). This does not mean being weak; on the contrary it means being aware of one's limitations and mistakes, being willing to learn from them, seeing the value that others bring to situations and not being an arrogant glory seeker.
- Seeing situations from a range of perspectives, bringing out into the open the tensions and moral dilemmas existing within them.
- Knowing one's own sense of right and wrong and adhering to personal standards in decisions and relationships. When times get difficult authentic leaders display the moral courage to act consistently and not sacrifice deeply held beliefs (Verbos *et al.*, 2007).

Activity 6.7

Think of the characteristics of authentic leaders and then see if you can relate them to any leaders that you know of. You may need to think of leaders of nations or social movements rather than organizations.

In our tour of leadership theories we have seen how they have evolved over time and, in a sense, we have returned to the beginning by describing characteristics of business leaders that are fit enough to lead organizations in the twenty-first century and fulfil the expectations of the people that work under them. Authentic leadership is a powerful theory and right now there are good grounds for thinking that business leadership will need to move in this direction if organizations are to enjoy support from their employees as well as from government and society. Recent crises blamed on poor leadership and the behaviour of extremely well paid leaders after they have stepped down (e.g. Sir Fred Goodwin resisting calls for him to pay back part of his unfeasibly large pension fund) appear to have dented public confidence in leaders who need to work hard to recover personal and corporate reputations.

Having summarized from a largely rational and normative view how thinking about leadership has evolved, the discussion now turns to take a look at more critical perspectives.

Critical approaches to leadership

Stories of leaders who are doing a great job for their organizations are commonly found in the management literature. We even found one journal running a 'leader of the month' page. A typical portrayal is shown in Illustration 6.8 to give readers a taste of what these stories are like.

Illustration 6.8

An interview with a leader

This *Sunday Times* interview was with Peter, a 50–something Austrian running German engineering giant Siemens. The story lead tells us that he is ruthlessly reorganizing a company racked by bribery and corruption scandals. We are told that he is the first non-German to head-up the 161-year-old conglomerate. He has achieved the 'astonishing feat' of changing the executive structure and personnel without hurting the company.

He is 'tall, stern and grey' and previously worked for one of Siemen's main rivals. After sorting out the executives, 17,000 job cuts were anticipated in an effort to raise profitability. He is also tackling the company's leadership culture which, it is implied, fostered the practices that courted bribery and corruption investigations. Part of that change is to restore a culture of responsibility in which people take and accept responsibility for their actions. He has worked in several different countries and is one of a handful of people with experience for his post. In his previous positions he built a reputation as a 'maker of

instant decisions'. One former colleague described him as 'relentless'.

He wakes at 0630 and is driven to work for 0800. He takes calls from key people and then goes into meetings and is rarely home before 2200. He travels extensively and follows strict routines to organize his time. The article is sprinkled with buzzwords; remodelling, culture, global network, responsibility, leadership, infrastructure, excellence, global footprint.

This is typical of the heroic leadership stories that are found. They tell of energetic and driven people who give no quarter in driving forward the changes they feel are needed for the good of shareholders and customers. Aspiring leaders may take inspiration from such stories and try to mimic the bold behaviour described but how indicative are they of how leadership really happens? We explore this question below.

Source: Based on: Davidson, A. (2008) 'Austrian Turns on Siemen's Lights', *Sunday Times*, 29 June, Business Section, p. 6.

Gendered leadership

Portrayals of the kind in Illustration 6.8 have attracted a critical and rather disbelieving literature and one angle on this is through exploration of gendered
narratives. Ann Rippin (2005), for instance, reinterprets the leadership history of
one of the UK's best known and perhaps best liked retailers, Marks and Spencer.
Marks and Spencer was founded in the late nineteenth century and has always
been led at the highest level by men. Rippin (p. 582) points out that in histories
written about M&S 'the absence of women is exceptional'. All the top action was
performed by men. Leadership was passed initially through the male family line
and when this had run its course other 'equally strong' men were brought in.
She draws a parallel with the story of *Sleeping Beauty* such that the organization
became, periodically, a sleeping princess waiting for a dashing and handsome
prince to rejuvenate it. She allies it to 'illness narratives', i.e., 'we are sick but
will be healed' (p. 584) by the arrival of Prince Charming. Later the prince displays his beautiful and fertile possession (the company, that is). Trouble is, they
don't often live happily ever after, as when the princess falls sick again or the
prince eyes a bigger prize the search for another prince resumes.

Rippin viewed M&S as a patriarchy (actually a phallocracy) that implies that
organizations are far from the rational systems we read about but can be 'locations of masculine violence' (p. 586). In M&S this violence took the form of
robust exchanges between senior male managers vying for position as the alpha
males. She sees M&S as gendered from birth and continuing so into its recent
struggles to maintain its high street position in a changing retail environment.
The cumulative effects of men of action at the top makes change in M&S a very
gendered thing and it is hard for her to imagine an alternative way of leading
becoming accepted.

Linstead and colleagues (2005, p. 543) noted that managing change is typically
'authoritative, patriarchal, competitive, confrontational and bullying' and when
managers speak and behave otherwise they are quickly labelled as going soft and
losing their grip – even, horror of horrors, as acting like a woman in a masculine
workplace. Studies of women as change agents are few as women are often
excluded from the male social networks outside work where big decisions can be
made and set in motion. So, why should gender have an influence on management theory and specifically organizational change? Most management texts
present theory and best practice as gender neutral and let men and women interpret it and apply it at work. The alternative view is that since management is
enacted by men and women and since the two enactors have different identities
there must be some sort of interaction or influence operating (Linstead *et al.*,
2005, p. 546). Although the differences are small, studies of gender and management suggest that men are more transactional and rely more on position power
to get results whereas women are more likely to be transformational and use relationships rather than power to motivate (Eagly *et al.*, 2003).

However, an additional overlay comes from the organizational context and the nature of the work. If work cultures are combative then whether male or female the manager will have to respond with matching behaviour. Indeed, drawing on person-organization fit theory and the aim of selection processes to seek people who fit with cultures, then organizations will recruit people who appear to fit. Assuming there is no direct discrimination against women in selection then both men and women with similar characteristics will tend to be recruited.

Linstead and colleagues see Western masculinity as being focused on control; control of self, of others and of the environment. However, it is important to note that not all men are comfortable with the display of control-oriented behaviour and it is clear that some women display masculine control orientations either by nature or through conformance to a culture. The characteristics that usually accompany control such as decisiveness and quickness to punish people are, however, less acceptable in contemporary society than they once were. While these characteristics have perhaps never been suited to managing professionals who seek autonomy to use their professional knowledge rather than close direction, they are unfashionable and unwelcome to the humblest of workers who deserve, and expect, to be treated with dignity and consideration.

It is reasonable to suggest that classic masculine management styles are being challenged by a feminization of management (Kerfoot and Knights, 1993). While opening up leadership positions to women is an important social goal it is far from clear that having more women in top jobs would deliver innovation, creativity and change any better than men.

Reanalyzing leadership stories

Collins and Rainwater (2005) offer an interesting reanalysis of a corporate transformation at giant US retailer Sears Roebuck, first told in the esteemed *Harvard Business Review* (Rucci *et al.*, 1988). First though, we need to remind ourselves of what happened in Beijing in April 1989. This was a time of crisis for communism with huge structural changes occurring in Eastern Europe. Following the death of a pro-democracy sympathizer in China people wanted to demonstrate in Tiananmen Square, Beijing but the Chinese government had little tolerance of demonstrations and of demonstrators. After demonstrations had taken place for some time and as numbers swelled in the Square the government sent in tanks to disperse protestors. An unknown 'rebel' stood in front of the advancing tank column and halted it – the photo of him appearing as if in conversation with the lead tank commander became an icon of resistance.

Collins and Rainwater use the Tiananmen Square 'tank man' incident to show that there are multiple ways of interpreting something like the Sears Roebuck change story. Did 'tank man' stand in front of the moving column and stop it or had it already stopped? Was he a people's hero defiant in the face of government oppression or was he an agitator who would undermine the harmonious society in which he lived? Why was he there? Was he just crossing the road with his shopping or are there more sinister explanations? Who ordered the tanks to stop advancing? Why did they stop? Had they already stopped? We don't know, but the point is that multiple stories can be written and told to explain the events that happened.

The Sears Roebuck story was written by company insiders and Collins and Rainwater criticize the paper as being an uncritical shrine to the transformational efforts of a new CEO. The new leader announced new strategic priorities and new task forces. Events were held to attune the workforce to the new position and revised 'total performance indicators' were introduced to measure performance. The paper's authors portray the transformation as an epic tale of heroic 'daring-do' with the chief hero the CEO. It is about bringing light where there was darkness. It is *Beowulf*, it is *Biggles*.

What Collins and Rainwater then bring is a perceptive and amusing sideswipe at the paper. First they show how the same story can be retold not as heroism but as a tragedy. What of the cast of thousands (the employees) who have only 'walk on' parts in the play. It is a tragedy that their role, which must have been more than a little, is neglected. The CEO cast in the leading role, they argue, can just as well be seen as a villain motivated by corporate profits who manoeuvres the main characters (employees) for his own ends.

The story is also recast as a comedy. Central to the transformation was a new set of 'total performance indicators' such that, we are told, 'our model shows that a 5 point improvement in employee attitudes will drive a 1.3 point improvement in customer satisfaction, which in turn will drive a 5% improvement in revenue growth ... these numbers are as rigorous as any others we work with at Sears' (Rucci *et al.*, 1988, p. 91). Really? Is business performance really this linear? Have we learned nothing from complexity theory? Can we not recast the main character as a fool leading willing dupes (senior management) into a Wonderland of cause and effect?

Management literature abounds with heroic stories of change. Some leaders are given nicknames to emphasize their superpowers; 'Neutron Jack' (so-called because he left the buildings standing but without any people in them, rather like neutron bombs do) and 'Chainsaw Al' who was famed for cutting through organizations, slashing jobs on the way, are but two examples.

The *Harvard Business Review* carried a similar piece to the Sears story only this time on German pharmaceutical company Siemens (Stewart and O'Brien, 2005). Again we are shown a picture of the clean shaven and well dressed CEO and told how the organization transformed from a technically strong but slow outfit to a fast and nimble giant. A 'top+' programme was introduced to reduce costs, innovate and grow and deliver cultural change. Mass meetings addressed thousands of employees where urgency was stressed. The CEO socialized with worker representatives. An annual business conference was held and at quarterly business meetings the heads of the worst performing units had to present their results first – perhaps not to humiliate them but certainly to make them aware of their performance. External benchmarking and joint-ventures were championed and worker hours were raised from 35 to 40 without extra pay. This dynamic story is, of course, about the same company that Illustration 6.8 tells us was becoming embroiled in dodgy practices at the same time.

We emphasize that our aim here is not to mock or deride the organizations we have used to illustrate our points, their managers who work hard to secure jobs for employees and profits for investors, or the authors of the heroic stories in which they feature. Rather it is simply to point out that stories of change are too often overly simple and sequential stories of heroism would have us overlook the true complexities and true contributions made by a largely anonymous cast.

Leading change

A common theme in discussions of leadership and change is the idea of linking different leadership approaches to different change situations. Greiner (1972) and Quinn (1988) proposed that different organizational life cycle stages (formation, growth, maturity and decline) need different leadership styles to take the organization forward. In the formative period when markets and structures are evolving quickly, for example, a creative and entrepreneurial style fits best.

Dunphy and Stace (1988, 1993) modelled approaches to change on two dimensions; the level of environmental readjustment needed to restore environmental fit and the style of leadership needed to realign it – see Figure 6.7. Their readjustment categories are:

- *Fine tuning* – typically at lower levels, e.g., clarifying goals, refining methods and procedures.
- *Incremental adjustment* – distinct changes but not on a radical scale, e.g., changing structure, using new production methods.
- *Modular transformation* – a major realignment of part of an organization, e.g., a major restructuring, expansion or contraction.
- *Corporate transformation* – changes across the organization to business strategy, e.g., revised mission, organization-wide restructuring, new top management.

Their categories of leadership are:

- *Collaborative* – wide participation of employees.
- *Communicative* – involving people in goal setting.
- *Directive* – managerial authority is the driving force.
- *Coercive* – change is forced and imposed.

Combining the environmental refitting and leadership categories above, Dunphy and Stace proposed the following approaches to managing change. When employees are in favour and support change then participative evolution is used when the amount of change needed is small. When environmental fit is low and when employees support radical change then charismatic transformation applies. When employees oppose change then forced evolution applies when small adjustments are needed whereas dictatorial transformation is needed when environmental fit is low and major realignment is needed.

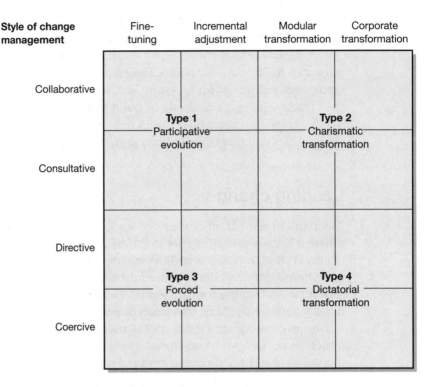

Figure 6.7 The Dunphy and Stace change matrix

Source: Reprinted by permission of Sage Publications Ltd from Dunphy, D. and Stace, D. (1993) 'The Strategic Management of Corporate Change', *Human Relations*, 46(8), p. 908. Copyright (© The Tavistock Institute, 1993).

A problem with typologies like this is that they imply that managers have a choice of change strategies almost as if they are picking from a toolkit. Indeed, Dunphy and Stace claim that the model has 'implications for the choice of strategies for managing organizational change in differing circumstances and for the training of change agents' (1988, p. 317). It assumes that change can be planned and implemented and implies that whatever outcomes are desired by top management will come to pass. There is no recognition of the employees' voices in, for instance, transformational change imposed in a dictatorial fashion. How smooth would that be?

As well as its prescriptive nature another problem lies in the model's treatment of the environment. Dunford (1990) points out that the model assumes that the environment is a determinable fixed reality 'out there' that can be accurately gauged before the organization is repositioned to fit it. While environments are definitely 'out there', what they are like and how organizations need to respond is imagined and enacted by managers and these perceptions shape their strategic thinking. To some extent then, environments are 'in here'.

Obstructing and facilitating change

If change is going to work then getting the right reactions from employees is critical. Indeed, employee reactions arguably have the biggest impact on the success of change initiatives. As we saw above however, much advice on change management offers prescriptions for matching leadership styles to levels of change in a highly formulaic and normative way and brushes over some deep issues that obviously exercise the minds of those whose lives others want to alter. The high failure rate of planned change initiatives alerts us to how difficult it is to manage employee reactions. But what exactly is resistance to change and why is it so common in relation to readiness to change?

Resistance to change

'Resistance to change' is a widely used phrase which captures a broad range of meaning. It applies to the individual employee who is asked to change their working practices and who puts up a fight and also to employees collectively, such as when the entire workforce of an organization takes industrial action. It is often seen as a negative thing that management should try to eradicate but this overlooks the fact that those who are doing the resisting might have good reason.

Piderit (2000) identifies behavioural, affective and cognitive forms of resistance. Behavioural resistance could manifest as endless questioning, non-compliance or disruption to planned changes. Alternatively people may stay silent and comply with change but with their emotions running high. Others resist by defending and arguing for preservation of their preferred routines. It is generally seen as a negative outcome but to more enlightened managers it can be a source of ideas. Ford and Ford (2009), for instance, recommend that resistors should not be overlooked but that resistance should be seen as a form of feedback that can enhance the change initiative (see Illustration 6.9).

Illustration 6.9

A fresh view of resistance: resistance as feedback

Managers blame resistors for not seeing the light, not being objective, being awkward. Maybe sometimes they are these things but sometimes perhaps it is the resistors who can see where plans are not joining up or see the flaws in management's assumptions. Resistance is a resource; an 'energy that can be channelled on behalf of the organization'. Ford and Ford (2009) suggest five ways of using resistance constructively.

Boost awareness – top managers, having convinced themselves of the benefits, are mostly immune to how changes affect the jobs of people far below them so they should 'drop down' a few layers and talk to those who are being affected. Even emotional exchanges may add value in keeping a dialogue open.

Return to purpose – communicate what needs to change and why. Middle managers need to be able to explain to their staff what needs to happen and they cannot do this unless the purpose is clear.

Change the change – resistors can identify serious points about what is being proposed so don't be afraid to change the change to take these points on board. Egos and position power may impede this so it is vital that

▶

Illustration 6.9 *continued*

senior managers don't allow junior managers to block new insights.

Build engagement – if communication channels are effective then worries and ideas can come to the surface. These can be managed in ways that enable individuals and groups to get involved in dealing with them and by so doing engage people in the changes.

Complete the past – many people in change situations have good memories of what happened the last time change was attempted. This means that today's resistance may not be much to do with today's change but with past change. Past failures need to be acknowledged.

Oreg (2003) approached the question of what resistance to change is by developing a scale to measure individual differences. Scales like this are used in research to see how resistance is related to other variables and this particular scale could be used in employee selection processes to assess how applicants fit with particular jobs. From theory he built up a four dimensional model of resistance which is summarized below with examples of the statements in the scale:

- *Routine seeking*, e.g. 'I'll take a routine day over a day full of unexpected events any time'.
- *Emotional reaction*, e.g., 'When things don't go according to plans it stresses me out'.
- *Short-term focus*, e.g., 'Once I've made plans I'm not likely to change them'.
- *Cognitive rigidity*, e.g., 'I often change my mind'.

Routine seeking is a behavioural component of resistance. Emotional reaction and short-termism are affective components reflecting people's unease with change and with the disturbances that being involved in change create. Cognitive rigidity is a cognitive component reflecting how willing an individual is to change their mind. When testing the resistance to change scale Oreg found moderate positive correlations with risk aversion and moderate negative correlations with tolerance of ambiguity. These were as expected, since the more risk averse a person is the more they would be expected to avoid change and the more tolerant of ambiguity they are the less resistant to change they would be.

Cynicism and scepticism

These two concepts are quite closely related but also quite different. Stanley *et al.* (2005, p. 436) consider that scepticism towards change is 'doubt about the viability of a change for the attainment of its stated objective'. Sceptics therefore do not believe that the intended change will bring about the intended benefits if it is implemented.

Cynicism towards change differs in that it is 'disbelief about a management's implied or stated motives for a specific organizational change'. Stanley *et al.* (2005) found that cynicism was a predictor of resistance to change, although the connection was not as strong as was anticipated. The link between cynicism and resistance implies that change agents should work on overcoming cynical reactions in communication strategies. If employees are disbelieving and distrusting of management in general then the ingredients of a problem are in place and cynical reactions can spiral out of control, as shown in Figure 6.8.

The importance of communicating with employees is well known and takes on a heightened importance when change is needed. Bordia and colleagues (2004) found that communication during change is vital to manage employee uncertainty and feelings of loss of control. While communication is clearly essential, having been on the inside of organizational changes this book's

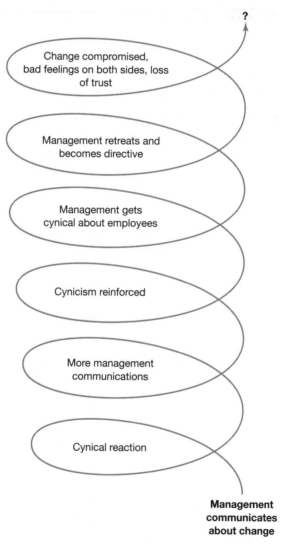

Figure 6.8 Cynicism spiral

authors have seen how the real reasons for changes are sometimes suppressed behind 'spin'. Indeed, taking a lead from governments and how they communicate with the electorate it looks to us as if organizations are routinely 'spinning' stories to employees and other stakeholders. Although cynicism and scepticism are negative feelings it is sometimes abundantly clear to organizational insiders why they arise. Management is not always 'squeaky clean' in its words and its deeds so it is important not to simply dismiss cynicism and scepticism as the reactions of people who cannot see the light. Combating cynicism may be helped if visible changes are made to organizational symbols such as pay structures or reporting relationships. This helps employees to see management's sincerity.

Readiness for change

Readiness for change is an important precursor to coping with resistance according to Armenakis, Harris and Mossholde (1993). Readiness involves shaping, perhaps conditioning, attitudes and beliefs to be favourable. Communication strategies need to emphasize two messages:

- The need for change, i.e., explaining the gap between what the organization needs to be doing and what it is doing.
- The affected parties' ability to change and the ability to do it well. This is important because if employees think they cannot achieve it then they will avoid putting effort into it.

Combining the concept of readiness with urgency (the amount of time before changes must be implemented) leads to the typology shown in Figure 6.9.

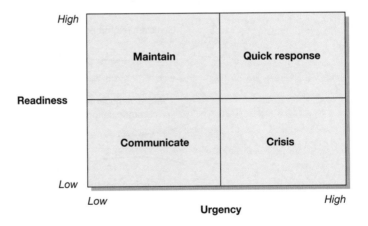

Figure 6.9 Organizational readiness for urgency

Source: Based on Armenakis , A., Harris, S.G. and Mossholde, K.W. (1993) 'Creating Readiness for Change,' *Human Relations*, 46(6), pp. 681–704.

- *Low readiness/low urgency* – calls for a communication strategy to enhance readiness. This could involve opinion forming and active participation of employees in events that raise readiness.
- *Low readiness/high urgency* – this is a crisis situation which may need a rapid injection of new personnel and reassignment of people to new tasks.
- *High readiness/low urgency* – the priority here is to keep messages about the discrepancy current.
- *High readiness/high urgency* – a quick response scenario exists in which high energy for change needs to be maintained.

Leader-member exchange

One of the limitations of leadership style theory is that it assumes that leaders display the same style towards their followers and those followers, in response, see and respond to a consistent style. But anyone who has been part of organization, club or society can see that the relationships between leaders and followers are often mixed. Leaders behave differently with different people. Some followers are held in high esteem and included in what goes on, others are treated with respect but perhaps not involved much, others are treated with disdain. This observable feature of organizational life led Graen *et al*. (Graen and Scandura, 1987; Graen and Uhl-Bien, 1995) to develop what has become known as leader-member exchange (LMX) theory. (Members in this context are people who are in groups working with a leader.)

Graen argued that the different types of social exchanges fall into two types; in-group and out-group. People in the in-group are involved in decision making and might be given projects to lead. Their opinions will be sought and the leader may well 'keep them in the know' and share confidences about people and plans with them. They are well placed to influence the leader in their favour for tasks, assignments and career advancement.

People in the out-group are kept at arm's length and only given the information needed to do their job. Their ideas are not much sought after and if they volunteer ideas, unless they are 'dynamite', they will struggle to be taken seriously. In-group members are likely to believe that they have better knowledge and competencies than 'outers' and that is why they are in the in-group. They can 'dis' out-group members who they perceive as being less capable. Out-group members may look at the in-group and think they are favoured not because of their enhanced competencies, but because they are ingratiating creeps or because they are 'old hands' who have been around for too long and who really need to be split up before they do any more damage.

The effects of LMX relationships are felt when organizations want to change, in large or small measure, because this is when leaders need to persuade followers to move in particular directions. While in-group members may be falling over each other in the rush to change something (they may have thought of it in the first place) the out-group typically takes much more convincing and could be an important source of resistance.

Attribution theory plays a part in situations like this (Furst and Cable, 2008). The quality of the leader-member relationship seems likely to have a big influence on how communications about change are interpreted by followers. If relations are poor then negative attributions towards the initiator could follow, for example, 'Why do they want me to do that?' When relations are good then the communications are likely to be seen much more constructively. Attributions also work the other way such that, where relations are poor, leaders may not bother to try and explain to someone what they need from them because they have already categorized them as a resistor. Furst and Cable (2008) found that LMX affects the relationship between leaders' use of different influence tactics and followers' outcomes. This explains why, for instance, coercion may be effective in one setting and ineffective in another.

A study of Dutch employees during a merger (Van Dam *et al.*, 2008) found that employees who reported high LMX also reported low resistance to change. They also found that giving information, giving people opportunities to participate, and trust in the people managing the change were all related to lower resistance. This implies that bottom-up approaches to change in which employees interact directly with leaders and change agents are likely to be more effective than top-down approaches characterized by remoteness and impersonal management. A further implication is that it is not enough to seek high LMX when change is needed but that it should be sought routinely so that it is in place to support change when it comes along. It needs to be a part of the daily work routines (Van Dam *et al.*, 2008).

Organizational citizenship

Organizational citizenship behaviour (OCB) (Organ, 1988) refers to the discretionary behaviour that people display (or not) in the workplace such as covering for a colleague off sick, being proactive and sorting out a problem before it escalates or helping out a colleague who is under pressure. Citizenship behaviour can be directed toward individuals or the organization and it is not part of any formal job description; it is above and beyond one's formal duties. The display of organizational citizenship is thought to have a big impact on performance in the workplace and logically connects with success in change initiatives. The presence of OCBs should catalyze change and their absence should hold it back.

The links between LMX and OCB have been explored and it was found that OCB directed towards the supervisor are stronger than OCB directed toward the organization (Ilies *et al.*, 2007). This means that high LMX is more likely to lead to reciprocation with behaviour helping individuals than behaviour helping the organization. Implications for change managers are that they need to focus on the health of dyadic (two person) relationships since any poor relationships will undermine change.

Force field analysis

Chapter 1 introduced the external forces that push organizations into change situations but counteracting, resisting forces often arise inside organizations when change is attempted. One technique for analyzing the range and strength of forces for and against change is *force field analysis* – see Figure 6.10. Developed by Kurt Lewin (1951), force field analysis is based on the idea that social situations can be seen as equilibria that are periodically disturbed when changes to the situations are attempted. Change is prevented when the situations exist in conditions of stable equilibria, where the two sets of forces are in balance, and when the opposing forces are stronger than the driving forces. If change is to happen then the equilibrium has to be shifted so that the driving forces are stronger than opposing forces.

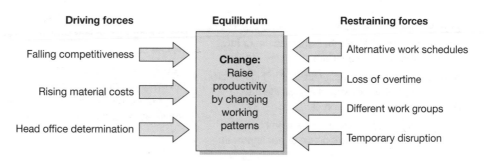

Figure 6.10 A force field diagram

Force field analysis is a way of identifying and bringing out into the open the forces that are impacting on a situation. It identifies power interests of actors involved and should lead to ideas about how to influence the actors to reduce the opposing forces and strengthen the driving forces. In the context of trying to implement planned change Lewin saw change as a three stage process; unfreezing, moving (changing) and refreezing. Unfreezing means understanding the forces that are operating in the system and realigning them (unfreezing them) so that the equilibrium is moved. The change stage is a process of communicating, support and development so that a different situation is created. Refreezing is a process of returning to stability as the actors become used to the new balance of forces.

This three stage process appears as rather simplistic and can be criticized for its portrayal of rigid (frozen) situations rather than the flexible situations that modern business rhetoric calls for. It also overlooks the politics of change. However, Burnes (2004a, 2004b) considers that the three stage process has parallels with complexity theory and that it still has much to offer in analyzing change situations and resistance to change. Recent applications of the technique include understanding how the nature of management has changed (Wilson and Thomson, 2006), understanding conflict in engineering project teams (Hayden, 2006) and understanding culture integration following acquisition (Elsass and Veiga, 1994). Illustration 6.10 outlines the steps in carrying out a force field analysis.

Illustration 6.10

Force field analysis

Step 1: Define the problem in terms of the present situation, with its strengths and weaknesses, and the situation you would wish to achieve. Define the target situation as precisely and unambiguously as possible.

Step 2: List the forces working for and against the desired changes. These can be based on power, symbols, procedures, resources, time, external factors and aspects of corporate culture.

Step 3: Rate each of the forces for and against change in terms of strength: high, medium or low. Numerical values can be given.

Step 4: Using a diagram such as that in Figure 6.10, draw lines of different lengths to indicate the different strengths of the forces.

Step 5: Label each line to indicate whether that force is very important, important or not important.

Step 6: For each very important and important force supporting the change, indicate how the force might be strengthened. Then do the same for those forces opposing the change, but in this case indicate how they could be weakened.

Step 7: Agree on those actions that appear most likely to help solve the problem of achieving change.

Step 8: Identify the resources that will be needed to take the agreed actions and how these resources may be obtained.

Step 9: Make a practical action plan designed to achieve the target situation, which should include timing of events, specified milestones and deadlines, specific responsibilities – who does what.

Paton and McCalman (2000) suggest that force field analysis, as well as operating as a technique in its own right, can be incorporated into other change situation analyses such as the TROPICS test discussed in Chapter 2. The results of such analyses help in deciding the extent to which an organization is open or closed to change. Strebel (1992, p. 67) offers the following advice on this:

1   Look for closed attitudes by examining what processes are in place for bringing new ideas into the sector, company or business unit, especially at the highest levels; and by probing whether management is aware of the change forces.

2   Look for an entrenched culture by examining what processes are in place for reflecting on values and improving behaviour and skills; and by enquiring to what extent behaviour and skills are adapted to the forces of change.

3   Look for rigid structures and systems, by examining when the organization, business system, the stakeholder resource base and the industry last changed significantly; and by enquiring to what extent the structures and systems are capable of accommodating the forces of change.

4   Look for counterproductive change dynamics by examining whether historical forces of change are driving the business; and by enquiring to what extent the historical forces of change have become the new force of resistance.

5   Assess the strength of the overall resistance to change by examining to what extent the various forces of resistance are correlated with one another; and by describing the resistance threshold in terms of power and resources needed to deal with the resistance.

If assessments of this kind can be achieved then Strebel's (1996) juxtaposition of the level of intensity of forces for change with the degree of resistance expected (that is, whether an organization is closed to change, can be opened to change, or is open to change) is useful for determining the leadership behaviour and overall management approach to implementing change (see Figure 6.11).

The role of leadership in Strebel's model is most clearly spelt out in the case of weak environmental change forces in an organizational situation of being closed to change (top left of Figure 6.11). In this situation, weak change forces imply proactive change. In an organization unused to and closed to change this implies radical leadership that breaks the dominant culture of resistance by starting with top management and continuing through a process of shaking-up others in the organization. The upshot of Strebel's ideas is that change agents need to adapt standard recipes – different recipes, strategies and paths are needed from situation to situation.

Activity 6.8 *Force field analysis*

Force fields are best analyzed in groups, so if possible do this activity with others. Choose a social situation where change is being attempted and identify the driving and opposing forces. Next, try to gauge the strength of the forces. Then identify strategies to diminish opposing forces and strengthen driving forces.

Resistance	PROACTIVE	REACTIVE	RAPID	
Closed to change	Radical leadership	Organizational realignment	Downsizing and restructuring	Discontinuous paths
Can be opened to change	Top-down experimentation	Process re-engineering	Autonomous restructuring	Mixed paths
Open to change	Bottom-up experimentation	Goal cascading	Rapid adaptation	Continuous paths
	Weak	Moderate	Strong	**Change force**

Figure 6.11 Contrasting change paths

Source: from 'Choosing the Right Change Path', Financial Times Mastering Management, Part 14, p. 17 (Strebel, P. 1996) 9th February 1996.

Responding to resistance

Leadership can be conceptualized in terms of its three main functions within a group or organization (Open University, 1996, p. 38):

1 the *strategic* function: developing a sense of direction in the group or organization;

2 the *tactical* function: defining the tasks necessary to achieve the group's or the organization's goals and making sure that these tasks are carried out effectively;

3 the *interpersonal* function: maintaining the morale, cohesion and commitment of the group or organization.

These functions do not divide among leaders at the top, middle and bottom of organizations; all functions are carried out by all leaders regardless of status.

Reducing or overcoming resistance to change depends on identifying the sources of resistance and on a leader's ability to be task oriented (both strategically and tactically) when the time requires but also relationship oriented to address the more individualized resistances to change. A first step is to recognize that individuals faced with change often go through a traumatic process of shock and denial before they come to acknowledge and adapt to it (Rashford and Coghlan, 1989; Clarke, 1994; Nortier, 1995). What must not be forgotten, however, is that change can be exciting and can bring new and positive opportunities for all. Although communicating a vision is important many other change catalysts and barriers need managing – see Illustrations 6.11 and 6.12. These illustrations clearly overlap in content and intent and the advice is offered by their creators as relevant to all situations.

Illustration 6.11

Six steps to effective change

1 Mobilize commitment to change through joint diagnosis of business problems.

2 Develop a shared vision of how to organize and manage for competitiveness.

3 Foster consensus for the new vision, competence to enact it and cohesion to move it along.

4 Spread revitalization to all departments without pushing it from the top.

5 Institutionalize revitalization through formal policies, systems and structures.

6 Monitor and adjust strategies in response to problems in the revitalization process.

Source: Beer, M., Eisenstat, R.A. and Spector, B. (1990) 'Why Change Programmes Do Not Produce Change', *Harvard Business Review*, November–December, 68(6), pp. 158–166.

Illustration 6.12

Why transformation efforts fail

According to Kotter (1995), transformation in an organization fails through:

1 not establishing a great enough sense of urgency;

2 not creating a powerful enough coalition;

3 lacking a vision;

4 undercommunicating in a big way;

5 not removing obstacles to the new vision;

6 not systematically planning for and creating short-term wins;

7 declaring victory too soon;

8 not anchoring changes in the corporation's culture.

Source: Kotter, J.P. (1995) 'Leading Change: why transformation efforts fail', *Harvard Business Review*, March–April, 73(2), pp. 59–67.

Conclusions

Leadership theory began with a search for universally applicable traits and styles but increasingly recognized that leadership approaches need to fit organizational contexts. Charismatic and transformational approaches were heralded but it seems clear that leaders fitting these descriptions can show a dark side. Recent corporate mismanagement has led to an emphasis on the moral, ethical and self-regulatory components captured in authentic leadership. Followers can also make good leaders and this recognition has stimulated interest in distributed leadership.

Our understanding of resistance to change, often seen as a challenge to the power and authority of leaders, is now better understood and good communication is one of the best strategies for dealing with it. Learning how to learn from resistors is a challenge to modern managers and leaders.

Leadership theory is dominated by studies from the US and this perhaps reflects its dominant industrial position and endemic culture of finding and championing the heroic figure that saves the day and gets the girl (or boy), even though they may inflict casualties along the way. Hopefully studies of leadership outside the North American context will increase and shed new light on ways of managing meaning and getting others to believe in an organizational vision.

Leadership, together with the other aspects of organizational life, comprise the context in which change takes place. With the context now in place we can proceed to the more practical considerations of how to design, plan and implement change in Part Three.

Discussion questions and assignments

1 Drawing on your own experience of organizational change, describe a situation where the leader was seen, or styled themselves, as a 'heroic' figure.

2 In the context of the discussion of different types of change in Chapter 2, and the idea that organizations must be alert to their ever-changing environments, debate the advisability of seeking managers at all levels who can act as transformational leaders.

3 Examine the concept of 'leaders of change' as it might apply across different societies and organizations.

4 Think of a change situation that you have been in. What were the sources of resistance? How did management try to combat them?

5 If you wanted to develop your own leadership skills/style what would you prioritize? What do you need to be better at? How might you begin to develop leadership qualities?

Case example ●●●

Making the transition from manager to leader: tough lessons on the road to leadership

The call for better quality leadership in politics and organizations is now widely heard and often repeated. Simply stated, leaders are people who establish new directions, gain the support, cooperation and commitment of those they need to move in that new direction and motivate them to overcome obstacles to gaol achievement. There's also good agreement about what leadership is not. Leadership differs from management, an equally valuable but different set of activities.

Leadership development is not a smooth, continuous or incremental process, but is punctuated by inflection points. These key junctures, which Herminia Ibarra (2004) calls leadership transitions, are the points in a person's career at which they either learn how to lead or become derailed. A transition is a move into a new role – whether formal assignment, a project, or a role imposed by an unexpected event such as a crisis – which is so fundamentally different that the old ways of operating are no longer valid or effective.

Consider the experience of Anne – after a steady rise through the functional ranks in logistics and dis-

tribution, Anne found herself blind-sided by a proposal for a radical reorganization that came from outside her division. Accustomed to planning for annual improvements in her basic business strategy, she failed to notice shifting priorities in the wider market. Although she had built a loyal, high-performing team, she had few networks outside her group to help her anticipate the new imperatives. Worse, she was assessed by her boss as lacking the broader business picture. Frustrated, Anne contemplated leaving. Anne's predicament is not unusual. The most common learning challenges for aspirational leaders are the following:

Learning to see, not just produce good ideas

Communicating clear messages that have emotional impact

Delegating and involving others

Improving social skills, such as empathy, listening and coaching.

Consider the experience of Jeff – he is a general manager of a consumer product subsidiary and was praised by his company for his turnaround skills. But after three or four successful assignments he found himself in trouble at all levels. His relationship with an older, more conservative colleague in marketing suffered from miscommunication and mutual lack of trust. At each point of disagreement Jeff had taken over, at times doing his colleague's job. After this, he received his first poor performance review. His manager questioned his ability to delegate and to communicate laterally with other groups within the company. He sought and gained the motivation, practice and feedback that ultimately broadened his leadership style.

These examples suggest that the leadership transition can provoke deep self-questioning. Who am I?

What do I want to become? What do I like to do? Do I have what it takes to learn a different way of operating? Is it me? Is it worth it?

Ibarra suggests that there are three things in particular that can help support leaders to change; motivation, practice and feedback, and coaching.

If we consider Anne and Jeff's transitions, in each case the most important changes to be made involved not skills but values. With greater attention to the leadership transition as a personal passage, organizations will better prepare promising managers for leading roles in the business.

Source: Ibarra, H. (2004) 'Tough Lessons on the Road to Leadership', *Financial Times*, 5 August, 2004, p. 11.

Case exercise

1 From definitions and discussion at the beginning of the chapter and key points raised in this illustration, what do you consider to be the main differences between management and leadership? Share your response with others to assess whether there is a general consensus.

2 The illustration suggests that leadership development 'is not a smooth, continuous or incremental process, but is punctuated by inflection points'. Do you agree or disagree with this statement? Support your arguments with theoretical frameworks and examples you may have from your own experience or through examples you have researched in the general business domain.

3 In relation to the 'management of change', is there anything that Anne and Jeff could have done in relation to their roles to have assessed their environment more effectively and help them better prepare for the changes within their organizations?

4 From areas discussed in this chapter, is there anything the organization could have done to better prepare Anne and Jeff for the changes in their roles?

●●●● Indicative resources

Armstrong, M. and Stephens, T. (2005) *A Handbook of Management and Leadership*, London: Kogan Page. This text provides information on key theories and best practice related to management and leadership. Included in this is the issue of delivering change and case examples that support management, leadership and change.

Harvard Business Review (2004) *Leadership in a Changed World*, Boston, MA: Harvard Business School Press. This book (not a text) is part of a series published by Harvard Business School to compile key writers' ideas in relation to different business areas. This particular part of the series offers eight 'leading thinkers' on leadership and the impact of leadership in a changing environment. The key thinking with this book is leadership and globalization and the future of leadership in an ever-changing global economy.

Useful websites

www.berr.gov.uk/whatwedo/regional/skills/management-and-leadership/ page10947.html The Department of Business Innovation and Skills website includes work on inspirational leadership. Some case studies are also included.

www.nhs.leadershipqualities.nhs.uk This site provides information on how the National Health Service sees leadership and describes the behaviour that the NHS seeks in its present and future leaders.

www.i-l-m.com This is the website of the Institute for Leadership and Management and contains research and comment in the field.

www.time.com/time/time100/leaders/index.html This site gives suggestions for the 100 people whose leadership has shaped our world.

www.northernleadershipacademy.co.uk This is a good site for information on a wide range of leadership issues.

> To click straight to these links and for other resources go to
> **www.pearsoned.co.uk/senior**

References

Anderson, L., Bennet, N., Cartwright, M., Newton, W., Preedy, M. and Wise, C. (2003) Study Guide, *Leading and Managing for Effective Education*, Milton Keynes: Open University Press.

Armenakis, A., Harris, S.G. and Mossholde, K.W. (1993) 'Creating Readiness for Change', *Human Relations*, 46(6), pp. 681–704.

Armstrong, M. and Stephens, T. (2005) *A Handbook of Management and Leadership*, London: Kogan Page.

Avolio, B.J. and Gardner, W.L. (2005) 'Authentic Leadership Development: getting to the root of positive forms of leadership', *Leadership Quarterly*, 16(3), pp. 315–338.

Baker, D.P. and Salas, E. (1997) *Team Climate Inventory Manual and User's Guide*, Windsor: ASE Press.

Bar-On, R. (1997) *Emotional Quotient Inventory: Technical Manual*, Multi-Health Systems, Toronto.

Bass, B.M. (1990) 'From Transactional to Transformational Leadership: learning to share the vision', *Organizational Dynamics*, Winter, pp. 19–31.

Bass, B.M. and Avolio, B.J. (1993) Transformational Leadership: a response to Critiques, in Chemers, M. and Ayman, R. (eds) *Leadership Theory and Research: Perspectives and Directions*, San Diego, CA: Academic Press, pp. 49–80.

Beer, M., Eisenstat, R.A. and Spector, B. (1990) 'Why Change Programmes Do Not Produce Change', *Harvard Business Review*, November–December, 68(6), pp. 158–166.

Beer, M. and Nohria, N. (2000) 'Cracking the Code of Change', *Harvard Business Review*, May–June, pp. 133–141.

Blake, R.R. and McCanse, A.A. (1991) *Leadership Dilemmas: Grid Solutions*, Houston, TX: Gulf Publishing.

Blake, R.R. and Mouton, J.S. (1964) *The Managerial Grid*, Houston, TX: Gulf Publishing.

Bono, J.E. and Judge, T.A. (2004) Personality and Transformational and Transactional Leadership: a meta-analysis, *Journal of Applied Psychology*, 89(5), pp. 901–910.

Bordia, P., Hunt, E., Paulsen, N., Tourish, D. and DiFonzo, N. (2004) 'Uncertainty During Organizational Change: is it all about control?' *European Journal or Work and Organizational Psychology*, 13(3), pp. 345–365.

Bottery, M. (2004) *The Challenges of Educational Leadership*, London: PCP.

Burnes, B. (2004a) 'Kurt Lewin and Complexity Theories: back to the future?' *Journal of Change Management*, 4(4), pp. 309–325.

Burnes, B. (2004b) Kurt Lewin and the Planned Approach to Change: a re-appraisal, *Journal of Management Studies*, 41(6), pp. 977–1002.

Burns, J.M. (1978) *Leadership*, New York: Harper & Row.

Clarke, L. (1994) *The Essence of Change*, Hemel Hempstead: Prentice Hall.

Collins, D. and Rainwater, K. (2005) 'Managing Change at Sears: a sideways look at a tale of corporate transformation', *Journal of Organizational Change Management*, 18(1), pp. 16–30.

Conger, J. (1993) 'Max Weber's Conceptualization of Charismatic Authority: its influence on organizational research', *Leadership Quarterly*, 4(3), pp. 277–288.

Cote, S. and Miners, C. (2006) 'Emotional Intelligence, Cognitive Intelligence and Job Performance', *Administrative Science Quarterly*, 51, pp. 1–28.

Dries, N. and Pepermans, R. (2007) 'Using Emotional Intelligence to Identify High Potential: a metacompetency perspective', *Leadership & Organization Development Journal*, 28(8), pp. 749–770.

Dulewicz, V. and Herbert, P. (1996) 'Leaders of Tomorrow: how to spot the high-flyers', *Financial Times*, 20 September, p. 16.

Dunford, R. (1990) 'Strategies for Planned Change: an exchange of views between Dunford, Dunphy and Stace', *Organization Studies*, 11(1), pp. 131–135.

Dunphy, D. and Stace, D. (1988) 'Transformational and Coercive Strategies for Planned Organizational Change: beyond the OD model', *Organization Studies*, 9(3), pp. 317–334.

Dunphy, D. and Stace, D. (1993) 'The Strategic Management of Corporate change', *Human Relations*, 46(8), pp. 905–920.

Eagly, A.H., Johannesen-Schmidt, M.C. and van Enge, M.L. (2003) 'Transformational, Transactional and Lassaiz-faire Leadership Styles: a meta-analysis comparing men and women', *Psychological Bulletin*, 129(4), pp. 569–591.

Elsass, P.M. and Veiga, J.F. (1994) 'Acculturation in Acquired Organizations: a force field analysis', *Human Relations*, 47(4), pp. 431–454.

Farkas, C.M. and Wetlaufer, S. (1996) 'The Ways Chief Executive Officers Lead', *Harvard Business Review*, May–June, pp. 110–122.

Fiedler, F.E. (1967) *A Theory of Leadership Effectiveness*, New York: McGraw-Hill.

Fiol, C.M., Harris, D. and House, R. (1999) 'Charismatic Leadership: strategies for affecting social change', *Leadership Quarterly*, 10(3), pp. 449–482.

Ford, J.D. and Ford, L.W. (2009) 'Decoding Resistance to Change', *Harvard Business Review*, Mar/April, pp. 99–103.

Furst, S.A. and Cable, D.M. (2008) 'Employee Resistance to Organizational Change: managerial influence tactics and leader-member exchange', *Journal of Applied Psychology*, 93(2), pp. 453–462.

George, J. and Jones, G. (2005) *Understanding and Managing Organizational Behaviour* (4th edn), Harlow: Pearson Prentice Hall.

Goleman, D. (1998) 'What Makes a Leader? IQ and technical skills are important, but emotional intelligence is the *sine qua non* of leadership', *Harvard Business Review*, November–December, pp. 93–104.

Gordon, J.R. (1999) *A Diagnostic Approach to Organizational Behaviour* (6th edn), Englewood Cliffs, NJ: Prentice-Hall.

Graen, G.B. and Scandura, T.A. (1987) 'Toward a Psychology of Dyadic Organizing', *Research in Organizational Behaviour*, 9, pp. 175–208.

Graen, G.B. and Uhl-Bien, M. (1995) 'Relationship-based Approach to Leadership: development of leader-member exchange (LMX) theory of leadership over 25 years', *Leadership Quarterly*, 6, pp. 219–247.

Greiner, L. (1972) 'Evolution and revolution as organizations grow', *Harvard Business Review*, July–August, pp. 37–46.

Hackman, R. (1994) 'Tripwires in Designing and Leading Workgroups', *The Occupational Psychologist*, 23, pp. 3–8.

Harvard Business Review (2004) *Leadership in a Changed World*, Boston, MA: Harvard Business School Press.

Hayden, W.M. (2006) 'Human System Engineering – A Trilogy, Part II: may the force be with you: anatomy of project failures', *Leadership in Management and Engineering*, 6(1), pp. 1–12.

Hersey, P. and Blanchard, K.H. (1993) *Management of Organizational Behavior: Utilizing Human Resources* (6th edn), Englewood Cliffs, NJ: Prentice-Hall.

Higgs, M. and Dulewicz, V. (2004) 'The Emotionally Intelligent Leader', in Rees, D. and McBain, R. (eds) *People Management: Challenges and Opportunities*, London: Palgrave-MacMillan.

House, R.J. (1971) 'A Path–goal Theory of Leader Effectiveness', *Administrative Science Quarterly*, September, pp. 321–338.

Ibarra, H. (2004) 'Tough Lessons on the Road to Leadership', *Financial Times*, 5 August, p. 11.

Ilies, R., Morgeson, F.P. and Nahrgang, J.D. (2005) 'Authentic Leadership and Eudaemonic Well-being: understanding leader-follower outcomes', *Leadership Quarterly*, 16(3), pp. 373–394.

Ilies, R., Nahrgang and J.D. Morgeson, F.P. (2007) 'Leader-Member Exchange and Citizenship Behaviors: a meta-analysis', *Journal of Applied Psychology*, 92(1), pp. 269–277.

Judge, T.A. and Piccolo, R.F. (2004) 'Transformational and Transactional Leadership: a meta-analytic test of their relative validity', *Journal of Applied Psychology*, 89(5), pp. 755–768.

Kanter, R.M. (1991) 'Change-motor Skills: what it takes to be creative', in Henry, J. and Walker, D. (eds) *Managing Innovation*, London: Sage.

Katzenbach, J.R. and Smith, K. (1993) *Wisdom of Teams: Creating the High-performance Organization*, Boston, MA: Harvard Business School Press.

Kerfoot, D. and Knights, D. (1993) 'Management, Masculinity and Manipulation: from paternalism to corporate strategy in financial services', *Journal of Management Studies*, 30(4), pp. 659–677.

Kirkpatrick, S.A. and Locke, E.A. (1991) 'Leadership: do traits matter?', *Academy of Management Executive*, May, pp. 48–60.

Kotter, J.P. (1990) *A Force for Change: How Leadership Differs from Management*, New York: Free Press.

Kotter, J.P. (1995) 'Leading Change: why transformation efforts fail', *Harvard Business Review*, March–April, 73(2), pp. 59–67.

Kotter, J.P. (1996) *Leading Change*, Boston, MA: Harvard Business School Press.

Landrum, N.E., Howell, J.P. and Paris, L. (2000) 'Leadership for Strategic Change', *Leadership and Organization Development Journal*, 21(3), pp. 150–156.

Lewin, K. (1951) *Field Theory in Social Science*, New York: Harper & Row.

Likert, R. (1961) *New Patterns of Management*, New York: McGraw-Hill.

Linstead, S., Brewis, J. and Linstead, A. (2005) 'Gender in Change: gendering change', *Journal of Organizational Change Management*, 18(6), pp. 542–560.

Lord, R.G., De Vader, C.L. and Alliger, G.M. (1986) 'A Meta-analysis of the Relation Between Personality Traits and Leadership Perceptions: an application of validity generalization procedures', *Journal of Applied Psychology*, 71, pp. 402–410.

Mann, R.D. (1959) 'A Review of the Relationship Between Personality and Performance in Small Groups', *Psychological Bulletin*, 56(4), pp. 241–270.

Martin, C.M. (2008) a Meta-analytic Investigation of the Relationship between Emotional Intelligence and Leadership Effectiveness', unpublished D. Ed. dissertation, East Carolina University.

McHugh, M. and Bennett, H. (1999) 'Introducing Teamwork within a Bureaucratic Maze', *The Leadership and Organization Development Journal*, 20(2), pp. 81–93.

Mintzberg, H. (1979) *The Nature of Managerial Work*, Englewood Cliffs, NJ: Prentice-Hall.

Murphy, K.R. (ed.) (2006) *A Critique of Emotional Intelligence: What Are the Problems and How Can They be Fixed?* Mahwah, NJ: Lawrence Erlbaum Publishers.

Nortier, F. (1995) 'A New Angle on Coping with Change: managing transition', *Journal of Management Development*, 14(4), pp. 32–46.

Open University (1996) Book 6, 'Managing People: a wider view', MBA Course, Milton Keynes: Open University.

Oreg, S. (2003) 'Resistance to Change: developing an individual differences measure', *Journal of Applied Psychology*, 88(4), pp. 680–693.

Organ, D.W. (1988) *Organizational citizenship behaviour: The Good Soldier Syndrome*, Lexington, MA: Lexington Books.

Parry, K.W. and Bryman, A. (2006) 'Leadership in Organizations', in Clegg, S.R., Lawrence, T.B. and Nord, W.R. (eds) *The SAGE Handbook of Organization Studies*, London: SAGE, pp. 447–467.

Paton, R.A. and McCalman, J. (2000) *Change Management: A Guide to Effective Implementation*, London: Sage.

Piderit, S.K. (2000) 'Rethinking Resistance and Recognizing Ambivalence: a multidimensional view of attitudes toward an organizational change', *Academy of Management Review*, 25(4), pp. 783–794.

Post, J.M. (1986) 'Narcissism and the Charismatic Leader–follower Relationship', *Political Psychology*, 7(4), pp. 675–688.

Quinn, R.E. (1988) *Beyond Rational Management: Mastering the Paradoxes and Competing Demands of High Performance*, San Francisco, CA: Jossey-Bass.

Rashford, N.S. and Coghlan, D. (1989) 'Phases and Levels of Organisational Change', *Journal of Managerial Psychology*, 4(3), pp. 17–22.

Reich, R.B. (1991) 'The Team as Hero', in Henry, J. and Walker, D. (eds) *Managing Innovation*, London: Sage.

Rippin, A. (2005) Marks and Spencer – waiting for the warrior, *Journal of Organizational Change Management*, 18(6), pp. 578–593.

Robbins, S.P. and Coulter, M. (2005) *Management* (8th edn), Englewood Cliffs, NJ: Prentice-Hall.

Rucci, A., Kirn, S. and Quinn, R. (1998) 'The Employee-customer Profit Chain at Sears', *Harvard Business Review*, January–February, pp. 82–97.

Runciman, W.G. and Matthews, E. (1978) *Max Weber: Selections in Translation*, Canbridge: Cambridge University Press.

Senior, B. and Swailes, S. (2007) 'Inside Management Teams: developing a teamwork survey instrument', *British Journal of Management*, 18(2), pp. 138–153.

Shamir, B. and Eilam, G. (2005) "What's your story?' A life-stories approach to authentic leadership development', *Leadership Quarterly*, 16(3), pp. 395–417.

Shin, Y.K. (1999) 'The Traits and Leadership Styles of CEOs in South Korean Companies', *International Studies of Management and Organization*, 28(4), pp. 40–48.

Smith, M. (1991) 'Leadership and Supervision', in Smith, M. (ed.) *Analysing Organizational Behaviour*, New York: Macmillan.

Stanley, D.J. Meyer, J.P., and Topolnytsky, L. (2005) Emploee Cynicism and Resistance to Organizational Change, *Jounal of Business Psychology*, 19(4), 429–459.

Stewart, T.A. and O'Brien, L. (2005) 'Transforming an Industrial Giant', *Harvard Business Review*, February, pp. 114–122.

Stodgill, R.M. (1948) 'Personal Factors Associated with Leadership: a survey of the literature', *Journal of Psychology*, 25, pp. 35–71.

Stodgill, R.M. and Coons, A.E. (1957) *Leader Behavior: Its Description and Measurement*, Columbus, OH: Ohio State University Bureau of Business Research.

Storey, A. (2004) 'The Problem of Distributed Leadership', *School Leadership & Management*, 24(3), August, pp. 251–265.

Strebel, P. (1992) *Breakpoints: How Managers Exploit Radical Business Change*, Cambridge, MA: Harvard Business School Press.

Strebel, P. (1996) 'Choosing the Right Change Path', *Mastering Management*, Part 14, *Financial Times*, pp. 5–7.

Tannenbaum, R. and Schmidt, W.H. (1973) 'How to Choose a Leadership Pattern', *Harvard Business Review*, 51, May–June, pp. 162–180.

Treviño, L.K., Brown, M. and Hartman, L.P. (2003) 'A Qualitative Investigation of Perceived Executive Ethical Leadership: perceptions from inside and outside the executive suite', *Human Relations*, 56, pp. 5–37.

Useem, M. (1996) 'Do Leaders Make a Difference?' *Mastering Management*, Part 18, *Financial Times*, pp. 5–6.

Van Dam, K., Oreg, S. and Schyns, B. (2008) 'Daily Work Contexts and Resistance to Organizational Change: the role of leader-member exchange, development climate and change process characteristics', *Applied Psychology: An International Review*, 57(2), pp. 313–334.

Verbos, A.K., Gerard, J.A., Forshey, P.R., Harding, C.S. and Miller, J.S. (2007) 'The Positive Ethical Organisation: enacting a living code of ethics and ethical organisation identity', *Journal of Business Ethics*, 76, pp. 7–33.

Watson, T. (1994) *In Search of Management*, London: Routledge.

Wensley, R. (1996) 'Mrs Beeton, Management Guru,' *Financial Times*, 26 April, p. 15.

Wilson, J.F. and Thomson, A. (2006) 'Management in Historical Perspective: stages and paradigms', *Competition and Change*, 10(4), pp. 357–374.

Woffard, J.C. and Liska, L.Z. (1993) 'Path–goal Theories of Leadership: a meta-analysis', *Journal of Management*, Winter, pp. 857–876.

Woodruffe, C. (2000) 'Emotional Intelligence: time for a time-out', *Selection and Development Review*, 16(4), pp. 3–9.

Wright, P. (1996) *Managerial Leadership*, London: Routledge.

Yukl, G. (2002) *Leadership in Organizations* (5th edn), Englewood Cliffs, NJ: Prentice-Hall.

Zaccaro, S.J. (2007) 'Trait-Based Perspectives of Leadership', *American Psychologist*, 62(1), pp. 6–16.

STRATEGIES FOR MANAGING CHANGE

Part Three turns to the practicalities of *doing* change in the sense of designing, planning and implementing change – in other words concentrating on the processes through which change comes about. Two different approaches to managing change processes, each encompassing various methodologies, are discussed in Chapters 7 and 8. These approaches relate directly back to the types of change discussed in Chapter 2, in particular, the concepts of hard and soft problems, difficulties and messes. Chapter 7 concentrates on change approaches that are based on rational–logical models of change which are most appropriate for situations of hard complexity where the 'people' issues are low. In contrast, Chapter 8 recognizes that many change situations involve issues of organizational politics, culture and leadership that dictate an approach to change which can deal more easily with situations characterized by soft complexity.

Finally, Chapter 9 considers issues that will affect work and organizations in the future and trends in researching change.

Chapter 7

Hard systems models of change

There are a number of models for handling change in situations of hard complexity. This chapter describes one and, in order to demonstrate its use, applies it to a particular change situation. The limitations of this type of model are discussed.

Learning objectives

By the end of this chapter you will be able to:

- recognize change situations (problems/opportunities) characterized mainly by hard complexity, where the use of hard systems methodologies are appropriate;

- describe the main features of hard systems methodologies for defining, planning and implementing change;

- explain the hard systems model of change (HSMC) as representative of hard systems methodologies of change;

- discuss the limitations of hard systems methodologies of change and, therefore, the need for other change methodologies more suited to situations of soft complexity.

Situations of change

In Chapter 2 a number of different ways of categorizing organizational change were discussed; from incremental to radical, frame-breaking or discontinuous changes. As Chapter 2 showed, expectations with respect to the ease with which change happens vary according to its perceived complexity. Consequently, change in situations that are characterized by hard complexity is more likely to be enacted easily and speedily than change in situations which show soft complexity, that is, where issues are contentious and there is a high level of emotional involvement on the part of those likely to implement the change and those who will be affected by it.

There are many approaches to planning and implementing change. Some are more appropriate to situations of hard complexity while others are more appropriate to situations of soft complexity or, as Chapter 2 characterized them, 'messy' situations. Flood and Jackson (1991), using a systems perspective, classify various methodologies in a similar way but use the terms 'simple system' and 'complex system' instead of difficulties and messes. What is of more interest, though, is that Flood and Jackson also classify these methodologies according to their appropriateness of use in situations characterized by different ideological viewpoints. Three ideological viewpoints, representing three types of relationships between people, are defined. Two of these (the unitary and pluralist viewpoints) have been discussed already in Chapter 5 (see Illustration 5.9); all three are described in Illustration 7.1.

Using an extensive list of different methodologies for problem solving and change, Flood and Jackson suggest which are most appropriate in situations characterized as simple or complex systems but modified by whether relationships between people tend to be of a unitarist, pluralist or coercive nature. It is not the intention here to consider all the possibilities. What is important is to note that different logics dominate each possibility in terms of suggesting a particular approach to change. Consequently, in situations of hard complexity (e.g. where simple systems and a unitarist ideology of relationships prevails), a particular type of change approach will be appropriate, whereas in situations of soft complexity (e.g. where complex systems and a pluralist ideology of relationships prevails), a different type of change approach should be used. This chapter concentrates on the first of these situations, to describe an approach to change that is representative of those approaches which are best applied in the relatively bounded situations described variously as difficulties, simple/unitarist systems or, in more straightforward terms, 'hard' situations.

Illustration 7.1

Characteristics of unitary, pluralist and coercive relationships

Unitary

People relating to each other from a unitary perspective:

- share common interests
- have values and beliefs that are highly compatible
- largely agree upon ends and means
- all participate in decision making
- act in accordance with agreed objectives.

Pluralist

People relating to each other from a pluralist perspective:

- have a basic compatibility of interest
- have values and beliefs that diverge to some extent
- do not necessarily agree upon ends and means, but compromise is possible
- all participate in decision making
- act in accordance with agreed objectives.

Coercive

People relating to each other from a coercive perspective:

- do not share common interests
- have values and beliefs that are likely to conflict
- do not agree upon ends and means and 'genuine' compromise is not possible
- coerce others to accept decisions.

Source: Based on Flood, R.L. and Jackson, M.C. (1991) *Creative Problem Solving: Total Systems Intervention*, Chichester: Wiley, pp. 34–35.

Systematic approaches to change

Most people have the capacity to think logically and rationally. Indeed, some would say this is the only way to approach problem solving or respond to opportunities and, therefore, there can be one basic way of planning and implementing change. It is upon this premise that the more systematic approaches to managing change are based. Derived from earlier methods of problem solving and decision making such as systems engineering methods and operational research (Mayon-White, 1993), these 'hard' approaches rely on the assumption that clear change objectives can be identified in order to work out the best way of achieving them. What is more, a strict application of these approaches dictates that these objectives should be such that it is possible to quantify them, or at least be sufficiently concrete that one can know when they have been achieved. For instance, consider the situation described in Illustration 7.2.

Illustration 7.2 provides an example of what appears to be a difficulty about which most people could agree – it appears to have fairly defined boundaries. There are clearly some problems with the way IT faults are reported to the IT support service and the way they are responded to when they are received. It is also clear that some quantitative indices could be devised on which to judge the system and that might give evidence of improvement if this were to take place. What follows is, first, a generalized description of a model of change which is most suited to situations such as this – that is, in situations which are more of a difficulty than a mess and, second, a more fully worked-out example of its use to plan and implement change in the Beautiful Buildings Company.

Illustration 7.2

Dissatisfaction with the system for providing IT support services

Susan, a member of staff of the Faculty of Art and Design at Northshire University, was making a telephone call to the office of the IT support service to report that the computer link from her office to the resource centre was not working. As usual, there was no one there – she supposed the staff employed in the office were somewhere in the Faculty fixing someone else's computer. She decided, therefore, to send an email but knew that because of the time it took to respond to individuals, it would not be dealt with by the IT support team before the next day. Even then, from past experience, she suspected that when it was received she would not get a response without at least one reminder and perhaps two. Overall she took a particularly dim view of the quality of IT support service provided and was sure that, if she were responsible for this service, she could improve its effectiveness without too much effort or many more resources.

The hard systems model of change

The methodology for change described here draws on a range of sources (Open University, 1984, 1994, 2000; Flood and Jackson, 1991; Paton and McCalman, 2008). To avoid confusion with the Open University's model, the 'systems intervention strategy' (SIS), and Paton and McCalman's 'intervention strategy model' (ISM), the approach described here is referred to simply as the 'hard systems model of change' (HSMC).

Change in three phases

The HSMC is a method that has been developed for designing and managing change. Its roots lie in methods of analysis and change associated with systems engineering, operational research and project management, that is, where there is an emphasis on means and ends – in other words, on the means with which particular set goals are to be achieved. The HSMC is especially useful when dealing with situations that lie towards the 'hard' end of the hard–soft continuum of change situations. It provides a rigorous and systematic way of determining objectives (or goals) for change; this is followed by the generation of a range of options for action; the last step is testing those options against a set of explicit criteria. The method is also useful where quantitative criteria can be used to test options for change. However, it is also possible to use qualitative criteria – a possibility that is discussed later in the chapter. The process can be thought of as falling into three overlapping phases:

1 the *description* phase (describing and diagnosing the situation, understanding what is involved, setting the objectives for the change);
2 the *options* phase (generating options for change, selecting the most appropriate option, thinking about what might be done);
3 the *implementation* phase (putting feasible plans into practice and monitoring the results).

Within these three phases a number of stages can also be identified. These are shown in Illustration 7.3. What follows describes the stages in more detail.

Illustration 7.3

Stages within the hard systems methodology of change

Phases	Stages	Actions appropriate for each stage
Description	1 Situation summary	• Recognize need for change either to solve a problem or take advantage of an opportunity • Test out others' views on the need for change • Using appropriate diagnostic techniques, confirm the presence of hard complexity and a difficulty rather than a mess
	2 Identify objectives and constraints	• Set up objectives for systems of interest • Identify constraints on the achievement of the objectives
	3 Identify performance measures	• Decide how the achievement of the objectives can be measured
Options	4 Generate options	• Develop ideas for change into clear options for achievement of the objectives • Consider a range of possibilities
	5 Edit options and detail selected options	• Describe the most promising options in some detail • Decide, for each option, what is involved, who is involved and how it will work
	6 Evaluate options against measures	• Evaluate the performance of the chosen options against the performance criteria identified in Stage 3
Implementation	7 Develop implementation strategies	• Select preferred option(s) and plan how to implement
	8 Carry out the planned changes	• Involve all concerned • Allocate responsibilities • Monitor progress

The stages

Illustration 7.3 shows how the stages relate to the phases and provides an indication of likely actions at each stage. An important point to note, however, is that although Illustration 7.3 presents the phases and stages as a series of sequential steps that follow on logically one from another, this rarely happens so neatly in reality. Nor is it desirable, as Paton and McCalman (2000, p. 84) make clear when they say of their version of this approach: 'Iterations will be required at any point, within or between phases, owing to developing environmental factors.' There will, therefore, be times when there is a need for iteration or 'backtracking', from one stage/phase to earlier stages/phases, as insights generated at later stages reveal the requirement for modifications to previous ones.

Phase 1: Description

Stage 1: Situation summary

The basic idea in Stage 1 is to start by describing the system within which change is going to be made. This is an important stage in the change process and should not be rushed. People who are centrally concerned with the change (those sponsoring it and those who will carry it out) should be consulted. Unless the specification of the problem and description of the situation are done carefully, the subsequent change objectives and process will be flawed. This stage includes the following:

- Stating the commitment to the analysis and the reason for doing it. For example, statements such as the following might be made:

  - A commitment to ensuring the current product range is maintained after the takeover.
  - A commitment to developing new markets while maintaining market share for existing services.
  - A commitment to reducing the amount of floor space occupied by merchandise not achieving at least a 25 per cent profit margin.
  - A commitment to moving to another site or offices.

- Describing, in words and with diagrams, the situation within which changes will be set.

At the end of this stage the scope of the study will be defined, as will the range of problems and issues to be addressed. Try to defer, until Stage 4, thinking about *how* the change(s) will be brought about.

Stage 2: Identification of objectives and constraints

In the context of Stage 2, an objective can be defined as something that is desired; a constraint is something which inhibits or prevents achievement of an objective. In reality, objectives are likely to be things over which members of organizations may have some control. Constraints are frequently things in an organization's environment (whether this is internal or external to the organization) over which it has little control. This stage addresses both objectives and constraints. It involves being clear about where the decision makers want to go and which ways might be impassable or perhaps temporarily blocked. This stage involves the following:

● Listing objectives that are consistent with the themes which emerged from the diagnostic stage.
● Arranging the objectives into a hierarchy of objectives – an objectives tree. An example of a generalized objectives tree is shown in Figure 7.1. This shows how the high-level objective comes at the top, with lower-level objectives (sub-objectives) arranged in descending order. Lower-level objectives 'lead to' or help the achievement of higher-level objectives.
● Listing constraints in terms of those that (a) are inviolable and (b) may be modified.

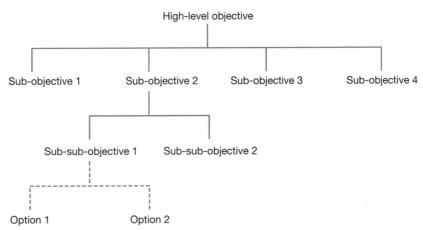

Note: Some objectives may not be compatible – achieving one may mean sacrificing another. In other cases, some objectives may be linked to others – achieving one or more may be necessary in order to achieve another.

Figure 7.1 The structure of an objectives tree

Stage 3: Identification of performance measures

The question here is: 'How will I know whether or not I have achieved my objective?' If at all possible, use quantifiable measures, e.g. costs (in monetary terms), savings (in monetary terms), time (years, days, hours), amount of labour, volume, etc. This stage includes the following:

● Formulating measures of performance, which can be put against the objectives on the objectives tree.

It is possible that some objectives cannot be quantified. In this case, some form of rating or ranking can be used as a measure of performance. Figure 7.2 is an

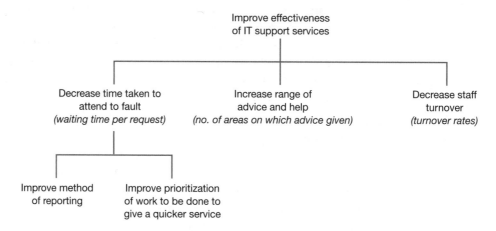

Figure 7.2 An objectives tree for improving the IT support services

example of an objectives hierarchy for improving the effectiveness of an organization's information technology support service. The measures of performance for each of the main objectives are in brackets.

Phase 2: Options

Stage 4: Generation of options (routes to objectives)

The setting of objectives to be achieved is based on the concept of *what* needs to be done to bring about change. By contrast, the generation of options stage is the stage of finding out *how* to achieve the objectives. If the objectives tree is well developed, as Figure 7.1 shows, some of the lower-level objectives may actually be options. There will, however, almost certainly be more. In addition, therefore, to any options that 'creep into' the objectives tree, this stage involves the following:

● Drawing up a list of options. This can be done by making use of any number of creative thinking techniques such as:

– brainstorming
– ideas writing
– questioning others
– focus groups
– interviews
– research
– meetings
– organizational comparisons/benchmarking
– gap analysis.

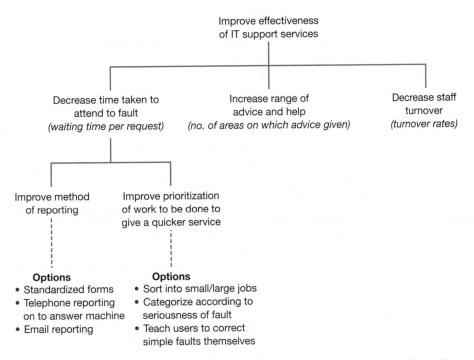

Figure 7.3 An objectives tree for improving the IT support services, with options generated for the two sub-sub-objectives

At the end of this stage a set of specific ideas should have been generated which will help the problem or opportunity – in the sense that they will further the achievement of the objective(s), rather than that they will break the constraints, and lead to beneficial changes to the situation described in Stage 1. Figure 7.3 gives a list of options for the sub-sub-objective of 'improve prioritization of work to be done to give a quicker service' – which is one of the objectives in an objectives hierarchy for improving the effectiveness of the service given by an organization's IT department in support of those who use computer-based programs to help with their work.

Stage 5: Editing and detailing selected options

At the stage of editing and detailing some options, it may be necessary to sort the options, in terms of those that are likely to be feasible given the particular situation described in Stage 1 and the constraints identified in Stage 2. The selected options should then be described in more detail – or 'modelled' – in terms of what is involved, who is involved and how it will work. It may be that some options cluster together and are better considered as a group. Other options will stand independently and must, therefore, be considered in their own right. There are many ways of testing how an option might work. The following are some possibilities drawn from a comprehensive list produced by the

Open University (1994, pp. 35–36).

(a) Physical models (architectural models, wind-tunnel test pieces, etc.).
(b) Mock-ups (make mock-ups of new products – sewing machines, aircraft, clothes dryers, etc.).
(c) Computer simulation models (for complex production systems, financial systems, etc.).
(d) Cashflow models (either manually produced or computer driven).
(e) Experimental production lines, or laboratory-scale plant.
(f) Scale plans and drawings (alternative office layouts, organizational structures, etc.).
(g) Cost/benefit analyses (as models of the likely trade-offs that would take place if a particular option were exercised; can be qualitative as well as quantitative).
(h) Corporate plans or strategies (any one plan or proposal represents a 'model' of how the corporation or organization could develop its activities in the future).
(i) Organization structure plans and proposals (for example, a chart of a new organization structure would show how the formal communication links or reporting channels would work if the structure were adopted).
(j) Organizational culture analyses (methods of describing organizational cultures as the means of identifying effects of different options on the culture of the organization).

Clearly, some of these processes can be time consuming and expensive. However, many options can be described or modelled through the use of diagrams (e.g. of different organizational structures, of input–output processes) or some form of cost-benefit analysis.

It is at this stage of the HSMC that each of the options generated for the objectives in Figure 7.3 would be explored in more detail, using the questions listed earlier about who would be involved, how it would work and what financial and other resources would be required for it to work. Some form of cost-benefit analysis could be used with costs and benefits being those of time as well as money.

Stage 6: Evaluating options against measures

The evaluation stage of the change process is a decision area. It allows choices of options to be made against the criteria identified in Stage 3. Figure 7.4 shows a generalized evaluation matrix that compares one option against another on the basis of the measures set during Stage 3.

Before making your recommendation, you should complete the following:

- Check that the model you have used is an accurate representation of the system.
- Consider whether the model seems to contain any bias or mistaken assumptions.
- Evaluate each option, or combination of options, according to how well it meets the performance measures. Rating the options overall on a scale (say of 1 for very good and 5 for very bad) is a useful guide.

Objectives and related measures of performance	Option A	Option B	Option C	Option D
Objective 1, measure 1				
Objective 2, measure 2				
Objective 3, measure 3				

Figure 7.4 An evaluation matrix

Figure 7.5 is a rough estimate of the desirability of some of the options generated from the objectives in Figure 7.3.

A more detailed examination of each option in Figure 7.5 would show more precisely the impact, in terms of the performance criteria, on each objective listed. For the purposes of this example, however, an estimate has been made. On the basis of these, it is clear from the evaluation matrix in Figure 7.5 that

Objectives and related measures of performance	Options			
	Telephone reporting on to answer machine	Email reporting	Categorization according to seriousness of fault	Use of written standardized reporting form
Sub-objective Decrease time taken to attend to fault *(waiting time per request)*	Low cut in waiting time	Medium cut in waiting time	High cut in time for serious faults; low cut for simple faults	Low cut in time – delays through need to post
Sub-sub-objective Improve method of reporting *(fault reporting received more quickly and accurately)*	High increase in speed of reporting	High increase in speed and some increase in accuracy of reporting	No effect	High increase in accuracy of reporting
Sub-sub-objective Improve prioritization of work to be done *(serious faults dealt with first)*	Difficult to estimate	Small improvement	Great improvement	Some improvement

Figure 7.5 An evaluation matrix for some options to improve the effectiveness of the IT support services

some of these options could be combined. For instance, the best method of reporting should be combined with the best method for prioritizing work to be done. On this basis, option 2 combined with option 3 seem to contribute most to the main objective. However, if an email standard format of reporting were to be used, this would also help speed and accuracy in reporting faults. It could also include space for indicating urgency in terms of lack of access to the particular program affected. The only problem with an email solution is it relies on this function not being the one at fault! If this is the case, written or telephone communication must be resorted to.

Phase 3: The implementation phase

Stage 7: Implementation

In problems of a definite 'hard' nature, implementation will rarely be a problem. With problems tending towards 'softness', implementation will be a test of how much people involved in the change have participated in its design.

There are three strategies for implementation:

1 pilot studies leading to eventual change
2 parallel running
3 big bang.

Pilot studies help sort out any problems before more extensive change is instituted, but they can cause delay – a factor that is particularly important in a fast-moving, dynamic situation.

Parallel running applies most frequently to the implementation of new computer systems, but can be applied to other kinds of change. The new system is run, for a time, alongside the old system, until confidence is gained that the new system is reliable and effective.

Big bang implementation maximizes the speed of change, but can generate the greatest resistance. Big bang implementations carry a high risk of failure unless planned very carefully.

Implementation often involves a blend of all three strategies.

Stage 8: Consolidation – 'carry through'

It takes time for new systems to 'bed in'. It is at this stage that there tends to be a decline in concentration on the need to support the change, and nurture both it and the people involved. Yet this is one of the most crucial stages if the change is to be accepted and successful. Even after the implementation process further changes can be forced on the situation at any time if the imbalance between the system and the environment becomes too great. There is no justification for 'sitting back'.

Using the hard systems model of change

Illustration 7.4 describes concerns about the way large plant and machinery is acquired and maintained for use on the building sites of the Beautiful Buildings Company. What follows is a description of the process Gerry Howcroft went through to identify a number of options for improving this situation to put before the senior managers' meeting. The description takes the form of notes made by Gerry, interspersed with comments on the method he used.

Illustration 7.4

Financial savings on the provision and maintenance of plant for use on building sites

'The next item on the agenda is the issue of the increasing costs of providing and maintaining major items of plant on the UK building sites. At our last meeting we saw an earlier draft of this paper. We must now come to some decision as to which option to follow and how it will be implemented.'

So spoke Gillian Lambeth, the Managing Director of the Beautiful Buildings Company, at one of its regular senior managers' meetings. The next item on the agenda was the increasing costs of purchasing and maintaining large items of plant (such as cranes, diggers and earth-moving equipment) used on the various UK building sites. The item had come to the fore because of the latest rises in the cost of purchasing and maintaining some of these large items of plant, which were necessary components in any building project. What was more, in the case of plant breakdowns, getting the specialist maintenance services to effect speedy repairs was always problematical.

Gerry Howcroft, who was responsible for overseeing management of all the UK sites, had prepared a number of options for change that he believed would reduce these costs and improve the maintenance problems. These had already been discussed in rough form at a previous meeting. He had now gained more information on the costs, etc. of following the different options and had distributed the latest version of these to the managers before the meeting. The meeting now settled down to discuss what to do.

Change at the BB Company

Gerry Howcroft's Note 1   21 May

Need to think back to that course on managing change.

Is this a difficulty or a mess?

Application of criteria discussed in the book they gave us (Senior, 'Organizational Change' – Chapter 2 – Illustrations 2.12 and 2.13) ... situation is: bounded in terms of problem definition, people involved, timescale and resources available.

Plus – situation is like Stacey's conditions of 'close to certainty' rather than conditions of 'far from certainty' (also mentioned in Senior's book – Chapter 2).

Think, therefore, that this is more of a difficulty than a mess.

So – think will have a go at using the HSMC.

Stage 1: Summarizing the BB Company's concerns

As overall sites manager, Gerry was responsible for the acquisition and mainte-nance of plant and equipment deemed necessary for carrying out the complex activities that take place on any building site. In this role, he had to make sure that large plant such as cranes and diggers were fit to carry out the required work. This entailed his finding the best suppliers in terms of cost and service back-up and ensuring proper maintenance of the plant. Recently, however, the costs of maintaining two large cranes and a digger, which were currently being used on two different sites, had begun to escalate and it seemed as if costs gener-ally for using plant such as this were rising. Gerry wondered whether the equipment had been ill-used or not well maintained or whether it was simply beginning to wear out. As part of the first stage of applying the HSMC he decided to visit the sites in question and talk to the site manager and any others who had views about the provision, use and maintenance of this type of plant. On his return he summarized his findings in another note (see Note 2).

Gerry Howcroft's Note 2   19 May

Visited Karen (site manager) at the Three Towers site. She said cranes such as these should last 'forever' if looked after. Think this far-fetched given the way the guys use them. Didn't seem to be anyone personally responsible for servicing and maintaining them – one of the men got some overtime each week to hose them down – if they broke down and the operator couldn't fix it, the service agent was sent for. On the other hand, Jed (who operated the crane all the time at the Riverside site) said his crane was just so old that, in spite of good maintenance it had 'had its day' – this in spite of Jed's obvious feelings of 'ownership' towards the crane!

Think there are many contributions to rising costs – a couple of diagrams might help – see Note 3.

Gerry Howcroft's Note 3   23 May

Looking at these diagrams, think I am dealing with a 'system for providing and maintaining plant for use on UK building sites'... which is different from what I first thought, which was 'a system for provision of plant for UK building sites'. The new definition includes the way plant is used as well as the way it is provided and maintained – as Karen reminded me when she saw the diagrams when she visited the office!

Jed reminded me that the weather matters!

Weather

Market for selling older plant

Site management

Work in progress

Site condition

Operators

PLANT

Changing technology

System for influencing maintenance and use of plant

Plant suppliers

Maintenance

System for provision and maintenance of plant and machinery for use on UK building sites

Higher maintenance costs

Increased overall cost of plant on UK sites

Higher replacement costs

Lower incentives to use plant carefully

Increased depreciation of plant and machinery

Increasing age of plant

No feelings of 'ownership' of plant

Fewer dedicated full-time operators

Lower level of plant use

Multiple-cause diagram of the issues involved

Stage 2: Setting up objectives to be achieved and recognizing constraints

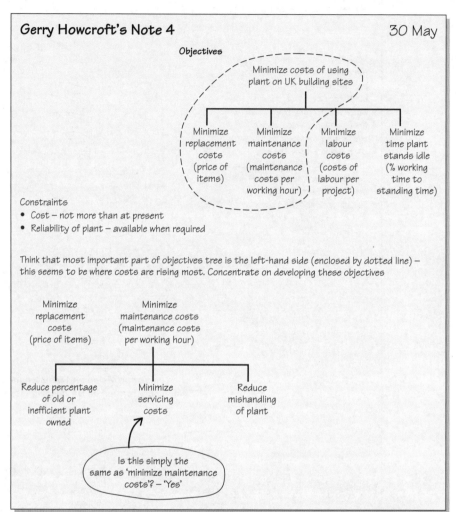

Having summarized the situation regarding the issue of plant costs, Gerry's next step was to build a hierarchy of quantifiable objectives. His Note 4 shows the results of this activity. Gerry did not find this activity particularly easy, given the requirement of the HSMC methodology that lower-level objectives should logically contribute to higher-level objectives and contribute overall to the top objective, in this case of 'minimizing the costs associated with the use of plant on UK building sites'. However, he recognized that some confusion of objectives was inevitable before a clear system of objectives began to emerge. Even so, he reminded himself that the characteristics of a good objective are as follows:

1 It should address the problem to be solved.
2 It must be relevant to the issues identified.

3 It should provide a guide on what needs to be done to make the change from the current situation to the desired situation.

4 It must be something that can feasibly be acted upon.

It can be seen from Gerry's Note 4 that he did not develop all the higher-level objectives into more detailed sets of sub-objectives. Given his knowledge of his management colleagues and their way of thinking, he made a decision to concentrate on the objective 'Minimize maintenance costs' to develop sub-objectives for further consideration, but also to consider the objective 'Minimize replacement costs'. With regard to the objectives 'Minimize labour costs' and 'Minimize time plant stands idle', he kept these 'in reserve' in case of need for further exploration of the issue.

Having developed his objectives hierarchy as far as he could in a direction thought feasible and achievable, the next step for Gerry was to develop further the measures of performance for the objectives identified (encircled) in Note 4.

Stage 3: Identify performance measures

Gerry Howcroft's Note 5	2 June
Objective	**Measure**
1. Minimize replacement costs	Cost of replacing item of plant over a specified period of time averaged out per year (assume cost of new plant for now).
2. Minimize maintenance costs	Cost of maintenance (includes servicing and repair) averaged out on a working hourly basis – i.e. does not include time standing idle.
3. Reduce percentage of old/ inefficient plant	Say no plant to be more than eight years old.
4. Reduce mishandling of plant	Difficult to measure. May have a look at training given – assuming training improves standard of plant handling. Another measure might be cost of maintenance per operator – easier to do when operator full time on plant. For now using a scale of 1 (low) to 5 (high) according to effect on plant might be okay.

Note 5 shows the table Gerry compiled to ensure he had some idea of how he would tell if and when an objective had been achieved. From Gerry's Note 5, it can be seen that some objectives are more difficult to quantify in *practice*, even if, theoretically, measures can be put upon them. In addition, the simple measure of 'price of items' for the objective 'Minimize replacement costs' was not sufficient. The cost needed to be expressed for a certain period of time, which could be related either to (say) a number of years or the period of a particular project. The measure for reducing mishandling of plant could, perhaps, have been formulated in monetary terms but, for the present, Gerry decided to use a scale to judge the likely effects of any option on this objective.

Stage 4: Generate options for change

Having set up some objectives to be achieved – hopefully, to improve the situation – Gerry's next step was to generate a range of options that would enable the objectives to be achieved. He did this by asking Kerry, one of the site managers, and the accounts manager to help in 'brainstorming' ideas for change. The results of this brainstorm are shown in Note 6.

Gerry Howcroft's Note 6   6 June

Options for change

Objective: Minimize replacement costs

Options: Find cheapest supplier
                  Stop buying plant
                  Increase replacement time
                  Get someone else to replace the plant
                  Hire not buy
                  Lengthen life of plant
                  Buy second-hand

Objective: Reduce percentage of old/inefficient plant owned

Options: Sell everything over a certain number of years old
                  Sell everything not used on a regular basis and hire
                       occasionally as required
                  Replace old plant with new plant more frequently
                  Don't own any plant
                  Borrow plant from others

Objective: Minimize servicing costs

Options: Reduce number of services per period of time (say
                       operating hours)
                  Obtain cheaper provision of services
                  Don't service at all
                  Operators do all servicing rather than just basics
                  Use other people's plant, which they service
                  Contract out servicing to lowest bidder

Objective: Reduce mishandling of plant

Options: Train operators in plant handling
                  Institute operator gradings (linked to pay) based on handling
                       performance
                  Contract out operating to operators employed by specialist
                       agencies

Stage 5: Edit options and detail selected options

Gerry considered all these options in the light of the constraint of maintaining a high level of reliability of plant. It seemed that the options might reduce to a few main themes. At this point Gerry decided to try out the options list on a couple of colleagues (one of whom was the company accountant) to see which they thought might be feasible. He also used his own judgement. He eventually arrived at a list that included some options as they stood, amalgamated others, and eliminated yet others (see Note 7).

Gerry Howcroft's Note 7   9 June

Themes emerging from options list

- Finding a cheaper source for buying plant (either new or second-hand)
- Don't buy plant – hire or borrow
- Use only plant which is less than eight years old (or whatever period seems appropriate considering rise in repair and maintenance as age increases)
- Increase the period of time before replacement
- Service plant less frequently than at present
- Train operators to do all servicing and maintenance
- Contract out operating to specialist firms
- Offer incentives for better operating practices

Comments

Some of these options contradict each other, so if one is taken up another might be automatically cancelled – e.g. 'Increase time before replacement' conflicts with 'Use plant eight years old or younger'.

Given the importance the MD attaches to safety on sites, I am going to go for options that are in line with her concerns and which meet the constraint of 'reliability of plant'.

For the time being, therefore, I am going to turn an objective into a constraint and work to have plant that is no older than eight years.

Within these constraints, the following seem worthy of further consideration.

1 Continue buying own plant (search for cheapest deals) with maintenance outsourced.
2 Continue buying own plant with maintenance done by own staff.
3 Continue buying plant that is used continuously and hire other for occasional use: maintenance of own plant done by own staff.
4 Continue buying plant that is used continuously and hire otherwise but outsource maintenance of own plant.
5 Hire all plant with maintenance as part of the deal.
6 Offer incentives for good performance in plant handling.

I guess there are more permutations but, depending on how the costings come out on these, we can look at those later.

As Note 7 indicates the options available seemed to range from, at the one extreme, the BB Company's owning and maintaining all plant to, at the other extreme, hiring (or leasing) plant that was maintained entirely by the suppliers. A number of possibilities were clearly possible between these two. The options listed as 1 to 5 are a mix of these. What is evident from the range of possible options is that some quite detailed information is required before one option can be evaluated against another. In addition, option 6 might only be relevant if one of options 1 to 4 were chosen. If option 5 were chosen, incentives to operate the plant well might not be thought relevant if all maintenance costs were included in the hire contract.

Stage 6: Evaluate options against measures

The method of evaluating options against the measures of performance associated with each of the objectives to be reached varies according to the type of options generated. For example, if the options are different production systems,

---

Gerry Howcroft's Note 8   16 June

Objectives and related measures of performance	Options					
	1 Continue buying own plant with maintenance outsourced	**2** Continue buying own plant with maintenance by own staff	**3** Continue buying continuously used plant and hire plant that is used only occasionally: maintenance of own plant done by own staff	**4** Continue buying continuously used plant and hire otherwise: outsource maintenance of own plant	**5** Hire all plant with maintenance as part of the deal	**6** Offer incentives for good plant-handling performance
Minimize replacement costs (£ per year)	High cost	Medium cost	Medium cost	Medium cost	Medium cost	Low cost
Minimize maintenance costs (£ per working hour)	High cost	Medium cost	Medium cost	Medium–high cost	Medium cost	Low cost
Reduce mishandling of plant (scale of 1 to 5 – 1 being least effective, 5 being most effective)	1	3	2	1	1	4

Need to give some information on this to the senior managers' meeting on 23 June – only a week away!
Have got only limited information on options – still, can make some guesses at this point and will take the views of colleagues as to which options to pursue – then must get better information on hiring etc.

not only would these have to be evaluated on cost measures, but they might also involve evaluation through building some simulations of the different systems. These could, of course, be physical models but they could also be computer models. For Gerry's purposes, it was possible to construct an evaluation matrix that allowed comparison of options one against another in terms of the measures of performance for the defined objectives. Note 8 is a record of Gerry's first attempt, on very limited information, at an evaluation matrix.

Gerry took copies of the first draft of the evaluation matrix to the senior managers' meeting. The outcome of the discussion of what he had prepared was that he should get more information on options 3, 4 and 5, which involved different levels of hiring plant instead of purchasing it. What Gerry had to do, in effect, was to go back to Stage 5 to get more detail about these options before preparing a final evaluation matrix. This took some time, what with getting information from the finance department (only to discover that it was not kept in a 'user-friendly' form!) and from companies that hired out plant and equipment. Eventually, however, having gathered as much information as he could, he prepared a final evaluation matrix for discussion at the meeting referred to in Illustration 7.4.

The outcome of that discussion is recorded in Gerry's Note 9.

Gerry Howcroft's Note 9   5 August

What a long discussion, which went round and round in circles – difficult to decide between one option and another – the evaluation matrix was very helpful but then decisions are not always perfectly logical!

Eventually, decided on the hiring option with maintenance all-in – however we could not change overnight to this from where we are at present – just purchased a new digger on the Blackton site.

Will need to do a thorough survey of the state of plant on all the sites to determine when to make the changeover to hiring.

Interesting that the meeting decided to retain our own operators for now (even though could get an agency to supply these) – so will start talks with Personnel as to how we might give extra training and/or offer incentives to improve operator performance – after all, the maintenance costs part of the hiring contract is dependent on the amount of maintenance needed – large repairs will incur extra cost.

Seems an implementation strategy is required!

Stage 7: Develop implementation strategy

Gerry realized that the 'big bang' strategy for implementing change was not viable for his situation. Some of the plant had only recently been purchased, while other items were some years old. Overall, plant on the various sites was in different states of repair. Gerry therefore decided to go for the 'parallel running' implementation strategy where older and/or poorly maintained plant was replaced first. This would also offer the opportunity of monitoring the costs of hiring against owning *in reality* as against the theoretical case that the options had presented. If, after all, the savings proved negligble or negative, another evaluation of options could be done.

One good thing about retaining the company's own operators was that there were likely to be few problems from the workforce on the changeover. What might happen, however, was the occasional hiring of plant plus operator when it was required for a limited, short period. This would give a chance to see how such hirings were received generally.

Stage 8: Carrying out the planned changes

For Gerry and the other senior managers the changes, when implemented, will need monitoring. Changing from purchasing plant to hiring it may not mean much change in the way plant is operated on the building sites. However, the changes in the way maintenance and repairs are carried out will require operators and site managers to learn a new system of reporting and getting these done.

One of the benefits of going through the processes involved in applying the HSMC methodology was that Gerry realized how little monitoring of the costs of plant usage had been done up to the change. When trying to obtain the costs of the different ways of providing and maintaining plant, he became very much aware of the diffuse nature of much of the information he wanted. From now on, he was going to make sure that the finance department arranged its systems so that monitoring of large expenditure such as this could be monitored. This would, of course, mean yet more change, but in a different part of the organization.

Further uses for the hard systems model of change

The HSMC has been posed as a methodology for change that is most appropriately used in situations of hard complexity, or what have been termed difficulties. The case study involving Gerry Howcroft and the BB Company illustrates this use. In Gerry Howcroft's case, there is reason to believe that resistance to the planned changes will not be high. However, this is not always the case, as the discussion in Chapter 6 showed. Whenever and wherever possible, therefore, those people who are likely to be affected by the change should be consulted as early as possible. In addition, support from senior management is essential for any but the most localized, operational types of change.

It was clear that, in Gerry's case, the information he needed to construct an informative evaluation matrix was not easily obtainable – particularly with regard to that which he required from his own organization. This stage of the methodology can, therefore, be quite long if a realistic evaluation of options is to be done. By the same token, it is possible to go through the stages of the methodology quite quickly to address key factors associated with the change situation. A small group of people could quickly drive a way through this methodology to suggest at least a tentative solution in a situation requiring change. In addition, as Paton and McCalman (2008, pp. 121–22) point out:

> A Q & D (quick and dirty) analysis can be a useful starting point for the change agents tackling a more complex problem. It will indicate key factors and potential barriers to change, it will highlight the principal players and give an indication of resource requirements. Such an analysis will at an early stage set the scene for things to come and provide the change agents with a valuable insight into the complexities of the transition process.

An example of using the HSMC in this 'quick and dirty' way, that is as a starting point to an analysis of more messy situations, is given in Illustration 7.5 and Figures 7.6 and 7.7. These demonstrate the early stages in considering how to expand the provision and delivery of open and resource-based learning in the further education colleges run by the local education authority of 'Shire County'.

Illustration 7.5

Change in the further education colleges of Shire County

The question of how to expand the position and delivery of learning brought forth the following commitment statement:

> In an environment of decreasing numbers of 16–19 year olds and limited numbers of adults participating in further education, the aim for the future is to make it possible for more people to participate in education and training through the expansion of open and resource-based learning (O&RBL) both as an integral part of mainstream provision as well as an alternative but equally credible way of facilitating and accrediting learning.

A causal-loop diagram (see Figure 7.6) was constructed to provide further information about the forces operating for and against the desire to expand O&RBL. From this a range of objectives were formulated, together with a list of possible measures of performance.

An initial attempt at an objectives hierarchy is shown in Figure 7.7.

Possible measures of performance (not particularly attached to specific objectives):

- Establish O&RBL centres by ? (date).
- Extend availability of provision to 48 weeks per year by ? (date).
- Achieve × % of open and resource-based learners by ? (date).
- ? (number) of companies using O&RBL by ? (date).
- ? (number) of staff trained in the delivery of O&RBL by ? (date).
- ? (number) of students gaining qualifications through O&RBL by ? (date).
- Complete changeover to providing mathematics instruction in modules by ? (date).
- ? % increase in use of O&RBL in all mainstream provision by ? (date).

Existing state of affairs

- Falling numbers of 16–19 year olds coming into further education (FE)
- Only small percentage of adults participating in FE
- Current FE provision not always accessible to needs of adults in terms of content, qualifications and mode of delivery

GAP

Desired state of affairs

- Increase proportion of 16–19 year olds in FE
- Significant increase in number of adults in FE
- Improve accessibility for all learners, but for adults in particular, i.e. greater choice of content, qualifications and mode of delivery relevant to educational and training needs

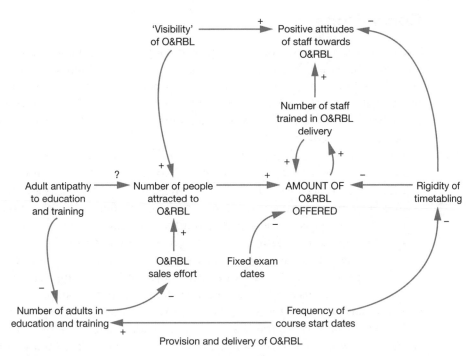

Note: The + signs denote a causal relationship in the same direction. The – signs denote a causal relationship in opposite directions

Figure 7.6 Causal-loop diagram of the situation facing Shire County further education services

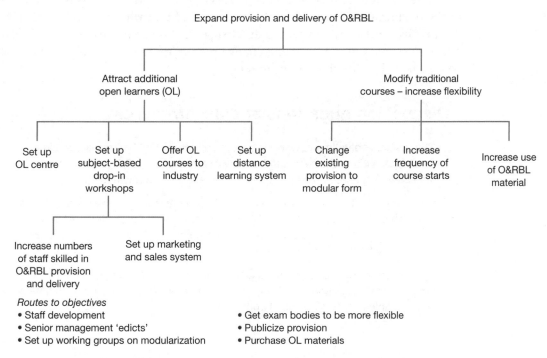

Figure 7.7 Hierarchy of objectives for expanding O&RBL provision in Shire County

Conclusions

The hard systems model for change provides a practical approach designed to be applied to situations – such as the Beautiful Buildings Company example – of low to medium complexity (difficulties). It is particularly useful when an area of the organization may need to be changed but may not infringe on other areas and when choices based on rational decision making can be made (see March's 1984 theories of choice and decision making).

The HSMC can also be effective to begin to diagnose a change situation (see Illustration 7.5) before categorizing it into more simple or more complex change. For instance, using the HSMC in the case of Shire County was useful for setting out the commitment to change, carrying out (with the help of diagrams) a situational analysis of the forces for and against the change and formulating some objectives and measures of performance in preparation for planning and implementing the change. What this methodology was less good at doing was identifying the political and moral issues surrounding the implementation of radical change of this kind. In addition, current organizational, professional and institutional cultures were clearly going to make changes of this kind difficult.

This was a case where the changes desired would take some time to come to fruition and would involve changes not only to the buildings and teaching areas (i.e. physical changes) but also to attitudes and behaviour – changes that would include both staff and students (present and potential students). The changes proposed here were more in line with what has been described as 'organizational development', that is, change that is ongoing, which involves most parts of the organization and most of its members and that will not succeed without the involvement of all concerned at all stages in the change process. The next chapter describes in more detail a change process more relevant to situations of soft complexity – in other terms, messes.

Discussion questions and assignments

1 Can you think of a time at work when a change that would be considered 'hard' or 'difficult' was not implemented as effectively as planned? If you were to apply the HSMC approach could you identify where things went wrong?

2 Can you think of change situations within your organization that are more difficult than messy, where the HSMC would be both appropriate and effective? What factors would you need to consider in order to ensure effective planning, decision making, implementation and review?

3 Considering issues raised in this chapter, under what circumstances might the HSMC not be appropriate and why? Could some of these issues be overcome so as to be able to use this phased approach?

Indicative resources

March, J.G. (1984) 'Theories of Choice and Making Decisions', in Paton, R., Brown, R., Spear, R., Chapman, J., Floyd, M. and Hamwee, J. (eds) *Organisations: Cases, Issues, Concepts*: London: Harper & Row. This text offers a critique of models for change which assumes that the process of choice is a rational one, based on having complete, or almost complete, knowledge of the alternatives which are generated. They argue that choices frequently involve moral as well as cognitive issues and that decisions about action, once made, are then overtaken by events which make implementation difficult if not impossible.

Open University (2000) *Managing Complexity: A Systems Approach*, Course T306, Milton Keynes: Open University, http://www3.open.ac.uk/courses/bin/ p12.dll?C01T306. This is an Open University course that draws on and extends a range of approaches to managing complexity which have been developed by internationally recognized systems practitioners. They include the soft systems method, the viable systems model and the hard systems method. Of particular relevance to the material in this chapter is Block 2, which discusses the hard systems approach.

Paton, R.A. and McCalman, J. (2008) *Change Management: A Guide to Effective Implementation* (3rd edn), Sage: London. This text reinforces the approach to change discussed in this chapter (see Chapter 5) and also discusses two more change approaches – 'Total project management' and 'The organization development model' (the latter of which is the subject of the next chapter). Particularly helpful is Chapter 4, 'Mapping change', which 'teaches' how to use diagrams effectively in diagnosing and implementing change.

Useful websites

www.open.ac.uk This is the Open University website. There are links from here to information about all the courses it offers.

http://www.ukss.org.uk/ The UK Systems Society (UKSS) website. The UKSS is a non-profit-making, professional society registered as an educational charity. The Society is committed to the development and promotion of 'systems' philosophy, theory, models, concepts and methodologies for improving decision making and problem solving for the benefit of organizations and the wider society.

To click straight to these links and for other resources go to
www.pearsoned.co.uk/senior

●●●● References

Flood, R.L. and Jackson, M.C. (1991) *Creative Problem Solving: Total Systems Intervention*, Chichester: Wiley.

March, J.G. (1984) 'Theories of Choice and Making Decisions', in Paton, R., Brown, R., Spear, R., Chapman, J., Floyd, M. and Hamwee, J. (eds) *Organisations: Cases, Issues, Concepts*: London: Harper & Row.

Mayon-White, B. (1993) 'Problem-solving in Small Groups: team members as agents of change', in Mabey, C. and Mayon-White, B. (eds) *Managing Change* (2nd edn), London: PCP.

Open University (1984) Block III, 'The Hard Systems Approach', Course T301, *Complexity, Management and Change: Applying a Systems Approach*, Milton Keynes: Open University Press.

Open University (1994) 'Managing the Change Process', Course B751, *Managing Development and Change*, Milton Keynes: Open University Press.

Open University (2000) *Managing Complexity: A Systems Approach*, Milton Keynes: Open University Press.

Paton, R.A. and McCalman, J. (2000) *Change Management: A Guide to Effective Implementation* (2nd edn), London: Sage.

Paton, R.A. and McCalman, J. (2008) *Change Management: A Guide to Effective Implementation* (3rd edn), London: Sage.

Chapter 8

Soft systems models for change

Through a revision of the concept of soft complexity, this chapter begins by challenging the notion of rationality as applied to organizational change. This is followed by a short description of Lewin's three-phase model of change as a prelude to a more detailed description and discussion of organizational development (OD) as an approach to change. Some limitations of organizational development as a change philosophy and as a change approach are discussed.

Learning objectives

By the end of this chapter you will be able to:

- recognize that some change situations (problems/opportunities), by nature of their complexity and particular characteristics, require soft rather than hard systems approaches to change;

- consider the philosophy, value orientation and theoretical underpinnings of organization development as a generalized example of soft systems models for change;

- outline and describe the processes and practices that comprise most OD approaches to designing and implementing organizational change;

- critically review the limitations of OD approaches to managing change.

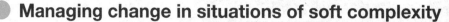 ## Managing change in situations of soft complexity

The previous chapter ended with an example of the need for change for which the hard systems model for change (HSMC) had limited applicability. This was because the situation that gave rise to the requirement to expand open and resource-based learning in further education colleges in Shire County was characterized by both hard and soft complexity. As Chapter 7 highlighted, it was possible, using the HSMC, to build an objectives hierarchy with measurable performance criteria and to generate some options for bringing about the necessary changes. However, while this was fine in theory, other factors – the organizational culture, entrenched power bases and established leadership styles, as well as the simultaneous reorganization of the county education service that was driving the change – combined to make the process of change much more complex, diffuse and confused than it appeared at first sight. In summary, what faced those charged with bringing about the changes was much more of a mess than a difficulty, implying that a different approach to planning and implementing change was required.

In a chapter aptly named 'The art and science of mess management', Ackoff (1993) identifies three different 'kinds of things' that can be done about problems. He says (p. 47): 'They can be *resolved, solved or dissolved.*'

According to Ackoff, 'to resolve a problem is to select a course of action that yields an outcome that is good enough, that *satisfices* (satisfies and suffices)'. This is an approach that relies on common sense, based on previous experience as to what might work or not and, to some extent, on trial and error. People who use this approach (and Ackoff says most managers are problem resolvers) do not pretend to be objective in their decision making. They use little specially collected data, either of a quantitative or qualitative nature, justifying their conclusions by citing lack of time or lack of information or too complex a situation for anything other than minimizing risk and maximizing the likelihood of survival. Ackoff calls this the 'clinical' approach to dealing with messes, a metaphor that emphasizes different people preoccupied with different aspects of the problem situation, but coming together to reach some consensus on how to proceed with resolving the problem. However, while this approach is likely to keep most people satisfied and 'on board' with the change, a major criticism is that, because of its commitment solely to qualitative thinking based on past experience and hunch, it lacks analytical rigour in its formulation of objectives and the means of evaluating them. Therefore it is never quite clear how far the objectives of the change have been met.

This criticism can certainly not be levelled at the 'solvers' of problems. By contrast with resolvers of problems, rather than using simple common sense and what might have been successful in the past, solvers of problems use approaches to problems that are much more heavily reliant on research-based scientific methods, techniques and tools. This means they eschew qualitative models in favour of quantitative models in their aspirations to be completely objective. Ackoff calls this the 'research' approach to mess management. It is much more likely to be used by management scientists and technologically oriented managers. This approach is akin to hard systems models of change in its emphasis on quantitative methods of analysis, objective setting and generation of options for change as demonstrated in the description of the HSMC in the previous chapter. However, while addressing the lack of 'hard' data in the clinical approach to mess management, the research approach is limited in that its techniques are more applicable to mechanistic systems (which lend themselves to performance definition and measurement) than to purposeful human behaviour (which includes many immeasurable elements). In addition, given that a mess is not just one problem but a complex set of problems interacting one with another, decomposing the mess to deal with one problem at a time (as this approach would suggest) loses the essential properties of the larger, more complex, whole. This is summarized well by Ackoff (p. 51):

> Therefore, when a research-orientated planner decomposes a mess by analysis, he loses its essential properties . . . As a consequence, what he perceives as the hard facts of the mess are really soft fictions of his imagination, abstractions only loosely related to reality.

From this it seems that both resolvers, with their clinical approaches to bringing about change, and solvers of problems, with their research approaches to change, are limited in their capacity to plan and implement change in unbounded soft situations characterized as messes. Consequently Ackoff suggests a third approach, based on the concept of *dissolving* problems. Of this approach to problem solving he says (p. 48):

> To *dissolve* a problem is to change the nature, and/or the environment, of the entity in which it is embedded so as to remove the problem. Problem dissolvers *idealize* rather than satisfice or optimize because their objective is to change the system involved or its environment in such a way as to bring it closer to an ultimately desired state, one in which the problem cannot or does not arise.

He calls this approach the 'design' approach in that problem dissolvers, in addition to using the methods and techniques of problem resolvers and problem solvers, seek to redesign the characteristics of the larger system containing the problem (for instance changing the organizational culture, structure, systems and/or processes). Thus they look for dissolution of the problem in the wider containing system rather than looking for solutions in the contained parts. Ackoff (p. 48) maintains that only a minority of managers uses this approach and they are those 'whose principal organizational objective is *development* rather than growth or survival, and who know the difference'. Of the concept of development he says (pp. 48–49):

> To develop is to increase and desire to improve one's quality of life and that of others. Development and growth are not the same and are not even necessarily related.

As an example of this he refers to the fact that a heap of rubbish can grow without developing and a person can develop without growing.

As the situation for change unfolded in the further education system in Shire County it became evident that this was not a problem to be resolved or solved, but a complex set of problems that was likely to require the wider system containing it to be redesigned, if progress was to be made towards achieving the stated objectives. These objectives themselves were, incidentally, somewhat unclear and by no means shared by all.

It is not usual to find reference to 'dissolving' problems in the literature on change. Yet most of the change models associated with 'soft' situations and systems (i.e. those characterized by soft complexity) imply a need for redesigning systems at many levels of the organization. These include issues associated with individuals and the groupings they form, as well as with organizational strategy, structure and processes. This means not only an emphasis on the *content* and *control* of change (as the hard systems models of change dictate), but also an emphasis on the *process* by which change comes about, or as Buchanan and Boddy (1992, p. 27) maintain, a need for 'backstaging' as well as 'public performance'. In other words, there is a need to be concerned with what Buchanan and Boddy (p. 27) call 'the exercise of "power skills", with "intervening in political and cultural systems", with influencing negotiating and selling, and with "managing meaning"'.

The consequences of this are that designing change in messy situations must also include attention to issues such as problem ownership, the role of communication and the participation and commitment of the people involved in the change process itself. It also means, as evidenced in the following section, challenging the notion that planning and implementing change can be wholly rational, a notion that the majority of hard systems models of change assume.

The challenge to rationality

For some time the literature on corporate strategy and strategic change (for example Balogun and Hope Hailey, 2008; Carnall, 2007; Stacey, 2008) has put forward arguments challenging the idea that people make decisions and choices according to some rational model of decision making. For example, Johnson (1993) argues strongly that rational models of change, with their associated scientific management techniques, overlook the significance of the cultural, political and cognitive dimensions of organizational life.

This is not to say, however, that people do not act rationally. It is to say (Carnall, 2007, p. 126) that they act according to their own view of what is rational for them. Carnall uses the example of 'clinical' rationality in healthcare, where rationality is apparent in the decisions of doctors that govern the pattern of care provided and the use of resources. This, however, does not mean that all doctors have the same views, beliefs or attitudes or that they would argue for the same vision of healthcare. This will include their particular perspective of the causes, consequences and need for change, moulded by their values, culture, attitudes and political position within the organization. Any case for change will not, therefore, be accepted according to some (supposedly) objective rational analysis. Change, in this scenario, will only be possible and effective if it is accompanied by processes that address, in particular, the feelings, needs and aspirations of individuals, the group processes that bind them together and the structures and systems that are forces for stability rather than change. Added to these are the cultural, political and symbolic processes that act to maintain the current organizational paradigm, or 'the way things are done around here'.

Given all this, it appears that hard systems models of change, although necessary in some defined and agreed situations, are not sufficient to explain organizational messes and are extremely limited in providing a model for planning and implementing change in these situations. For instance, hard systems approaches to change require the setting of quantifiable objectives against which they can be judged. This assumes that there is little argument about *what* the change objectives are. These approaches are useful in situations where change is sought to the *means* whereby things are done and where a problem can be *solved* in the terms discussed by Ackoff in the previous section. By contrast, one of the distinguishing features of organizational messes is that there is no agreement on what constitutes the problem, let alone what changes are required. Consequently it is more likely that those involved in these types of situations are looking to challenge not just the *means* of doing things, but also the *purposes* and *why* things are done and even if they should be done *at all*. In other words, they are searching for ways to *dissolve* rather than just *solve* problems, in Ackoff's terms. In summary, therefore, what this latest discussion leads to is an argument for an approach to change that can cope more effectively with situations of soft complexity – in other words some type of soft systems model for change.

There is neither the space nor the necessity to illustrate here all the different variants of models for bringing about change in soft, messy situations. What follows, therefore, is a generalized description of 'organizational development' (more commonly known as the OD approach) – an umbrella term for a set of values and assumptions about organizations and the people within them that, together with a range of concepts and techniques, are thought useful for bringing about long-term, organization-wide change; that is, change which is more likely to dissolve problems than resolve or solve them.

●●●● Organizational development – philosophy and underlying assumptions

According to French and Bell (1999, pp. 25–26) organization development is:

> a long term effort, led and supported by top management, to improve an organization's visioning, empowerment, learning and problem-solving processes,

through an ongoing, collaborative management of organization culture – with special emphasis on the culture of intact work teams and other team configurations – using the consultant–facilitator role and the theory and technology of applied behavioral science, including action research.

Cummings and Worley (2009, p. 1) see organization development as:

A process that applies behavioural science knowledge and practices to help organizations build the capacity to change and achieve greater effectiveness, including increased financial performance and improved quality of work life. OD differs from other planned change efforts, such as technological innovation or new product development, because the focus is on building the organization's ability to assess its current functioning and to achieve its goals. Moreover, OD is oriented to improving the total system – the organization and its parts in the context of the larger environment that affects them.

More succinctly, they offer the following (Cummings and Worley, 2009, p. 1):

Organizational development is a systematic application and transfer of behavioural science knowledge to the planned development, improvement, and reinforcement of the strategies, structures and processes that lead to organizational effectiveness.

An examination of these definitions confirms some distinguishing characteristics of the OD approach to change:

1 It emphasizes goals and processes but with a particular emphasis on processes – the notion of organizational learning (Senge, 1990; Pedler, Boydell and Burgoyne, 1991; Argyris and Schon, 1996) as a means of improving an organization's capacity to change.
2 It deals with change over the medium to long term, that is, change that needs to be sustained over a significant period of time.
3 It involves the organization as a whole as well as its parts.
4 It is participative, drawing on the theory and practices of the behavioural sciences.
5 It has top management support and involvement.
6 It involves a facilitator who takes on the role of a change agent (Buchanan and Boddy, 1992 and French and Bell, 1999).
7 It concentrates on planned change but as a process that can adapt to a changing situation rather than as a rigid blueprint of how change should be done.

In addition, French and Bell (1999, p. 29) give the following ten OD principles:

1 OD focuses on culture and processes.
2 OD encourages collaboration between organization leaders and members in managing culture and processes.
3 Teams of all kinds are particularly important for accomplishing tasks and are targets for OD activities.
4 OD focuses on the human and social side of the organization and in so doing also intervenes in the technological and structural sides.

5 Participation and involvement in problem solving and decision making by all levels of the organization are hallmarks of OD.

6 OD focuses on total system change and views organizations as complex social systems.

7 OD practitioners are facilitators, collaborators, and co-learners with the client system.

8 An overarching goal is to make the client system able to solve its problems on its own by teaching the skills and knowledge of continuous learning through self-analytical methods. OD views organization improvement as an ongoing process in the context of a constantly changing environment.

9 OD relies on an action research model with extensive participation by client system members.

10 OD takes a developmental view that seeks the betterment of both individuals and the organization. Attempting to create 'win–win' solutions is standard practice in OD programmes.

The discussion that follows develops these definitions and underlying philosophy and assumptions.

The significance of people in organizations

The OD approach to change is, above all, an approach that cares about people and which believes that people at all levels throughout an organization are, individually and collectively, both the drivers and the engines of change. Consequently one underlying assumption is that people are most productive when they have a high quality of working life. In addition there is an assumption that, in many cases (and perhaps the majority), workers are under-utilized and are capable, if given the opportunity, of taking on more responsibility for the work they do and of contributing further to the achievement of organizational goals.

Paton and McCalman (2008, p. 166) offer three 'fundamental' concepts with respect to the management of people and gaining their commitment to their work and organization:

1 Organizations are about people.

2 Management assumptions about people often lead to ineffective design of organizations and this hinders performance.

3 People are the most important asset and their commitment goes a long way in determining effective organization design and development.

These assumptions are not new. Even so, many managers continue to practise Taylorism and scientific management – which in Matsushita's (1988) words means: 'executives on one side and workers on the other, on one side men [sic] who think and on the other men [sic] who can only work'. Yet Matsushita, drawing on his experience as head of the Sony organization, went on to say:

We are beyond the Taylor model; business, we know, is so complex and difficult, the survival of firms so hazardous in an environment increasingly so unpredictable, competitive and fraught with danger, that their continued existence depends on the day-to-day mobilization of every ounce of intelligence.

The OD approach to change is entirely in line with these sentiments. What is more, these sentiments extend to a number of assumptions regarding people in groups. The first of these is that people are in general *social* beings. They will, therefore, form groups – whether these are legitimized by the organization in terms of formal work teams or whether they are the more 'informal' groupings that form part of every organization's functioning. French and Bell (1999, p. 68) reinforce this assumption by saying that: 'One of the most psychologically relevant reference groups for most people is the work group, including peers and boss.' Consequently the work group becomes increasingly important in any attempt at change. Yet in many cases work groups do not effectively utilize resources for collaboration. For instance, the formal leader of any group cannot perform all the leadership functions at all times and in all situations. Thus, for a group to become effective, all group members must share in problem solving and in working to satisfy *both* task and group members' needs. If work groups are managed in such a way as to engender a climate of mistrust and competition between participants, then any change will be seen as a threat rather than an opportunity and all the negative aspects of group functioning will come to the fore to work against the change. OD approaches to change assume, therefore, that work groups and teams are an essential element in the process of designing and implementing change. However, as individuals interact to form groups and other collective working relationships, so do groups interact and overlap to form larger organizational systems that, in their turn, influence an organization's capacity to learn and change.

The significance of organizations as systems

One of the characteristics of OD approaches to change mentioned earlier in the chapter is that it involves the organization as a whole as well as its parts – a characteristic exemplified by Pugh (1993, p. 109) when he refers to organizations as 'coalitions of interest groups in tension'. Chapter 1 introduced the idea that organizations are systems of interconnected and interrelated subsystems and components that include more formal organizational structures and processes as well as culture, politics and styles of leadership which are closely bound up with the values and attitudes people bring to their workplaces.

This idea is one of the most important assumptions of OD as a process of facilitating change. This is because, first, it reinforces the systemic nature of organizational life and the fact that changes in one part of the organization will inevitably impact on operations in another part. For instance, the multiple-cause diagrams used in previous chapters to depict a number of different change situations are good illustrations of the *interconnectedness* of causes and consequences of complex messy situations.

Second, and related to this, OD challenges the assumption that a single important cause of change with clear effects can be found, as well as the assumption that any cause and its effects are necessarily closely related in space and time. This is most clearly stated by Carnall (2007, p. 131):

> [The] causes of a problem may be complex, may actually lie in some remote part of the system, or may lie in the distant past. What appears to be cause and effect may actually be 'coincidental' symptoms.

Third, any organization is a balance of forces built up and refined over a period of time. Consequently, proposed change of any significance will inevitably change this balance and will, therefore, almost certainly encounter resistance. Consequently, OD approaches assume that no single person or group can act in isolation from any other. For instance, if win–lose strategies are common to the behaviour of management then this way of dealing with conflict will permeate other workers' attitudes to settling disputes and disagreements. By way of contrast, if managers openly discuss problems and take views on how these might be addressed, then this culture of trust and cooperation will reach into other parts of the organization's functioning – hence the belief that OD activities need to be led by top management if they are to succeed in bringing about successful change.

Fourth, because organization development as a concept is assumed to operate throughout an organization, the OD process is most definitely not a 'quick fix' to the latest management problem. This is articulated by French and Bell (1999, p. 75), who say that change 'takes time and patience, and the key movers in an OD effort need to have a relatively long-term perspective'.

Finally, OD approaches to change are essentially processes of facilitating *planned* change. Consequently, an effective manager of change:

> *anticipates* the need for change as opposed to reacting after the event to the emergency; *diagnoses* the nature of the change that is required and carefully considers a number of alternatives that might improve organizational functioning, as opposed to taking the fastest way to escape the problem; and *manages* the change process over a period of time so that it is effective and accepted as opposed to lurching from crisis to crisis.
>
> (Pugh, 1993, p. 109)

The significance of organizations as learning organizations

The ideas in the previous two sections (the significance of people in organizations and the significance of organizations as systems) come together in the assumptions that, for organizations operating in increasingly complex and turbulent environments, the only way to survive and prosper is to be a *learning organization*.

The concept of a learning organization is built upon the proposition that there is more than one type of learning. In support of this proposition Argyris (1964, 1992) and Argyris and Schon (1996) distinguish between *single-loop* and *double-loop* learning or, as Senge (1990) terms them, *adaptive* and *generative* learning. The concepts of single- and double-loop learning can be explained in terms of systems for change that are either goal oriented or process oriented (Open University, 1985). In brief, a goal-oriented approach to change is directed towards changing the means by which goals are achieved. By contrast, those who subscribe to a process-oriented approach to change, while still concerned with goals, focus more on fostering a change process that enables the goals to be challenged. In other words, goal-oriented approaches are concerned with doing things better, while process-oriented approaches are concerned with doing the right things.

With a goal-oriented approach, the problem or issue is likely to be seen as an interesting, though possibly substantial *difficulty;* that is, it is perceived primarily as a technical and financial matter with a specific time horizon and hence fairly well bounded. The main focus is on increased efficiency of goal achievement. Management of this type of change is frequently done through a project team led by more senior managers concerned primarily with cost-benefit aspects (goals and constraints). A goal-oriented approach is analogous to thermostatically controlling the temperature of a heating system. The temperature is predetermined and the thermostat merely alters the means through which the temperature is maintained. In essence, what is not questioned is the initial setting of the goal. It is not difficult to see that goal-oriented approaches to problems, issues and change are basically congruent with hard systems models of change. Once the objective is identified, then the issue that remains is to establish the most efficient means of achieving it – hence the function of objectives trees as described in the previous chapter.

By contrast, within a process-oriented approach the problem is likely to be seen as distinctly *messy*. The changes might have long-term and, as yet, unforeseen ramifications, which make the formulation of goals and constraints problematic. The problem is much more concerned with changing the behaviour of people and the structures and cultures within which they work. A process-oriented approach starts by identifying who must be involved in the process, what sort of issues should be addressed and how all this can be facilitated. The phases of the project are by no means as clearly defined as in a goal-oriented approach. It may take some time before the problem itself is agreed, which will most likely challenge the goal itself. In these situations single-loop learning is necessary as a means of monitoring the performance of organizational systems and subsystems in relation to the objectives set for them. However, single-loop or adaptive learning, which depends mainly on individualistic learning, is not sufficient in situations that require creative thinking to develop new visions and ways of doing things.

Elkjaar (1999, pp. 86–87) speaks of 'social learning' and that it is necessary to participate and be engaged in organizational projects. In a good exposition and critique of the learning organization, Paton and McCalman (2008, pp. 296–297) summarize the views of double-loop or generative learning as expressed by the main writers on learning organizations/organizational learning as follows:

They emphasize a collaborative, participative approach centred on team processes. They demonstrate a commitment to the creation of a shared vision of the future direction of the company and the necessary steps, structural and behavioural, to achieve that vision. They stress a proactive approach to learning, creating new experiences, continuous experimentation and risk-taking. Finally, they each emphasize the role of leaders to facilitate the change process and to foster a commitment to learning.

This quotation indicates that process-oriented/double-loop/generative learning involves issues associated with organizational structures, cultures and styles of leadership in terms of the capacity of these aspects of organizational life to support and facilitate this type of learning. It certainly draws attention to many of the issues discussed in Part Two, the importance of people and the concepts associated with organizations as collections of subsystems interacting and reflecting the organizational system as a whole – concepts that are wholly in line with the organizational development approach to change.

Figure 8.1 summarizes the philosophy and underlying assumptions of OD as a process for facilitating organizational change. The remainder of this chapter attempts to spell out in more detail the nature of the OD process itself.

The OD process

OD is at heart a process of facilitation of organizational change and renewal. It operates at all levels of the organization – individual, group and organizational. It is a relatively long-term process for initiating and implementing planned change. It takes into account the messy nature of many organizational problems, which involve unclear goals and differing perspectives on what constitutes the problems, let alone how to solve them. It recognizes organizations as social entities where political as well as intellectual responses to change can be expected. It agrees with Benjamin and Mabey's (1993, p. 181) statement that: 'While the primary stimulus for change in organizations remains those forces in the external environment, the primary motivator for *how* change is accomplished resides with the people in the organization.'

On the basis of these assumptions, organization development as a process for instigating and implementing change has two important characteristics. The first is that it is a process of change which has a framework of recognizable phases that take the organization from its current state to a new more desired future state. Second, within and across these steps, the OD process can be perceived to be a collection of activities and techniques that, selectively or accumulatively, help the organization and/or its parts to move through these phases. The idea of phases can be most clearly demonstrated through a consideration of Lewin's (1951) three-phase model of change. This is followed by a more detailed description of OD as it has developed in more recent times.

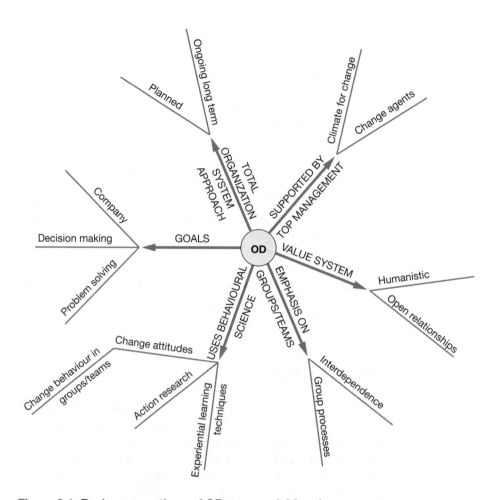

Figure 8.1 Basic assumptions of OD as a model for change

Lewin's three-phase model of change

Most OD models of change consist of a series of phases or steps. One of the earlier and most influential models of planned change that is still referred to extensively in the literature on change is Lewin's (1951) model of the change process (see Chapter 6). This consists of the three phases of *unfreezing, moving* and *refreezing*.

Unfreezing

The first of these phases – unfreezing – concerns the 'shaking up' of people's habitual modes of thinking and behaviour to heighten their awareness of the need for change. According to Cummings and Worley (2009, p. 22), this implies disturbing the *status quo* by either strengthening the forces that could *push* for change and/or weakening the forces which are maintaining the situation. This is likely to include the introduction of information showing discrepancies between desirable goals and modes of operating and what is currently happening. According to Goodstein and Burke (1993), it might even include selectively promoting employees or terminating their employment. For instance, in the case of Pitford College in Shire County (see Chapter 7, Illustration 7.5) a member of staff was promoted to Director of Open and Resource-based Learning (O&RBL). Other staff had their responsibilities changed to include 'tutoring' (rather than teaching) students working mainly in a self-service type of learning environment. All staff received news that a new O&RBL centre was to be built and that the timetables of all full-time students would be altered so that at least 20 per cent of their time would be spent learning in the new centre, using multimedia materials on a 'pick and mix' basis according to their needs. Part of this unfreezing process was the extensive consultation with heads of departments and other decision makers to discuss the new developments – which were seen as challenging the prevailing wisdom of how education and training in the further education sector should happen.

Another example of the application of OD to a 'frame-breaking' or 'transformational' change occurred when the 'Regional College', a student nurse training establishment, was forced to change the way it operated. Illustration 8.1 describes the beginnings of this process.

Illustration 8.1

Change at the Regional College of Psychiatric Nursing

Lewin's unfreezing process was evident in the environmental pressures which caused a school of nursing to review its entire mode of operation when the whole system of education for trainee nurses was changed. The courses leading to graduate status were to be centralized in another institution. Instead of simply allowing this school to close down, the Director set out a case, to the relevant authorities, for the development of courses that would lead to the award of postgraduate masters level degrees, allowing the undergraduate level courses to move to the central institution. Her case was accepted which meant she had to set about the task of convincing her staff of the benefits of what was essentially 'frame-breaking/transformational' change. She recognized what the unfreezing phase of change would entail. Staff would be 'shaken up'

and their professional roles changed. Although some individuals might look forward to the change, others might not, fearing the additional training they would have to do to bring themselves up to a standard to teach at postgraduate rather than undergraduate level. All members of staff were to have their roles and terms of employment changed. She had to face the fact that some staff might leave or be 'persuaded' to do so. During the unfreezing process staff were likely to grieve for what they were losing in spite of those who might welcome the change.

Source: Grateful thanks go to Esther Warnett of the Berufsschule fur Pflege, Switzerland for allowing us to draw on her experiences whilst researching and preparing her Open University Doctorate in Education thesis.

Moving

The second phase of Lewin's change process – moving – is essentially the process of making the actual changes that will move the organization to the new state. As well as involving new types of behaviour by individuals, this includes the establishment of new strategies and structures, with associated systems to help secure the new ways of doing things. In Shire County this involved a number of different activities. First, a series of staff seminars on the concept and operation of O&RBL were carried out. As a result staff were concerned with redesigning their courses to include at least 20 per cent delivery of learning on O&RBL principles. In fact, some staff planned to deliver certain learning programmes as *predominantly* O&RBL programmes.

In addition, in Pitford College and one of the other two colleges in Shire County, large new O&RBL centres were built with multimedia teaching and learning facilities. Dignitaries representing education, industry and commerce were invited to the opening ceremonies, which were used as a symbol for change as well as advertising the facilities to those who might support them. The inclusion of local employers' representatives emphasized the importance of providing for the needs of adult learners as well as those of the youngsters who had, traditionally, been the main 'customers' of these colleges. What is more, in the redefinition of teaching as 'facilitating learning' it was recognized that the managers of these new O&RBL centres did not necessarily have to be academics. This was further reinforced by associating the new centres very closely with existing library and computer services whose staff were not classed as academics.

Refreezing

Lewin's final phase in the change process – refreezing – involves stabilizing or institutionalizing the changes. This requires securing the changes against 'backsliding' and may include recruitment of new staff who are 'untainted' by the old habits. The continuing involvement and support of top management is crucial to this step. All of the elements of the cultural web (see Chapter 4) are important in establishing new ways of doing things. Once strategy, structure and systems have been changed it is equally important to reinforce the changes through symbolic actions and signs such as a change of logo, forms of dress, buildings design and ways of grouping people to get work done. The use of continuous data collection and feedback is essential to keep track of how the change is progressing and to monitor for further change in the light of environmental changes.

As an example of Lewin's three-phase change process, Goodstein and Burke (1993) make reference to the change British Airways (BA) made in 1987, from being a government-owned enterprise to being privately owned – a change that involved moving from a bureaucratic and militaristic culture to a service-oriented and market-driven culture. Regarding the refreezing step, they mention how the continued involvement and commitment of top management helped ensure that the changes were 'fixed' in the way BA did business. Promotion was given to those employees who displayed commitment to the new values with a 'Top Flight Academy' being established to train senior management according to the new way of doing things. In addition, Goodstein and Burke (pp. 169–170) say: 'Attention was paid to BA's symbols as well – new, upscale uniforms; refurbished aircraft; and a new corporate coat of arms with the motto "We fly to serve".'

In the case of the colleges in Shire County, although the move to a culture of open and resource-based learning continued to some degree, it was constrained by a slackening off of commitment from top management as the environment in which the colleges operated changed yet again and brought new imperatives. Included in this were changes in the economic environment that brought changes in the political environment. These were increasing unemployment rates among young people and, as a result, a commitment on the part of government to increase training opportunities through funding further education provision for the 16–19 age group. In addition, there was an increase in training opportunities for adults. These opportunities operated outside the further education system, thereby, perhaps, lessening the requirement for more flexible provision within the further education colleges themselves. Consequently the phase of 'moving' the current situation to the desired future one was never fully completed and the follow-through of refreezing – absorbing the change into the culture of the organization – was put in jeopardy.

Lewin's three-phase model of organizational change can be criticized mainly for its concept of refreezing, that is, the idea of cementing the changes in place to create a new organizational reality. While this aim to prevent the backsliding mentioned earlier is laudable, it tends to ignore the increasingly turbulent environment within which many modern organizations operate and the need for *continuous* change. In addition, Burnes (2004, p. 997), in his critique of the model, said that it assumed organizations operate in a stable state, it was only suitable for small-scale change projects, it ignored organizational power and politics, and was top-down management driven.

This should not, however, detract from the debt that current OD approaches owe to the work of Lewin and his colleagues. This debt is summarized by French and Bell (1999, p. 44) when they say: 'Lewin's field theory and his conceptualizing about group dynamics, change processes, and action research were of profound influence on the people who were associated with the various stems of OD.' This remains the case today.

Lewin's concept of organizational change as a *process* dominates much of OD theory, a view supported by Burnes (2004) in his recognition of Lewin's contribution to understanding group behaviour and the roles groups play in organizations and society. In addition, there is widespread recognition that organizations must carry out an assessment of where they are now, where they want to be in the future and how to manage the transition from the one state to the other. Where current theories of OD are leading, however, is to a realization that change is a process that is not linear and is itself complex and messy, including many loops back and forth from one stage in the process to another. The following description tries to capture the essence of this. However, because of the limitations of difficulties of describing something that is so dynamic the process may appear more mechanistic than it is in reality. It should be remembered that what is being proposed is only a framework within which many variations may occur.

OD – an action research based model of change

According to Paton and McCalman (2008, p. 217), 'change is a continuous process of confrontation, identification, evaluation and action'. They go on to say that the key to this is what OD proponents refer to as an action–research model. French and Bell (1999), Coghlan and Brannick (2007) and Cummings and Worley (2009) give detailed descriptions of action research. Succinctly, it is a *collaborative* effort between leaders and facilitators of any change and those who have to enact it. In simplified form, it involves the following steps:

1 management and staff perception of problem(s)
2 data gathering and preliminary diagnosis by those concerned with leading the change (who can be internal and/or external to the organization)
3 feedback to key client, management and those involved in the change
4 joint agreement of the problem(s)
5 joint action planning
6 implementation
7 reinforcement and assessment of the change.

Therefore action research is, as its name suggests, a combination of research and action. This means collecting data relevant to the situation of interest, feeding back the results to those who must take action, collaboratively discussing the data to formulate an action plan and, finally, taking the necessary action. Figure 8.2 shows the action research cycles in their relationship to the major stages of the OD model shown in Figure 8.3.

A number of elements distinguish this approach from the hard systems model of change discussed in Chapter 7. First, it is not a 'one-off' event, which ends when a change has been completed. In describing the application of OD in an American electricity utility, Alpander and Lee (1995) illustrate this by saying: 'Organizations which are successful in maintaining their competitiveness have learned to view change not as a one-time event, but an ongoing process necessary to remain on the cutting edge in meeting customer needs.' This includes the ideas within the concept of a learning organization discussed earlier. Second, it is an iterative or cyclical process that is continuous and which, if OD is taken as part of an organization's philosophy of action, continues as part of everyday organizational life. Third, each of the components of the model (diagnosis, data gathering, feedback to the client group, data discussion and work by the client

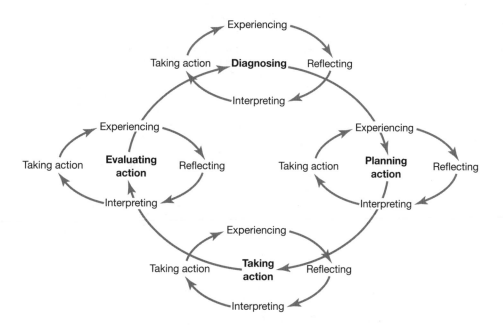

Figure 8.2 Doing action research in your own organization

Source: Coghlan, D. and Brannick, T. (2007) *Doing Action Research in Your Own Organization* (2nd edn), London: Sage, 2007, p.35.

group, action planning and action) may be used to form each of the phases that make up a typical OD process. Furthermore, these components may, collectively, form cycles of activity *within* each stage of the OD process. Finally, the OD approach to change is firmly embedded in the assumption, that all who are or who might be involved in any change should be part of the decision-making process to decide what that change might be and to bring it about. It is not, as some hard systems models of change suggest, a project planned and implemented by senior managers or some designated project manager, with the assumption that other workers in the organization will automatically go along with it.

Building on the concept of action research, Figure 8.3 illustrates the major stages of the OD model. These are now described in more detail. It is important to note that change on the scale involved in most OD efforts does not succeed without some established facilitation function. Hence the emphasis on the role of the facilitator, or as termed here the *change agent*, as evidenced by positioning this person or group in the centre of the diagram. The role of the facilitator or change agent, who can be internal or external to the organization, is discussed later in the chapter. What follows first is a more detailed description of the stages that make up the OD model itself.

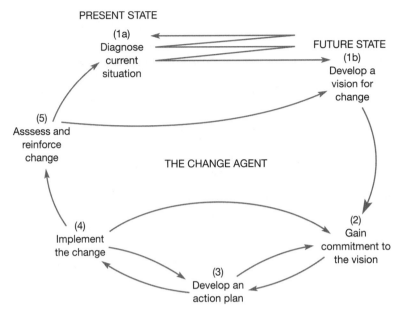

Figure 8.3 The OD model for change

Stages 1a and 1b: The present and the future

An examination of Figure 8.3 shows two stages strongly linked together in a symbiotic relationship. Hence the labelling of them as 1a and 1b – that is, two processes that are, in effect, intertwined and which could be regarded as one. The reason for this is that it is never clear whether a change process should start with the development of a vision for change (that is, where the organization wants to be), followed by a diagnosis of where the organization is at present; or whether a start should be made with diagnosing 'what is', followed by statements about 'what could be'. For instance, Buchanan and McCalman (1989), in their four-step model of perpetual transition management, pose the 'trigger layer' (which examines environmental opportunities and threats) before the 'vision layer' (which defines the future). In contrast, Mabey and Pugh (1995) put as the first stage the process of agreeing the organization's purpose/mission. This is followed by an assessment of the organization's external and internal environments.

In reality, as the zigzag arrow in Figure 8.3 shows, these two processes act in parallel, with each process feeding the other as it proceeds until some idea of a future direction is achieved. However, for ease of description, Stages 1a and 1b are discussed separately.

Stage 1a: Diagnose current situation

This stage is where environmental analysis and the metaphor 'winds of change' (see Chapter 1) are useful as tools for diagnosing triggers for change. In addition the temporal and internal environments must be assessed. In an ideal world this would be done on an ongoing basis: (a) to detect strategic drift and (b) to gather data on the organization's capacity to respond to a change in direction or ways of operating. However, sometimes it takes a crisis to trigger this type of diagnosis.

Diagnostic processes such as these clearly call upon the data-gathering component of the action–research aspects of the OD model and the feedback of the results for discussion and verification by those concerned with, and involved in, the subsequent change. As mentioned earlier, in addition to data gathering about the organization's external environment, there is also a need for a more detailed examination of such things as:

- organizational purposes and goals
- organizational structure and culture
- prevailing leadership approaches and styles
- recruitment practices, career paths and opportunities
- reward structures and practices
- individuals' motivation and commitment to their work and organization
- employee training and development provision
- intra- and inter-group relationships.

The diagnostic stage forms the foundation for all the subsequent stages of the OD cycle. It is the beginning of the data collection process that will continue throughout the change process. It should provide information about the 'total system'. Data gathering, therefore, is done at the individual, group and organizational levels and should include those things that form barriers to organizational performance as well as those which contribute to organizational success. Table 8.1 provides a comparison of different methods of data collection.

Table 8.1 Comparison of different methods of data collection

Method	Major advantages	Potential problems
Questionnaires	1 Responses can be quantified and easily summarized 2 Easy to use with large samples 3 Relatively inexpensive 4 Can obtain a large volume of data	1 No empathy 2 Predetermined questions/ missing issues 3 Over-interpretation of data 4 Response bias
Interviews	1 Adaptive – allows data collection on a range of possible subjects 2 Source of 'rich' data 3 Empathic 4 Process of interviewing can build rapport	1 Expense 2 Bias in interviewer responses 3 Coding and interpretation difficulties 4 Self-report bias
Observations	1 Collects data on behaviour, rather than reports of behaviour 2 Real time, not retrospective 3 Adaptive	1 Coding and interpretation difficulties 2 Sampling inconsistencies 3 Observer bias and questionable reliability 4 Expense
Unobtrusive measures	1 Non-reactive – no response bias 2 High face validity 3 Easily quantified	1 Access and retrieval difficulties 2 Validity concerns 3 Coding and interpretation difficulties

Source: Nadler, D. (1977) *Feedback and Organization Development: Using Data-based Methods*, Reading, Mass: Addison Wesley, pp. 156–158. Reprinted in Cummings and Worley (2009, p. 159) by permission – Pearson Education, Inc., Englewood Cliffs, NJ.

The data collected, particularly from carrying out interviews, making observations and engaging in other unobtrusive methods of data collection can be put together in a 'rich picture' (see Checkland's (1981) description of soft systems). This can be constructed by the change leader or change agent but, as importantly, should also include those involved in the change. Rich pictures are particularly useful in identifying issues regarding how people *think*, *feel* and *what they do* in terms of the *tasks* they perform, their *ways of working* and the *relationships* they have with each other. Many of the illustrations and activities in the chapters in Part Two are useful diagnostic tools for use at this stage in the change process. Illustration 8.2 is a summary of the situation facing the Hardwater Mineral Water Company. This is also depicted in Figure 8.4 as a rich picture. From looking at the rich picture it can be seen that much more can be displayed than is evident in the account. However, this picture is a single person's first reaction to the situation they found themselves in. Rich pictures are tyically drawn by more than one person in the situation and, from these, a composite picture will emerge.

Illustration 8.2

The Hardwater Mineral Water Company Ltd

Part 1: The context of the change situation

The Hardwater Mineral Water Company Ltd (HMWC) was a regional bottler of mineral water located in an English region. The company was formed in the early 1990s and grew steadily and profitably over the ensuing ten years under the ownership of the founders. Although it had some sales across the UK, the HMWC was essentially a regional company having the majority of its sales within a single region. In 2001, the HMWC was acquired by the 'Fishy Group', since when it consistently failed to make a profit. At the time of the acquisition, the Fishy Group was a well established family business that for many years had been prominent in the regional fishing industry. As this industry declined, the company had diversified into the business of ice production and was one of the largest suppliers of ice-cubes in the UK, supplying most of the major retailers. It was the increasing demand for mineral water ice-cubes that led to the acquisition of the HMWC.

At the time of this acquisition, the Fishy Group owners, and family members and friends who were also employed, knew nothing about the UK bottled water industry and market. Consequently, the chairman brought in a new managing director and sales director (at very high salaries) with the task of bringing in new business and returning the company to a profitable trading situation. However, these two directors were nearing the end of their working careers and were more interested in the title of 'director' and associated salary and fringe benefits, than working to develop the business.

Meanwhile, whilst the ice-cube business continued to operate profitably, the HMWC's products of flavoured water, which contained additives including preservatives and sweeteners, were losing market share fast. This was exacerbated by consumers and schools (where products with additives were banned) increasingly demanding additive-free products, but which the company had failed to introduce. The lack of effort on the part of the directors meant that much of the responsibility for bringing in new business fell on the sales manager with little support from those at a senior level. The sales manager's situation was not helped by the chairman's threats to close the business down unless it could generate a profit. Even if the HMWC had won a national contract, it would not have had the economies of scale necessary to compete on pricing, particularly given market competition from national and multinational brands.

By 2006, the chairman had sold off all the Fishy Group's fishing vessels and was spending most of his time aboard his private yacht. He effectively handed over the day-to-day control of the HWMC business to his daughter, who took over the role of Managing Director whilst still employing the 'other' managing director and the sales director, as well as the several family members and friends. In spite of now having three directors, HMWC had no sales and marketing strategy nor did it conduct market research to establish why sales and profitability were down. Instead they blamed the situation on the Sales Manager and sacked him. Not long after that the original Managing Director and Sales Director left the company and the Chairman's daughter, as the new Managing Director, took over management of the sales staff. This certainly lowered some costs. However, without a realistic sales strategy based on the changing market demands for additive-free products, together with a competent sales manager and 'field' based sales executives experienced in the industry, sales continued to decline.

Figure 8.4 is a rich picture of the diagnosis of the 'messy' situation facing the HMWC, its Managing Director and staff.

Source: We are grateful to Andrew Cressey for this summary account and for the rich picture shown in Figure 8.4.

A more self-explanatory rich picture is that shown in Figure 8.5. This rich picture was the result of a group of people working together to depict how they perceived the situation they were in and which needed to change.

Activity 8.1

Go back to Part Two of the book and, in conjunction with the list in Table 8.1, list those illustrations and activities you think might be useful for the process of carrying out a diagnosis of the current state of your organization or one with which you are familiar. On the basis of what you know about your place of work or one familiar to you, and if necessary in consultation with others, attempt to construct a rich picture. If this is not possible, imagine you are one of the sales staff at the Hardwater Mineral Water Company Ltd and use the account in Illustration 8.2 to construct a rich picture from your point of view.

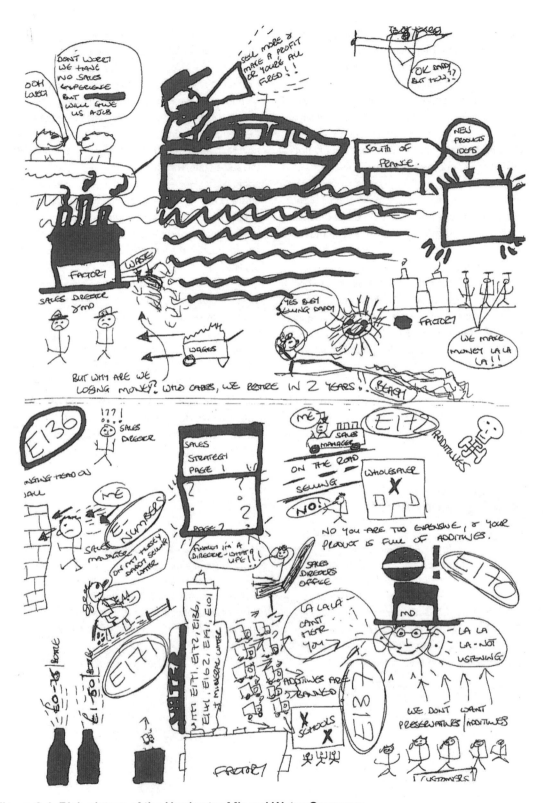

Figure 8.4 Rich picture of the Hardwater Mineral Water Company

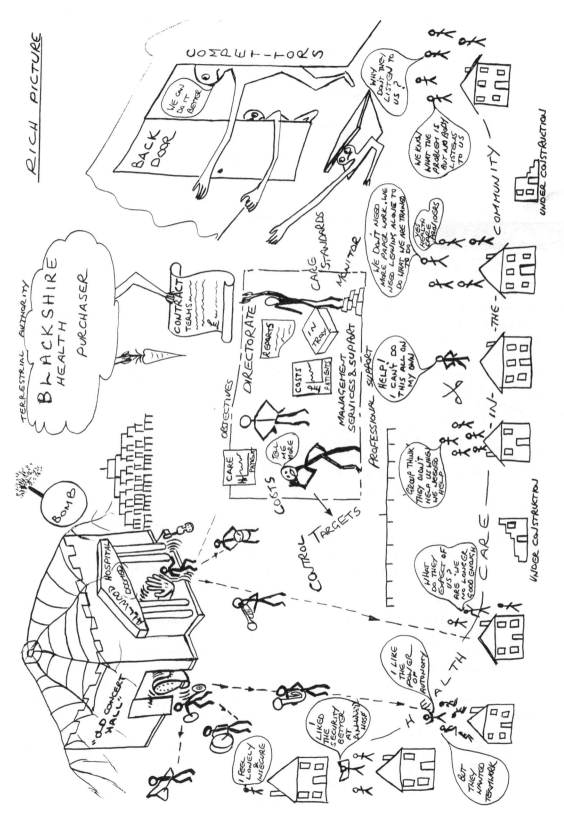

Figure 8.5 Rich picture of changes in the organization of services for people with learning disabilities

It is clear that data collection and analysis are crucial to this stage in the OD process. It is important to note, however, the necessity for giving feedback on the findings to those from whom the data came, for further discussion and verification – a process particularly important in the case of data gained from the administration of questionnaires and through observation, where there is little interaction between questioner and questioned. This feedback process also serves the purpose of developing a vision for change – that is, where the organization wants to be in the future. Illustration 8.3 describes the techniques of data collection and feedback used by the Director of the Regional College as she carried out the diagnostic phase of the change with her staff.

Illustration 8.3

Diagnosing the situation facing the Regional College of Psychiatric Nursing

In order to diagnose the situation facing the Regional College, the Director undertook a series of exercises with her staff. First, she met with her four departmental heads (who with the Director formed the School Committee) to analyze the external context for the change. Secondly, she used the concepts of 'difficulties' and 'messes' to identify those issues (difficulties) that were more easily managed and those (messes) that would be more problematical both for themselves and particularly for the other staff members. A month later, she called together all the 20 members of staff for a team day. She showed and discussed with them the results of the PEST analysis and shared and received their perceptions of the implications of the 'mess' they faced. In particular the staff agreed that they faced a situation that had: 'serious and worrying implications for all concerned' (see Chapter 2, Illustration 2.12). Most importantly, she was able to agree with the staff that the nature of change is sometimes perceived subjectively, as more 'frightening' than it is in reality.

Two months after she started the diagnostic stage, the Director brought her heads of department together to take part in an exercise similar to constructing a 'rich picture', except this exercise used objects that could be arranged and rearranged to depict, in a three-dimensional way, what the group thought and felt about the problems and issues in which they were and would be involved. The fact

that the objects could be picked up and moved about, allowed the group participants to change their representations and those of others and build on each other's ideas. In addition to these meetings and group exercises the Director carried out one-to-one interviews with members of staff. She also had the results of an official questionnaire showing the staff and students' perception of the learning climate and the strategy and leadership of the College.

The diagnostic stage of this first cycle in Regional College's change process ended with a meeting of the Director and Heads of Departments to carry out a SWOT analysis (see Johnson, Scholes and Whittington, 2008): that is, an exploration of the organization's external environment for Opportunities and Threats and the internal environment for Strengths and Weaknesses. This process took account of the results of the meetings, exercises, interviews and the results of the questionnaire.

As the arrows in Figure 8.3, between the diagnosis and developing the vision stages show, during these three months the vision for the College of becoming a postgraduate institution was accepted even though, as the Director's reflections on this process show: 'the workload at the moment seems almost insurmountable'.

Source: Grateful thanks go to Esther Warnett of the Berufsschule fur Pflege, Switzerland for allowing us to draw on her experiences whilst researching and preparing her Open University Doctorate in Education thesis

Stage 1b: Develop a vision for change

An organization's sense of what needs to change comes out of the process of organizational diagnosis and creative thinking. However, as we have already seen, this does not happen only when the diagnosis is complete. As the diagnosis proceeds and problem and success areas emerge, theories of what should be changed begin to form. These, in turn, bring demands for new information that will eventually move the process towards some definition of what the future should look like.

One way of looking at this stage of activity is to perceive it as a *creative* phase, in the sense that 'something new' is being looked for. This might imply a different strategy in terms of products, services or markets. It might also imply a change in structure and culture – including the way people are managed and led. Flood and Jackson (1991) and Morgan (1997) suggest the use of metaphors as organizing structures to help people think about their organizations. The examples given are: organizations as machines, organisms, brains, cultures, teams, coalitions, prisons, instruments of domination and organizations in flux and transformation. Thus, Stage 1a would be concerned with identifying what metaphor most matched the current organization and Stage 1b would identify a metaphor to which its members might aspire. One implication of course is that where these two metaphors changed, so too would the underlying values of the organization.

Cummings and Worley (2009, pp. 169) say that:

> The vision that an organization has describes the core values and purposes that guide the organization as well as an envisioned future toward which change is directed. It provides a valued direction for the designing, implementing, and assessing of organizational changes.

They also suggest that a vision can energize commitment as people will be working towards a common goal. And as the discussion in the previous chapter shows, vision plays a key role in effective leadership.

> A vision can be described as a living picture of a future, desirable state. It is living because it exists in the thoughts and actions of people, not just in a written document. It is a picture because it is composed not of abstractions but of images.
>
> (Burnside, 1991, p. 193)

On the concept of 'images', Burnside quotes Lievegoed (1983, p. 75) as saying: 'Images are more meaningful than abstract definitions. Images always have a thought content, an emotional value, and a moral symbolic value' and goes on to say: 'A vision is thus integrative because it brings these dimensions together.' According to Burnside there are two main aspects to visions – the strategic picture, which he calls the 'head' side, and the relational picture, which he calls the 'heart' side. Illustration 8.4 refers to a company that conforms closely to these ideas.

Illustration 8.4

The Body Shop's values

In 1976, reflecting the principles and vision of its main creator, Anita Roddick (now deceased), the first Body Shop, a retailer of skin care and fragrance products was opened. From this small beginning the company grew to its present size (as a manufacturer as well as retailer) of approximately 56 markets, 2,265 stores, 1,200 products, and 10,034 employees (some working through its franchise system). In 1997, the website (www.thebodyshop.co.uk) set out the company's charter and mission statements (see Activity 8.2). Whilst the website does not currently list these in this form, the essence of them is still evident in the Chairman and CEO's 'Values Report' and the range of value statements titled: 'activate self-esteem'; 'against animal testing'; 'protect our planet'; 'support community trade'; and 'defend human rights'. He concludes his statement by saying:

Our values are not just things we do, but who we are. Being an employee, a consultant or a franchisee here is to make a difference every day. The achievements and aspirations in this report are a result of our people's passionate work and our customers' dedicated support. Whether we operate in new areas of the world, through new channels or under new ownership, our values are in our DNA and we will continue our efforts to make a difference.

The company also has a charitable foundation that was launched in 1990. It exists to:

... give financial support to pioneering, frontline organizations that otherwise have little hope of conventional funding. The Foundation's focus is to assist those working to achieve progress in the areas of human and civil rights, environmental and animal protection.

Source: The Body Shop, www.thebodyshop.co.uk

Activity 8.2

How far do you think the following statements made by The Body Shop go towards meeting the definitions of a vision as given above?

THE BODY SHOP'S TRADING CHARTER
We aim to achieve commercial success by meeting our customers' needs through the provision of high quality, good value products with exceptional service and relevant information which enables customers to make informed and responsible choices.

Our trading relationships of every kind – with customers, franchisees and suppliers – will be commercially viable, mutually beneficial and based on trust and respect.

THE BODY SHOP'S MISSION STATEMENT – OUR REASON FOR BEING
- To dedicate our business to the pursuit of social and environmental change.
- To CREATIVELY balance the financial and human NEEDS of our stakeholders: employees, customers, franchisees, suppliers and shareholders.
- To COURAGEOUSLY ensure that OUR business is ecologically sustainable, meeting the needs of the present without compromising the future.

- To MEANINGFULLY contribute to local, national and international communities in which we trade, by adopting a code of conduct which ensures care, honesty, fairness and respect.
- To PASSIONATELY campaign for the protection of the environment and human and civil rights, and against animal testing within the cosmetics and toiletries industry.
- To TIRELESSLY work to narrow the gap between principle and practice, while making fun, passion and care part of our daily lives.

This example of employee involvement in the development of an organization's vision underlines the close linking of Stages 1a and 1b and their combined outputs in identifying an organization's present and desired states in terms of two aspects of its functioning. These outputs are: first, the gap that represents the difference between an organization's current strategy and goals and those to which it must aspire in order to respond to the forces and circumstances of changing internal and external environments; second, the gap between what Benjamin and Mabey (1993, p. 182) call: 'the core values as they are related internally to the ethos of the organization'.

Stage 2: Gain commitment to the vision and the need for change

It is at the second stage of the process that feedback from the results of Stages 1a and 1b is most important. Unless those concerned and involved with the change have been consulted and have participated in the process to this point, there will be little incentive for them to 'buy into' the new vision and the change process that will follow it.

Illustration 8.5

Pugh's principles and rules for understanding and managing organizational change

Principle 1: *Organizations are organisms*
This means the organization is not a machine and change must be approached carefully, with the implications for various groupings thought out. Participants need to be persuaded of the need for change and be given time to 'digest' the changes after implementation.

Principle 2: *Organizations are occupational and political systems as well as rational resource-allocation ones*
This means that thought must be given to how changes affect people's jobs, career prospects, motivation and so on. It also means paying attention to how change will affect people's status, power and the prestige of different groups.

Illustration 8.5 *continued*

Principle 3: *All members of an organization operate simultaneously in the rational, occupational and political systems*
This means that all types of arguments for change must be taken seriously. It is not sufficient merely to explain different points of view. Rational arguments for change are as important as those which involve changes in occupational and political systems.

Principle 4: *Change is most likely to be acceptable with people who are successful and have confidence in their ability and the motivation to change*
This means ensuring an appropriate place (or set of people) from which to start the change and to ensure the methods used are relevant to those who are 'first in line' in accepting the change.

Source: Based on Pugh, D.S. (1993) 'Understanding and Managing Change', in Mabey, C. and Mayon-White, B. (eds) *Managing Change* (2nd edn), London: PCP, pp. 109–110.

This stage is akin to the 'conversion layer' in Buchanan and McCalman's (1989) model of perpetual transition management – the one that follows the trigger and vision layers which were mentioned earlier. However, gaining recruits for the change is not easy, as Pugh's (1993) four principles for understanding the process of organizational change show (see Illustration 8.5 and Activity 8.3). These principles in turn draw attention to the need for managers to use many different and interacting ways to gain the commitment and involvement of all concerned in the change programme.

Activity 8.3

Identify a major change in an organization with which you are familiar – preferably one in which you have been involved.

Consider each of Pugh's principles and make notes regarding the following in terms of gaining people's commitment to the need for a new vision and associated change.

Principle 1
- *Were the implications for different groupings thought out?*
- *What (if any) methods were used to persuade people of the need for change?*

Principle 2
- *Was thought given to how the changes might impact on people's:*
  - *Positions and prospects?*
  - *Status?*
  - *Power?*

Principle 3
- *Were the comments (supportive or otherwise) of different people and groups taken seriously and acted upon?*

Principle 4
- *How much effort was made to increase people's confidence in the new vision?*
- *How much effort was made to identify those people and groups who were most likely to 'spearhead' the change?*

Pugh's four principles draw attention to the need for not just two-way but many-way communication as part of the process of gaining commitment to the vision and the need for change. This is one of the reasons why most descriptions of OD-type models of change emphasize the importance of managing resistance through discussion, negotiation and active participation of those likely to have to make the changes. Established work groups and teams become particularly important at this stage, as is evidenced by French and Bell's (1999, p. 155) statement that:

> Collaborative management of the work team culture is a fundamental emphasis of organization development programmes. This reflects the assumption that in today's organizations much of the work is accomplished directly or indirectly through teams. This also reflects the assumption that the work team culture exerts a significant influence on the individual's behaviour . . . Teams and work groups are thus considered to be fundamental units of organizations and also key leverage points for improving the functioning of the organization.

Consequently the process of gaining commitment to change must include working at the group level of the organization and recognizing the strength of influence of both formal and informal group leaders. In addition, it is more efficient of time and effort to communicate with individuals as groups than with them solely as individuals – even though this should not be the only means of communicating with them. It is not, however, sufficient merely to inform people of the vision and the necessity for change. This is because visions for change are rarely so clearly structured that information from all levels of the organization can be ignored. As Smith (1995, p. 19), writing on the realities of involvement in managing change, says: 'No top manager can know at the outset [of any change] exactly what needs doing, what information is needed, or where it is located.'

Jones (1994, p. 49) talks of 'listening to the organization'. Reporting research with top management on the reasons why large-scale programmes of change often fail, Smith (1995) says that nearly all the managers interviewed reported on how much they had underestimated the importance of communication. However, as Jones says, this is not simply a question of senior management shouting louder from the top. This will not identify and bring to the surface the doubts that people have and their fears of what change might mean for them. Neither will it bring to the surface any problems with implementing the vision that top management may not be able to see for themselves.

Far from shouting from the top, the action–research cycle of collecting and analyzing data and feeding back the results should be maintained here, as in the previous stages, to avoid widespread alienation of the workforce from the need to change and the vision to which it relates. Lloyd and Feigen (1997, p. 37) neatly summarize the dangers of not doing this when they say: 'Vision statements only work when the needs of those at the bottom of the organization are integrated upwards with the needs of the market.' Accomplishing this means being sensitive, not only to people's worries about the way tasks and structures may be affected by the change, but also to what Mabey and Pugh (1995, p. 36) term the 'emotional readiness for change, the quality of existing relationships and the latent commitment to new ways of working'. Otherwise, any plan for action has little chance of being successfully implemented.

Stage 3: Develop an action plan

The development of an action plan can be thought of as beginning the phase of managing the transition from an organization's current state to its desired future state, as shown by the 'journey to the future' zigzag in Figure 8.3. However, it also continues the process of gaining commitment to the vision but with a somewhat changed emphasis on *how* that vision can come about.

A number of issues are important in this stage of the OD process. One is the issue of *who* is to guide the planning and, later, the implementation of the change. Another is the issue of precisely *what* needs to change to achieve the vision, while a third is *where* any intervention should take place. The following explores these issues in more detail.

The role of a change agent

The success of using an OD approach to facilitate change rests on the qualities and capabilities of those who act as the facilitators of change. Moving organizations from current to future changed states is not easy and requires knowledge and skills that some managers might not possess. In addition, many managers are often so close to the day-to-day issues and problems of managing that they find it difficult to stand back from the current situation of *managing* to take on the role of change agent as well. For these and other reasons, such as the need for managers, themselves, to learn how to manage change, many writers on change advise that a change agent, who is external to the organization, is necessary. However, the change agent as facilitator of change does not necessarily have to be from outside the organization, as the Director of the Regional College of Psychiatric Nursing (see Illustrations 8.1 and 8.3) demonstrates. She was the Director of the organization and the change it had to make, as well as the change agent within an OD process. Coghlan and Brannick (2007) discuss the issues involved in a single person occupying dual organizational and change agent roles. They discuss how internal change agents' existing relationships with others will alter alongside changes in the agents themselves. Whilst Figures 8.2 and 8.3 do not explicitly demonstrate the role of reflection in each stage of the process, both external and internal change agents should keep a reflective diary that records their thoughts and emotions as well as actions proposed during the change cycles.

Apart from engaging an external change agent or using an internal change agent, it is not unusual to involve someone from another part of the organization, not the one that is the focus of the change. Indeed some large organizations have departments or divisions that are specifically set up to act as OD consultants to the rest of the organization. What should also be borne in mind is that all the skills and competencies required of a change agent might not reside in one individual. It might, therefore, be preferable to use more than one person or, in the case of large-scale change, a team of people.

Buchanan and Boddy (1992) give a helpful list of the competencies of effective change agents, based on research on how managers deal with change (see Illustration 8.6) which is reminiscent of the characteristics of 'transformational' leaders (see Chapter 6). However, this list must be considered in the context of how it came about. The evidence for constructing the list came mainly from questioning project managers – that is *internal* change agents who were concerned with changes in their own project areas. Perhaps, because of this, it emphasizes more the *content* of the change and how to get ideas accepted, rather than the *process* skills of consultation and participation which form an essential part of the facilitation role. In this respect it can be compared with Paton and McCalman's list of the roles taken on by effective change agents:

1 to help the organization define the problem by asking for a definition of what it is;
2 to help the organization examine what causes the problem and diagnose how this can be overcome;
3 to assist in getting the organization to offer alternative solutions;
4 to provide direction in the implementation of alternative solutions;
5 to transmit the learning process that allows the client to deal with change on an ongoing basis by itself in the future. (Paton and McCalman, 2008, p. 232)

Illustration 8.6

Competencies of an effective change agent

Goals

1 Sensitivity to changes in key personnel, top management perceptions and market conditions, and to the way in which these impact the goals of the project in hand.
2 Clarity in specifying goals, in defining the achievable.
3 Flexibility in responding to changes out with the control of the project manager, perhaps requiring major shifts in project goals and management style and risk taking.

Roles

4 Team-building activities, to bring together key stakeholders and establish effective working groups and clearly to define and delegate respective responsibilities.
5 Networking skills in establishing and maintaining appropriate contacts within and outside the organization.
6 Tolerance of ambiguity, to be able to function comfortably, patiently and effectively in an uncertain environment.

▶

Illustration 8.6 *continued*

Communication

7 Communication skills to transmit effectively to colleagues and subordinates the need for changes in project goals and in individual tasks and responsibilities.

8 Interpersonal skills, across the range, including selection, listening, collecting appropriate information, identifying the concerns of others and managing meetings.

9 Personal enthusiasm, in expressing plans and ideas.

10 Stimulating motivation and commitment in others involved.

Negotiation

11 Selling plans and ideas to others, by creating a desirable and challenging vision of the future.

12 Negotiating with key players for resources or for changes in procedures and to resolve conflict.

Managing up

13 Political awareness, in identifying potential coalitions and in balancing conflicting goals and perceptions.

14 Influencing skills, to gain commitment to project plans and ideas from potential sceptics and resisters.

15 Helicopter perspective, to stand back from the immediate project and take a broader view of priorities.

Source: Buchanan, D. and Boddy, D. (1992) *The Expertise of the Change Agent*, Hemel Hempstead: Prentice Hall, pp. 92–93.

In contrast to the concept of a change agent, Kotter (1996) uses the concept of a 'guiding coalition' and suggests four key characteristics as being essential for it to be effective:

1 *Position power*: Are enough key players on board, especially the main line managers, so that those left out cannot easily block progress?

2 *Expertise*: Are the various points of view – in terms of discipline, work experience, nationality, etc. – relevant to the task at hand adequately represented so that informed, intelligent decisions will be made?

3 *Credibility*: Does the group have enough people with good reputations in the firm so that its pronouncements will be taken seriously by other employees?

4 *Leadership*: Does the group include enough proven leaders to be able to drive the change process? (Kotter, 1996, p. 57)

It is clear, however, that the guiding coalition cannot, by itself, cause widespread change to happen. What it can do is to set targets for change that, collectively, will move the organization and its members much closer to realizing the vision which was developed in Stage 1b and further refined in Stage 2. Having done this, the issue becomes: *'Who is to do what, with what kind of involvement by others?'*

Responsibility charting

Beckhard and Harris (1987, pp. 104–108) developed a technique called 'responsibility charting' that assesses the alternative behaviours for each person or persons involved in a series of actions designed to bring about change. They describe the making of a responsibility chart as follows:

> Responsibility charting clarifies behaviour that is required to implement important change tasks, actions, or decisions. It helps reduce ambiguity, wasted energy, and adverse emotional reactions between individuals or groups whose interrelationship is affected by change. The basic process is as follows:
>
> > Two or more people whose roles interrelate or who manage interdependent groups formulate a list of actions, decisions, or activities that affect their relationship (such as developing budgets, allocating resources, and deciding on the use of capital) and record the list on the vertical axis of a responsibility chart [see Figure 8.6]. They then identify the people involved in each action or decision and list these 'actors' on the horizontal axis of the form.

The actors identified can include:

R = the person who has the *responsibility* to initiate the action and who is charged with ensuring it is carried out.

A = those whose *approval* is required or who have the power to veto the decision. This could be the responsible person's superiors.

S = those who can provide *support* and resources to help the action to take place.

I = those who merely need to be *informed* or consulted but who cannot veto the action.

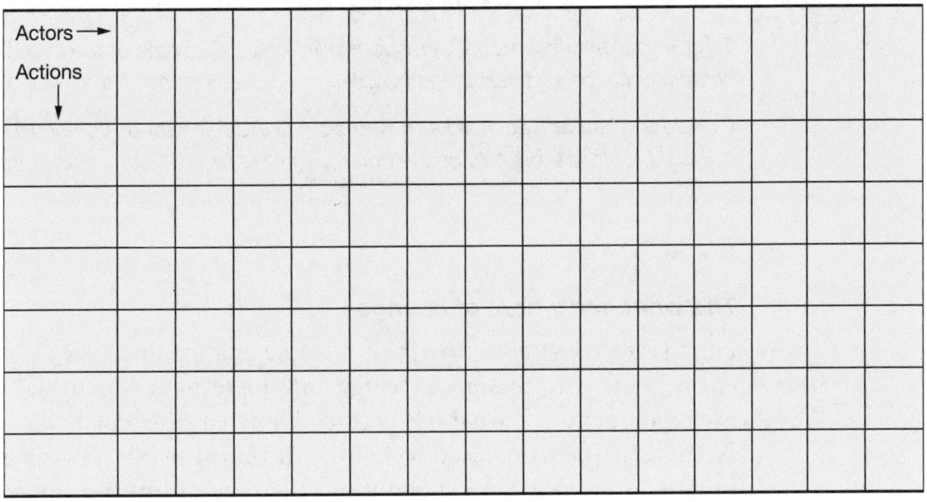

Key:
R = Responsibility (not necessarily authority)
A = Approval (right to veto)
S = Support (put resources towards)
I = Inform (to be consulted before action but with no right of veto)

Figure 8.6 Example of a responsibility chart

Certain ground rules are set out when making a responsibility chart. French and Bell (1999, pp. 172–173) summarize these as follows:

> First, assign responsibility to only one person. That person initiates and then is responsible and accountable for the action. Second, avoid having too many people with an approval–veto function on an item. That will slow down task accomplishment or will negate it altogether. Third, if one person has approval–veto involvement on most decisions, that person could become a bottle-neck for getting things done. Fourth, the support function is critical. A person with a support role has to expand resources or produce something that is then used by the person responsible for the action. This support role and its specific demands must be clarified and clearly assigned. And, finally, the assignment of functions (letters) to persons at times becomes difficult. For example, a person may want A–V (approval–veto) on an item, but not really need it; a person may not want S (support) responsibility on an item, but should have it; or two persons each want R (responsibility) on a particular item, but only one can have it.

This discussion of responsibility charting illustrates the 'chicken and egg' nature of planning organizational change. While it is right to consider who will lead and participate in implementing change, this has to be done in conjunction with what needs to change.

Activity 8.4

Identify a change initiative in which you have been involved (or one with which you are familiar). You may find it helpful to use the example identified in completing Activity 8.3.

To give you practice in using a responsibility chart, list some of the actions associated with that change and assign the people involved according to their responsibility role(s).

Consider whether Beckhard and Harris's ground rules for assigning roles were adhered to. If not, did this cause confusion of responsibilities and/or impede action?

The what and where of change

Pugh (1986) devised a matrix of possible change initiatives based on the different issues that can hamper change and the level at which they occur. Figure 8.7 is a reproduction of what has become known as the 'Pugh OD matrix'.

The matrix can be used to help with action planning (as represented by the initiatives listed in italics) about: (a) the type of intervention required to facilitate change in line with the organization's vision (represented by the columns), and (b) the level at which it should take place (represented by the rows). For instance, at the level of the individual, problems may be occurring because there are few opportunities for promotion from the job of factory floor supervisor to

	Behaviour (What is happening now?)	Structure (What is the required system?)	Context (What is the setting?)
Organizational level	General climate of poor morale, pressure, anxiety, suspicion, lack of awareness of, or response to, environmental changes *Survey feedback, organizational mirroring*	Systems goals – poorly defined or inappropriate and misunderstood; organization structure inappropriate – centralization, divisionalization or standardization; inadequacy of environmental monitoring – mechanisms *Change the structure*	Geographical setting, market pressures, labour market, physical condition, basic technology *Change strategy, location, physical condition, basic technology*
Inter-group level	Lack of effective cooperation between sub-units, conflict, excessive competition, limited war, failure to confront differences in priorities, unresolved feelings *Inter-group confrontation (with third-party consultant), role negotiation*	Lack of integrated task perspective; sub-unit optimization, required interaction difficult to achieve *Redefine responsibilities, change reporting relationships, improve coordination and liaison mechanism*	Different sub-units' values, lifestyle; physical distance *Reduce psychological and physical distance; exchange roles, attachments, cross-functional groups*
Group level	Inappropriate working relationships, atmosphere, participation, poor understanding and acceptance of goals, avoidance, inappropriate leadership style, leader not trusted, respected; leader in conflict with peers and superiors *Process consultation, team building*	Task requirements poorly defined; role relationships unclear or inappropriate; leader's role overloaded, inappropriate reporting procedures *Redesign work relationships (socio-technical systems), self-directed working groups*	Insufficient resources, poor group composition for cohesion, inadequate physical set-up, personality clashes *Change technology, layout, group composition*
Individual level	Failure to fulfil individual's needs; frustration responses; unwillingness to consider change, little chance for learning and development *Counselling, role analysis, career planning*	Poor job definition, task too easy or too difficult *Job restructuring/modification, redesign, enrichment, agree on key competencies*	Poor match of individual with job, poor selection or promotion, inadequate preparation and training, recognition and remuneration at variance with objectives *Personnel changes, improved selection and promotion procedures, improved training and education, bring recognition and remuneration in line with objectives*

Figure 8.7 The Pugh OD matrix

Source: from Course P679 'Planning and Managing Change', Block 4, Section 6. Copyright © The Open University.

higher levels of management, salespeople see no reason to change given their current bonus plan and many middle managers have made their jobs to suit their own needs rather than those of the organization. Problems at the inter-group level might include marketing and production arguing about the feasibility of setting up a new production line to satisfy what the marketing staff consider to be a market opportunity. Intervention is frequently required at the organizational level when an organization's structure prevents the emergence of, let alone action upon, initiatives that could be beneficial to the organization as a whole.

Beckhard and Harris (1987, p. 73) suggest the following organizational subsystems – any of which can be considered as a starting point for change:

- *Top management:* the top of the system.
- *Management-ready systems:* those groups or organizations known to be ready for change.
- *'Hurting' systems:* a special class of ready systems in which current conditions have created acute discomfort.
- *New teams or systems:* units without a history and whose tasks require a departure from old ways of operating.
- *Staff:* subsystems that will be required to assist in the implementation of later interventions.
- *Temporary project systems:* ad hoc systems whose existence and tenure are specifically defined by the change plan.

Activity 8.5

What similarities and differences can be found between Pugh's levels of analytical focus and Beckhard and Harris's list of subsystems for intervention?

In addition to the issue of where change interventions might take place, the planning of OD interventions must also take account of the degree of change needed that is the scope of the change activities. In terms of Pugh's OD matrix, this means considering whether:

(a) people's *behaviour* needs to change, and/or
(b) the *organization's structure and systems* need to change and/or
(c) the *context or the setting* needs to change.

According to Mabey and Pugh (1995, pp. 40–1):

> The first (left-hand) column is concerned with current behaviour symptoms which can be tackled directly. Since it suggests methods and changes which address the symptoms without intervening into the required system or setting, this column comprises the least radical of the development strategies. Indeed in some cases the results may not be recognized as change at all – merely as

overcoming some difficulties in the proper workings of the current system. Thus in one application, as the result of a team-building exercise with a Ward Sister and her staff, the functioning of the ward, the morale of staff, and the standard of patient care all improved. The Hospital Management Committee regarded this process not as a change, but one of getting the organization to work properly.

But it may be that this degree of intervention is not sufficient to achieve the required aims. It could be that, however improved the group atmosphere and leadership style, the group will not function well because it is not clear what the organization requires of it, adequate information to carry out the group task is not available at the appropriate time, and the tasks are inappropriately divided and poorly allocated to the members of the group. In these circumstances, the second column, concerned with organizing the required system, is the appropriate degree of intervention. This is a greater degree of intervention because it may require change in the structure, systems, information flows, job design, etc., which inevitably affects a much wider range of the 'organizational environment' of the particular group.

Even this degree of intervention may be insufficient. The problems may lie in the contextual setting (changing market pressures, physical distance, poor group composition, poor promotion procedures, etc.). Then the degree of intervention in the third (right-hand) column is appropriate. This is a still greater degree of intervention requiring strategy changes, considerable expenditure of resources (both financial and human), and carrying with it greater likelihood of disruption with its attendant costs. It is not, therefore, to be undertaken lightly.

Mabey and Pugh go on to say that, as action moves from the left through to the right-hand column, a greater degree of intervention and commitment is required. Consequently, they suggest starting at the left column of the matrix and moving towards the right only as it becomes necessary because of the dictates of the problem. Activity 8.6 offers an opportunity to become more familiar with the content of the matrix and how it might be used in planning change.

Activity 8.6

The best way to understand the Pugh OD matrix is to apply its different 'cells' to a real organizational example.

Choose a situation from your own experience where a need for change has been established.

Go through the matrix and note which cells are appropriate for starting interventions that will help in the change process.

If you find this too difficult to start with, look at the following list of organizational problems and activities and note in which of the Pugh matrix cell(s) you would place them.

1 *The accounts department who 'lived' on the top floor always seemed to be at loggerheads with the research and development team who were 'housed' in an outside annex.*

2 *Since the redundancies, which were mentioned wherever you went in the organization, people were moaning about the amount of work they had to do and the lack of recognition of this by senior management.*

3 *The staff in the post room appeared bored with their jobs. Admittedly, the work was rather repetitious.*

4 *It took too long to get an answer to queries, because the boss had always to be informed.*

5 *The members of the project group felt abandoned and without leadership.*

As stated earlier, the process of developing an action plan for change should be done through consultation and collaboration with those who will implement the change, thus reinforcing commitment to change. Beckhard and Harris's (1987, p. 72) concept of the action plan being a 'road map' for the change effort is a useful one. In addition, they say that an effective action plan should have the following characteristics:

● *Relevance*: activities are clearly linked to the change goals and priorities.
● *Specificity*: activities are clearly identified rather than broadly generalized.
● *Integration*: the parts are closely connected.
● *Chronology*: there is a logical sequence of events.
● *Adaptability*: there are contingency plans for adjusting to unexpected forces.

The last of these characteristics is particularly important. As anyone knows, it is all well and good setting out on a journey with the route well defined beforehand. However, because of the many things that exist to thwart the best-laid plans (in the case of the journey: traffic, passenger sickness, road works, accidents and so on), the plan must be flexible enough to adapt to the changing circumstances of not only *what* needs to change, but also possible changes in the transition process itself. Consequently, as Figure 8.3 shows, the development of an action plan must always be linked closely to its subsequent implementation.

Stage 4: Implement the change

Any text dealing specifically with organization development as a change methodology contains details of different techniques and methods for initiating and implementing change (see, for instance, French and Bell, 1999; Cummings and Worley, 2009). For the present purposes, the activities in italics in the Pugh OD matrix in Figure 8.7 can be used to illustrate ways of initiating organizational change. As the matrix illustrates, these relate to the different levels of analytical focus and the scope of the change activities. The following gives additional details of those activities. It should be noted however that, because these activities are mainly concerned with the behaviour column of the matrix, it *does not mean* that they are, necessarily, any more important than the activities concerned with structure and context. They are selected for further explanation simply because they may not be as familiar as some of the others.

Survey feedback

Surveys can be used to assess the attitudes and morale of people across the organization and are used at different stages in the OD process. At the implementation stage they are important for the effective management of the change. Feedback from surveys of those involved in the change activities helps stimulate discussion of what is working and what is not and should result in modifications to the action plan or the way it is being implemented or, sometimes, to a reorientation of the vision.

For example, Lloyd's of London, one of the City's prestigious financial institutions, carried out an employee opinion survey on the progress of a large-scale change programme, the results of which were fed back to the staff involved for further discussion and appropriate action. Clarke, Hooper and Nicholson (1997, p. 29), writing about this, say:

> The process was designed to demonstrate to people that the corporation was not just saying: 'Your views are important', but that it actually meant it. Not only was the management team prepared to listen, it would also distribute the results openly and honestly. More importantly it would act on the views expressed. Sophisticated timetabling, communications, objective-setting and measurement ensured that this happened.

The survey was repeated 18 months later to identify progress on actions resulting from the first survey.

Organizational mirroring

'The organization mirror is a set of activities in which a particular organizational group, the host group, gets feedback from representatives from several other organizational groups about how it is perceived and regarded' (French and Bell, 1999, p. 186). Organizational mirroring is different from interventions at the inter-group level, being concerned with relationships between three or more groups. It is a technique that benefits from the services of a change consultant who is not connected with any of the groups involved in the process. A 'fishbowl' technique is frequently used as part of organizational mirroring. This is where the group asking for feedback (the host group) first sits and listens to what the other group representatives have to say (without interruption). The representatives of the host group and the other group then exchange places to allow the host group to have their say (ask for clarification, information, etc.) without interruption. Finally, the representatives of both groups are divided into small sets to work together on problems that emerge before all coming together to devise action plans, assign people to tasks and set target dates for improvements to be completed.

The techniques of survey feedback are most frequently associated with gaining information on people's attitudes and behaviour. It should not be forgotten, however, that other types of information gathering will be just as important – for instance with regard to progress against financial and other quantifiable measures of organizational performance.

Inter-group confrontation (with third-party assistance)

Although a technique of 'confrontation' sounds alarming it enables two groups, which have their unique specialties, to confront organizational issues that go beyond their particular expertise. Mabey and Pugh suggest that an exercise such as this might require two days of work away from distractions and be helped by a 'neutral' facilitator. The objective is to help the members of the two groups increase their awareness of the importance of each other's activities to the overall organizational performance and thus reduce a sense of 'them and us'.

French and Bell and Mabey and Pugh suggest a process where each group is asked to produce two lists. The first is the complaints 'we' have against 'them'. The second is the complaints that 'we' think 'they' would have about 'us'. Lists are then shared between the two groups. According to Mabey and Pugh, two characteristics usually emerge. First, some of the complaints can be dissolved fairly quickly, being the result of simple misunderstandings or lack of communication. Second, the lists of both groups show a surprising degree of congruency; in other words 'we' know what they think about 'us' and 'they' know what we think about 'them'. The lists form the basis for further discussion and exploration of how conflict can be resolved and more positive working relationships established.

Role negotiation

Role negotiation is a technique developed by Harrison (1972). Basically it involves individuals or groups negotiating to 'contract' to change their behaviour on a *quid pro quo* basis. In general it requires the help of a facilitator and (typically) during a day's workshop session, each set of participants is asked to say what they want the others to *do more of, do less of or maintain unchanged*. A follow-up meeting a month or so later assesses progress and, if necessary, renews or sets up new contracts. It is important to note that this *does not* involve probing people's likes and dislikes about each other. It concentrates solely on the roles they play and their behaviour as part of these.

Process consultation

Schein (1998) regards process consultation (PC) as a central part of organizational development. According to French and Bell (1999, p. 164): 'The crux of this approach is that a skilled third party (consultant) works with individuals and groups to help them learn about human and social processes and learn to solve problems that stem from process events.' The kinds of interventions that are part of process consultation are: agenda-setting; feedback of observational data; coaching and counselling of individuals and suggestions about group membership; communication and interaction patterns; allocation of work, responsibilities and lines of authority. French and Bell say (p. 163):

> The process consultation model is similar to team-building interventions and intergroup team-building interventions except that in PC greater emphasis is placed on diagnosing and understanding process events. Furthermore there is more emphasis on the consultant being more nondirective and questioning as he or she gets the groups to solve their own problems.

French and Bell imply, in this discussion, that the consultant is someone external to the organization. This process, however, is also essential for internal change agents with the recognition that greater effort might be needed in order to undertake 'nondirective questioning'.

Team building

Team building is an essential part of the OD process. Individuals working together do so in many different ways – not all of which contribute to team effectiveness. Consequently issues such as the overall size of the team, the characteristics of its members, the focus and direction of the team and its role within the organization are important. In situations of change any or all of these might also need to change. Team changing and team building techniques can help in this.

Team building techniques can be used for established long-term groups as well as for special, shorter-term project groups. Processes included in team building are:

(a) diagnosis of the task together with individuals' and group needs;
(b) diagnosis and negotiation of roles;
(c) responsibility charting;
(d) understanding and managing group processes and culture.

Usually a change agent or independent consultant/facilitator is used to help in team building.

Life and career planning

There are a number of exercises that can help in career planning, which is part of life planning. One is to draw a lifeline representing the past, present and future. Past events are positioned according to important things that have happened in life, including things done well and things done not so well – 'ups' as well as 'downs'. Future desired events are also recorded on the line, and some indication is given of time of achievement. Another exercise is to write one's obituary as if death were to occur now and then as if death were some years in the future. The last exercise is intended to give some idea of what is hoped for in the near and far future. The use of a life coach or mentor can be helpful in the application of these techniques.

Activity 8.7

Think back to the change which you identified for Activity 8.4. Which of the techniques (at any level or scope) in Pugh's OD matrix were used as the change was implemented? Were they appropriate?

The role of short-term wins

Implementing change that will ultimately transform an organization is a *long-term process* and it is understandable if commitment to the vision becomes somewhat weakened on the way. Consequently the achievement of 'short-term wins' (Kotter, 1996) is important, both as a motivating factor and as a mechanism for tracking the progress towards the longer-term goals. However, Kotter (1996, p. 123) goes further than this in identifying six ways in which short-term wins can help organizational transformations. These are:

- *Provide evidence that sacrifices are worth it:* wins greatly help justify the short-term costs involved.
- *Reward change agents with a pat on the back:* after a lot of hard work, positive feedback builds morale and motivation.
- *Help fine-tune vision and strategies:* short-term wins give the guiding coalition concrete data on the viability of their ideas.
- *Undermine cynics and self-serving resistors:* clear improvements in performance make it difficult for people to block needed change.
- *Keep bosses on board:* provides those higher in the hierarchy with evidence that the transformation is on track.
- *Build momentum:* turns neutrals into supporters, reluctant supporters into active helpers, etc.

Short-term wins do not, however, happen automatically as part of the change process. They have to be planned *deliberately* so that they become much more probabilities than possibilities. According to Kotter (pp. 121–122), a short-term win has three characteristics:

1 It is visible: large numbers of people can see for themselves whether the result is real or just hype.
2 It is unambiguous: there can be little argument over the call.
3 It is clearly related to the change effort.

An example of a short-term win is when a company reduces delivery time on one of its main products by a predetermined percentage in a predetermined time; or when the number of customer complaints reduces by (say) 50 per cent during the first half of the year; or when the jobs of a group of employees become easier to do because they are getting more relevant information in a more timely way. Short-term wins are not targets, for example, 'We expect to increase our sales in the next couple of months'; neither is the fact that two previously sworn enemies are now talking pleasantly to each other a short-term win, unless the outcome is some further improvement in morale and organizational performance.

The setting and assessment of short-term wins links the implementation stage of the OD process to the more all-embracing assessment of the organization's progress towards its vision and the continuing reinforcement of the change process itself.

Stage 5: Assess and reinforce the change

Assessing change

In organizational situations of hard complexity it is relatively easy to assess the extent to which change has been achieved. So the setting of 'hard' objectives and quantifiable performance measures makes this a more straightforward process. However, in the softer, more 'messy' situations where change methodologies of the OD type tend to be used, change is an evolving process concerned not only with changes in quantifiable performance objectives, but more frequently with changes in attitudes, behaviours and cultural norms where measurement is bound to be less precise. Even so, measurement of these things is possible. It is also desirable in terms of its role in providing positive feedback that the change process is 'working' and in testing how far the organization has moved towards achievement of its vision.

A number of ways are available for measuring the softer issues associated with change:

1 *A survey or cultural audit*, which can potentially cover all staff. Its results can be quantified and quickly disseminated. The audit can be done at regular intervals to provide repeated snapshot measures of an organization's progress towards its change objectives. The Nationwide Building Society is an example of an organization that uses such a system as part of its commitment to continuous improvement.

2 *Interviews with individuals or focus groups*, which allow the collection of more qualitative, in-depth information. An example of testing what a company's vision and values statement meant to staff was the exercise carried out by The Body Shop just after a public challenge to its integrity regarding its stance of being socially responsible in its policies and practices. The Body Shop called it 'gazing into the mirror'. It consisted of 44 meetings, each with 20 different staff and managers from all parts of the organization. All the meetings were attended by a board member and a moderator who later summarized the discussions to produce a report of the main themes arising and subsequent recommendations for action.

3 *An examination of turnover and absenteeism rates* as an indication of general morale and well-being.

4 *An analysis (through observation or questionnaire) of group performance* in terms of task achievement, but also in terms of the quality of meetings (including number of meetings and length) and leader performance.

5 '*Re-picturing the organization*', that is, asking staff to re-draw any rich pictures that they might have produced at stages (1(a))/(1b) of the OD process (see Figure 8.3). Re-picturing might also include the use of metaphors in line with those suggested by Morgan (1997) in Chapter 4 or Flood and Jackson (1991) (see Stage 1b earlier in this chapter). In contrast to the pictures and metaphors that depict the pre-change situation, the rich pictures that are drawn at this stage in the change process should relate more closely to the change vision. If this proves to be so, then management can have some confidence that the change has been successful in respect of how employees feel about it.

Reinforcing and consolidating change

Farquhar, Evans and Tawadey (1989, p. 49) noted that, 'A real danger in the process of organizational change is the failure to carry it through sufficiently far. Companies may be tempted to relax when the immediate crisis recedes while they still have not addressed the deeper organizational problems which generated the crisis.' The lesson from this is that the new order resulting from any change needs to be institutionalized. This is well put by Mabey and Pugh (1995, p. 50):

> Individuals need to be held personally accountable for prescribed initiatives; new working relationships and boundaries between different working groups need to be negotiated; ways of recognizing and rewarding desirable behaviours and attitudes need to be devised to demonstrate that the organization is serious about the change strategies that have been set.

It is pointless expecting people's behaviour to change if this is not reinforced by concomitant changes in personnel policies and practices, including appraisal, career development and reward systems. In addition, staff training and development needs to reorient itself to the needs of the new vision and the changes that help guide its attainment. According to Farquhar *et al.* this is particularly important with regard to middle managers. While change can happen fast at the top (often through bringing in new people) and be accepted at the lower levels of an organization (particularly if the rewards for change are clear), middle managers, who perform the bridging function between the two, may be slower to accept new cultures, policies and practices. Yet it is middle management that must make change work. They must, therefore, be given the new skills they will need – particularly when structures and cultures are expected to change.

More generally, the action–research model of data collection, data analysis and feedback for action is just as important at this stage of OD as at any other. Any change programme is stressful, but if employees continue to *own* change this stress will become not negative stress but, rather, positive pressure to accept that change can be the norm, with the adoption of innovative, change-oriented behaviour.

An assessment of the OD model for change

The model of OD presented here departs to some extent from early OD models that emphasized mainly the attitudinal and behavioural aspects of organizational life and gave insufficient attention to aspects such as strategy, structure, technology and, in particular, the needs of customers or clients, let alone shareholders, and the financial environment within which most organizations operate. Not only has it drawn from these earlier models, but it has used elements of other, more directive change models such as Kotter's (1996, Part 2) eight-stage change process and Paton and McCalman's (2008, p. 12) model of perpetual transition management.

Even so, organization development as a philosophy and a process can be critiqued according to a number of criticisms. The following are examples.

OD does not always face up to harsh realities of change

Almost all models of change include, in one form or another, the underlying concept of unfreezing. From an OD point of view this would be achieved through a typical action–research process of data collection, analysis and feedback as part of a participatory process of education for change. Yet authors such as Clarke (1994) and Johnson (1990) describe this process of unfreezing in much harsher terms.

Clarke (pp. 147–148) talks of 'speeding up the unfreezing process' through *destabilizing* people to detach them from the old order. She quotes the example of Centraal Beheer, an insurance company in the Netherlands, 'creating an anxiety greater than the risk of doing something different'. She goes on to say (p. 149): 'Pent-up anger and discontent are the motivators for change; no significant change is possible without them.' Clarke talks the language of crisis and even of engineering a crisis in order to speed up the unfreezing process.

Johnson (p. 190) goes further than Clarke with his talk of 'symbolic acts of questioning or destruction' to start the unfreezing process. He gives examples of John de Lorean trying to change his division of General Motors by promulgating stories to ridicule the dominant culture and of Lee Iacocca firing 33 out of 35 vice-presidents within three years of taking over at Chrysler. Johnson continues this line of thinking by saying (p. 190): 'As conflict and debate grows, managers may actually foster it by symbolic acts of conflict, destruction and degradation.'

However, care must be taken that crisis is not seen merely as a threat and, as Ferlie and Bennett (1993) point out, paradoxically reduces energy, creativity and flexibility. From an OD point of view crisis would be seen as an opportunity that, in Ferlie and Bennett's (p. 270) words, 'forces awkward issues up the

agendas [when] we are likely to see continuing pressure from pioneers, the formation of special groups who evangelize the rest of the organization, high
energy and commitment levels, and a period of organizational plasticity in
which anything seems plausible'.

Alternatively, as Farquhar *et al.* (1989, p. 37) point out: 'Not all companies see
crisis as a prerequisite for major organizational change.' Triggers for change
could come from the aspirations of top management, perhaps through anxiety
about an uncertain future including a downturn in results or fear for their own
positions. Monitoring the internal and external organizational environments on
a regular basis can detect potential crises in their early and most treatable
phases. What needs to be recognized is that change without crisis is most frequently incremental and time is needed to build the momentum for larger-scale,
more radical change.

OD is limited when change situations are 'constrained'

OD has been promoted as a change model for coping with situations of soft
complexity where goals and also the means of achieving them are unclear.
However, there are situations which have many of the characteristics of soft
complexity yet are constrained in the sense that the goals are predetermined
and the means of achieving them are to some extent set. In other words change
is dictated by top management or the precise requirements of some part of the
organization's external environment. For instance, healthcare is proscribed by
the need to safeguard the public against malpractice and legislation regarding
the use of treatments and drugs. Setting up a new doctor's practice must adhere
to many different forms of regulatory requirement. Franchisees must often run
their businesses according to the dictates of the franchiser.

It may be, of course, that, when change is desirable, a hard systems model of
change is most appropriate. However, 'dictated' or 'forced choice' change is
likely to bring resistance from those who must implement it. Therefore,
although the earlier stages of the OD model may not be applicable, there is still
the requirement to develop an action plan, and implement, assess and reinforce
change. In addition, gaining commitment to, and participation in, this part of
the change process by those who must make the change is of the utmost importance. Consequently, even in highly constrained situations of change,
implementation must be as collaboratively executed as in any other OD process.

OD requires 'out of the ordinary' leadership

Over many years of teaching MBA students and asking them to identify what
leadership style they use or aspire to use, transformational leadership (see
Chapter 6) is the one that gets named most often. Very few said they aspired to
be authoritative, coercive or directive. However, the culture of many organizations makes it difficult to involve others continuously whilst trying to manage

medium and large-scale change. Some leaders do not have the personality or persistence that prepares them for the 'long haul' of frame-breaking change. Couple this with what Coghlan and Brannick (2007) term *denial* that change is required or relevant, and *dodging*, which is an effort to divert the change, then an argument could be made that a more directive style of leadership is needed.

In her account of leading the change in the Regional College of Psychiatric Nursing, the Director comments that her original plan to be a distributive leader (see Chapter 6) had to be reassessed as her staff went through a period of resistance to what they envisaged happening to their roles and identities. Leading change is itself a complex process and the skill is not always to be a transformational leader but to know when to use one style of leadership compared to another.

OD fits uneasily with the structures and culture in the public sector

Burns and Stalker (1961) illustrated the differences between mechanistic and organic organizational structures (see Chapter 3) and an organic structure, rather than a mechanistic structure, is more suited to organizations embracing an OD model of change. Consequently the application of OD in the mechanistically structured, bureaucratic organizations that are typical of governmental and publicly accountable organizations can be a problem. Writing on organizational development in the public sector, McConkie (1993, pp. 634–642), from a North American perspective but one that applies generally, discusses a number of reasons why the application of OD in public sector organizations is likely to give rise to problems. These, together with others, are the following:

1 The basic philosophical differences between the assumptions and values of OD and those of the bureaucratic model (which is typical of most public sector organizations) are significant because public sector organizations typically reflect strong adherence to bureaucratic norms and behaviour patterns – forms and patterns foreign to those of OD – therefore making OD application difficult and sensitive, though not impossible.

2 Public sector organizations have multiple authoritative decision makers and multilevel accountability and reporting relationships. They are also 'supervised' by many interests, such as the general public, other government agencies, interest groups, the media and so on. All these make it difficult, first, to get support and gain approvals for an OD initiative and, second, to guide OD designs to fruition because so many people and interests 'get in the way'.

3 Financial support is difficult to obtain for OD work in public sector organizations. This is because, first, funding for consultancy (i.e. external change agents) is limited compared with that available in the private sector and, second, so many different people have to agree to the spending of funds.

4 In public sector organizations the large variety of different and frequently conflicting interests, different political allegiances, reward structures and values make OD, as a system-wide effort, difficult to apply. OD interventions

are, therefore, more likely to be of a small-scale nature in single departments or work groups.

5 McConkie (p. 640) drawing on Golembiewski (1989), says: 'Five aspects of the public "habit background" . . . make it an inhospitable host for OD: public patterns of delegation, the legal habit, the need for security, the procedural regularity and caution, and the developing image of the "professional manager".'

6 Decision making in public sector organizations tends to be pushed upwards towards the top. This contrasts with OD objectives that seek to increase self-control and self-direction of organization members, something which is difficult if decisions must always be passed to upper levels of management. What is more, deciding where the 'top' is can be confusing. It might be the highest level of the administration, but it may be necessary also to take account of elected and appointed political interests – which may be at both local and national level. The generally accepted assumption that OD-type interventions should have the support of top management and, frequently, should be led by them, sits uneasily with the realization that, in some instances, for political reasons the top may not want to be seen to be involved.

These points paint a depressing picture for the likelihood that OD models for change could succeed in public sector organizations. However, as the public sector has moved towards market principles OD models for change become more realistic and easier to apply. Indeed, because of the extreme complexity of these organizations and the massive changes they have to face, change models that do not take account of the soft, messy situations they face have little likelihood of succeeding.

Illustration 8.7 is an extract from the 'Employers' Organization for Local Government' website where it makes the case for the use of OD in the context of the large-scale changes faced by institutions of local government in the United Kingdom.

Illustration 8.7

Making sense of change – saying goodbye to 'initiative fatigue'

Why should we be interested in Organisation Development?

Councils are facing unrelenting pressure to provide better quality services at a time when they are under unprecedented scrutiny. The introduction of the corporate governance and capacity assessment presents a further challenge, not least because it comes on top of other government initiatives, such as best value.

Change initiatives often fail because organisations try to implement a number of activities too quickly and without proper coordination or thought about the implications for people management. This leads to 'initiative fatigue' where staff become disillusioned and more resistant to change.

Many authorities are beginning to consider the importance of Organisation Development as part of preparing for e-government. So far, there has generally been more emphasis on ICT, systems and the use of technical experts, yet more than 50 per cent of ICT projects fail because of cultural or organisational problems. E-government will demand support at the top and people with organisational development expertise helping to plan and implement ICT and related changes strategically throughout the local authority.

During recent years 'Organisation Development' (OD) has re-emerged as a key element in the strategic management of change, providing a focus for the cultural and organisational change needed for continuous improvement, aligning systems, culture and activities to the achievement of organisational goals. It enables better use of financial, human and technological resources, fosters a greater sense of organisational purpose and it is therefore more likely to deliver the required performance improvement.

What sorts of activities are integral to Organisation Development?

These include linking OD with council objectives, finding and developing staff with the right skills to help champion OD throughout the organisation and encouraging wide participation and ownership of the continuous improvement process among staff and elected members. Building in this perspective at the beginning will mean that changes are grounded and sustainable, with people

management considerations integrated into the process.

Where is Organisation Development located within local authorities?

In principle OD can be located anywhere in an authority structure, though recent research shows that where posts are located within the Chief Executives' Department there is closer liaison and a more flexible organisational response to wide-ranging demands. But wherever the function is located there are a wide range of behaviours, skills and knowledge that will be needed across the organisation.

Taking it forward – What next for you?

- Have you got commitment and involvement at the top of the organisation?
- Is there someone in your organisation who is coordinating OD activities?
- Have you got a 'map' of the OD activities happening in your organisation?

Source: This is an extract from the local government employer's organization website that appeared in 2006. The site address is no longer available. However, the sentiments expressed appear to be relevant to organizations in the public sector now.

More recently, Parkes (2008, p. 44), director of HR and OD at Croydon Council, discusses how the council Human Resources OD consultancy team brought about change to reduce sickness levels across the council workforce. Parkes notes that, what was then a newly formed team learnt a number of lessons for the future. These include:

- Make sure you have a strong leadership from the top.
- Involve managers in setting the policy – don't just impose it upon them.
- Be consistent in your approach right across the organization.
- Train everyone you need to in what is expected from them.
- Accurate, timely communications are essential so people understand what you are trying to achieve.
- Stick at it and don't give up.

OD does not 'work' in all cultures

This chapter and Chapter 7 have described at least three ways of designing and implementing organizational change and ways of dealing with resistance and conflict have been addressed. What must be recognized, however, is the predominantly western bias of much that is written about organizations and change. Consequently, not all change methods and techniques are transportable across national boundaries or even to different ethnic groupings within single countries (Adler, 2007; Jaegar, 1986). This is particularly the case with the range of techniques associated with OD as a philosophy and a methodology for bringing about change.

In an extensive discussion of organizational development and national culture, Jaegar links typical OD values with each of Hofstede's (1980) dimensions of culture and concludes that they have a low correspondence with high power distance, high uncertainty avoidance, high masculinity and moderate individualism. Consequently, some OD-type interventions will struggle to be accepted in societies that score highly on these dimensions.

The title of Jack's (1997) article 'Caste in stone' and his comment, 'Challenge French corporate hierarchies at your peril', say much of French managers' attitudes to the participative styles of leadership that are typical of OD approaches to change.

One consequence of these reservations about the degree to which OD approaches can be used wherever change occurs is that there is a need for OD-type techniques to vary according to whether an organization operates in what Keegan (1989) terms an *ethnocentric* or *geocentric* way. Organizations with an ethnocentric orientation are those that tend to offer a standard product across the world and operate with centralized decision making from the home country base. Managers, wherever they are located, are usually chosen from home country nationals on the basis that operations and ways of managing 'abroad' should mirror those in the home base.

By contrast, organizations with a geocentric orientation accept that things might be done differently in different countries. Consequently, although there is still a degree of overall centralized coordination of activities, products, operations and methods of management are tailored to the different conditions in each country. In this type of organization, instead of managers being 'sent out' (e.g. as expatriates) from the home country, the organization trains and develops host country managers to operate in a decentralized, mainly autonomous way.

The consequences of this distinction are that similar approaches to change are more likely to be used in ethnocentrically operated organizations than those that organize on geocentric principles where approaches to change are more likely to be tailored to the cultures in which they are being used. Cummings and Worley's (2009) extensive discussion of the application of OD in different parts of the world demonstrates how the cultural context in which organizations exist has to be considered when any change process is proposed.

Having noted these views, globalization of business and trade in recent years has brought, to a considerable extent, a conversion of strategies and ways that organizations operate. Global communications allow the transfer of ideas and processes found to be effective in one environment to be tried in another. Consequently, there are many OD techniques that can be used in spite of there existing less than propitious attitudes and beliefs on the part of those involved. Citing Harrison (1972), French and Bell (1999) use the concept of 'depth of intervention' to distinguish those techniques that interact mainly with the more formalized organizational systems (such as job enrichment, management by objectives, role analysis and attitude surveys) and those that go deeper into exploring the informal and more personal organizational systems – for instance team building, encounter groups and interpersonal relationship explorations. Depth of intervention is a useful concept for deciding how 'deep' to go in the use of OD-type interventions as part of the process of change that involves people from different cultures. It is particularly relevant for those organizations that operate outside their home country environment.

Conclusions

Soft systems models for change, of which OD is a well-known example, contrast with hard systems in being able to address the issues of soft complexity inherent in 'messy' situations. Soft systems approaches to change emphasize not just the content and control of change but also the *process* by which change comes about. They require consideration of the cultural and political aspects of organizations as much as the structure and systems. 'Change agents' facilitating change using these approaches require influencing skills and the skills of negotiation. Because different individuals respond to their different *perceptions* of events, which will differ one from another, change agents need to understand the aspirations and feelings of those working in change situations as well as the group processes that bind them together.

Soft systems models of change are, essentially, *planned* approaches to change. This does not mean, however, that they cannot account for unexpected and surprising events. Indeed the requirement to iterate frequently around and across the different phases and stages of the model takes account of the probability that there will be 'changes within changes' occurring. Taken together, hard and soft systems models of change offer those working with change ways of addressing issues in their simplicity and complexity to enhance the work of organizations and the lives of those working in them.

Discussion questions and assignments

1 Debate the pros and cons of using external change agents compared to internal ones.

2 Compare and contrast the HSMC and OD approaches to change. Give examples of types of change situations where each may be appropriate.

3 Draw a rich picture of life as experienced by you in your organization.

4 If your manager is looking for a 'quick fix' to manage a change process, how might you justify using an OD approach to change?

Indicative resources

Cummings, T. and Worley, C. (2009) *Organization Development and Change* (9th edn), Mason, OH: Thomson South-Western. Part of this is dedicated to the effective implementation of OD and how it can be used in both public and private sectors. There are numerous case studies as examples of issues associated with OD and applications of it in a variety of organizations.

French, W.L. and Bell, C.H. (1999) *Organization Development* (6th edn), Upper Saddler River, NJ; Prentice-Hall. French and Bell have dedicated much of their time to promoting and educating in the field of OD. This text offers a good introduction to OD and guidance in using this approach.

Useful websites

www.actionlearningassociates.co.uk This site is helpful for those who have further interest in action learning. It provides a working definition, offers examples of how action learning can be used, how the groups operate and how to use 'in-house' sets for the purposes of OD.

www.ifal.org.uk This is the UK's official action learning site.

To click straight to these links and for other resources go to **www.pearsoned.co.uk/senior**

References

Ackoff, R.L. (1993) 'The Art and Science of Mess Management', in Mabey, C. and Mayon-White, B. (eds) *Managing Change*, London: PCP.

Adler, N.J. (2007) *International Dimensions of Organizational Behavior*, Cincinnati, OH: South-Western College Publishing, ITP.

Alpander, G.G. and Lee, C.R. (1995) 'Culture, Strategy and Teamwork: the keys to organizational change', *Journal of Management Development*, 14(8), pp. 4–18.

Argyris, C. (1964) *Integrating the Individual and the Organization*, New York: Wiley.

Argyris, C. (1992) *On Organizational Learning*, Oxford: Blackwell.

Argyris, C. and Schon, D. A. (1996) *Organizational Learning II*, Reading, MA: Addison-Wesley.

Balogun, J. and Hope Hailey, V. (2008) *Exploring Strategic Change* (3rd edn), Harlow: Financial Times Prentice Hall.

Beckhard, R. and Harris, R.T. (1987) *Organizational Transitions: Managing Complex Change* (2nd edn), Reading, MA: Addison-Wesley.

Benjamin, G. and Mabey, C. (1993) 'Facilitating Radical Change: a case of organization transformation', in Mabey, C. and Mayon-White, B. (eds) *Managing Change* (2nd edn), London: PCP.

Buchanan, D. and Boddy, D. (1992) *The Expertise of the Change Agent: Public Performance and Backstage Activity*, Hemel Hempstead: Prentice Hall.

Buchanan, D. and McCalman, J. (1989) *High Performance Work Systems: The Digital Experience*, London: Routledge.

Burnes, B. (2004) *Managing Change: A Strategic Approach to Organisational Dynamics* (4th edn), Harlow: Financial Times Prentice Hall.

Burns, T. and Stalker, G.M. (1961) *The Management of Innovation*, London: Tavistock.

Burnside, R.M. (1991) 'Visioning: building pictures of the future', in Henry, J. and Walker, D. (eds) *Managing Innovation*: London: Sage.

Carnall, C. (2007) *Managing Change in Organizations* (5th edn), Harlow: Pearson Education.

Checkland, P. (1981) *Systems Thinking, Systems Practice*, Chichester: Wiley.

Clarke, J., Hooper, C. and Nicholson, J. (1997) 'Reversal of Fortune', *People Management*, 20 March, pp. 22–26, 29.

Clarke, L. (1994) *The Essence of Change*, Hemel Hempstead: Prentice Hall.

Coghlan, D. and Brannick, T. (2007) *Action Research in Your Own Organization* (2nd edn), London: Sage.

Cummings, T.G. and Worley, C.G. (2009) *Organization Development and Change* (9th edn), Mason, OH: South-Western.

Elkjaar, B. (1999) 'In Search of a Social Learning Theory', in Easterby-Smith, M., Burgoyne, J. and Araujo, L. (eds) *Organizational Learning and the Learning Organization: Development in Theory and Practice*, London: Sage, pp. 75–91.

Farquhar, A., Evans, P. and Tawadey, K. (1989) 'Lessons from Practice in Managing Organizational Change', in Evans, P., Doz, E. and Laurent, A. (eds) *Human Resource Management in International Firms: Change, Globalization, Innovation*, London: Macmillan.

Ferlie, E. and Bennett, C. (1993) 'Patterns of Strategic Change in Health Care: district health authorities respond to AIDS', in Hendry, J., Johnson, G. and Newton, J. (eds) *Strategic Thinking, Leadership and the Management of Change*, Chichester: Wiley.

Flood, R.L. (1995) *Solving Problem Solving: a Potent Source for Effective Management,* Chichester: Wiley.

Flood, R.L. and Jackson, M.C. (1991) *Creative Problem Solving: Total Systems Intervention*, Chichester: Wiley.

French, W.L. and Bell, C.H. (1999) *Organization Development: Behavioural Science Interventions for Organizational Improvement* (6th edn), Upper Saddle River, NJ: Prentice-Hall.

Golembiewski, R.T. (1989) *Organizational Development: Ideas and Issues*, New Brunswick: Transaction Publishers.

Goodstein, L.D. and Burke, W.W. (1993) 'Creating Successful Organization Change', in Mabey, C. and Mayon-White, B. (eds) *Managing Change*, London: PCP.

Harrison, R. (1972) 'When Power Conflicts Trigger Team Spirit', *European Business*, Spring, pp. 27–65.

Hofstede, G. (1980) *Culture's Consequences: International Differences in Work-related Values*, London and Beverley Hills, CA: Sage.

Jack, A. (1997) 'Caste in Stone: challenge to French corporate hierarchies at your peril', *Financial Times*, 10 April.

Jacobs, B. (2004) 'Using Soft Systems Methodology for Performance Improvement and Organisational Change in the English Health Service', *Journal of Contingencies and Crisis Management,* 12(4), December, pp. 138–149.

Jaegar, A.M. (1986) 'Organization Development and National Culture: where's the fit?' *Academy of Management Review*, 11(1), pp. 178–190.

Johnson, G. (1990) 'Managing strategic action; the role of symbolic action', *British Journal of Management*, vol. 1, pp. 183–200.

Johnson, G. (1993) 'Processes of Managing Strategic Change', in Mabey, C. and Mayon-White, B. (eds) *Managing Change* (2nd edn), London: PCP.

Johnson, G., Scholes, K. and Whittington, R. (2008) *Exploring Corporate Strategy Texts and Cases* (8th edn), Harlow: Financial Times Prentice Hall.

Jones, P. (1994) 'Which Lever Do I Pull Now?: the role of "emergent planning" in managing change', *Organisations & People*, vol. 1, no. 1, January, pp. 46–49.

Keegan, W.J. (1989) 'International-multinational-global Marketing: a typology', Chapter 1 in Keegan, W. J. (ed.) *Global Marketing Management* (4th edn), Englewood Cliffs, NJ: Prentice-Hall.

Kotter, J.P. (1996) *Leading Change*, Boston, MA: Harvard Business School Press.

Laurent, A. (1983) 'The Cultural Diversity of Western Conceptions of Management', *International Studies of Management and Organisations*, XIII(1–2): pp. 78–96.

Lewin, K. (1951) *Field Theory in Social Science*, New York: Harper & Row.

Lievegoed, B. (1983) *Man on the Threshold*, Driebergen: Hawthorne Press.

Lloyd, B. and Feigen, M. (1997) 'Real Change Leaders: the key challenge to management today', *Leadership & Organization Development Journal*, (1): pp. 37–40.

Mabey, C. and Pugh, D. (1995) Unit 10, 'Strategies for Managing Complex Change', Course B751, *Managing Development and Change*, Milton Keynes: Open University Press.

Matsushita, K. (1988) 'The Secret is Shared', *Manufacturing Engineering*, March, pp. 78–84.

McConkie, M.L. (1993) 'Organization Development in the Public Sector', in Cummings, T.G. and Worley, C.G., *Organization Development and Change* (5th edn), St. Paul, MN: West.

Morgan, G. (1997) *Images of Organization*, London: Sage.

Open University (1985) Unit 8, 'Process', Course T244, *Managing in Organizations*, Milton Keynes: Open University Press.

Parkes, P. (2008) 'How I Make a Difference at Work', *People Management*, August, p. 44.

Paton, R.A. and McCalman, J. (2008) *Change Management: A Guide to Effective Implementation* (3rd edn), London: Sage.

Pedler, M., Boydell, T. and Burgoyne, J. (1991) *The Learning Company*, London: McGraw-Hill.

Phillips, L. (2007) 'Skills Training for OD Specialists? That's a bright idea', *People Management*, November, p. 12.

Price, C. (1987) 'Culture Change: the tricky bit', *Training and Development*, October, pp. 20–22.

Pugh, D. (1986) Block 4, 'Planning and Managing Change', *Organizational Development*, Milton Keynes: Open University Press.

Pugh, D. (1993) 'Understanding and Managing Change', in Mabey, C. and Mayon-White, B. (eds) *Managing Change* (2nd edn), London: PCP, pp. 108–112.

Schein, E. (1998) *Process Consultation Revisited: Building the Helping Relationship*, Reading, MA: Addison-Wesley.

Senge, P. (1990) *The Fifth Discipline: The Art and Practice of the Learning Organization*, New York: Doubleday Currency.

Smith, B. (1995) 'Not in Front of the Children: the realities of "involvement" in managing change', *Organisations & People*, 2(2), pp. 17–20.

Stacey, R. (2008) *Strategic Management and Organisational Dynamics: The Challenge of Complexity* (5th edn), Harlow: Financial Times Prentice Hall.

Whitney, D. and Trosten-Bloom, A. (2003) *The Power of Appreciative Inquiry*, San Francisco, CA: Berrett-Koehler.

www.thebodyshop.co.uk

Chapter 9

Future directions and challenges

Change exists at both macro levels such as restructuring a multinational organization and at micro levels such as when individuals see their jobs being redesigned. This chapter identifies the key trends that will continue to prompt macro and micro level changes in organizations and at the effects they are having. It also looks at the act of changing and introduces the idea of organizational capacity for changing and at how people make sense of the changes going on around them.

Learning objectives

By the end of this chapter, you will be able to:

- Identify and discuss the contemporary economic and social forces that are pressuring organizations to change;

- identify and discuss organizational capacity for change;

- summarize the contributions of sensegiving, sensemaking and appreciative inquiry;

- discuss the main challenges facing change researchers.

Introduction

Part One examined the way organizations and the context in which they operate have changed throughout time and discussed how political, economic, social and technological forces impact on the way that organizations operate. The concept of organizational change was shown to be heterogeneous in that there are many types of change occurring both sequentially and simultaneously, sometimes predictable and sometimes unexpected.

Part Two elaborated on this by addressing aspects of organizational life that influence change outcomes in one way or another. Part Three introduced two major methodologies for change. Given all this it would be ideal if the overall outcome was an all-embracing, widely accepted theory of change with agreed guidelines on 'how to do it'. Unfortunately this is not the case and it seems unlikely that it ever will be.

The purpose of this final chapter is, therefore, to look more closely at the act of changing and recent thinking on how it happens and how best to catalyze it. First though, we begin by summarizing the main social and economic forces that will continue to push organizations into change.

Future organizations

Environmental forces

As we saw earlier there are many triggers of change, such as the appointment of a new top manager or falling organizational competitiveness. Over and above internal factors, external factors continue to push organizations into change situations and the major trends that will continue affecting businesses, lifestyles and social structures and which, in turn, will affect organizations, are summarized below (Arnold *et al.*, 2005; DTI, 1999).

Choice – an increase in the choice we have between home, work and leisure. As wealth increases then an increasing proportion of people can choose between leisure and work. However, the benefits of increasing choice seem unlikely to be shared equally. Increasing self-employment is a consequence of rising choice.

Falling birth rates and rising longevity – this trend is producing an older workforce, on average, with an increasing number of older people being able to, and often needing to, work past normal retirement age. There are also implications for the creation of new products and services for an ageing but relatively active population and for healthcare providers who face constantly rising demand for services within budgets that are not rising in proportion. The ageing population and higher mobility between occupations and organizations has put pressure on occupational and employer-based pension schemes. Traditional final salary schemes are being closed to new employees, increasing the pressure on people to make their own pension arrangements.

Mobility – increasing mobility, for example of workers in the European Union, has implications for the use of migrant labour which can fill skills gaps and lower labour costs. Mobility also leads to an infusion of cultural differences into the workplace.

Independence – increased freedom from traditional obligations leads to more self-centred, self-indulgent and hedonistic psychologies. This has implications for the ways employees see authority and power in organizations since increased independence is likely to lead to much higher confidence in one's own judgements and decisions, and the questioning of line management and others in authority when their decisions differ from those judgements. Management is partly about trying to control what others are doing and this basic function becomes more difficult as people become more self-aware and confident.

Creativity – increased focus on individuality and self-interest is likely to encourage personal creativity. This has implications for the quality of management – is it good enough to recognize and leverage the employee creativity that is available into the workplace? It also impacts upon the design of organizational reward systems such that they need to be flexible enough to reward and retain those employees who show innovation and creativity in the workplace but who will not be convinced by promises of promotion in the future. Reward systems traditionally geared to status and position will need greater recognition of a person's contribution than their grade.

Information and communication technology – increasing capability of ICT is enabling new forms of organization (e.g. more networked organizations) and organizing (e.g. job sharing) and is allowing management to put systems into place to increase the monitoring, control and regulation of how employees work and what they can do. ICT will continue to promote homeworking and other ways of working away from a traditional permanent and fixed place of work where this does not detract from adding value.

Technology – continuing advances in human biology and genetic engineering provide new commercial opportunities for biotechnology companies that can organize to harness knowledge and production facilities. Biotechnology is also increasing the availability of costly medical treatments that will cure or alleviate previously untreatable conditions and will put immense pressure on healthcare providers to find ways of funding them. At a broader level, changing technology impacts upon the skills that employers need from the labour market.

Social structures – changing attitudes to marriage, high levels of divorce and the viability of single parent households mean that there are higher numbers of smaller family units and this has implications for job design though flexible, temporary and part-time working arrangements particularly, although not exclusively, for women. Increasing gender and ethnic diversity in the workforce means that organizations and individuals have to adjust to new attitudes and new expectations. Where entrenched attitudes to selection, job performance and promotion exist they look set to be challenged by injections of different cultural norms.

National competitiveness – as developed economies increasingly rely on knowledge-based and service sectors for jobs and value creation, forecasts show that the UK economy at least will need more people in managerial, technical/professional and service jobs and fewer people in administrative and manual work. Outsourcing of relatively low-cost and low-skilled functions to lower-cost providers will continue. Within the context of national competitiveness organizations will be seeking structural changes through the further elimination of layers of management and reduction in workforce headcount, together with moves to increased teamwork and pressures for individuals to work harder and longer.

The changing psychological contract

The psychological contract (Rousseau and Parks, 1993; CIPD, 2004) is a framework to analyze the relationship between an employee and their employer that can be traced back to the 1960s and interest in social exchange theory. The concept attracted much attention in the 1990s as it offered a powerful way of analyzing the feelings and reactions of the victims of mergers, takeovers, redundancy, downsizing and other sometimes brutal employer behaviour witnessed at the time. These corporate changes often led to new terms and conditions of employment and Cooper (1998, p. 98) remarked that in total they added up to 'the most profound changes in the workplace since the industrial revolution'.

Rousseau and Parks (1993, p. 19) offer a clear definition of the psychological contract; the psychological contract represents 'an individual's beliefs regarding terms and conditions of a reciprocal exchange agreement between that person and another party'. For most of the time, as employees perform their normal routines, the contract usually remains hidden. However, it quickly becomes visible and expressed when it is broken or when one side feels that a breach of contract has been attempted (Sparrow, 2000, p. 171). Breaches often come about when change is attempted.

When employees grumble about something their employer (or someone they believe is one of its representatives) has said or done, this is often a reaction to the employees' perceived breach of their psychological contract. Yet each employee has a uniquely individual mental picture of their contract such that what upsets one employee may not be a problem to another. Shore and Tetrick (1994, p. 103) identify three types of contract violation.

- *Violation of distributive justice* – this could occur where an employee sees co-workers selected for development that will help their careers but is not selected themselves. Another example is where an employee's job grade is selected for job evaluation, with the risk of pay regrading, but where other grades, perhaps higher ones, are not selected.
- *Violation of procedural justice* – this occurs when the procedures leading to particular outcomes are deemed unfair. Being selected for redundancy is bad enough but if people think the manner in which they were selected was

biased it aggravates a bad situation. If an employee feels that an internal promotion opportunity was not a fair and open process and that it was a 'done deal' or was discriminatory in favour of a particular person or group, then they will perceive that procedural justice was not done.

- *Violation of interactional justice* – this happens when the ways that people are treated and informed while something is being decided or implemented are deemed unacceptable. Stories of employees receiving text messages informing them of redundancy when they are on their way to work are gross violations of interactional justice.

Minor breaches of psychological contracts are usually dealt with by use of voice, i.e., an employee talking about the breach with people who can restore the balance of exchange, e.g., a supervisor or higher manager. Goodwill can often be restored and peace returns. Major breaches of contracts lead to much more serious and sometime irretrievable reactions including retreats into negative emotional states, attribution of blame to individuals and withdrawal from the workplace. People who believe they have suffered a major violation will often leave the organization if they can. If they cannot they remain as a disgruntled and disaffected employee.

Managers involved with change need to be alert to what their organizations are doing that shape the formation of contracts. For new employees the contract begins to be formed early in recruitment when they interact with organizational literature and websites and then later in selection processes when they interact with the people they will work with in interviews or assessment centres. In the first few weeks and months of working in a new place the new employee's experiences will shape the contract they are building; the behaviour of co-workers and the stories they tell are influential. They see the performance of others and hear stories of what to do and what not to do. Performance management systems have a big impact upon expectations of work and rewards. What is the general performance climate and how well does the organization distinguish between poor, average and top performers and how are they rewarded differently?

The psychological contract therefore has a big influence on employee acceptance of change and when change is in the air managers need to be alert to how employees will perceive things. Given the pervasiveness and urgency of change today (Guest, 2004) there are implications for how organizational practices act to shape contracts. While it is far too simple to suggest that organizations can put into place experiences that will shape psychological contracts so that employees will readily accept change it is clear that certain organizational actions do act to shape contracts. Careful management of selection and socialization procedures could be used to set expectations of working life that are at least conducive to change.

Innovation

Miles *et al.* (2000) emphasize the importance of innovation and their basic message is that in the emerging era of continuous innovation, knowledge is the key asset, the exploitation of which will determine the success of many organizations. The issue which challenges them is, however, that they perceive no existing organizational model which is sufficiently worked out to ensure that sufficient innovation takes place. For example, they say (p. 301): 'Innovation cannot be managed hierarchically because it depends on knowledge being offered voluntarily rather than on command.' Furthermore, they maintain that approaches to facilitating innovation require investments that often appear to be unjustified within current organizational accounting systems.

Their argument is that models of organizing that involve standardization and, more recently, customization which have required, respectively, 'meta-capabilities' of coordination and delegation are no longer sufficient for innovation to flourish. This is because organizations of the future need not just knowledge but knowledge generation and transfer, which in turn require social interaction and exchange between organizational members. The logical outcome of this, they argue, is that *collaboration* is the key to innovation – what Miles *et al.* call the new 'meta-capability'. Acknowledging that collaboration is not entirely natural in many organizational cultures, they suggest three conditions for collaboration to happen:

1 People need *time* to discuss ideas, reflect, listen and engage in a host of activities that might produce fresh ideas.
2 They need to develop strong bonds of *trust* between each other – a willingness to expose one's views without the fear of being exploited and to probe more deeply for new insights and perspectives.
3 People need a sense of *territory* marking one's place in the outcomes of the collaborative process. These visible stakes might be stock ownership, stock options, visible awards, collegial recognition amongst others.

In organizational terms, they also maintain that the organizational model of the future will go beyond the functional, divisional, matrix and network organizations (discussed in Chapter 3) and will involve alliances, spin-offs and federations – organizations operating more in virtual structures, with large degrees of self-management and self-directing teams.

Miles *et al.* assume a style of leadership that is participative, caring of followers, and which recognizes the role of everyone in the efforts to make any organization successful. This is exemplified by Bennis (2000) and McGill and Slocum (1998) who argue for the demise of 'top-down' leadership. Bennis (p. 73) says: 'The most urgent projects require the coordinated contributions of many talented people working together' and (p. 74): 'No change can occur without willing and committed followers.' He maintains that it is only in the solving of relatively simple technical problems that top-down leadership is effective. For the resolution of 'adaptive', complex, messy problems many people at all levels of the organization must be involved and mobilized. Two further quotations (Bennis, 2000, p. 76) suffice to make the point:

> Post-bureaucratic organization requires a new kind of alliance between leaders and the led. Today's organizations are evolving into federations, networks, clusters,

cross-functional teams, temporary systems, ad hoc tasks, lattices, modules, matrices – almost anything but pyramids with their obsolete TOPdown leadership.

The new reality is that intellectual capital, brain power, know-how, human imagination have supplanted capital as the critical success factor and leaders will have to learn an entirely new set of skills.

A look back at the list of general trends posed at the beginning of this chapter and a summary of the discussion so far paints the following scenario. On the one hand there is a picture of people becoming more individualistic, independent, hedonistic, living for some of their adult lives alone, communicating increasingly through ICT and with more choice in respect of their lifestyle. This attitude to life and work is reinforced by the increase in 'non-standard' working that is frequently insecure and which does not engender commitment to any particular organization and it goals. On the other hand there are business thinkers arguing for more organic, network and virtual organizations that require collaborative attitudes and behaviour so that innovation can flourish. Organizational commitment is an antecedent of many positive behaviours in the workplace including innovation, so we appear to have a paradox – are changing career patterns undermining the key attitudes and behaviour that employers need?

Empowerment is part of the answer but in spite of the emphasis put on empowering employees to work in organic, network and virtual forms of organizations, many large organizations continue to conform to hierarchical principles of structure and accountability. The skills that managers need to be successful in this type of organization are not those which comfortably agree with the principles of empowering subordinate levels of staff. Even if empowering abilities are developed, they are unlikely to be rewarded or acknowledged. Behaving in empowering ways does not support the culture and processes that make these managers successful. Many of the characteristics – such as showing determination, drive/energy, leading from the front, objective decision making and personal achievement – are not among the key empowering characteristics.

Schein (1999) notes how the concepts of organizational learning and the learning organization together with those of 'generative' or double-loop learning, require employees to develop new thinking skills, new concepts and points of view and cognitively to redefine old categories and change standards of judgement. Such changes increase individuals' capacity to deal with situations in new ways and lay the basis for developing radically new skills.

By comparison with single-loop learning, which socializes individuals into specific attitudes, double-loop learning requires collaboration, but also a change in values and assumptions about how the world operates and what is good and what is bad. According to Schein, however, requiring individuals to learn to think and behave in these ways is essentially asking them to put themselves through transformational culture change – coming as they frequently have from organizational cultures suited more to traditional bureaucratic norms of command and control – not least because these types of systems discourage creativity and innovation. He goes on to say (p. 7): 'But paradoxically, when we speak of "culture change" in organizations we are typically demanding levels of cognitive redefinition that can probably only be achieved by some version of coercive persuasion.' This is because these individuals are being asked to *disconfirm* what they have believed is *right* – what they have been used to doing for much of their organizational life.

This seems a worrying scenario given the belief, as Miles *et al.*, Bennis and others assert, in alternative, more satisfying and effective ways of running organizations.

Changing

In Chapters 7 and 8 we looked at ways of changing and we extend that discussion now by looking in more detail at what happens during change. In contrast to the many n-step recipes around that are let down by their normative and simplistic approaches, one relatively recent method that overcomes these concerns and which builds on Chapter 8 is *appreciative inquiry*.

Appreciative inquiry

Traditional approaches to organizational change involve a few managers diagnosing a problem, gathering data about it and deciding what needs to be done to fix it. Data typically come from management information systems and the managers' general knowledge of their environments. Interpretation of data is likely to be heavily influenced by the managers' conversations with others in power positions.

Appreciative Inquiry (AI) is an organizational change methodology that takes a radically different view from traditional approaches, being a far more collective method that focuses on the 'positive psychology' generated by asking positive questions rather than concentrating on negative questions and issues. The basic idea is that asking positive questions creates a positive atmosphere that is more likely to generate fresh ideas and employee engagement towards solutions.

Introduced by David Cooperrider, AI is a search for the best in people and what is happening in their organizations (Cooperrider and Whitney, 2005). It is about capturing their imagination of what is most effective and of using that imagination to create a possible future. Eight principles serve to explain how AI should be implemented (Dunlap, 2008).

1 *The constructionist principle* – this maintains that reality is constructed through social interactions. An individual or group in a workplace will experience a countless number of interactions and these interactions create a particular reality for that person or group. This reality then becomes institutionalized and reproduced through action. Reality, therefore, is only one possible reality; it is socially constructed.

2 *Simultaneity* – in contrast to the normal approach of analyzing data and then deciding what to do, simultaneity expresses the idea that inquiry and change

occur together. When people are involved in thinking about positive questions the ensuing discussions and stories begin to change their attitudes and behaviour.

3 *The poetic principle* – this expresses the notion of organizations as narratives, continually being co-authored by the people in them together with outsiders who work with them. The past is written and shapes what is to be written but what is written next (metaphorically speaking) is open and depends on what is inquired about and what stems from the inquiry. The language of the inquiry also influences future outcomes.

4 *Anticipation* – the images (anticipations) of the future that people create begin to shape their constructions and discourses about the future. Imagine, for instance, how anticipation of a stormy meeting with your boss might influence your behaviour compared to anticipation of an upbeat meeting. A gloomy future makes for a gloomy present; a positive future makes for a positive present.

5 *Being positive* – positive climates create conditions for change far more than negative climates. Healthy social relationships between people create atmospheres of trust and support and are therefore important to underpin positive interactions relating to work.

6 *Wholeness* – all groups and stakeholders connected to a change should be involved to maximize the capacity for creative outcomes. If some stakeholders are excluded then the whole story is not narrated.

7 *Enactment* – individuals and groups must enact changes that they want to see. It is about living the future in the present.

8 *Free choice* – people should not be constrained in terms of how they contribute to an inquiry. They need to be free to decide how they will contribute as free choice will raise commitment and creativity.

Appreciative inquiry is a form of action research that can involve a large number (potentially thousands) of participants to create a learning community and shape possible futures. It is suited to situations where large numbers of participants are involved in working across an organization(s) that needs to innovate its way towards some new reality. It has been used in profit-seeking and public service organizations on a wide range of change situations such as enhancing shareholder value in BP (Gilmour and Radford, 2007), transforming a nursing culture (Moody *et al.*, 2007), improving services in healthcare (Baker and Wright, 2006) and cultural change (Van Oosten, 2006).

The eight principles of AI are used to underpin a four stage (4-D) cycle to engage people. The first stage is *Discovery* of what is done well in the group or organization and what makes it happen. The second stage is *Dreaming* of possible futures based on the exceptional experiences identified in Discovery. The third is *Designing* what should be done to implement the shared view of the future and the fourth stage is *Destiny*, which is a collective agreement on the systems to support the desired future state (Watkins and Mohr, 2001).

Although it has an intuitive appeal stemming from its inclusive and democratic ethos, AI is not a panacea and does have some limitations; being labour intensive is among them. Evaluating AI as a way of raising citizen participation in local government uncovered the following issues (Schooley, 2008).

- Very skilful facilitators are required to accentuate the positive and prevent regression to negative thinking.
- The overt focus on the positive could suppress the voices of people with genuine grievances.
- Some decisions and intentions would need referral back to the council who could 'put out the fires' lit by AI processes.

Despite the popularity of AI little research has evaluated how effective it is. However, an examination of 20 cases where AI had been used found that 7 were judged to have produced transformational outcomes although not all cases had intended to be transformational (Bushe and Kassam, 2005). Where transformational change was observed, Bushe and Kassam suggested that two qualities of AI were instrumental in the process:

- the focus on changing how people think and not what they do; and,
- the focus on creating an environment in which ideas lead to self-organizing change.

However, this meta-analytic approach to AI implies that it is possible to evaluate AI in some objective sense in that there is some reality out there to be found (e.g., it is or is not effective). Since AI is based on principles of social constructionism (e.g., what is positive is a social construction) it follows that whether it is successful or not in a particular setting is also a social construction. Evaluation of AI is an ongoing part of an AI intervention.

This summary of AI presents a general methodology for change that is capable of getting people engaged in shaping their futures. But do all workplaces share a similar capacity for change or are some more ready than others?

Illustration 9.1

Using AI at the BBC

Appreciative Inquiry was used at the BBC to help a culture change project with a basic aim of moving further towards a culture of creativity, teamwork, better leadership and less competition among staff. Using a 'Just Imagine' banner, over 10,000 employees voluntarily participated in over 200 meetings. Three questions were asked; what was your most creative experience here, what made it possible and what has to be changed to make those experiences the norm? In groups of about 10 people these questions were discussed by employees in pairs. Their stories were shared and the most uplifting reported back. Ideas for action were captured in each meeting and about 15,000 distinctive ideas were put forward, leading to 35 initiatives for change.

Some ideas could be implemented quickly (easy wins) whereas others took longer to put in place. The use of AI is said to have created a culture in which employees remained willing to be involved and to have built communication within teams. The BBC's use of AI did not extend to the full 4-D model – it was only used in the Dreaming stage to generate ideas that top management could work with. Had they persevered with the full approach then teams would have retained ownership of ideas and worked through how to implement them.

Source: Based on Berrisford, S. (2005) 'Using Appreciative Inquiry to Drive Change at the BBC', *Strategic Communication Management*, April–May, 9(3), pp. 22–25.2

Capacity for change

We can see by looking at organizations in the same sector that although they face similar pressures for change they embark on different change programmes, have different journeys and arrive at different destinations. Some organizations may evolve into market leaders whereas others wither and die. The different ways in which organizational leaders interpret environmental signals offer one explanation for this but so does the idea that organizations have different capacities to change (Meyer and Stensaker, 2006). This refers to their ability to undertake 'large-scale changes without compromising daily operations or subsequent change processes' (p. 218), i.e., the positive effects of change outweigh the negative effects. If the idea that organizations carry a certain change capacity is accepted then it makes sense to ask how that capacity can be expanded. Building on the extensive advice there is on successful change Meyer and Stensaker offer the following prescriptions.

- *Framing* communication of the reasons for change, including use of symbols and metaphors to reinforce and simplify messages. The way the change is framed by management has a big influence on how people see it.
- *Participation* of employees in the design and implementation of change is now accepted as inescapable. However, employees must see that their participation is genuinely wanted (and is not a result of management tokenism) and that it has an impact in the workplace otherwise cynical reactions will result, poisoning change processes.
- *Pacing and sequencing* relate to the speed at which change is attempted and the timing of different stages in a change process. Slow change gives opportunities to learn about what is happening but slowness could be seen as lack of urgency and it gives resistors the best chance to mount a defence. Fast change can accelerate the benefits but could crash and burn if poor decisions are made. Getting the pace and sequencing (the timing of different interventions) right is a key challenge to management.
- *Routinizing* calls for the use of existing or new structures and processes to introduce change because these are the things that connect people, and offer support and understanding.
- *Recruiting* people specifically to help implement changes; consultants, change agents or perhaps new appointments to key positions. There are also implications for the organization's general approach to selection and in particular the competences that it seeks in new appointments. Hiring people with experience of change and/or selection that methods suggest are not typically resistors of change, should add to capacity.

Meyer and Stensaker argue that by focusing on these issues the organization's capacity for change will increase. Change capacity is a dynamic capability that underpins the ability to manage change over a period of time (Meyer and Stensaker, 2006; Klarner *et al.*, 2008). Klarner *et al.* (2008) offered a model of change capacity as shown in Figure 9.1.

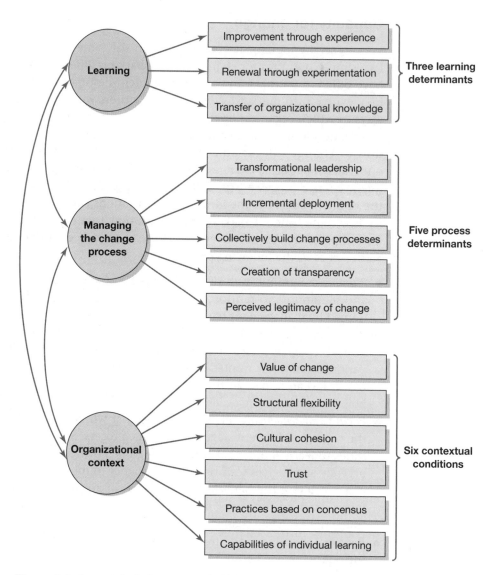

Figure 9.1 A model of change capacity

Source: Based on Klarner, P., Probst, G. and Soparnot, R. (2008) 'Organizational Change Capacity in Public Services: the case of the World Health Organization', *Journal of Change Management*, 8(1), pp. 57–72.

Change capacity is conceptualized as comprising three correlated dimensions; learning, change process and organizational context. These dimensions are thought to mutually reinforce each other and each dimension is assessed through the determinants or conditions shown in Figure 9.1. The basic idea is that change agents can assess each of the 14 determinants and conditions to see how far they are present in the organization as a forerunner to intervening and strengthening where there are weaknesses – see Illustration 9.2.

Illustration 9.2

Dr WHO?

The model of change capacity shown in Figure 9.1 has been applied to the World Heath Organization (WHO) (Klarner et al., 2008). The WHO is on a mission to see that people the world over enjoy the best possible health but in the face of new health problems (HIV/AIDS) and funding issues it had become a touch too bureaucratic. A new Director General set out on a drive to make the WHO more flexible and responsive. A classic case of realigning with the environment, it seems. A programme of change was evaluated after 18 months using a case study methodology.

Klarner and colleagues judged that all three learning dimension determinants were present in full measure. The organizational context dimension was judged lacking on structural flexibility, practices based on consensus and individual learning capabilities. The change process dimension was found wanting on incremental deployment, building change processes and creating transparency. Despite some rather big omissions in relation to the model, they say the changes intended had been mostly met and overall were thought to have had a 'positive impact' and conclude that the WHO's capacity for change was 'moderate'.

Models of this type are limited in that we cannot escape having to reach some rather judgemental conclusions about the extent to which the proposed catalysts of change are present. Nevertheless, they can act as useful templates to stimulate thinking around some important factors that influence the success of change initiatives.

A repeated finding in research on episodic change is that the frequency of past change increases the likelihood of future change (Beck et al., 2008). It is a repetitive momentum theory; past change predicts future change. The basic reason for this (Beck et al.) is that organizations are governed by formal and informal routines. Sticking to routines saves time as they act as short cuts to decisions. They also act as standardized solutions to day-to-day problems. Routines also influence change processes as some develop in response to previous change attempts. The more routines are changed then the more conducive the organization becomes to further change – so goes the theory. However, Beck et al. are not convinced by this theory and put forward an opposite view. Their point is that since change is aimed at improving things then, if these things are improved, there should be less need for future change. They support their theory with a series of simulations and improved investigative methods, the results of which (in their view) contradict the 'change breeds change' hypothesis and support a deceleration hypothesis in which change leads to less change. It is worth noting here that this research is based on episodic change which is perhaps less indicative of reality now than continuous change.

Sensegiving and sensemaking

When organizations embark on change, planned or otherwise, employees' routines are challenged. They are asked to sign-up to new values, unlearn and discard practised ways of doing things and learn how to do new things. If you have been in change situations you may have sometimes paused for thought; 'What's going on around here and how do we make sense of what we are supposed to be doing?' This question had been overlooked in change theory until *sensemaking* became a distinctive area of research in its own right (Weick, 1995).

Sensemaking is a way of discovering meaning and is a key ingredient in understanding how organizing takes place and the organization that results from it. It involves 'turning circumstances into a situation that is comprehended explicitly in words and that serves as a springboard into action' (Weick *et al.*, 2005, p. 409). Further, 'to focus on sensemaking is to portray organizing as the experience of being thrown into an ongoing, unknowable, unpredictable streaming of experience in search of answers to the question, "what's the story?"' (Weick *et al.*, 2005, p. 410).

Sensemaking is a social process that occurs through interactions and conversations with others who are also trying to make sense of what is happening. It occurs at all levels; top managers carry out environmental scanning and try to make sense of signals they pick up. It is not about discovering some precise and accurate way forward; rather it leads to a pragmatic, workable interpretation to take another step forward. It is a bridge between getting information on what to do (e.g. from top managers or peers) and figuring out what to do next. The bridge is made up of narratives that are created, shared, deconstructed and recreated until eventually the narratives provide sufficient meaning to enable people to move forward. As we have seen earlier, change in its early stages at least has much to do with changing the conversations that people are having. If this can be achieved then change is set in motion. Sensemaking, however, does not happen in some single grand 'eureka' moment, rather it is punctuated by a series of smaller moments of discovery and meaning.

Sensemaking is influenced by the actions of others who play a 'sensegiving' role. Good leaders, for instance, do a good job at sensegiving which means influencing others so that they move towards some concept of organizational reality (Maitlis, 2005). Maitlis's study of a range of change situations identified four different types of sensemaking which were determined by the extent to which leaders and stakeholders engage in sensegiving.

Maitlis found that high levels of leader sensegiving produced environments where sensemaking was highly controlled. Control manifested in the form of formal committees, meetings, events and private discussions between leaders. Where leaders relaxed and gave more control to stakeholders then high stakeholder sensegiving relied upon using less formal, animated and continuous arrangements based on extensive sharing and reporting of information. The most productive form of sensemaking, 'guided organizational sensemaking', occurred, when there were high levels of leader and stakeholder sensegiving. Outomes of guided sensemaking were thorough in that they incorporated the views of all stakeholders and they were unitary in the sense that they were agreed upon by all parties. Where both leader and stakeholder sensegiving were low then a 'minimal' level of sensemaking occurred, leading to shallow and less effective outcomes. More research is needed to understand the reasons why different patterns of sensemaking occur. How much does the issue itself play a part in determining levels of control and animation?

One trigger for sensemaking is when our identity is challenged. At any point in time we perceive a particular identity for ourselves, perhaps as a caring and high performing employee. We think that others share that perception but if an event happens that makes us question it then we will set off on a sensemaking trail. An interesting account of this is Margaret Vickers' (2007) autoethnographic account of bullying in the workplace and how the experience of bullying brought about for her an identity shift. Other illustrations of the role played by identity include Bean and Eisenberg's (2006) study of change from traditional to 'nomadic' working patterns in a telecoms company which made employees question their 'taken for granted' views of who they were and how they were valued, and Bird's (2007) study of a women's network in a large corporation.

Challenges for future research on change

Despite being among the most studied aspects of organizations, there is much more to understand about change and organization development. Much of the earlier theorizing led to prescriptive, 'how to' models that neglect crucial aspects of context such as micro politics and workforce skills. As this book nears an end, therefore, it is worth looking at some of the gaps and limitations in change research as a way of understanding where research is needed. Pettigrew, Woodman and Cameron (2001) suggest six issues.

1 *Multiple contexts and levels of analysis*. Early studies were typically of one-off change events but these overlooked the contextual factors that 'were shaping these particular episodes' (p. 698). Since the 1980s there has been more focus on contextualism and on 'changing' rather than on finding out what can be understood by researching single change events. The emphasis moved to exploring change while it was happening to detect the complex embedded nature of historic, political and environmental factors bearing on change outcomes. The key point is that the processes of change can only be studied in context and therefore a way of understanding contexts is needed. Pettigrew and colleagues identify two choices for researchers; how many levels of analysis should be studied in order to understand context and how many different processes across the multiple levels need investigating. This approach to conceptualizing change moves away from seeing it as something that is influenced by a set of variables that researchers can measure towards seeing it as 'interaction between context and action' (p. 699). Illustration 9.3 relates sector level change in a declining manufacturing industry to multiple contexts.

But achieving this level of analysis calls for an understanding of how time and history have shaped the context as it is today.

2 *Time, history, process and action.* Most studies of management are cross-sectional. They are snapshots of situations and as such they are incapable of separating cause from effect. Many organizations of course have existed for a long time so any snapshot study excludes the past and how it shaped the situation captured in the photograph. However, it is not just a case of seeing history as a chronological sequence of events, as it needs to be understood in terms of how it shaped prevailing processes: 'The past is alive in the present and may be shaping the emerging future' (p. 700). Implications therefore are for the inclusion of time in understanding of change and this can be achieved by historical studies of sectors and organizations or by research programmes that follow change over time.

3 *Change processes and organizational performance.* Whereas many studies of change unravel the processes going on, Pettigrew *et al.* point out that in few studies is much account taken of the link between capacity for change and organizational performance. The key point is about judging whether and to what extent change is successful through some assessment of performance. This poses considerable challenges to researchers, however, as measures of performance specific to the change situation being studied are called for. Easy quantitative measures may not be available and so judgements of the success of change may have to rely on subjective criteria.

4 *International comparative research.* Most change research takes place in single organizations or at best in a few organizations in the same country. For understandable practical reasons the field lacks studies of change on a cross-national scale although these are needed to help understand innovation, new ways of organizing, the influence of national cultural differences and the limitations of normative theory.

5 *Reciprocity, customization, sequencing and pace.* While there is much theory and advice available to change agents, deciding where and how to start a change initiative is difficult. How receptive will people be? How much should change agents customize change to fit different contexts within an organization? Where is the start point and what is the optimum linking (sequencing) of events and interventions? What is the optimum amount of urgency and pace to inject into proceedings? Answers to these questions cannot, of course, be generalized and are context specific.

6 *Scholar-practitioner engagement.* Management research is often carried out by a lone researcher, maybe a small team of researchers, conceptualizing and designing studies in the first place, gathering and analyzing data. There is little interaction with the research setting although, depending on the topic being researched, in some research studies not much interaction is needed. However, the study of change needs research strategies that engage with participants in agreeing how problems are described, the data that is needed, how it should be collected and interpreting what the data mean. Hence, far

more interaction between researcher(s) and what is being researched is needed to explore the multi-layered and multi-context nature of change. Teams of researchers working alongside organizations over a long time frame are needed.

Illustration 9.3

The multi-level nature of sector change

Footwear manufacturing in the UK, the US and other high labour cost countries was once a substantial employer, providing jobs across the entire supply chain (materials, components, machinery, manufacturing and retail). From the late 1960s onwards, however, the domestic manufacturing base in these countries has contracted steadily so that only a handful of niche suppliers and producers remain capable of turning enough profit to survive. But people buy more shoes now than ever, so what happened?

The most often cited explanation is that domestic production was displaced by cheaper and sometimes more fashionable imports. Basic styles could be made far more cheaply in places like China and Taiwan whereas Italy and Portugal had reputations for producing high fashion shoes at a good price. So a simple answer is that the retailers in the UK, the US and elsewhere placed their orders overseas and imported cheaper goods. This is an inescapable truth but it does not represent the full context of the change very well.

Shoemaking has a long history and was largely clustered on a regional basis. In the UK, Leicestershire and Northamptonshire were historic shoemaking centres, among others. The work, though, was for most operatives not much fun – operating the same machine day after day, year after year on relatively low wages based on piece-rates in factory conditions that were often noisy, untidy and with a background of leather dust and solvent fumes.

For decades this was not questioned much but with increasing prosperity in the 1960s people began to reassess the quality of working life and the sector began to develop a 'last resort' image in the labour market. What parent would want their child to work in a shoe factory? A small proportion of factory owners and others who made it to management jobs could do well but for the majority it had little to offer.

Industry structure was also a factor in the decline. UK retailing was very concentrated in the hands of a few large companies. For instance, the biggest retailer controlled about 25 per cent of the retail market and five retailers controlled over 40 per cent of footwear sales. Importers only had to knock on a few doors in Leicester to get access to a big slice of the retail market and this made importing to the UK much easier than to other countries where shoe retailing was much less concentrated.

There is a political context such that cries for protection against imports by UK producers fell on the deaf ears of government ministers committed to free market principles (the heyday of Prime Minister Thatcher and President Reagan). If a sector was not inherently competitive then why should the government bale it out? The sector, too, had little political 'clout'. Despite being a substantial employer it is clear that politicians were not sorry to see it decline and were more concerned with supporting the survival and growth of higher value adding sectors. Many manufacturers increasingly relocated some or all of their production overseas and then imported cheaper shoes back into the UK – this strategy probably did not endear them to government when the same manufacturers called for protection.

▶

Illustration 9.3 *continued*

UK producers periodically set off on a 'Buy British' campaign appealing to patriotic values but these never had any effect. Consumers were more concerned with price and style than loyalty to home producers in high streets where imported consumer goods were everywhere. Producers also seemed stuck on tramlines in terms of fashion reflecting the historic position of the UK as a maker of well made but not particularly fashionable shoes. At a time when consumers wanted more fashion they could not respond.

Producers did innovate at a technical level – automated cutting of fabrics and formulating new plastics and rubbers for components and the machines for moulding them. But so many footwear styles relied upon manual work to cut materials, sew, stitch and box the goods and, despite efforts to automate, labour costs as a share of total manufacturing costs remained too high. It is hard to imagine another product that contains so many components in so many colours and which comes in so many sizes and sells so cheaply. This inability to simplify the product proved too much.

Conditions and change in shoe manufacturing are superbly portrayed in the British comedy film *Kinky Boots*. The film shows how an old, small town shoe factory was on the point of failing with a lacklustre product range. A chance encounter leads the new factory owner to see a market for high leg boots for male transvestites. The film is a great portrayal of pushing radical change on a traditional workforce; asking people to make things that push their skills to the limit and questioning their parochial attitudes to sexuality.

Activity 9.1

Following from Illustration 9.3, watch a DVD of the film Kinky Boots. Enjoy it, and think about what the film says about the events pushing for change and how to manage resistance to change.

The classic and still widely used approach to management research, including change and organization development, relies upon positivistic approaches to defining and investigating research questions. From the 1980s onwards alternative ways of seeing change have emerged and are captured in Table 9.1.

The classical approach sees change situations as possessing a single truth and reality which needs to be discovered and then told to the waiting world. Ways of discovering the true situation rely on objective methods of collecting data (e.g., top managers know best, management information is valid). Data analysis shows the way forward to a new organizational position. Change, like TV shows, occurs as episodes and in between the episodes there are periods of no change.

Table 9.1 Trends in organization development

Classic organization development	New organization development
Based in classical science and modern thought and philosophy	Influenced by the new sciences and postmodern thought and philosophy
Truth is transcendent and discoverable; there is a single objective reality	Truth is immanent and emerges from the situation; there are multiple, socially constructed realities
Reality can be discovered using rational and analytic processes	Reality is socially negotiated and may involve power and political processes
Collecting and applying valid data using objective problem solving methods leads to change	Creating new mindsets or social agreements, sometimes through explicit or implicit negotiation, leads to change
Change is episodic and can be created, planned and managed	Change is continuous and can be self-organizing
Emphasis on changing behaviour and what one does	Emphasis on changing mindsets and how one thinks

Source: Marshak, R.J. and Grant, D. (2008) 'Organizational Discourse and New Organization Development Processes', *British Journal of Management*, 19, Special Issue, p.S8. Reproduced with permission.

In contrast to the classical approach, new perspectives drawing on postmodernism have emerged (Marshak and Grant, 2008). Rather than seek to understand a simple objective reality, multiple realities are recognized – for example, appreciating the ways different groups of actors involved in a situation will differ and that each interpretation has its own validity. Power and the exercise of political energy are used to shape reality. Change is seen as a continuous phenomenon (not episodic) and is grounded in changes to how people think, not changes to how they behave. Of course, how people think does influence their behaviour but the key difference is that classical approaches target behavioural change whereas postmodern and constructivist approaches target how people think.

Makshak and Grant suggest that five practices are being used in contemporary organization development situations to take us beyond classical positivist approaches and their limitations.

1 *Appreciative inquiry* – see above.
2 *Changing mindsets and consciousness*. Rather than rely on enticing people with rewards and changes to systems and relationships this approach focuses on changing how people think about the situations they are in. New found consciousness in turn leads to modified behaviour. There is a bit of a problem with this approach, namely that political manipulation could be used to create favourable mindsets around situations that are, by everyday standards of decency and integrity, rather unsavoury. For instance, persuading people that a situation is in their favour when they will be disadvantaged by it in the future.

3 *Diversity and multicultural realities.* This approach recognizes that when organizations feel moved to change there is often a backdrop of barriers to development, e.g., biased promotion and job assignment processes that stop people contributing their best. The recognition of power and the dominance of powerful lobbies in shaping realities is emphasized.

4 *Different models of change.* Moving from the simplistic unfreeze/move/refreeze approaches to narratives of continuous and transformational change.

5 Marshak and Grant conclude that the new approaches to organizational change centre around *changing discourses* on the basis that it is through discourse that people develop and live out the realities that shape their behaviour. Change agents need to appreciate how power and politics shape discourses, for example by perpetuating dominant views and suppressing contrasting views.

Activity 9.2

For an organization that you know well, identify what you see are barriers that put a ceiling on employee performance. Barriers could exist in the way people are rewarded, allocated work and promoted although they can lurk anywhere.

When you have identified what you see are barriers, think how other constituents and constituencies in the organization would see them. For instance, what would top management say about them?

This thinking is reflected in modernist, sophisticated modernist or postmodernist views of change (Kirkbride, Durcan and Obeng, 1994). A *modernist* view of the world sees change as incremental, evolutionary, constantly developing, following a linear path and worked out according to a known recipe about what should change and how. Thus modernists tend to believe in change models based on simple cause and effect: if the right levers are pulled in relation to desired outcomes, those outcomes should surely follow.

A *sophisticated modernist* view of the world would see change as transformational, revolutionary, periodic, following a circular path (i.e. 'moving in a complex and dynamic fashion from emerging strategy to deliberate strategy and back again' (p. 157)) and one where the end point can change as the change process unfolds. As a result, this view recognizes that the world does not stand still for long. The *postmodernist view* of change is summed up as follows (Kirkbride *et al.*, pp. 158–159):

> The post-modern world can . . . be seen as one characterized by randomness and chaos, by a lack of certainty, by a plethora of competing views and voices, by

complex temporalities, and where organizations are unable to produce recipes for dealing with the unstable environment.

A cursory examination of some of today's organizations will show that there is 'truth' in all these views of change – the 'trick' is to know when and where one or the other is current. For instance, in limited, constrained situations, a modernist view of change may be most appropriate and might loosely be linked to the hard systems model of change, which implies transition rather than transformation and planned rather than emergent change.

The version of an OD model of change presented in the previous chapter is more congruent with a sophisticated modernist view of the world – provided the presence of continuous feedback loops is stressed and it is recognized that the vision and its associated change goals are not fixed – in the sense that the change process is never complete.

The postmodernist view does not easily attach itself to any recognizable model of change. What it does point towards, however, is a model of organization that is organic, flexible, niche market-oriented, where jobs are highly de-differentiated, de-demarcated and multi-skilled in a context of employment relationships based on subcontracting and networking (see Clegg, 1990). Change, in this context, could take on any number of faces and forms.

Conclusions

Understanding change and changing have become one of the biggest preoccupations for management theory reflecting the situation now that change and changing exercise the minds of most managers most of the time. Whether planned or emergent, change takes a number of different forms, each of which requires a different type of action. Building capacity to change and using collective methods of action research and appreciative inquiry to involve people in changing are promising approaches that appear to offer more than conventional approaches.

While there is no one best way to achieve successful organizational change, making efforts to understand the wide variety of change situations and to be familiar with the different characteristics of change itself will help organizations and their members negotiate appropriate paths to change and face the future with some confidence. There are key areas that should be considered in relation to the diagnosis, implementation and review of change situations:

1 *Multiple paths to change*
   - Continuous environmental scanning (internal and external) to get early warning of change triggers.
   - Understanding the different types of change.
   - Adopting a contingency approach to developing plans for managing change based on an understanding of the change scenario being faced.

2 *The challenge of diversity*
- Regarding differences between people as something to be valued.
- Recognizing that interacting with people across different cultures is essential to effective organizational effectiveness.

3 *Empowerment and control*
- Change is more likely to be a success if those it affects are willing collaborators.
- The effective collaboration of employees/stakeholders is more likely if they are involved at all stages of the change process and not just its implementation.
- Behaviour linked to empowerment should be reinforced through appropriate reward mechanisms.

4 *Creativity and innovation*
- Creative and innovative approaches to change are more likely to flow from a diverse workforce.
- Creativity and innovation require a creative organizational climate if they are to flourish.
- The organization and its managers need to foster structures and processes that facilitate creativity.

Change calls for high levels of persistence. This means persisting in the face of an ultra-unstable environment; persisting in the face of systems that are built for stability rather than change; persisting in the face of plans which are out of date as soon as they are formed. It means recognizing that nothing is perfect and that people will act in infuriating and annoying ways but that, when necessary, will bring the genius of their humanity to solve apparently insoluble problems. For organizations, it is learning that change is necessary and often very effective even when business is good. Change is not easy but it can be interesting. It is certainly worth the journey, even if the place we arrive at is surprising.

Discussion questions and assignments

1 What are the benefits of using approaches such as appreciative inquiry to stimulate change?

2 For an organization that you know well, what changes will it have to face up to in the near future? What is the organization's capacity for change and how would you recommend it approaches the changes?

3 Think of a change situation that you have been in and discuss the sensegiving and sensemaking processes that took place. How effective were they?

Indicative resources

Arnold, J. with Silvester, J., Patterson, F., Robertson, I., Cooper, G. and Burnes, B. (2005) *Work Psychology* (4th edn), Harlow: Pearson Education. This book is extremely useful when focusing on present and future trends that employers and managers are facing given its emphasis on behaviour in the workplace and change.

Whitney, D. and Trosten-Bloom, A. (2003) *The Power of Appreciative Inquiry*, San Francisco, CA: Berrett-Koehler. Based on the principles of OD (people and their potential) this book in particular supports the ideas and concepts associated with learning organizations.

Useful websites

http://www.technobility.com/docs/article036.htm This is a consultant's site which contains views and thoughts on managing change.

http://www.new-paradigm.co.uk/Appreciative.htm Gives a useful summary and links to articles.

http://ai-consulting.co.uk/ This is a consultant's website containing further information of AI.

To click straight to these links and for other resources go to **www.pearsoned.co.uk/senior**

References

Arnold, J., Silvester, J., Patterson, F., Robertson, I., Cooper, C. and Burnes, B. (2005) *Work Psychology: Understanding Human Behaviour in the Workplace*, Harlow: Pearson Education.

Baker, A. and Wright, M. (2006) 'Using Appreciative Inquiry to Initiate a Managed Clinical Network for Children's Liver Disease in the UK', *International Journal of Health Care Quality Assurance*, 19(7), pp. 561–574.

Beck, N., Bruderl, J. and Woyode, M. (2008) 'Momentum or Deceleration? Theoretical and methodological reflections on the analysis of organizational change', *Academy of Management Journal*, 51(3), pp. 413–435.

Bennis, W. (2000) 'The End of Leadership: exemplary leadership is impossible without the full inclusion, initiatives, and cooperation of followers', *Organizational Dynamics*, pp. 71–80.

Berrisford, S. (2005) 'Using Appreciative Inquiry to Drive Change at the BBC', *Strategic Communication Management*, Apr/May, 9(3), pp. 22–25.

Bird, S. (2007) 'Sensemaking and Identity', *Journal of Business Communication*, 44(4), pp. 311–339.

Bushe, G.R. and Kassam, A.F. (2005) 'When is Appreciative Inquiry Transformational? A Meta Case Analysis', *Journal of Applied Behavioral Science*, 41(2), pp. 161–181.

Capon, C. (2004) *Understanding Organisational Context: Inside and Outside Organisations* (2nd edn), Harlow: Pearson Education.

CIPD (2004) *Managing the Psychological Contract*, December, London: CIPD.

Clegg, S.R. (1990) *Modern Organization: Organization Studies in the Postmodern World*, London: Sage.

Cooper, C. (1998) Editorial: 'The Changing Psychological Contract at Work', *Work & Stress*, 12(2), pp. 97–100.

Cooperrider, D.L. and Whitney, D. (2005) 'A Positive Revolution in Change: appreciative inquiry, in Cooperrider, D.L., Sorenson, P.F., Whitney, D. and Yaeger, T.F. (eds) *Appreciative Inquiry: Rethinking Human Organization Toward a Positive Theory of Change*, Champaign, IL: Stipes.

DTI (1999) *Britain Towards 2010: The Changing Business Environment*, London: Department of Trade and Industry.

Dunlap, C.A. (2008) 'Effective Evaluation through Appreciative Inquiry', *Performance Development*, 47(2), pp. 23–29.

Gilmour, D. and Radford, A. (2007) 'Using Organization Development to Enhance Shareholder Value: delivering business results in BP Castrol Marine', *Organization Development Journal*, 25(3), pp. 97–102.

Guest, D.E. (2004) 'The Psychology of the Employment Relationship: an analysis based on the psychological contract', *Applied Psychology: An International Review*, 53(4), pp. 541–555.

Kirkbride, P.S., Durcan, J. and Obeng, E.D.A. (1994) 'Change in a Chaotic World', *Journal of Strategic Change*, 3, pp. 151–163.

Klarner, P., Probst, G. and Soparnot, R. (2008) 'Organizational Change Capacity in Public Services: the case of the World Health Organization', *Journal of Change Management*, 8(1), pp. 57–72.

Maitlis, S. (2005) 'The Social Processes of Organizational Sensemaking', *Academy of Management Journal*, 48(1), pp. 21–49.

Marshak, R.J. and Grant, D. (2008) 'Organizational Discourse and New Organization Development Processes', *British Journal of Management*, 19, Special Issue, S7–S19.

McGill, M. E. and Slocum, J.W., Jr (1998) 'A Little Leadership, Please?', *Organizational Dynamics*, 26(3), pp. 39–49.

Meyer, C.B. and Stensaker, I.G. (2006) 'Developing Capacity for Change', *Journal of Change Management*, 6(2), pp. 217–231.

Miles, R.E., Snow, C. and Miles, G. (2000) 'The Future.org', *Long Range Planning*, 33, pp. 300–321.

Moody, R.C., Horton Deutsch, S. and Pesut, D.J. (2007) 'Appreciative Inquiry for Leading Complex Systems: supporting the transformation of an academic nursing culture', *Journal of Nursing Education*, 46(7), pp. 319–324.

Rousseau, D.M. and Parks, J.M. (1993) 'The Contracts of Individuals and Organizations', in *Research in Organizational Behavior*, Greenwich, CT: JAI Press, 15, pp. 1–43.

Schein, E. (1999) 'Empowerment, Coercive Persuasion and Organizational Learning: do they connect?' *The Learning Organization*, 6(4), pp. 1–11.

Schooley, S. (2008) 'Appreciative Democracy: the feasibility of using appreciative inquiry at the local government level by public administrators to increase citizen participation', *Public Administration Quarterly*, 32(2), pp. 243–282.

Shore, L. M. and Tetrick, L.E. (1994) 'The Psychological Contract as an Explanatory Framework in the Employment Relationship', in Cooper, C.L. and Rousseau, D.M. *Trends in Organizational Behaviour*, New York: John Wiley & Sons Ltd, pp. 91–109.

Sparrow, P.R. (2000) 'The New Employment Contract: psychological implications of future work', in Burke, R.J. and Cooper, C.L. (eds), *The Organization in Crisis: Downsizing, Restructuring and Privatisation*, London: Blackwell, pp. 167–187.

Van Oosten, E.B. (2006) 'Intentional Change Theory at the Organizational Level: a case study', *Journal of Management Development*, 25(7), pp. 707–717.

Vickers, M. (2007) 'Autoethnography as Sensemaking: a story of bullying', *Culture and Organization*, 13(3), pp. 223–237.

Watkins, J.M. and Mohr, B.J. (2001) *Appreciative Inquiry: Change at the Speed of Imagination*, San Francisco: Jossey Bass.

Weick, K.E. (1995) *Sensemaking in Organizations*, Thousand Oaks, CA: Sage.

Weick, K.E., Sutcliffe, K.M. and Obstfeld, D. (2005) 'Organizing and the Process of Sensemaking', *Organization Science*, 16(4), pp. 409–421.

Name index

Subject index